International conflict is neither random nor inexplicable. It is highly structured by antagonisms between a relatively small set of states that regard each other as rivals. Examining the 173 strategic rivalries in operation throughout the nineteenth and twentieth centuries, this book identifies the differences rivalries make in the probability of conflict escalation and analyzes how they interact with serial crises, arms races, alliances and capability advantages. The authors distinguish between rivalries concerning territorial disagreement (space) and rivalries concerning status and influence (position) and show how each lead to markedly different patterns of conflict escalation. They argue that rivals are more likely to engage in international conflict with their antagonists than nonrival pairs of states and conclude with an assessment of whether we can expect democratic peace, economic development and economic interdependence to constrain rivalry-induced conflict.

Michael P. Colaresi is Assistant Professor in the Department of Political Science at Michigan State University.

Karen Rasler is Professor in the Department of Political Science at Indiana University.

William R. Thompson is Rogers Professor of Political Science in the Department of Political Science at Indiana University.

Strategic Rivalries in World Politics

Position, Space and Conflict Escalation

Michael P. Colaresi, Karen Rasler, and
William R. Thompson

CAMBRIDGE
UNIVERSITY PRESS

CAMBRIDGE
UNIVERSITY PRESS

University Printing House, Cambridge CB2 8BS, United Kingdom

Cambridge University Press is part of the University of Cambridge.

It furthers the University's mission by disseminating knowledge in the pursuit of education, learning and research at the highest international levels of excellence.

www.cambridge.org
Information on this title: www.cambridge.org/9780521707619

© Michael P. Colaresi, Karen Rasler and William R. Thompson 2007

First published 2007

A catalogue record for this publication is available from the British Library

ISBN 978-0-521-88134-0 Hardback
ISBN 978-0-521-70761-9 Paperback

To our kids, Cam, Lieu, and Landon

Contents

Part V   Strategic rivalries and conflict

Figures

Tables

APPENDICES: TABLES

Acknowledgments

We are indebted to Blackwell Publishing for permission to reprint revised versions of the following articles: Karen Rasler and William R. Thompson, "Explaining Rivalry Escalation to War: Contiguity, Position and Space in the Major Power Subsystem," *International Studies Quarterly* 44 (September 2000): 503–30; William R. Thompson, "Identifying Rivals and Rivalries in World Politics," *International Studies Quarterly* 45 (December 2001): 557–86; Michael Colaresi and William R. Thompson, "Hot Spots or Hot Hands?: Serial Crisis Behavior, Escalating Risks and Rivalry," *Journal of Politics* 64 (2002): 1175–98; Michael Colaresi and William R. Thompson, "Alliances, Arms Buildups, and Recurrent Conflict: Testing a Steps-to-War Model," *Journal of Politics* 67 (2005): 345–64; Karen Rasler and William R. Thompson, "Contested Territory, Strategic Rivalry, and Conflict Escalation," *International Studies Quarterly* 50 (March 2006): 145–67. Thanks are due as well to Sage Publications for permission to republish a revised version of Michael Colaresi and William R. Thompson, "Strategic Rivalry, Protracted Conflict and Crisis Behavior," *Journal of Peace Research* 39, 2 (March 2002): 263–87.

We are also grateful for National Science Foundation funding to Thompson in 1995–7 that underwrote the collection of data on strategic rivalries. At various points, a number of individuals have commented on earlier parts of the manuscript or provided assistance in acquiring pertinent data. For services rendered along the way, we thank Todd Allee, Terry Boswell, Eric Chang, Derekh Cornwell, Jonathan DiCicco, Paul Diehl, Gary Goertz, Paul Hensel, Paul Huth, David Kelly, Brian Lai, Jack Levy, Sara Mitchell, Joachim Rennstich, Bruce Russett, Brandon Valeriano, and John Vasquez. All are absolved from any errors we may have committed or advice that we may have ignored.

Part I

About strategic rivalries

1   An introduction to strategic rivalries

The advent of explicit interstate rivalry analysis in the past few years has raised serious questions about the wisdom of assuming that any two states have an equal probability of engaging in war. Most wars are related to protracted, ongoing conflicts between long-term adversaries and rivals. A very small number of rivalry dyads, therefore, are disproportionately responsible for a great deal of interstate conflict. Strategic rivalries, in turn, are relationships in which decision-makers have singled out other states as distinctive competitors and enemies posing some actual or potential military threat.[1] It is not unusual for state leaders to perceive threats from states with which they do not feel particularly competitive. The Israel–Lebanon dyad is a good example. Israeli decision-makers may feel threatened by activities that originate within Lebanese space but they do not worry much about an attack from the Lebanese army. Should Israel decide to attack targets in Lebanon, there is little the Lebanese state *per se* can do to deter such attacks.

It is also not unknown for two states to be competitive without appearing to pose a military threat. The French–German dyad, after 1955, provides another illustration. Both states compete for leadership in the European Union, as well as elsewhere, but they no longer regard each

---

[1] Strategic rivalries should not be confused with enduring rivalries that are identified by specifying some number of militarized interstate disputes occurring within a finite interval of time, as in Diehl and Goertz (2000) or Maoz and Mor (2002). For most questions pertaining to rivalry formation and conflict escalation, we prefer a conceptual approach, outlined in Chapter 2, that is independent of a dyad's militarized dispute history. Strategic rivalries can be formed in the absence of any militarized disputes. Whether militarized disputes are involved in their escalation to higher conflict levels are separate theoretical and empirical questions that are difficult to pursue if one starts with some level of dispute density. The use of dispute densities also asks a different question by focusing on moving from a state of affairs below the threshold to above it. That is a question about why some dyads engage in more disputes in a short period of time than others do. If strategic rivalries do not necessarily engage in any militarized interstate disputes, information on dispute densities is unlikely to help account for their formation. To the extent that escalation is about fighting more often, it would be extremely awkward to try to explain an increase in dispute behavior in dispute-density terms.

other as threats to their respective national security. Rivalry requires the combination of competition and the perception of threat from an enemy. The US-USSR-dominated Cold War is the outstanding illustration in recent world politics. The Cold War ended, from the US perspective, when the Soviet Union was perceived to be no longer either particularly competitive or threatening to the United States.[2]

Calling pairs of states "strategic rivals" is one thing. Explaining the dynamics of their relationships is quite another. While ground is certainly gained by recognizing rivals when we find them, the real question is what difference rivalry relationships make to world politics. Answering this question is what this book is mainly about. But before outlining how we proceed to generate our answer, some further illustration of what sort of phenomena we are attempting to explain is in order. Brief summaries of four rivalries should help in this regard. Moving from west to east, we will quickly scan the behavior of Ecuador–Peru, Greece–Turkey, India–Pakistan, and the two Koreas, focusing primarily on the relationship of the pairs of rivals – as opposed to various types of participation in the conflicts by actors outside the rivalry. The immediate question is what do these dyadic relationships seem to have in common?

We think that there are at least four common denominators that are susceptible to analysis, generalization, and theory-building/testing.

First, these strategic rivalries are competing over largely unresolved, distinctive goal incompatibilities. Both sides want things that the other side denies them and they have not devised a way to compromise. Second, the competitive actions within each rivalry combine to form a stream of conflict, rather than wholly separable events. Third, this stream of conflict alters the way objective events are perceived, increasing the escalatory potential of even presumably innocuous events. Adversaries believe that they have ample reason to mistrust the opposite side. Fourth, there is considerable variation in the intensity of competition over time in each case, as conflict is punctuated with periods of cooperation.

Four illustrations

Peru–Ecuador

In 1995, Peru and Ecuador fought a war on the Cenepa River. Exactly how many people died remains unclear but the death count probably

---

[2] With the advantage of hindsight, one can argue that the USSR was much less competitive than it seemed all along. But what matters is how decision-makers perceive the extent of competitiveness and threat at the time – not what we may conclude years later.

ranged between 500 and 1,500, with perhaps the lower number com-ing closest to the actual body count. Between 1995 and 1999, Peru and Ecuador then negotiated what appears to represent a compromise agree-ment that both sides appear to find reasonably satisfactory. A resumption of intense conflict, now, seems unlikely.[3]

The basic issue that had divided the two South American states was a combination of ambiguous boundaries and access to the Amazon Basin. Between 1824 and 1830 first Peru and then Ecuador emerged as indepen-dent states. From the outset, their boundaries were disputed and occa-sionally fought over. Wars between Peru and Ecuador were fought in 1859–60 (although not over boundaries) and 1941. Two crises in 1981 and 1991 might have erupted into full-scale wars but did not due in part to external mediation. Peru thought that the 1941 war outcome had resolved decisively the question of boundary delineation in their favor. Ecuadorians did not see it that way and, in fact, resented the coercion exerted successfully against them in 1941. There also remained some remote areas in which the exact boundary demarcation was less than clear.

Boundary disputes in South America were numerous in the nineteenth and early twentieth centuries. Ambiguous borders were inherited from the Spanish and Portuguese imperial era and few South American states initially had much capability to resolve these questions. Those states with more capability tended to take disputed territories away from weaker states. Both Peru and Ecuador could claim that they had lost territory to stronger neighbors in the past and were unenthusiastic about suffering any more losses.

Over the years, moreover, a distinctive behavioral pattern had emerged in boundary dispute processes. Protracted negotiations, punctuated by military clashes, and a return to negotiations were one dimension of this pattern. Another facet is revealed by Klepak's (1998: 76) summary evalu-ation of the nature of Latin American boundary negotiations: "a great deal of talking and little concrete action." Still another characteristic of these interactions is that some sort of military presence in the disputed area was considered useful (Herz and Pontes Nogueira, 2002). This meant that both sides would attempt to insert patrols and small military camps or posts in disputed areas. From time to time, these detachments would col-lide in contested space with one or both sides claiming that their competi-tors were attempting to expand their control into the sovereign territory of

---

[3] This sort of statement is always highly vulnerable to being contradicted by activities in the real world. Rivalries often de-escalate and terminate only gradually. Sporadic conflicts of low intensity should not be ruled out in the winding-down phase.

the other state. Any such clash had some potential for escalation, depending on how quickly reinforcements could arrive and some inclination to press the issue. In this fashion, even previously negotiated settlements might be overturned if the losing side decided its chances of doing better had improved (Klepak, 1998).

Each of the incidents in 1981, 1991, and 1995 began with some military movement into contested space. One difference in 1995 may have been that the Ecuadorians were better prepared for and, as a consequence, more ready to engage in a military confrontation than they had been in earlier encounters. While both sides allowed the clash to escalate into something bigger, the Ecuadorians remained aware of Peruvian military superiority and were open to negotiations.[4] Some military maneuvering continued in the next few years but a compromise emerged that gave Peru the definitive boundary it desired while also allowing Ecuador access to the Amazon Basin. It probably also helped that Ecuadorians felt that they had avenged their defeat in 1941 by exhibiting more martial competence in 1995 than had previously been the case (Klepak, 1998).

Greece–Turkey

Turkey and Greece have not fought a war recently although they have approached the brink on more than one occasion in the past several decades.[5] The two states have the rare distinction of actually having resolved earlier tensions in the 1930s as greater threats loomed. But they fell back into a relationship of mutual threat and recriminations after the mid-1950s changes in the future status of Cyprus. Since that time, militarized clashes and major crises have punctuated the relations of the two states that also happen to be members of the North Atlantic Treaty Organization and therefore allies.

For Greece, Turkey is the former colonial power from whom independence had to be gained the hard way. From the outset of independence in the early nineteenth century, Greek decision-makers have also been devoted to the idea of bringing all Greeks within a Greek state. Most of the target population for this irredentism happened to reside in Turkish territory. Greek expansion, therefore, could only occur at the expense of the Turks. Yet even as this problem had begun to recede in the second half of the twentieth century, Cyprus with its predominantly Greek population but with a sizeable Turkish minority emerged from British

---

[4] A fourth characteristic of Latin American boundary disputes is that both sides, once engaged in a military confrontation, seem to be particularly open to third party intervention/mediation.

[5] Greece and Turkey fought wars in 1897, 1912–13, 1917–18, and 1919–22.

control as a continuing symbol of the possibilities of Greek unification. The Turkish reaction to the threat of a plot to link Cyprus closely to Greece in 1974 led to a Turkish military occupation of northern Cyprus. From the Turkish point of view, Cypriot schemes reflected attempts at continuing Greek expansion at Turkish expense. From the Greek point of view, the Turkish occupation provided new evidence of Turkish predation and coercive aggression. Turkey ascended to the head of the list of Greek security threats as a consequence.

Subsequent frictions over the legal status of the Aegean and the definition of airspace and territorial waters escalated in the 1980s and 1990s. Greeks perceive Turkish interference with the rights accorded to the many outlying Greek islands near the Turkish coast. The Turkish perspective is that Greece wants to transform the Aegean into a Greek lake. Add to this formula for continuing foreign problems, the existence of a small and historically not well-treated, Turkish minority within Greece. From the Turkish perspective, these compatriots deserve protection from Greek repression. From the Greek perspective, the minority has frequently been seen as a potential fifth column that represents an internal security threat.

Greco-Turkish relations have improved in the past few years in part because both states desire a closer relationship with the European Union. To achieve better linkages to Europe, a variety of images and reflexes have to be moderated. EU members are expected to be democratic political systems with civilian control over the military. Economic growth and stability should be a primary state goal. High defense costs and feuding over adjacent territory are most undesirable. The altered regional environment – Yugoslav disintegration, new states, old communist states struggling to develop new foreign policies – has also contributed both to new venues for Greco-Turkish competition and a rationale for more cautious behavior. Yet while both states appear to be becoming more closely linked to Europe, significant resistance on both sides remains to resolving the major Greco-Turkish grievances. Some Greek observers (Dokos and Tsakonas, 2003: 16) have attributed this reluctance primarily to inertial opposition in Ankara while Turkish observers (Sonmezoglu and Ayman, 2003: 39) point to what they describe as a Greek tendency to tangle with Turkey as "like an addiction, a routine, a way of political life for Greece." It is the one constant upon which most politicians and parties of various ideological stripes can agree.

India–Pakistan

Since their independence shortly after World War II, India and Pakistan have fought four wars and appear to have come close to going to war on several other occasions.[6] In many respects, the two states represent the odd couple of South Asia, if not the world. India is one of the largest states in the world and has always possessed a substantial military capability advantage over smaller Pakistan. Thanks in part to more than a half century of competition with the leading state in its region, Pakistan is a weak state with an even weaker economy. India, in contrast, has remained surprisingly democratic and entertains aspirations of participating in the twenty-first century's development of high technology. One attribute they both share now is that they are also armed with nuclear missiles. As a consequence, they have the greatest potential for testing the debated notion that nuclear weapon proliferation will deter small state warfare.

The British partition of South Asia into primarily Hindu and Muslim areas led to the independence of India and Pakistan, with several major caveats. One is that partition led to a mass migration of people from one part of South Asia to other parts that were deemed less hostile, thereby practically ensuring Hindu–Muslim conflict from the outset. A second problem concerned the nature of British control of South Asia. In most parts of the sub-continent, it had become the direct ruler. In a few enclaves, its rule was officially more indirect via native princes. These princes were invited to choose between the two new states in 1948. Most did on the basis of co-religious and/or geographical principles. A few balked. One of these princely states, Jammu and Kashmir, has remained a contentious issue for India and Pakistan ever since.

One initial structural problem was that the Kashmiri prince was Hindu while most of his population was Muslim. He declined to choose between India and Pakistan until a local tribal rebellion with Pakistani support forced him to seek Indian military assistance. The price for the military support was adhering to India. The Kashmiri fighting escalated into the first war between India and Pakistan without a clear resolution. Both sides ended up holding onto the territory that they controlled at the time of the 1948 cease-fire.

After 1948, Indo-Pakistani troop maneuvering and probes along their mutual borders occasionally escalated into major troop mobilizations and crisis situations (1950–1, 1965, 1987, 1990, 1999, 2001). In 1965 and 1999, Pakistani probes expanded into higher levels of warfare but without ever resolving the question of control of Kashmir.[7] Another war broke out in 1971 over the non-Kashmiri issue of Pakistani control over what was once East Pakistan. A separatist movement/civil war prompted Indian

---

[6] Ganguly (2001) argues that the Kargil fighting in 1999 exceeded the minimal death count required for wars and therefore should be regarded as the fourth Indo-Pakistani war.

[7] In addition, Kashmir is subject to its own internal conflict dynamic that interacts with the preferences and schemes of various external actors.

military intervention that led to the capitulation of Pakistani forces and, ultimately, to the creation of Bangladesh.

Indo-Pakistani relations move back and forth between overt tensions and hostility and discussions about de-escalating their feuding history. The threat of nuclear warfare has added an extra dimension since the late 1990s without necessarily leading to more cooperation. Indeed, the Pakistani decision to develop a nuclear capability is thought to have stemmed from its defeat by India in 1971 and the perceived need for an equalizer. Otherwise, the overall capability gap between India and Pakistan has continued to grow in India's favor. While this expanding chasm and the nuclear dimension should make Indo-Pakistani warfare less likely, it does not seem to have worked that way between 1947 and 1999. It remains unclear whether much has changed substantially in the early twenty-first century.

People's Democratic Republic of Korea–Republic of Korea

Japan's surrender in World War II led to the presence of Soviet troops in the northern part of the Korean peninsula and US forces in the south. Without much apparent premeditation or discussion, this ad hoc division became more concrete when two Korean states were announced in 1948. Both states claimed legitimacy as the sole Korean state. The North and South also professed genuine interests in reunification. However, the division institutionalized a more industrialized North characterized by a Marxist regime organized around Kim Il Sung and an agrarian South ostensibly operating eventually within a relatively democratic regime that has oscillated between civilian and military rule over the last half-century.

In 1950, the better-armed North attempted a coercive reunification of the Korean peninsula. Three years of highly destructive warfare ensued that brought in military intervention by the United States and China, among other states. The 1953 armistice merely solidified the cleavage between the two Koreas. It also forced both sides to devote considerable resources to repairing the wartime devastation for the next twenty years. Initially, the more industrialized Northern economy was more successful in realizing growth but developed serious problems in the 1970s while at the same time it lost some of its external support and suffered from a string of environmental catastrophes. Southern industrialization and economic growth was initially slower but ultimately more spectacular and certainly successful in establishing a modern, competitive economy.

Throughout these economic gains and vicissitudes, the bilateral relations between the two Koreas have alternated between episodes of relative harmony and negotiations toward reunification and intense hostility.

Their history is also characterized by an unusually long series of Northern raids and incursions, listed in Table 1.1, that have always stopped short of a resumption of warfare. At the same time, both sides have maintained large military forces and prepared for a renewed outbreak of intense conflict – mitigated primarily by the presence of a large number of US troops stationed in the South intended to serve as a deterrent to another Northern invasion.

In the past decade or so, international attention has focused on North Korean attempts to build nuclear weapons that could threaten Japan and even the United States. At the same time, the Northern economy has continued to deteriorate and political control was passed from father to Kim Jong Il, his son. Even so, the two Koreas continue to talk about reunification while preparing for the possibility of renewed warfare either of an intra-Korean nature or, possibly, a US preemptive strike on the North.[8] North Korean incursions into South Korean territory have also continued. Yet South Korean official strategy persists in downplaying the threat presented by the North. A greater concern, perhaps peculiar to the Korean peninsula, is that the Kim regime might collapse thereby causing more problems for the South (and prematurely accelerating reunification) than if the Kim regime survived.

Common denominators

What, if anything, do these four cases share? There are actually several common traits in evidence. One is that these state pairs have fought repeatedly. In all four cases, the pairs have regarded their rival as an adversary from the independence of one or both states. Two of the cases date from the early nineteenth century while the other two emerged shortly after the conclusion of World War II. The main reason that they conflict repeatedly is a second shared trait. Whatever the issues that strain their relationship, they have been unable to resolve completely the source(s) of conflict. The most obvious exception appears to be the Ecuadorian–Peruvian case, which may well have resolved their long-running boundary dispute at long last. The Greeks and Turks were able to terminate their traditional rivalry in the 1930s only to have it flare up again in the 1950s. The Greco-Turkish rivalry has de-escalated in the early twenty-first century and may be in the process of terminating. The Koreans presumably will have protracted yet probably constrained conflict as long as there are

---

[8] Manyin (2002) notes four "thaws" in inter-Korean relations (1972, 1985, early 1990s, and 2000). North Korea, however, had also been publicly announcing the need for peaceful reunification when it launched its invasion in 1950.

Table 1.1 *Korean interactions*

Activity	Year
Establishment of the Republic of Korea and the Democratic People's Republic of Korea	1948
Korean War	1950–3
South Korean plane hijacked to North Korea	1958
Shooting incident on demilitarized zone (DMZ)	1966
South Korean frigate sunk, shooting incidents along DMZ, North Korean gunboat sunk	1967
South Korean fishing vessels captured by North; Northern commando raid on South Korean presidential palace unsuccessful; North Korean spy vessel captured by South; North Korean guerrilla raid on eastern coast	1968
Several North Korean ships suspected of infiltration sunk or captured; South Korean plane hijacked to North	1969
South Korea captures infiltration ship and kills agents setting explosives	1970
North Korean assassination attempt on South Korean president kills the wife of the president	1973
Discovery of DMZ Northern infiltration tunnel announced	1974
North–South maritime clash in the west; discovery of another infiltration tunnel announced	1975
Shooting incident on DMZ; Southern aircraft hijacked to North	1977
Another infiltration tunnel discovery announced	1978
North Korean spy rings arrested	1979
North Korean spy rings arrested	1982
A number of South Korean politicians killed in Myanmar bombing attributed to North Korea and presumably focused on South Korean president; North Korean spy rings arrested	1983
South Korean air liner blown up, possibly linked to Olympic Games, later attributed to North Korea	1987
Another infiltration tunnel discovery announced	1990
North Korean army incursion in DMZ; North Korean espionage submarine runs aground on east coast of South Korea	1996
Military intrusion and exchange of fire across DMZ	1997
North Korean submarine trapped in fishing nets off South Korean east coast; North Korean vessel sunk	1998
Serious naval clashes by North and South Korean gunboats in Yellow Sea linked initially to crabbing activities	1999
North Korea threatens military retaliation if US and South Korea enter Yellow Sea area claimed by North Korea	2000
Twelve North Korean intrusions into South Korean waters and exchange of fire across the DMZ	2001
Continued naval intrusions and clashes	2002
North Korea threatens to abandon 1953 Korean War armistice if US imposes trade sanctions	2003

Source: Hoare and Pares (1999: 231–40); updated using Oberdorfer (2001), Manyin (2002), and Nanto (2003).

two states claiming sole legitimacy on the Korean peninsula. India and Pakistan might be able to de-escalate their feud if the status of Kashmir could be resolved to everyone's satisfaction but, so far, a settlement of the Kashmir problem remains elusive. It is also conceivable that the rivalry might persist even if the Kashmir issue went away.

Given the development of these protracted conflict sets, each one characterized by a mix of idiosyncratic and general features, the participants acquire a set of self-fulfilling expectations concerning their adversaries. As enemies, they cannot be trusted. Conciliatory gestures are likely to be ruses. Moves that might seem threatening are definitely so and only confirm expectations that the opponent is up to no good. The third common denominator then is a relationship framed in expectations and beliefs that are prone toward exaggerating possibly hostile actions and downplaying the sincerity of possibly cooperative gestures. This setting is especially conducive to the maintenance of a conflictual relationship. If you cannot trust your adversary to operate in good faith, why should one bother with meaningful negotiations to resolve differences and grievances? Rivalry termination often means somehow overcoming the accumulated expectations of hostility and mistrust that accompany the history of the relationship. That is never easy to do but it is not impossible.

A fourth trait is that these pairs do not fight continuously. They fight at best intermittently. Every so often tensions escalate, troops are mobilized, and a shooting war either breaks out or comes close to breaking out. One or both antagonists may back down or they may be pressured into backing down. But from time to time, prudence, diplomacy, and major power sanctions fail to stop the escalation of conflict from taking place. War is the outcome. Moreover, we maintain that most wars occur in precisely this fashion. Table 1.2 lists all wars that have taken place since the end of World War II through the year 2000. The same table also identifies the rivalries at work in each case. The point is not that every war involves rivals exclusively. Every war does not, yet most do. Only three of the twenty-seven cases (the Russo-Hungarian, Turco-Cypriot, and Kosovo wars) in Table 1.2 deviate from this generalization.[9] Rivalries are very much involved in all of the other cases even if the rivals identified are not always the only or even the central actors involved. For instance, it is not an uncommon occurrence for rivals to join ongoing wars between

---

[9] In the first two exceptions, there was some deliberation, albeit limited, as to whether the main rival of the USSR or Turkey should intervene to oppose the invasions. One of the concerns about Serbian treatment of its Albanian minority was linked to the potential for drawing in other Balkan states and preexisting rivalries in the area. So, even the few exceptions have definite rivalry linkages.

Table 1.2 *Warfare in the second half of the twentieth century*

War name	Date	Rivalries
First Kashmir	1948–9	India–Pakistan
Palestine	1948	Egypt–Israel; Iraq–Israel; Israel–Jordan; Israel–Syria
Korean	1950–3	North Korea–South Korea; China–United States
Russo-Hungarian	1956	NA
Sinai	1956	Egypt–Israel
Assam	1962	China–India
Vietnamese	1965–75	North Vietnam–South Vietnam
Second Kashmir	1965	India–Pakistan
Six Day	1967	Egypt–Israel; Israel–Jordan; Israel–Syria
Israeli–Egyptian	1969–70	Egypt–Israel
Football	1969	El Salvador–Honduras
Bangladesh	1971	India–Pakistan
Yom Kippur	1973	Egypt–Israel; Iraq–Israel; Israel–Jordan; Israel–Syria
Turco-Cypriot	1974	NA
Vietnamese	1975–9	Cambodia–Vietnam
Ethiopian–Somali	1977	Ethiopia–Somalia
Sino–Vietnamese	1979	China–Vietnam
Iran–Iraq	1980–8	Iran–Iraq
Falklands	1982	Argentina–United Kingdom
Israel–Syria	1982	Israel–Syria
Sino–Vietnamese	1987	China–Vietnam
Gulf War	1990–1	Iraq–Kuwait; Egypt–Iraq; Iraq–Saudi Arabia; Iraq–Syria
Nagorno–Karabakh	1991–4	Armenia–Azerbaijan
Yugoslav Disintegration	1991–5	Bosnia–Croatia; Bosnia–Serbia; Croatia–Serbia
Eritrea–Ethiopia	1998–2000	Eritrea–Ethiopia
Kosovo	1999	NA
Kargil	1999	India–Pakistan

Source: The entries through the 1990–1 Gulf War are taken from the Correlates of War inventory (Sarkees, 2000). We will be surprised if all of the events listed after the Gulf War appear on a future Correlates of War listing of wars. We do assume that the Ecuador-Peruvian war failed to exceed the conventional battle death threshold used by the Correlates of War project. There are also major ambiguities about how best to treat the complicated and multiple state fighting in Zaire and Central Africa in general and, therefore, we have omitted this war from the list above.

an enemy and some other state.[10] This is one succinct way to explain the presence of the United States and China in the Korean War or Egypt and Syria in the first Gulf coalition against Iraq.

If most wars have strong roots in rivalry dynamics, then it seems fair to conclude that we need to have a decent understanding of these rivalry dynamics if we are to understand why wars break out. While that may appear to be an obvious conclusion, the irony is that scholars of war causality have virtually ignored rivalry dynamics altogether until quite recently. The normal tendency has been to either take each war as a singular event or all wars as interchangeable manifestations of the same phenomenon. In both extremes, the ideas that the main participants have a history and that that history probably has some bearing on whether and when conflict escalates get overlooked or pushed aside. But not only do most of the main war participants have histories of conflict with their adversaries, so, too, do the wars that they fight. If rivals have fought three or four wars, it is usually very difficult to explain, say, the third war without reference to the first and second. Often, the earlier wars make subsequent wars more probable. In particular cases, something may happen during or immediately after the "last" war in a rival series that makes subsequent wars less probable. The 1995 war between Ecuador and Peru seems to be a case in point.

Not all wars are serial in nature. Table 1.3 highlights this facet by demonstrating that only six of the twenty-three rivals that appear in Table 1.2 have experienced more than one war in the last half-century or so. But their rivalries encompass thirteen (50 percent) of the wars. It is also worth noting, at the same time, that some of the most intense blood-letting has been associated with the (so far) one-time wars between rivals (Korean, Vietnamese, and Iran–Iraq). The point here is not that only serial conflict is of interest. What is of interest is why and how rivals fight. Some do it repeatedly. Some fight very intensely for long periods of time. Some do not fight at all. All of these various tendencies are of interest. In short, to enhance our explanations of war, we need to know why rivals sometimes engage in staring contests and other times fisticuffs.

The rest of this book offers an explanation of why rivals fight sometimes. Yet it attempts more. It first establishes a foundation for identifying rivals and rivalries (Chapter 2). One of the advantages of rivalry analysis is that it can focus on the small number of feuding dyads that cause a disproportionate amount of the trouble in world politics. The prevailing assumptions that all actors are equally likely to clash and that they do so independently of previous clashes can also be amended

---

[10] This question of war joiners is reconsidered in Chapters 6 and 7.

Table 1.3 *Rivalries in contemporary warfare*

Rivalry	Number of appearances in war
Egypt–Israel	5
India–Pakistan	4
Israel–Syria	4
Israel–Jordan	3
China–Vietnam	2
Iraq–Israel	2
Argentina–United Kingdom	1
Armenia–Azerbaijan	1
Bosnia–Croatia	1
Bosnia–Serbia	1
Cambodia–Vietnam	1
China–India	1
Croatia–Serbia	1
Egypt–Iraq	1
El Salvador–Honduras	1
Eritrea–Ethiopia	1
Ethiopia–Somalia	1
Iran–Iraq	1
Iraq–Kuwait	1
Iraq–Saudi Arabia	1
Iraq–Syria	1
North Korea–South Korea	1
North Vietnam–South Vietnam	1

or abandoned. But the value added of this approach will hinge in part on how rivalries are identified. Earlier rivalry dyads have been identified primarily by satisfying thresholds in the frequency of militarized disputes occurring within some pre-specified period of time. But this dispute-density approach implies a number of analytical problems including the possibility that rivalry analyses are simply being restricted to a device for distinguishing between states that engage in frequent and infrequent conflict. An alternative approach defines rivalry as a perceptual categorizing process in which actors identify which states are sufficiently threatening competitors to qualify as enemies. The question, then, is who do decision-makers think of as their external rivals?

Answers to this question can be gleaned from historical analyses of foreign policy. A systematic approach to identifying these perceived strategic rivalries yields 173 rivalries in existence between 1816 and 1999. The rivalries named by this perceptual approach can be compared to the rivalry identification lists produced by several dispute-density approaches. The point of the comparison is not necessarily to assert the superiority of one approach over others as much as it is to highlight the very real costs and benefits associated with different operational assumptions. The question must also be raised whether all approaches are equally focused on what we customarily mean by rivalries. In the absence of anything resembling a consensus on what rivalries are, moreover, the additivity of findings will prove to be impossible. This particular problem cannot be resolved in this volume. The best that we can do is to establish a sufficiently solid foundation for our specific conception in the hope that others may also find it worthwhile to adopt.

Chapter 3 proceeds from this foundation to describe the nature of the 173 rivalries that we think have dominated conflict since 1816. How rare are they? Are they becoming more common or less so? What is the nature of the grievances that lead to rivalry relationships? Who participates in them? The second half of the chapter examines questions pertaining to timing, conflict, and distribution. Are rivalries something that happen "at birth" or as soon as independence is declared or do they emerge only gradually? Once in play, how long do they last? What proportion of rivalries actually experience militarized disputes and wars? Finally, we ask where these rivalry relationships occur. Are some regions more rivalry-prone than others? Have some regions become less rivalry-prone while others have become more prone to protracted conflicts between adversaries?

The first three chapters construct a conceptual, descriptive, and empirical foundation for a discussion of what difference strategic rivalries make in world politics. It will become clear that we think that one of the main answers to why rivalries matter is that they are critical to an understanding of conflict escalation processes. The remaining seven chapters are thus devoted to examining the processes of conflict escalation in several ways. Chapters 4 and 5 take on the task of demonstrating empirically whether information on rivalries makes some difference to our ability to account for variation in crisis behavior. Underlying the emerging interest in the role of rivalry processes as antecedents to interstate conflict, for instance, is the simple idea that conflict within the constraints of rivalry works differently than conflict outside of rivalry.

In Chapter 4, we examine the concepts of protracted conflict, as developed within the International Crisis Behavior (ICB) project (Brecher and Wilkenfeld, 1997), and rivalry, and discuss some of their applications to crisis escalation processes. The protracted conflict and rivalry concepts are not identical but they do overlap in terms of their emphases on historical context, serious goal incompatibilities, and stakes that might be resolved coercively. Developing an argument for the concept of rivalry possessing fewer limitations than the protracted conflict one, we proceed to evaluate the interaction between rivalry and other international and domestic conditions. We make use of an ICB escalation model when predicting crisis escalation to war. Throughout, our basic question concerns what role interstate rivalry plays in crisis behavior. Are the crises of rivals more lethal than those of nonrivals? If so, can we pinpoint why that is the case? We find that strategic rivalry not only makes escalation more likely, but also significantly changes the way we think about more traditional predictors of conflict, such as capability ratios, the number of actors in a crisis, democracy, and the issues under contention.

Chapter 5 takes these ideas and findings one step further. Responding to the debate concerning the relationship between conflict events over time between the same disputants, we acknowledge that the evidence to date on whether crises are related serially is fairly weak. To fill these lacunae, we examine four hypotheses relating past crisis behavior and sequences of crises to subsequent conflict, using the ICB data examined in the previous chapter. Our results support the serial crisis hypothesis, and suggest that the probability of subsequent crises and wars increases with each past crisis. Our findings also reinforce the inclination to give more emphasis to the analysis of rivalries. Thus, the combination of Chapters 4 and 5 establishes a solid foundation for claims that strategic rivalries matter. Clearly, they matter very much to the study of crisis and war escalation.

Chapters 6 and 7 make a case for differentiating rivalries according to the nature of their adversarial differences. John Vasquez's (1996) rivalry escalation theory stresses territorial disputes as the principal focus for a two-path explanation of war. Neighbors fight over adjacent space and non-neighbors sometimes join ongoing wars between neighbors. But major powers are also much concerned with positional issues. Expanding the war motivation focus to encompass both spatial and positional issues facilitates the development of a new, more elaborate theory in Chapter 6 from which several new hypotheses can be derived, in addition to the older ones. Evaluation of the new theory strongly supports the two-path, two-issue interpretation. In the major power subsystem, noncontiguous rivals outnumber contiguous rivals, dyadic wars are scarce, and war joining has been the norm. Spatial issues alone would have a hard time accounting for this pattern. Variable mixes of spatial and positional issues are able to account for it and a number of derived hypotheses reasonably well.

Chapter 7 takes this line of inquiry one step further by looking at the role of spatial and positional issues in rivalry initiation and escalation in the full universe of cases – that is, all states, not solely major powers within which positional issues are most likely to be manifested. We also assess the extent to which the late Stuart Bremer's (1992) dangerous dyad attributes (predicting which states are most likely to go to war) serve as potential predictors of rivalry. Do attributes found to identify war-proneness in general also tell us which states are most likely to become strategic rivals? This seems a reasonable question to raise given some apparent overlap between rivalry initiation and war-proneness. But there are also reasons for anticipating that Bremer's dangerous state profile, while no doubt highlighting important variables, will require some modification for use in rivalry analyses.

The findings put forward in Chapter 7 suggest that Bremer's dangerous dyad notion is of only limited assistance in delineating which pairs of states become rivals. Controlling for other factors, we also find that spatial rivalries are more prone to war, but not lower-level violence, than are positional rivalries. As found in Chapter 6's more restricted focus on major powers, positional rivals are more apt to join ongoing disputes than are spatial rivals. In this respect, the combination of Chapters 6 and 7 lays a concrete foundation for there being more than one escalatory path to war. Different types of rivals possess different behavioral propensities and, therefore, are likely to become entangled in warfare in different ways.

Why do spatial and positional rivalries sometimes intensify? Why do their conflicts escalate to war? We have already explored rivalry and crisis escalation in more general terms in Chapters 4 and 5. Chapters 6 and 7 examine a specific argument about spatial and positional rivalry escalation. Chapters 8 and 9 take this latter question even further by developing the implications of John Vasquez's (1993) steps-to-war theory. This theory organizes an understanding of international conflict into an interactive complex of factors, including contested territory, interstate rivalry, recurrent crises, alliances, military build-ups and the onset of war. Chapter 8 begins our examination of this construction by examining information on rivalry, crises, alliances, and military build-ups. In the context of rivalry and recurrent crises, military build-ups and asymmetrical external alliance situations combine to make escalations to war more probable. Indeed, the linkage between recurring crises, military build-ups and alliance making is so close that there is little variance left to be accounted for in the main relationship between crises and war once the interactions between crises and build-ups/alliances have been controlled.

Chapter 9 then steps back to take a closer look at territorial contests given the strong emphasis bestowed on them in the Vasquez theory. Bringing together independent information on territorial contests, rivalries, and conflict escalation (militarized interstate disputes [MIDs] and war), an examination of the timing and temporal order of the three processes is first conducted. Contrary to conventional expectations, the contested territory-militarized dispute-rivalry ordering is found to be rare. Rivalries and contested territory often begin at the same time. Second, a unified model of MIDs and war is constructed in which the triadic combination of contested territory, contiguity, and strategic rivalry is found to be a quite strong explanatory combination, both over time and in contrast to other explanatory factors such as the regime type and major power status. These findings provide strong support for arguments such as Vasquez's steps-to-war theory that are predicated precisely on these sources of conflict escalation.

Combining our arguments and theory-testing of steps-to-war theory to create a single model encompassing contested territory, rivalry, recurrent crises, military buildups and alliances that can be used to construct a relatively parsimonious but very powerful explanation for crisis and war escalation is the task of the second half of Chapter 9.[11] While we contend that this is a major step forward in unraveling the complicated dynamics involved in escalatory processes, we do not anticipate that this will be the last word on conflict spirals.

We think this improved understanding of interstate escalatory dynamics can serve as both a foundation and stimulus for more interactive attempts to unravel the puzzles of conflict escalation and war causation. Whether this proves to be the case or not, our ninth chapter makes a strong case for viewing the onset of war as a multivariate process, predicated on a restricted set of dynamics and theoretically grounded in Vasquez's theory, that also depends on what type of rivalry is involved. Positional and spatial rivalries do not necessarily follow the same interactive path to war escalation.

Chapter 10 summarizes the substantive influence of our work on rivalry and the steps to war, and compares it to the liberal constraints of economic development, economic interdependence, and democratization in restraining conflict escalation. We take part of the model developed in Chapter 9 that emphasizes the interactions among territorial conflicts, proximity, and rivalry and compare its explanatory weight to the liberal constraints. In doing so, we elaborate an argument initiated by Russett (2003) that advocates distinguishing between inducements to conflict and various factors that serve to facilitate or suppress conflict escalation. We see the territorial conflict–proximity–rivalry interaction as a major inducement to conflict. The evidence on this question proves to be quite

---

[11] Unlike a number of earlier analyses on these questions, we can also claim to have avoided as much as possible the endogeneity problems associated with an overreliance on various facets of militarized interstate disputes to measure rivalry, crisis, crisis recurrence, and war. Most of our variables are conceptualized and operationalized independently.

strong. These inducements, and facilitators such as capability asymmetry, play at least as important a role in conflict as liberal constraints and suppressors.

In general, then, interstate conflict in world politics is unlikely to be captured by a single model. There are multiple paths to conflict escalation. We make what we think is a strong case for differentiating between rivals and nonrivals. Another case is made for distinguishing between positional and spatial rivalries. Toward the end of this study, we also distinguish among inducements, facilitators, and suppressors, connecting this work to the broader literature on international conflict. These distinctions are demonstrated in this volume as having quite significant utility in explaining escalation in militarized disputes and crises to war. Yet our arguments and findings hardly constitute the end of the rivalry story. Major research challenges await in further delineating the dynamics of rivalry interactions. We have focused on conflict escalation, no doubt the most dramatic facet of rivalries, but that is only part of the landscape. The next challenge is to explain why and how rivalries run hot and cold. Literally, some rivals at one point are discussing peace and cooperation and, in the next, shooting at one another. Other sets of rivalries remain intensely hostile for prolonged periods of time. Still others settle their differences. Explaining these differences in behavior will constitute a major test for international relations theory and analysis.[12] As in the arguments advanced in this study, we doubt very much that future researchers will discover a singular explanation of fluctuations in rivalry interactions. Multiple paths, once again, are far more likely to emerge. Yet we seem to be on the right track(s).

---

[12] For example, see Colaresi (2005).

2 Defining and identifying strategic rivalries in world politics

We have tried to suggest in the preceding chapter that the analysis of rivalry in world politics possesses some considerable potential for revolutionizing the study of conflict. Rather than assume that all actors are equally likely to engage in conflictual relations, a focus on rivalries permits analysts to focus on the relatively small handful of actors who, demonstrably, are the ones most likely to generate conflict vastly disproportionate to their numbers. For instance, strategic rivals, a conceptualization that will be developed further in this chapter, have opposed each other in 58 (77.3 percent) of 75 wars since 1816. If we restrict our attention to the twentieth century, strategic rivals opposed one another in 41 (87.2 percent) of 47 wars. A focus on the post-1945 era yields an opposing rival ratio of 21 (91.3 percent) of 23 wars. Moreover, their conflicts are not independent across time – another frequent and major assumption in conflict studies. They are part of a historical process in which a pair of states create and sustain a relationship of atypical hostility for some period of time. What they do to each other in the present is conditioned by what they have done to each other in the past. What they do in the present is also conditioned by calculations about future ramifications of current choices. Rivalries thus represent a distinctive class of conflict in the sense that rivals deal with each other in a psychologically charged context of path dependent hostility in ways that are usually absent in conflicts that occur in more neutral contexts.

We cannot yet say that we know as much as we would like to know about how conflict in rivalry operates differently than conflict in nonrivalry contexts. That is, after all, one of the main reasons for undertaking the studies presented in this volume. Unfortunately, we have not really been sensitive to the significance of rivalry relationships for all that long a time. Much remains to be learned. However, before we are likely to make significant headway in reducing our collective ignorance about rivalry relationships, the problem of what rivalries are and how best to measure them must be confronted. It is no doubt expecting too much that we could develop a quick consensus on this matter. At the very least, though, we need to come to terms with the choices being made in undertaking the study of rivalry. One of the most fundamental issues relates to how we know a rivalry when we see one. The basic tension that is analyzed here is between an interpretative emphasis on perceptions about threatening competitors who are categorized as enemies (strategic rivalries) and an empirical emphasis on satisfying a minimal number of militarized disputes within some time limit (enduring and interstate rivalries). Must relationships become sufficiently militarized before we recognize it as a rivalry? A related question is what do we do with this recognition to translate it into a systematic data set for empirical analysis purposes? The interpretative approach requires a labor-intensive investigation of historical sources. The empirical approach requires manipulating an existing data set according to various rules. Unless we can come to some early understanding about these questions, the findings of rivalry analysis will simply not be comparable in any meaningful sense.

While the study of rivalry has been characterized by a large number of relatively casual, historical references to the phenomenon, there is also a burgeoning empirical literature that, in most cases, has developed a convention of relying on data on militarized interstate disputes (MIDs; see Jones, Bremer, and Singer, 1996) to identify rivalry relationships.[1] Essentially, analysts require X number of disputes within Y number of years to tell them that a rivalry exists. They then employ this information as a filter for various studies of conflict onset, escalation, and termination. Even though the approach seems quite straightforward, there are in fact a host of problems associated with this practice. One of the problems is whether the dispute-density approach measures rivalry relationships *per se* or simply greater-than-average disputatiousness?

Moreover, the last two decades have seen a number of formulae put forward for capturing the right dispute-density. How do we assess rivalry findings if they are predicated on a bewildering variety of different operational thresholds? Another problem is whether relying on information on the occurrence of disputes distorts our understanding of when rivalries begin and end. Does a reliance on dispute activity discriminate against places and times where and when militarized dispute activity is less visible?

There are definite limits on how well we can answer these questions at this time. But they need to be addressed early on rather than later.

---

[1] In addition, case studies that are sensitive to rivalry processes are beginning to appear. See, for example, Lieberman (1995), Stein (1996), Mares (1996/7), Colaresi (2005), a number of chapters in Diehl (1998) and Thompson (1999), Hensel (2001), Mares (2001), Rasler (2001), Thompson (2001), and the contents of Paul (2005).

Fortunately, it is also possible to address them in the context of an alternative way to identify rivalries. Rather than relying on data sets already in existence that were put together for other purposes, it is feasible to cull information from historical sources about when and with whom decision-makers thought they were in rivalry relationships. This approach emphasizing perceptions rather than disputes is not without its own problems. It requires a great deal of interpretation that renders replication difficult. But the question remains whether it is a more suitable approach to the substantive questions associated with rivalry analyses than the dispute-density approach.

Without knowing which type of approach is more accurate in capturing the "true" rivalry pool, the best that can be done is to look for the apparent biases exhibited by the alternative approaches. Accordingly, the remainder of this chapter is devoted to a more detailed examination of the problems linked to alternative approaches to rivalry identification. The examination is conducted within the concrete context of six identifications of rivalry: five versions utilizing a dispute-density approach (Diehl and Goertz's [2000] 63 enduring rivalries, Klein, Goertz, and Diehl [2006] 290 enduring rivalries, Bennett's [1996, 1997a] 34 interstate rivalries, Bennett's [1997b, 1998] 61 rivalries, and Maoz and Mor's [2002] 110 enduring rivalries) in contrast to a new data set on 173 strategic rivalries that is predicated on systematizing historical perceptions about competitors, threats, and enemies. The sequence of discussion is to first discuss the definition and operationalization of strategic rivalry – the measurement approach that we will be relying upon in subsequent chapters. A second section is devoted to comparing the six sets of rivalry identifications in terms of conceptualization, identification agreement, spatial and temporal coverage, and other types of characteristics. This is not a tournament in which one approach will be determined to be the victor. Each approach starts with a certain conceptualization and then proceeds to measure that conceptualization in distinctive ways. The ultimate question, therefore, cannot be which operational path is right or wrong. Rather, the fundamental question is what analytical price or payoff is likely to be associated with pursuing one path versus another.

Strategic rivalries

Strategic rivalries are very much about conflict. Thus, one needs to begin with some elementary assumptions about conflict. Inherently, conflicts are about relative scarcity and overlapping interests and goals. We cannot have as much as we would like of objects with value because there are usually not enough of them to go round. If desired objects are scarce, someone's gain usually means somebody else's loss. We cannot attain all of our goals because to do so would interfere with somebody else's maximal goal attainment. Hence, conflicts are about real incompatibilities in attaining material and nonmaterial goals. We accept the assumption that they do not exist unless they are perceived by actors. Perceptual pathologies or misperceptions may also make conflicts worse than they might otherwise have been. But conflicts still tend to be based on some inability to occupy the same space, share the same position, or accept the superiority of another's belief system. Disputes about territory, influence and status, and ideology, therefore, are at the core of conflicts of interest at all levels of analysis, but especially between states.[2]

Conflicts of interest vary in intensity. Conflicts can be mild or extreme. Yet state behavior is not universally consumed by conflict. Actors also cooperate, and they do so in varying amounts. One way to visualize the array of behavior is to imagine a conflict–cooperation continuum. At one end are extreme cases of intense conflict; at the other, extreme cases of intense cooperation. In between are varying mixes of conflict and cooperation of the relatively milder sorts. The relationships between most pairs of states can be located around the center of this continuum. That is, their relationships are normal and encompass some combination of conflict and cooperation. Some pairs of states have especially cooperative relationships (often called "special relationships"), because they share certain affinities of culture, race, and language, or because they share important goals, or because one of the states in the dyad has no choice but to be highly cooperative.

In the intense conflict zone of the continuum, pairs of states regard each other as significant threats to goal attainment. However, there are essentially two types of dyadic situations at this end of the continuum. Dyads encompass either roughly comparable states or circumstances in which one of the states is much more powerful than the other. When the dyad encompasses states with roughly equal capabilities, the conflicts of interest are likely to persist because it is less likely that one part of the dyad will be able to impose its will on the other actor successfully. When the dyad encompasses states with highly unequal capabilities, the conflicts of interest are less likely to persist, all other things being equal, because the more powerful actor can contemplate coercing the other actor to accept its superior position. If those same factors remain equal, the weaker party is likely to have incentive to yield on the question(s) at hand.

---

[2] There is no reason rivalry analysis might not also prove fruitful in applications to domestic political processes.

Of course, other things are not always equal. Stronger states do not always win their contests with weaker states. Weaker parties do not always knuckle under to stronger foes. Hence, it cannot be assumed that conflicts of interest will not persist in cases of dyads with unequal capability. They may not be the norm, but it is possible for conflicts to emerge in these circumstances and, given the appropriate conditions, to persist. It is also possible for decision-makers in weak states to delude themselves temporarily into believing that they have more capability to act in international politics than it turns out they really have. Decision-makers in strong states are also quite capable of exaggerating the menace posed by weaker neighbors. Finally, relatively weak actors may for a time "overachieve" – that is, act beyond the limits of their own capability base. In such cases, they promote themselves into the next capability tier and can become legitimate threats to otherwise stronger adversaries.

Strategic rivalries might be thought of as the reverse image of the cooperative special relationships. All dyads located toward the intense conflict end of the continuum are not strategic rivalries. A very weak state confronted with an intense threat from a very strong state is unlikely to see the very strong state as a rival. Nor is the strong, threatening state, other things being equal, likely to see the very weak state as a rival. Capability asymmetry does not preclude rivalry but it does make it somewhat less probable.

Nor are rivals defined solely by intense conflicts of interest. Rivals must be selected. Three selection criteria appear to be most important. The actors in question must regard each other as (a) competitors, (b) the source of actual or latent threats that pose some possibility of becoming militarized, and (c) as enemies. These criteria are not options. All three must be present to create rivalry.

Most states are not viewed as competitors – that is, capable of "playing" in the same league. Relatively weak states are usually capable of interacting competitively only with states in their immediate neighborhood, thereby narrowing the playing field dramatically. Stronger actors may move into the neighborhood in threatening ways but without necessarily being perceived, or without perceiving themselves, as genuine competitors. If an opponent is too strong to be opposed unilaterally, assistance may be sought from a rival of the opponent. Other opponents may be regarded more as nuisances or, more neutrally, as policy problems than as full-fledged competitors or rivals.

Scandinavia was once a theater dominated by the strategic rivalry between Sweden and Denmark. As new and more powerful states, Prussia and Russia in particular, entered the Baltic subsystem, the central rivalry was gradually supplanted and wound down as the traditional Baltic rivals found themselves outclassed by the new and greater power of their neighbors. At the same time, Sweden and Denmark ultimately came to a territorial arrangement that brought them less into conflict than had been the case in the past. Thus, several processes worked to de-escalate the Danish–Swedish rivalry without simply transforming the traditional rivalry into new ones.[3] Sweden attempted to be a rival to Russia for a time but was forced to concede that it was no longer sufficiently competitive. Denmark and Prussia never really became rivals despite the contentious Schleswig-Holstein dispute and the two nineteenth-century wars over the issue. Denmark was too weak and Prussia was more concerned about its Austrian and French rivals.

Relatively strong states are apt to perceive more competition than are weak states and to engage in wider fields of interaction. Yet only some limited portion of this wider field is likely to generate strategic threats. Even the strongest states find it highly taxing in resources and energy to cope with several rivals simultaneously. As a consequence, decision-makers, of both major and minor powers, are apt to downgrade old rivals once new ones begin to emerge. Taking on a new adversary often means putting some of one's old conflicts on the back burner. Both the supply and demand for rivals thus work toward actors being highly selective in whom they choose to threaten and from whom they choose to perceive strategic threats. As already noted, most states are unable to project threats very far in the first place. That fact of life also helps narrow the selection pool immensely.

The outstanding example of rivalry downgrading occurred prior to World War I. Faced with an emerging German threat, British decision-makers negotiated significant reductions in the level of hostility associated with their main rivals of the nineteenth century: France, Russia, and the United States. Two of these de-escalations proved to be permanent. Only the Anglo-Russian strategic rivalry resumed when decision-makers found it more convenient once again to act on their conflicts of interest. The other intriguing dimension of this British example is that a case can be made that the source of Britain's greatest threat emanated from the United States, not Germany. It would not have been totally implausible if British decision-makers had decided to ally with Germany and to oppose their mutual, traditional rivals, France and Russia. But they did not; nor was the United States placed at the top of the external threat list. That place was reserved for Germany. British decision-makers selected Germany to be Britain's principal rival, just as the Germans selected Britain as one of their primary rivals.[4]

---

[3] On the Danish–Swedish rivalry, see Lisk (1967), Barton (1986), and Fiztmaurice (1992).
[4] See, for instance, Kennedy (1976, 1980).

Similarly, Israeli decision-makers have done much the same thing by drawing concentric circles around their state boundaries.[5] Subject to some qualifications, Israel's rivals have been located in the most immediate geographic circle. Those located farther away are, or at least were once, less worrisome. Within the inner circle, further rank ordering took place, with Egypt and Syria regarded as more dangerous than Jordan. Much the same process was at work in southern Africa prior to the end of apartheid. States, such as Tanzania, that were not proximate to South Africa's borders were much less likely to be targets of South African attacks. Angola, Mozambique, Zimbabwe, and Zambia were a different story.

It is precisely in that context that the most important criterion for identifying rivalries is their non-anonymity.[6] Actors categorize other actors in their environments. Some are friends, others are enemies. Threatening enemies who are also adjudged to be competitors in some sense, as opposed to irritants or simply problems, are branded as rivals. This categorization is very much a dynamic process. Actors interpret the intentions of others based on earlier behavior and forecasts about the future behavior of these other actors. The interpretation of these intentions leads to expectations about the likelihood of conflicts escalating to physical attacks.

Strategic rivals anticipate some positive probability of an attack from their competitors over issues in contention. One side's expectations influence their own subsequent behavior toward their adversary and the process continues from there. Both sides expect hostile behavior from the other side and proceed to deal with the adversary with that expectation in mind. One round of hostility then reinforces the expectation of future hostility (and rivalry) and leads to some likelihood of a further exchange of hostile behavior in cyclical fashion. Whether or not the level of hostility spirals increasingly upward, the rivalry relationship, with time and repeatedly reinforced expectations, develops a variety of psychological baggage from which it is difficult to break free. The expectations become more rigid, less sensitive to changes in adversary behavior, and less in need of continued reinforcement.

This is not a mystical process in which somehow the rivalry takes over like a runaway train. The cognitive biases and expectations that are constructed to justify and maintain rivalries have their domestic political

---

[5] Brecher (1972) pursues this topic.

[6] This element is stressed especially in Kuenne (1989). See, as well, McGinnis and Williams (1989), McGinnis (1990), Vasquez (1993), Thompson (1995), Levy and Ali (1998), Levy (1999), and Rapkin (1999) for other definitions of rivalry that could be said to overlap on this issue. The enemy criterion follows the thread suggested some time ago by Finlay, Holsti, and Fagan (1967).

process counterparts. Rivalries develop their own domestic constituencies and those constituencies lobby for maintaining the rivalry (Colaresi 2005). Leaders may find that their room for external maneuver is circumscribed severely by the influence of these domestic constituencies. For that matter, leaders openly opposed to maintaining a prominent rivalry are less likely to be selected for major decision-making posts in the first place.

The combination of expectations of threat, cognitive rigidities, and domestic political processes makes strategic rivalry a potent factor in world politics. They create and sustain dyadic relationships of structured hostility, with or without a great deal of continuous, external reinforcement. Once in place, they develop substantial barriers to cooperation and conflict de-escalation. Some level of conflict and distrust becomes the norm. Dealing with one's rivals entails juggling very real conflicts of interest within a charged context especially prone to various decision-making pathologies (in-group solidarity, out-group hostility, mistrust, misperception, and self-fulfilling prophecies).

As a consequence, rivalry relationships should be particularly conducive to at least intermittent and serial conflict escalation. Not all interstate conflicts are embedded in their own history but those of rivals definitely are. Conflict de-escalation should thus also be much less likely within rivalry contexts than outside of them. To fundamentally alter this state of affairs becomes a matter of somehow overcoming expectational inertia – never an easy process in the political or any other type of arena. It is not impossible to do so. Yet, observers are often caught by surprise, for good reasons, when it is achieved. Very few observers, for instance, foresaw the ending of the US–USSR rivalry despite its being the most central conflict axis in the world system for some forty-five years.

Operationalizing strategic rivalry

This perceptual perspective on rivalry can be translated into operational terms by examining the appropriate evidence about who actors themselves describe as their rivals at any given point in time. Foreign policy-makers not only talk and write explicitly about their identification of rivals, but they also bias their activities by concentrating considerable energy on coping with their selected adversaries. Not surprisingly, then, we have an extensive foreign policy/diplomatic history literature well stocked with clues as to which, and when, states are strategic rivals. Culling the information constitutes a major task, to be sure, but it is possible to extract such information, systematize it, and generate a schedule of rivalries for all states in the international system as far back in time as one has the resources and inclination to do so.[7]

We no longer think twice about coding information on the existence and dates of onset and termination of wars, crises, deterrence attempts, alliances, or trade.[8] Collecting information on strategic rivalries is not really all that different an enterprise. No phenomenon is so clearcut that counting it does not require some level of interpretation. What is a war? If the definition hinges on battle deaths, how does one assess the number of troops actually killed? If a crisis must pose a severe threat to the existence of a state, how do we tell what decision-makers engaged in responding to the challenge are really thinking? If we want to know whether a deterrence attempt was successful, how do we go about determining whether an aggressor was really deterred from doing something that had been intended? What should we do with long-standing informal alignments that seem to be more meaningful than some formal alliances? Whose trade estimates should we trust: the importing state, the exporting state, or the vertically integrated, multinational corporation that evades labeling its production somewhere else as "trade"?

The point remains that measurement choices rarely boil down to interpreting the raw information versus allowing the facts to speak for themselves. Some interpretation of the raw information is inevitable. In the case of identifying strategic rivalry relationships, some more interpretation of the raw data is required than is normally the case with wars, alliances, or trade. The reason for this is that one is attempting to codify decision-maker perceptions without ever expecting to have direct access to these perceptions. In looking for proxies, minimal thresholds of violence or verbal threats as in the case of wars or crises have limited utility. These indicators may tell us something about the level of hostility at any given point in time but they are unlikely to tell us how long the rivalry has been in existence. Wars and disputes may come and go but rivalries can persist for generations. Strategic rivalries are not usually formally announced, as in the case of alliances, although official justifications for defense spending can approximate these formalities. Rivalries are sometimes declared to be over and sometimes the declarations can be taken at face value – but only sometimes.

---

[7] Data on major power rivalries going back to 1494 were also collected as part of this National Science Foundation funded project but they are not analyzed in this volume. Two applications are found in Colaresi (2004, 2005) and Rennstich (2003). Another application will be developed in Thompson (forthcoming).

[8] "Thinking twice" means only that we are not intimidated by the task, not that we can do it perfectly well.

The bottom line is that collecting information on strategic rivalries is not completely different from collecting systematic information on other topics of interest in world politics.[9] The phenomenon being measured must be delineated as carefully and accurately as possible. Data collection rules and sources must be made as explicit as possible. But as long as the rivalry definition demands that we focus on decision-maker perceptions and categorizations of other states, the need for more interpretation than usual should be anticipated. The following coding rules were employed to generate data on strategic rivalries for the 1816–1999 period:

1. Strategic rivals must be independent states, as determined by Gleditsch and Ward's (1999) inventory of independent states.[10]

2. Beginning and ending dates are keyed as much as possible to the timing of evidence about the onset of explicit threat, competitor, and enemy perceptions on the part of decision-makers. Historical analyses, for instance, often specify that decision-makers were unconcerned about a competitor prior to some year just as they also provide reasonably specific information about the timing of rapprochements and whether they were meaningful ones or simply tactical maneuvers. For instance, one might have thought there was a strong likelihood that some form of Spanish–US rivalry over Cuba preceded the 1898 war. Yet one is hard pressed to find any evidence of much US official concern about Spanish activities as a threat after the American Civil War. While Spanish decision-makers may have felt threatened by the presence and growing strength of the United States, US decision-makers often can be characterized as simply preferring the Cuban problem to go away. Alternatively, they also worried that Spanish colonies would be taken over by some other European power (see, for instance, Langley, 1976; Combs, 1986). The two wars between Spain and Morocco, prior to World War I and very contrary to what one might expect, also do not seem to have been preceded by a sense of rivalry (Burke, 1976; Parsons, 1976).

More often the identification problem is one of assessing a variety of different dates advanced as beginning and ending candidates. However, the candidates are not put forward in the relevant sources on the basis of a rivalry definition involving threat, competitor, and enemy criteria (or dispute-densities, for that matter). In actuality, it is often unclear

---

[9] Collecting data on rivalries is very much like collecting information on military coups (Thompson, 1973) or ships-of-the-line (Modelski and Thompson, 1988).

[10] Basically, the prime value of the Gleditsch–Ward approach is that it incorporates a number of non-European states earlier than do the conventions that have hitherto prevailed. This is important if one finds that a state engaged in an external rivalry is not considered to exist by prevailing Correlates of War conventions. Those who wish to employ a more restrictive system membership need only remove the rivalry cases that do not match.

what any given historian or decision-maker means by the terms "rival" and "rivalry." The mere utterance of the terms by appropriate sources, therefore, is not sufficient evidence of the existence of a rivalry. The operational question is one of deciding whether all three rivalry criteria have been met. Of the three criteria, perceived threat and enemy categorization are the most straightforward to identify. The competitor status identification can be murkier and tends to hinge on how the threat is perceived. If the threat is too great to be met by the threatened state acting alone or in conjunction with other states of similar capability, or if the threat is too insignificant to worry much about, the source of threat is not usually viewed as a competitor.

Denmark's decision-makers probably felt threatened by the Soviet Union during the Cold War, for instance, but there would not be much that Denmark could do alone or in alliance with half-a-dozen other states of similar capability to meet the threat. Denmark was not in the same league as the Soviet Union and neither Danish nor Soviet decision-makers were likely to think otherwise. Britain, on the other hand, had a long-lasting rivalry with Russia and the Soviet Union that persisted after the end of World War II despite Britain's diminished capacity after 1945. As long as Britain tried to maintain its great power status and as long as the Soviet Union and others treated Britain as a competitor, Britain was able to maintain some semblance of its traditional competitor status until the Suez Crisis in 1956. After 1956, Britain continued to regard the Soviet Union as a threatening enemy but no longer could be viewed as a competitor, as evidenced by Britain's gradual retreat from great powerhood and the winding down of its once-global security strategy.

Another illustration of the way in which these terms require interpretation is offered by the Franco-German rivalry. One might have thought that 1945 would have sufficiently altered Germany's competitor status to end the rivalry but it did not. French decision-makers persisted in treating Germany in terms of its potential to regain competitive status until the French strategy toward Germany underwent a radical shift in the early 1950s. Why that happened is too complicated a story to try to explain quickly (see, among others, Milward, 1984: 126–67; Heisbourg, 1998; Sturmer, 1998). Suffice it to say that the French acted as if the Franco-German rivalry was still alive for nearly a decade after the German defeat in World War II. The initial French strategy, predicated on ensuring that a strong Germany did not reemerge, evolved reluctantly into constraining the implications of the German reemergence through regional integration. One of the implications of this change in strategy was a reduction in the emphasis on the perceived threat of a nascent Germany. Thus, Germany began to regain its competitive status *vis-à-vis* France, but with much less of the threatening enemy image of the previous eight decades. Accordingly, the termination date for this rivalry is interpreted as 1955 and French acceptance of the official emergence of a West German state.

The changes of status experienced by major powers offer good examples of the need for interpretation. But the problem is not restricted to major powers. Cambodia/Kampuchea had never been competitive with Vietnam and most of the time, especially in the early nineteenth century, served as a buffer between Vietnam and Thailand. Yet Cambodian decision-makers, including both Lon Nol in the early 1970s and Pol Pot in the mid 1970s, apparently came to believe that they could compete with Vietnam, despite a capability ratio of roughly 10:1 in the Vietnamese favor when the Vietnamese invaded Kampuchea (Porter, 1990; Alagappa, 1993). Objectively, the evidence indicates that Cambodia and Vietnam should not have regarded each other as competitors but Cambodian decision-makers chose to ignore the objective evidence and act in a contrary fashion. The Vietnamese obviously did not choose to ignore or excuse this presumption. Something similar seems to have happened to Paraguay in the second half of the 1860s when it was crushed by Argentina and Brazil (Lynch, 1985; Perry, 1986). Objective capability ratios do not always govern the way decision-makers behave. The only recourse is to treat each potential case on a case-by-case basis in an attempt to assess decision-maker perceptions at the time. More often than not, though, and the Cuban–US case is clearly another exception, threat perceptions and competitor/enemy status are closely correlated, and tend to rise and fall in tandem.

As a general rule, the competitor criterion restricts rivalries to their own class within the major–minor power distinction. Major (minor) power rivalries are most likely to involve two major (minor) powers. Definitely, there are exceptions to this rule. Major–minor power rivalries emerge when minor powers become something more than nuisances in the eyes of major power decision-makers. Capability asymmetry may still be quite pronounced but that does not mean that the major power is in a position to, or is inclined toward, the use of its capability advantage. Minor power dyads can also be characterized by high asymmetry in capability and one might think that rivalry in such cases is unlikely. For instance, India and Nepal, China and Kazakhstan, or Israel and Lebanon suggest unlikely dyadic circumstances for the emergence of rivalry. Yet the India–Pakistan, China–Taiwan, China–Vietnam, and Israel–Jordan dyads are also characterized by unequal capabilities that have not prevented the emergence of rivalry perceptions. Ultimately, it depends on the decision-makers and their perceptions of sources of threat and who their enemies are.

3. No minimal duration is stipulated in advance. While one can certainly contend quite plausibly that longer-enduring rivalries are likely to possess greater expectations of threat, cognitive rigidities, and domestic pressures, as compared to shorter ones, there may be a variety of reasons why some rivalries are nipped in the bud, so to speak. For instance, one state might eliminate its rival in fairly short order. We would not wish to suppress this information by definition. Assessments of the effects of rivalry duration will proceed more efficaciously, presumably, if we allow the rivals themselves the opportunity to establish the minimum and maximum duration of hostility.

4. Various constituencies within states may have different views about who their state's main rivals are or should be. Unless they control the government, constituency views are not considered the same as those of the principal decision-makers. If the principal decision-makers disagree about the identity of rivals, the operational problem then becomes one of assessing where foreign policy-making is most concentrated and/or whether the disagreement effectively paralyzes the rivalry identification dimension of foreign policy-making. More likely in such cases, the identity of the leading rival fluctuates with the political fortunes of domestic competitors (e.g., Caps and Hats in eighteenth-century Sweden or Tories and Liberals in nineteenth-century Britain).

5. If two states were not considered rivals prior to the outbreak of war, they do not become rivals during the war unless their rivalry extends beyond the period of war combat. This rule is designed to avoid complications in assessing the linkages between rivalry and intensive forms of conflict. If every two states that opposed one another in a war became rivals by definition, we would be hard pressed to distinguish between genuine prewar rivals and states that were never rivals yet nevertheless found themselves on opposite sides of a battlefield. We would also find it difficult to trace the linkage between rivalry and warfare.

6. One needs to be especially skeptical about dating rivalry terminations. Some rivalries experience short-lived and highly publicized rapprochements that turn out to be less meaningful than one might have thought from reading the relevant press accounts at the time. In other cases, decision-makers become too distracted by other pressing events such as a civil war or other external adversaries to pay much attention to sustaining an external rivalry. Some rivalries enter long periods of hibernation only to erupt suddenly as if nothing had changed. All of these situations may share the outward appearance of rivalry termination. What needs to be manifested is evidence of some explicit kind of a significant de-escalation in threat perceptions *and* hostility. In the absence of such information, it is preferable to consider a rivalry as ongoing until

demonstrated explicitly otherwise. Nevertheless, one must also be alert to genuine de-escalations of hostility that resume at some future point. In such cases, the interrupted periods of threatening competition by enemies are treated as separate rivalries. For example, Greece and Turkey's first rivalry ended in 1930. The primary motivation for the de-escalation may well have been tactical – to meet mutual threats from third parties – but it is clear that the two long-time rivals suspended their dyadic hostility for a number of years. A second rivalry reemerged in 1955 initially over the status of Cyprus and remains ongoing.

Another example is provided by the relationships among several north-western African states. Morocco became independent in 1956 with aspirations toward creating a Greater Morocco – not unlike similar aspirations observed at times in other parts of the world (for example, Bulgaria, Greece, Somalia, Syria, Serbia, China). A newly independent or less constrained state may initiate a foreign policy agenda that entails expanding its territorial boundaries to encompass land controlled or thought to have been controlled in an earlier era. In the Moroccan case, Spain controlled small enclaves within Morocco and considerable territory to the south. The border between Algeria (not independent until 1962) and Morocco to the south-east was poorly defined. Mauritania (independent in 1960) also lay within the claimed southern scope of Greater Morocco. In all three cases, Morocco threatened to retake territory by force if necessary. Irregular actions against Spanish enclaves began as early as 1956, with the needling at Spain shifting south towards Ifni and the Western Sahara in the 1960s. Pressures on Spain to withdraw from its Saharan territory built up in the 1970s, both from Morocco and other sources, and ultimately led to a Spanish evacuation in 1976. Morocco had renounced its claim on Mauritania in 1969 and gained occasional Mauritanian collusion in controlling the former Spanish Sahara. However, Spanish–Moroccan conflict over the northern Spanish enclaves (Ceuta, Melilla) continued intermittently, with some possibility of militarized clashes remaining tangible and aggravated by fishing rights disputes off the Atlantic coast of Morocco. Only in the early 1990s did Spanish decision-makers seem to become less apprehensive of a military attack by Morocco.

Algerian and Moroccan troops began clashing over the disputed Tindouf region as early as 1962. While a resolution of the border dispute was eventually reached in the early 1970s, Algerian and Moroccan forces had also clashed over Algerian support for resistance against Moroccan expansion into the Western Sahara region. Once Spain withdrew, the main local opposition to Moroccan expansion became the indigenous Polisario movement, bolstered by unofficial Algerian financial and military support. Moroccan–Algerian military clashes appear to have continued intermittently in the Western Sahara without either side choosing to admit it. Diplomatic relations between Algeria and Morocco have blown hot and cold but there is as yet no indication that Algeria is prepared to concede to Moroccan expansion and a stronger Moroccan position in northwest Africa.

Three strategic rivalries have emerged from these relationships. The Algerian–Moroccan one began with Algerian independence in 1962 and has yet to end. The Mauritanian–Moroccan rivalry lasted only from 1960 to 1969. The Spanish–Moroccan rivalry began in 1956 and appears to have terminated by 1991. It could resume because the enclave-fishing rights problems persist but there is no indication that decision-makers on either side are prepared to press their grievances. As long as that remains the case on both sides, the level of threat perception is reduced substantially – at least as far as one can tell looking in from the outside.

7. The most valuable sources for information pertinent to identifying strategic rivalry are political histories of individual states' foreign policy activities.[11] Authors are not likely to identify rivalries precisely in ways a coder might desire because the concept of rivalry is not uniform in meaning. Nor do most historians consider it part of their job description to prepare their analyses in ways that political scientists can transform into systematic data. Yet for many rivalries, the problem is not an absence of information but too much information and information that is in disagreement. In the end analysis, the data collector must make a best judgment based on the information that is available and the explicit definitional criteria that are pertinent.

8. Reliance on students to collect data may be inevitable in large N circumstances. In cases requiring interpretation and judgment across a smaller number of cases, however, student input should be restricted as much as is feasible. In this particular case, all of the decisions made about how to code the strategic rivalry data were made by the author based on a direct reading of all of the sources employed for each case, as well as a number of other sources used to reject potential cases. Whether other analysts might have reached exactly the same conclusions about the identity of rivalry relationships must await subsequent studies by individuals prepared and equipped to take on the examination of nearly two centuries of conflict throughout the planet, or perhaps to concentrate on specific sections of the planet. It should be assumed that errors of interpretation

---

[11] The list of references exceeds some fifty pages. Most rivalries are quite capable of generating a dozen or more pertinent sources. In addition, Keesing's Contemporary Archives was examined for the 1990–9 period in order to compensate for any paucity of discussion in published sources for the last decade of the twentieth century. The sources for each rivalry are reported in Thompson (forthcoming).

have been made and, hopefully, they will be revealed in time by the closer scrutiny of other analysts. Just how much error should be anticipated and/or tolerated is not clear. Ultimately, error assessments are both absolute and relative. One question is how much error is associated with the 173 identifications of rivalry. While some termination dates are clearly debatable, publication of these identifications assumes that most of the specifications will survive closer scrutiny. The most likely source of error lies in omissions of rivalries about which we know very little in the corners of the globe that are not well covered by historians or journalists. Late twentieth-century Central Africa is one good example. Nineteenth-century Central America is another.

The relative error question is how well the 173 identifications fare in comparison with identifications made by other approaches to the rivalry question. This is a question to which we will return in the next section by comparing the strategic rivalry identifications with those of several other rivalry lists that appear to constitute the principal alternatives at this time. Yet since the principal alternatives are intended to measure distinctly different phenomena, there are major constraints on how far we can take comparisons of the multiple data sets' relative accuracy. If no one can claim to know what the full dimensions of the rivalry circle or pool are, it is rather awkward to assess relative accuracies. At the same time, it is also extremely awkward to simply leave the question of accuracy entirely open-ended. It should be made clear, at the very least, that there are implicit and explicit costs involved in choosing among the available measurements of rivalry between states.

Six approaches to measuring rivalry

Table 2.1 lists the 173 strategic rivalries that emerge from an identification process predicated on a rivalry definition that combines competitor status, threat perception, and enemy status and focuses on the extraction of information about decision-maker perceptions from historical analyses. Along with the 173 strategic rivalries, information on the varying identification of what are usually called enduring rivalries in some form (Bennett, 1996, 1997a, 1997b, 1998; Diehl and Goertz, 2000; Maoz and Mor, 2002; Klein, Goertz, and Diehl, 2006) is also provided in Table 2.1.[12] There is certainly more than one way to look at the contrasts

---

[12] Studies employing dispute-density approaches to constructing rivalry variables other than the ones to be examined more closely here have employed or endorsed different mixes of dispute and duration thresholds, as well as different versions of the MIDs data set. See, for instance, Gochman and Maoz (1984); Diehl (1985a, 1985b, 1985c, 1994); Diehl and Kingston (1987); Goertz and Diehl (1992b, 1995, 2000a, 2000b); Geller (1993, 1998); Huth and Russett (1993); Huth (1996a); Vasquez (1996); Maoz

suggested by the six columns of alternative identification. One slant is to simply say that each type of rivalry conceptualization must be looking at something quite different given the extensive disagreements characterizing the comparison of any two columns (about which more will be said below). If that is the case, users should simply adopt the identifications that come most closely to their own conception of rivalry. The problem with this approach is that there is much more agreement among these approaches in defining rivalry than may be apparent. Where they really part company is in measuring their concepts. Evaluating the relative utility of conflicting approaches to measurement is a different process than comparing conceptual definitions. Each approach has advantages and disadvantages that need to be made as explicit as possible. The ultimate questions are whether the advantages outweigh the disadvantages and whether such an outcome is equally true of all possible approaches.

Diehl and Goertz (2000: 19–25), the best known and most utilized measurement of enduring rivalry, begin their conceptual definition by stating that rivalries consist of two states in competition that possess the expectation of future conflict. This beginning point overlaps well with the notion of threatening enemy competitors associated with strategic rivalries. The expectation of future conflict is an important dimension in rivalries and can be conceptualized in various ways, including the synonymous concept of threat perception. At this point, then, the main conceptual difference between strategic and enduring rivalries is the absence of the enemy identification criterion found in the strategic definition.

However, a genuine parting of the conceptual ways occurs when Diehl and Goertz choose to introduce two additional measurement criteria: the severity of competition and time. They restrict the competitions in which they are interested to militarized ones. For them, rivalry equals militarized competition because the recourse to military tools of foreign policy demonstrates the severity of the conflict. They go one step further empirically and require that competitors engage in at least six militarized disputes. Moreover, the disputes must also take place within a minimal interval of twenty years. The rationale is that the frequency of militarized competition establishes the expectation of further conflict and also creates another important dimension of rivalry, a history of past conflict. Brief encounters preclude much in the way of history establishment. Nor is there sufficient time to create expectations of future conflict.

and Mor (1996, 1998); Wayman (2000); Gibler (1997); and Cioffi-Revilla (1998). A related conceptualization, examined in Chapter 4, is the idea of "protracted conflicts" found in ICB crisis studies (Brecher, 1984; 1993; Brecher and Wilkenfeld, 1997). Huth, Bennett, and Gelpi (1992) developed an alternative form of the labor-intensive approach to acquiring rivalry data but appear to have abandoned the further analysis of their rivalry data.

Table 2.1 Six identifications of rivalries in world politics

Rivalries	Strategic rivalries	Enduring rivalries I	Enduring rivalries II	Interstate rivalries I	Interstate rivalries II	Enduring international rivalries
Afghanistan–Iran I	1816–1937					
Afghanistan–Iran II	1996					
Afghanistan–Pakistan	1947–1979	1949–1989	1979–1999	1949–	1974–	40 years
Afghanistan–Russia			1949–2001			
Afghanistan–Tajikistan			1980–2001			
Afghanistan–Uzbekistan			1993–2001			
Albania–Greece	1913–1987		1993–2001			65 years
Albania–Italy[a]			1946–1949			
Albania–Italy[b]			1914–1939			
Albania–Yugoslavia			1952–1957			74 years
Albania–Yugoslavia[b]			1915–1921			
			1992–2001			
Algeria–Morocco	1962–	1962–1984	1962–1984		1984–	31 years
Angola–South Africa	1975–1988					
Angola–Zaire	1975–1997		1975–1978			
Argentina–Brazil	1817–1985		1872–1875			
Argentina–Britain[a]			1842–1846			
Argentina–Britain[b]	1965–		1976–1983			
Argentina–Chile[a]	1843–1991	1873–1909	1873–1909	1873–1984	1897–1984	151 years
Argentina–Chile[b]		1952–1984	1952–1984			150 years
Argentina–France			1842–1846			
Argentina–Paraguay	1862–1870		1992–2001			
Armenia–Azerbaijan	1991–		1950–1971			
Australia–China						
Austria–France	1816–1918					137 years
Austria–Greece			1886–1897			

Austria–Italy[a]	1848–1918		1848–1877	1843–1919	1926–1930	98 years
Austria–Italy[b]	1816–1918		1904–1918			
Austria–Ottoman Empire			1876–1905			
Austria–Papal States	1816–1870		1847–1849			
Austria–Prussia	1816–1918					
Austria–Russia II	1903–1920					
Austria–Serbia/Yugoslavia			1908–1918			
Bahrain–Iraq	1986–					
Bahrain–Qatar			1986–1994			
Bangladesh–India			1976–2001			17 years
Belgium–Germany		1914–1940			1938–1954	54 years
Belgium–Yugoslavia			1992–2000			
Belize–Guatemala	1981–1993		1993–2001			
Bolivia–Chile	1836–		1857–1884	1857–1904		135 years
Bolivia–Paraguay	1887–1938			1886–1938	1927–1938	78 years
Bolivia–Peru	1825–1932					
Bosnia–Croatia	1992–		1992–1996			
Bosnia–Serbia	1992–					
Botswana–South Africa			1984–1988			
Botswana–Zimbabwe			1969–1979			
Brazil–Britain		1838–1863			1849–1965	24 years
Brazil–Paraguay	1862–1870		1850–1870			140 years
Britain–Burma	1816–1826					102 years
Britain–China	1839–1900		1950–1968			95 years
Britain–Colombia			1836–1857			
Britain–Egypt			1942–1958			
Britain–France II	1816–1904	1887–1921	1888–1898			136 years
Britain–Germany I	1896–1918		1887–1921	1899–1955	1919–1955	114 years
Britain–Germany II	1934–1945		1938–1945			

(cont.)

Table 2.1 (*cont.*)

Rivalries	Strategic rivalries	Enduring rivalries I	Enduring rivalries II	Interstate rivalries I	Interstate rivalries II	Enduring international rivalries
Britain–Greece			1886–1897			
Britain–Guatemala			1972–1977			
Britain–Haiti			1883–1887			
Britain–Iceland			1958–1976			
Britain–Indonesia			1951–1966			
Britain–Iran			no dates given			
Britain–Iraq		1958–	1958–2001		1984–	54 years
Britain–Italy	1934–1943		1927–1943			79 years
Britain–Japan[a]	1932–1945		1862–1865			107 years
Britain–Japan[b]			1932–1945			
Britain–Ottoman Empire/Turkey		1895–1934	1876–1881		1905–1926	133 years
Britain–Russia[a]	1816–1956	1876–1923	1849–1861	1833–1907	1876–1907	158 years
Britain–Russia[b]			1876–1923			
Britain–Russia[c]		1939–1985	1939–1999			
Britain–Taiwan			1949–1955			
Britain–United States[a]	1816–1904	1837–1861	1837–1861	1816–1903	1858–1903	127 years
Britain–United States[b]			1902–1903			
Britain–Venezuela			1881–1903			
Britain–Yemen			1949–1967			
Britain–Yugoslavia			1992–2000			
Bulgaria–Greece	1878–1953	1914–1952	1914–1952		1940–1954	62 years
Bulgaria–Ottoman Empire/Turkey[a]	1878–1950		1908–1915			80 years
Bulgaria–Ottoman Empire/Turkey[b]			1935–1952			
Bulgaria–Ottoman Empire/Turkey[c]			1986–1987			

Dyad						
Bulgaria–Romania	1878–1945					
Bulgaria–Russia			1912–1917, 1941–1951			
Bulgaria–United States						58 years
Bulgaria–Yugoslavia	1878–1954	1913–1952			1940–1956	72 years
Burkino Faso–Mali	1960–1986		1974–1986			
Burma–China			1956–1969			
Burma–Thailand	1816–1826		1953–2001			38 years
Burundi–Rwanda	1962–1966		1964–1973			
Burundi–Tanzania			1995–2000			
Cambodia–Thailand		1953–1987	1953–1998	1953–		40 years
Cambodia–Vietnam (South)	1956–1975		1956–1998			40 years
Cambodia–Vietnam (North)	1976–1983		1969–1979			
Cameroon–Nigeria	1975–		1981–1998		1975–	
Canada–United States			1974–1997			
Canada–Yugoslavia			1998–2000			
Chad–Libya	1966–1994		1976–1994			
Chad–Sudan	1964–1969					
Chile–Peru[a]	1832–1929		1852–1921	1871–1929		93 years
Chile–Peru[b]			1976–1977			
Chile–Spain			1862–1866			
Chile–United States	1884–1891					
China–France[a]	1844–1900	1870–1900	1870–1927		1898–1929	108 years
China–France[b]			1949–1953			
China–Germany	1897–1901		1897–1901			
China–India	1948–	1950–1987		1950–	1971–	40 years
China–Japan[a]	1873–1945	1873–1958	1873–1958	1874–1951		104 years
China–Japan[b]			1978–1999			
China–Korea					1894–1951	42 years
China–Laos			1961–1979			
China–N. Korea			1993–1997			
China–Nepal			1956–1960			
China–New Zealand			1950–1971			

(cont.)

Table 2.1 (*cont.*)

Rivalries	Strategic rivalries	Enduring rivalries I	Enduring rivalries II	Interstate rivalries I	Interstate rivalries II	Enduring international rivalries
China–Philippines			1950–1971			
China–Russia I	1816–1949	1862–1986	1862–1994	1857–	1898–	130 years
China–Russia II	1958–1989					
China–S. Korea	1950–1987	1950–1987	1950–1994			
China–S. Vietnam			1956–1974			
China–Taiwan	1949–		1949–2001	1949–	1976–	42 years
China–Thailand			1951–1971			
China–United States	1949–1972	1949–1972	1926–1972	1949–1972	1969–1972	92 years
China–Vietnam	1973–		1975–1998			18 years
Colombia–Ecuador	1831–1919		1857–1863			
Colombia–Italy			1885–1898			
Colombia–Nicaragua	1979–1992					
Colombia–Peru	1824–1935		1898–1913	1899–1934		61 years
Colombia–Venezuela	1831–		1982–2000			
Congo–Brazzaville–Zaire		1963–1987	1976–1994		1987–	30 years
Costa Rica–Nicaragua I	1840–1858		1948–1957			
Costa Rica–Nicaragua II	1948–1992		1977–1998			45 years
Costa Rica–Nicaragua[c]						
Costa Rica–Panama	1921–1944					
Croatia–Serbia/Yugoslavia	1991–		1992–2000			
Cuba–United States[a]	1959–		1912–1934		1979–	81 years
Cuba–United States[b]		1959–1990	1959–1996		1988–	
Cyprus–Turkey		1965–1988	1965–2001			
Czechoslovakia–Germany	1933–1939		1938–1939			
Czechoslovakia–Germany (West)			1984–1986			
Czechoslovakia–Hungary	1919–1939					
Czechoslovakia–Poland	1919–1939					

Czechoslovakia–United States			1953–1961		
Czechoslovakia–Yugoslavia			1999–2000		
Denmark–Yugoslavia			1998–2000		
Dominican Rep.–Haiti	1845–1893		1986–1994		74 years
Dominican Rep.–United States			1900–1917		85 years
Ecuador–Peru[a]	1830–1998	1891–1955		1911–	102 years
Ecuador–Peru[b]		1977–1998			
Ecuador–United States	1952–1981	1952–1981		1972–	88 years
Egypt–Ethiopia	1868–1882				
Egypt–Iran I	1955–1971				
Egypt–Iran II	1979–				
Egypt–Iraq	1945–				
Egypt–Israel	1948–	1948–1989	1959–1962	1948–1979	32 years
Egypt–Jordan	1946–1970	1948–1962			
Egypt–Libya	1973–1992	1975–1985		1968–1979	16 years
Egypt–Ottoman Empire	1827–1841				
Egypt–Saudi Arabia	1957–1970	1962–1967			
Egypt–Sudan	1991–	1991–1996			
Egypt–Syria	1961–1990		1956–1973		
Egypt–United States					
El Salvador–Guatemala	1840–1930	1876–1906			115 years
El Salvador–Honduras	1840–1992	1969–1993			
El Salvador–Nicaragua	1907–1909				
Eq. Guinea–Gabon	1972–1979				
Eritrea–Ethiopia	1998–				
Eritrea–Sudan	1993–				
Eritrea–Yemen			1995–1999		
Ethiopia–Italy	1869–1943	1923–1943			
Ethiopia–Somalia	1960–1988	1960–1985		1980–	115 years
Ethiopia–Sudan	1965–	1967–1988	1967–1997	1987–	26 years
Finland–Russia					51 years
France–Germany II[a]	1816–1955	1830–1887	1830–1945	1866–1955	115 years

(cont.)

Table 2.1 (*cont.*)

Rivalries	Strategic rivalries	Enduring rivalries I	Enduring rivalries II	Interstate rivalries I	Interstate rivalries II	Enduring international rivalries
France–Germany II[b]		1911–1945				
France–Greece			1916–1922			
France–Iran			1985–1988			
France–Iraq			1990–1999			
France–Italy[a]	1881–1940		1860–1866			110 years
France–Italy[b]			1925–1940			107 years
France–Japan			1863–1865			
France–Libya			1978–1987			
France–Morocco			1904–1911			
France–Russia II	1816–1894		1830–1856			162 years
France–Russia II[b]			1918–1920			
France–Russia II[c]			1939–1961			
France–Thailand			1940–1952			
France–Tunisia			1957–1961			
France–Turkey[a]		1897–1938	1827–1833		1920–1939	137 years
France–Turkey[b]			1880–1938			
France–United States II	1830–1871					
France–Vietnam	1858–1885					
France–Yugoslavia			1992–2000			
Georgia–Russia			1992–2001			
Germany (West)–Germany (East)	1949–1973		1961–1971			
Germany–Greece			1886–1897			58 years
Germany–Haiti			1872–1942			
Germany–Italy		1914–1945	1914–1945		1939–1956	100 years
Germany–Norway			1911–1918			
Germany–Ottoman Empire/Turkey			1876–1897			

Germany–Poland	1918–1939				
Germany–Russia II[a]	1890–1945	1914–1920	1908–1970		
Germany–Russia II[b]		1936–1945			
Germany (West)–Russia		1961–1984			32 years
Germany–Saxony		1864–1866			
Germany–Sweden					
Germany–United States I	1889–1918	1915–1918			32 years
Germany–United States II	1939–1945	1939–1945			59 years
Germany–Yugoslavia[a]		1940–1941			
Germany–Yugoslavia[b]		1992–2000			
Ghana–Guinea		1966–1966			
Ghana–Ivory Coast	1960–1970				
Ghana–Nigeria	1960–1966	1961–1994			
Ghana–Togo	1960–1995				
Greece–Italy		1886–1897			
Greece–Ottoman Empire/ Turkey I	1827–1930	1866–1925	1829–1923	1878–1923	165 years
Greece–Russia	1879–1954	1886–1897			
Greece–Serbia	1955–				
Greece–Turkey II		1958–2001	1958–	1978–	
Greece–Yugoslavia		1992–2000			
Guatemala–Honduras	1840–1930				
Guatemala–Mexico	1840–1882				
Guatemala–Nicaragua	1840–1907				
Guinea–Portugal		1962–1973			
Guinea-Bissau–Senegal	1989–1993				
Guyana–Suriname		1976–2000			
Guyana–Venezuela	1966–	1966–1999			27 years
Haiti–United States	1895–1962	1869–1915	1891–1915		80 years
Honduras–Nicaragua I		1907–1929	1929–1962		86 years
Honduras–Nicaragua II	1980–1987	1957–2001			
Hungary–Romania	1918–1947	1919–1923			64 years
Hungary–Yugoslavia[a]	1918–1955	1938–1952			57 years

(cont.)

Table 2.1 (*cont.*)

Rivalries	Strategic rivalries	Enduring rivalries I	Enduring rivalries II	Interstate rivalries I	Interstate rivalries II	Enduring international rivalries
Hungary–Yugoslavia[b]			1991–2000			
Iceland–Yugoslavia			1998–2000			
India–Nepal			1962–1969			
India–Pakistan	1947–	1947–1991	1947–2002	1947–	1967–	40 years
India–Portugal			1954–1961			
India–Sri Lanka			1984–1992			
Indonesia–Malaysia	1962–1966		1963–1965			
Indonesia–Netherlands	1951–1962		1951–1962			
Indonesia–Papua New Guinea			1982–1990			
Iran–Iraq I	1932–1939		1934–1999			
Iran–Iraq II	1958–	1953–		1953–	1973–	49 years
Iran–Israel	1979–		1981–2000			
Iran–Ottoman Empire/Turkey	1816–1932					
Iran–Russia	1816–1828	1908–1987	1908–1993		1933–	85 years
Iran–Saudi Arabia	1979–		1961–2001			13 years
Iran–United States			1979–1997			45 years
Iraq–Israel	1948–	1967–1991	1948–1998		1991–	31 years
Iraq–Kuwait	1961–	1961–	1961–2000		1990–	
Iraq–Saudi Arabia I	1932–1957		1961–2000			
Iraq–Saudi Arabia II	1968–		1976–1991			
Iraq–Syria	1946–		1958–2001			
Iraq–Turkey			1990–1999			35 years
Iraq–UAE			1987–2001			
Iraq–United States	1948–1994					34 years
Israel–Jordan	1948–1973	1948–1973	1948–1973	1948–	1968–	42 years
Israel–Lebanon			1948–1975		1985–	40 years

(cont.)

Israel–Russia			1956–1974			
Israel–Saudi Arabia	1957–1981		1957–1981		1981–	
Israel–Syria	1948–	1948–1986	1948–2001	1948–	1968–	44 years
Italy–Russia	1936–1943		1918–1920			
Italy–Spain			1927–1944			
Italy–Turkey	1884–1943	1880–1924	1880–1924	1880–1923	1908–1928	44 years
Italy–Yugoslavia[a]	1918–1954	1923–1956	1923–1956		1953–1956	57 years
Italy–Yugoslavia[b]			1992–2000			
Japan–Korea						40 years
Japan–Mongolia			1935–1945			
Japan–Russia	1873–1945	1895–1984	1861–2001	1853–	1917–	122 years
Japan–S. Korea		1953–1982	1994–1999		1977–	45 years
Japan–United States	1900–1945		1932–1945			
Jordan–Saudi Arabia	1946–1958					
Jordan–Syria	1946–	1949–1991			1971–	40 years
Kazakhstan–Uzbekistan	1991–					
Kenya–Somalia	1963–1981		1963–1989			
Kenya–Sudan	1989–1994					
Kenya–Uganda	1986–1995	1965–1989	1965–1997		1989–	27 years
Korea–Russia			1994–1999			34 years
N. Korea–Japan						
N. Korea–S. Korea	1948–	1949–	1949–2001	1949–	1970–	44 years
N. Korea–United States		1950–1985	1950–2000		1975–	42 years
Laos–Thailand		1960–1988	1960–1988		1980–	33 years
Laos–Vietnam			1958–1973			
Lebanon–Israel			1948–2001			
Lebanon–Syria			1963–1969			
Liberia–Sierra Leone			1991–2001			
Libya–Sudan	1974–1985	1974–1985	1972–1984			
Libya–Tunisia			1977–1985			
Libya–United States			1970–1996			19 years
Lithuania–Poland	1919–1939					

Table 2.1 (cont.)

Rivalries	Strategic rivalries	Enduring rivalries I	Enduring rivalries II	Interstate rivalries I	Interstate rivalries II	Enduring international rivalries
Malawi–Tanzania	1964–1994					
Malawi–Zambia	1964–1986					
Malaysia–Philippines	1960–1969		1968–1988			
Mauritania–Morocco	1989–1995		1980–1987			
Mauritania–Senegal						
Mexico–United States[a]	1821–1848	1836–1893	1836–1893	1836–1923	1859–1927	108 years
Mexico–United States[b]			1911–1920			
Morocco–Spain[a]	1956–1991	1957–1980	1907–1911		1979	90 years
Morocco–Spain[b]	1975–1979		1957–1980			
Mozambique–Rhodesia	1976–1991					
Mozambique–South Africa			1983–1987			
Netherlands–Venezuela			1849–1969			
Netherlands–Yugoslavia			1993–2000			
Nicaragua–United States[a]			1909–1926			
Nicaragua–United States[b]			1982–1988			
Norway–Russia		1956–1987	1956–2001		1978–	37 years
Norway–Yugoslavia			1998–2000			
Oman–S. Yemen	1972–1982		1972–1982			
Ottoman Empire/Turkey–Russia[a]	1816–1920		1817–1821	1816–1923		170 years
Ottoman Empire/Turkey–Russia[b]			1849–1856			
Ottoman Empire/Turkey–Russia[c]		1876–1921	1876–1921		1898–1923	
Ottoman Empire/Turkey–Yugoslavia	1878–1957		1878–1941			
Ottoman Empire/Turkey–Yugoslavia[b]			1944–2004			
Peru–Spain			1859–1866			

Dispute					
Peru–United States			1955–1992	1992–	88 years
Poland–Lithuania	1918–1939		1919–1938		
Poland–Russia			1919–1920		
Poland–Russia[b]			1938–1939		
Poland–Yugoslavia			1998–2000		
Portugal–Senegal			1961–1973		
Portugal–Yugoslavia			1998–2000		
Portugal–Zambia			1966–1973		
Rhodesia–Zambia	1965–1979				
Romania–Russia			1940–1951		89 years
Romania–United States					63 years
Romania–Yugoslavia					78 years
Russia–South Korea			1959–1983		
Russia–Sweden[a]			1943–1964		
Russia–Sweden[b]			1981–1982		
Russia–Taiwan			1949–1958		
Russia–Ukraine			1992–1996		
Russia–United States	1945–1989	1946–1986	1918–1920	1966–	75 years
Russia–United States[b]	1948–1955		1946–2000	1946–	
Russia–Yugoslavia			1991–2001		
Rwanda–Uganda					59 years
Saudi Arabia–S. Yemen	1932–1934				
Saudi Arabia–Yemen I	1990–		1931–1934		
Saudi Arabia–Yemen II		1962–1984	1962–1984		24 years
South Africa–Zambia	1965–1991		1984–1988		
South Africa–Zimbabwe	1980–1992				
Spain–United States[a]	1816–1819	1850–1875	1816–1825	1850–1898	108 years
Spain–United States[b]			1850–1898	1873–1898	
Spain–Yugoslavia			1992–2000		
Sudan–Uganda I	1963–1972		1968–2001		
Sudan–Uganda II	1994–				
Syria–Turkey			1955–1998		42 years
Syria–United States			1970–1996		

(cont.)

Table 2.1 (*cont.*)

Rivalries	Strategic rivalries	Enduring rivalries I	Enduring rivalries II	Interstate rivalries I	Interstate rivalries II	Enduring international rivalries
Taiwan–S. Vietnam			1956–1974			
Tanzania–Uganda	1971–1979		1971–1979			
Thailand–Vietnam I	1816–1884					
Thailand–Vietnam II	1954–1988	1961–1989	1961–1995		1980–	34 years
Trinidad and Tobago–Venezuela			1996–1999			
Turkey–Yugoslavia			1992–2000			
Uganda–Zaire			1977–2001			
Uganda–Zambia						27 years
United States–N. Vietnam			1961–1973			
United States–Yugoslavia			1992–2000			
Vietnam (North)–Vietnam (South)	1954–1975		1960–1975			
Yemen–S. Yemen	1967–1990		1971–1994			
Zaire–Zambia						18 years
Zaire–Zimbabwe						25 years
Zambia–Zimbabwe			1965–1979			

Note: Indicators *a*, *b* and *c* indicate that for a given pair of states the different rivalry identification procedures identified distinct but potentially overlapping periods of rivalry. Roman numerals indicate that a dyad has engaged in more than one period of rivalry. In some major power cases, the earlier manifestation of the rivalry preceded the 1816 starting point for this data set. Similarly, all rivalries designated as beginning in 1816 actually began before the 1816 starting point.

The emphases on the history and future dimensions of rivalry are extremely well taken. Participants in rivalries are prisoners of the past and future. They select adversaries on the basis of past encounters, convert their interpretations of the past encounters into current and future expectations about the behavior of the adversary, and worry as well about how current decisions may benefit or penalize adversaries in the future. The problem, from our perspective, lies in the six militarized disputes and twenty-year threshold. The obvious advantage is that such a threshold can be applied to an existing data set on militarized disputes to create a list of enduring rivalries. Some variation can also be created by developing multiple thresholds. Diehl and Goertz (2000) also generate lists of what they call "isolated" and "proto" rivalries which have less dispute-density over time than enduring rivalries.[13] This procedure generates 1,166 "rivalries" and allows analysts to compare increasing levels or at least densities of dispute militarization.

The basic conceptual problem is that the Diehl and Goertz approach assumes that a fairly substantial amount of militarized disputation must occur in order to create rivalry histories and futures. While it may be true that more explicit conflict generates stronger expectations of future conflict and threat perception, the Diehl and Goertz approach rules out a full test of this proposition. We can only compare among different dispute frequencies at a number higher than 1. We cannot compare how non-militarized rivalries might be different from those that become militarized for non-militarized rivalries do not even exist by definition. Non-militarized rivals are implicitly grouped with nonrivals. Yet it is less than clear that militarized disputes of any frequency are necessary to the creation of conflict expectations.[14] The theoretical question is whether a sense of rivalry can precede actually coming to blows or the explicit

---

[13] "Isolated rivalries" have only one or two disputes. "Proto rivalries" fall in between the criteria for isolated and enduring rivalries.

[14] In contrast, slightly more than half (94 or 54 percent) of all strategic rivalries have yet to experience a war. All but 25 (14.4 percent) have experienced one or more militarized disputes but most have not had many of them. About three quarters (72 percent) of the 173 rivalries have engaged in ten or fewer years in which militarized disputes were ongoing between them. In this respect, the strategic rivalry approach endorses Goertz and Diehl's (1993: 155) argument that rivalry analysts should seek to avoid precluding "a priori any class of protracted hostile interaction from consideration as a rivalry." As Goertz and Diehl (1993) observe in the same article, an emphasis on high conflict thresholds can cause problems for studying the origins, continuation and endings of rivalries. In their own words (Goertz and Diehl, 1993: 163), "enduring rivalries definitions that use dispute data will [have problems detecting] truncation [starting a rivalry too late because an operational threshold is slow in being breached], censoring [not knowing when a rivalry actually ends because operational information is either missing – that is not yet collected – or because a fixed, post-conflict period has not yet been completed], and peaceful interludes [brief interruptions in intense conflict]."

(as opposed to implicit) threat thereof. The answer would seem to lie in the affirmative as long as actors are allowed to anticipate trouble. The Diehl and Goertz approach effectively eliminates this possibility in favor of requiring actors to find themselves embroiled in a sequence of conflict before the recognition of rivalry occurs.

It follows from this observation that the Diehl and Goertz rivalry identifications are likely to be slow in specifying beginning points. If one does not equate frequent militarized disputes with rivalry, and this is the critical assumption, the Diehl and Goertz identifications are also apt to be too quick in specifying termination points.[15] It seems also probable that some of the identifications will not focus on rivalries *per se* but, instead, identify dyads that merely have a sequence of militarized disputes. Similarly, any rivalries that lack a sequence of militarized disputes would be ignored entirely. Finally, one should expect some bias in a militarized dispute-based identification toward stronger actors that are most capable of foreign policy militarization and, as well, a bias toward areas in which these actors are most active.

This last expectation also suggests that the Diehl and Goertz listing is likely to "over sample" situations in which strong actors apply coercion to weaker actors repeatedly. There is debate in the rivalry literature over whether capability asymmetry is absolutely necessary to rivalry development and maintenance. Vasquez (1993), for instance, argues that it is necessary. Others, including Diehl and Goertz, suggest that it should remain an open empirical question. The position taken here (and employed in the development of the strategic rivalry data set) is that, other things being equal, symmetrical capabilities should be expected to make rivalry more likely and more enduring, but that it is not a necessary requirement. For instance, a weaker member of a rivalry dyad may possess a roughly equal capability position in a local arena in which the stronger member of the dyad is projecting some portion of its capability over considerable distance. At the same time, rivalries with asymmetrical capabilities are not likely to be all that common because both sides of such dyads are less likely to accord competitor status to the other side than they are in dyads with symmetrical dyads. That does not mean it cannot happen, but only that it is not the norm. More specifically, we should expect major (minor) powers to form rivalry relationships with other major (minor) powers and major–minor combinations should be more rare than major–major or minor–minor rivalry dyads.

---

[15] According to Diehl and Goertz (2000: 46), an enduring rivalry ends ten years after the last dispute.

While the list generated by Diehl and Goertz (2000) appears to be the one most utilized in enduring rivalry analyses, Klein, Goertz, and Diehl (2006) have generated another operationalization for rivalry analyses by significantly altering the Diehl and Goertz operational criteria and the basic list of enduring rivalries. What had been 64 rivalries is now almost five times as large at 290 rivalries. Without changing their conceptual definition, the new list is formed by focusing on all dyads with three or more MIDs between 1816 and 2001. This set is considered a pool of potential rivals. Narratives of the disputes were generated and examined for continuity over time in terms of the issues being contested. As long as the same issues were disputed without long periods (40–50 years) of peace intervening, the dyads are categorized as enduring rivals.[16] In essence, dispute-density has been supplanted by issue linkage or continuity. Some uncertainty persists, nevertheless, about when these enduring rivals begin and end. The duration of the rivalries is specified (see Table 2.1) but Klein, Goertz and Diehl acknowledge that the only information they have is when the first dispute begins and when the last dispute ends. They use this information, with rivalries ending 10–15 years after the last dispute, on a provisional basis. Greater dating precision, we are told (Klein, Goertz, and Diehl, 2006: 339), awaits further analysis.[17]

The measurement changes vault Klein, Goertz and Diehl into the lead for the most rivalries identified. While it is very clear that the latest enduring rivalry approach has been designed to stress issue recidivism, it is not clear what users of the earlier data are supposed to make of the new list that is about four times as long as the earlier one focusing on 64 rivalries. Should earlier studies using the "old" approach be invalidated? Just what difference does it make to switch from a rivalry N of 63 to 290?

One thing is reasonably clear. By expanding the net and dropping the temporal density measurement criteria, many more odd couples are identified as rivals. The new list in fact makes it most evident that the enduring rivalry concern is really with dyads that have some higher-than-usual level of militarized conflict. How else are we to explain all of the members of NATO involved in Kosovo operations as rivals of Yugoslavia, including at least one (Iceland) that prides itself on not having military forces? Coast guard clashes with fishing boats make Canada and the United States enduring rivals for a time. Nineteenth-century gunboat diplomacy makes France, Britain, and Italy the rivals of various South American and Caribbean states. The Haitian–US rivalry is back after being dropped by

---

[16] That still leaves problematic what one would do with a long rivalry characterized by the sporadic outbreak of disputes involving different issues at different times.

[17] Presumably, this promise also implies still another rivalry list at some future date.

Diehl and Goertz (2000) from an earlier rivalry list. All of these cases are intermixed with a number of other dyads many of which analysts would certainly recognize as classical rivalries. Whatever else one might say about this new set of identifications, it is unlikely to contribute to the resolution of disagreements about which cases to count as rivalries.

Bennett (1996, 1997a) defines interstate rivalries as dyadic situations in which states disagree over issues for an extended period of time to the extent that they engage in relatively frequent diplomatic or military challenges. The issues that are contested must be the same or related to preclude capturing situations in which states simply are disputatious. The outbreak of multiple disputes, continuing disagreement, and the threat of the use of force reflects long-term hostility, the seriousness of the policy disagreements, and the likelihood that states will consider each other as sources of primary threat. Bennett's empirical threshold for the interstate rivalries I data, in addition to the issue continuity, is five militarized disputes over at least twenty-five years. Rivalries end when the parties cease threatening the use of force and either compromise over the issues in contention or surrender their earlier claims. These terminations are recognized when a formal agreement is signed or claims are renounced publicly.

In Bennett (1997b, 1998) a second rivalry identification procedure is advanced. Starting with an older Goertz and Diehl (1995) identification of forty-five rivalries based on an earlier version of the MIDs data set, an interstate rivalries II is any dyad that satisfies a six MIDs criterion within a twenty-year interval, as long as there is no more than a fifteen-year gap between disputes.[18] In this approach, rivalries begin only after the dispute-density criteria have been fully established, they end when the issue in contention is settled and no more militarized disputes occur in the ensuing ten years – although the actual ending date is then backdated to the formal agreement to terminate the rivalry.

Bennett makes a telling observation when he notes that while continuing militarized disputes indicate an unwillingness to resolve issue conflicts, the absence of militarized disputes does not necessarily tell us whether the disagreements have been resolved. For this reason, he requires a formal agreement or renunciation to demarcate a rivalry termination in addition to the dispute termination. But if the absence of

---

[18] Actually, there appear to be two versions of interstate II. In Bennett (1997b), the starting dates of the rivalry identifications are based on the first dispute that begins the dispute-density qualification sequence. In Bennett (1998), the starting date of the rivalry identifications are based on the first year after the dispute-density qualifying sequence has been established. In both articles, it should also be noted that Bennett has dropped the "interstate" modifier and simply refers to the identification as rivalries.

militarized disputes cannot be equated with the absence of serious disagreement, then why should we assume that the presence of multiple
militarized disputes is necessary for the existence of a rivalry? Yes, multiple disputes suggest the presence of conflict quite explicitly. But, as
argued above, conflict, the expectation of conflict, and the perception of
serious levels of threat can exist without the prerequisite of five or six militarized disputes. Bennett's (1996, 1997a) approach, therefore, ends up
duplicating Diehl and Goertz's focus restricted to explicitly militarized
competitions.

Finally, Maoz and Mor's (2002) approach to enduring international
rivalries also falls clearly within the dispute-density class. Their definition of a dyadic rivalry emphasizes four dimensions: major issues that go
unresolved, the calculation of strategic plans based on what the other side
is thought to be planning, psychological indicators of hostility (including
suspicion, mistrust, and demonization), as well as recurring militarized
conflict of considerable intensity and severity. Despite a very rich definition, they fall back on a dispute-density measurement procedure that
overtly privileges the fourth of the four definitional components. Pairs
of states that persist for ten years or more and have six or more MIDs,
of which no two are separated by more than thirty years, are considered
rivals. This particular approach generates a list of 110 rivals.

We should expect Bennett's and Maoz and Mor's rivalry identifications
to possess many of the same disadvantages as Diehl and Goertz's list.
Beginning and end points may not possess much face validity if they are
geared to the occurrence of militarized dispute behavior. If they must
complete six disputes in twenty years before they even begin, as in the
Bennett case, their life cycle will look vastly different than if the first
dispute had been used as a starting point (Klein, Goetz, and Diehl),
or if one begins in some pre-militarized phase. Bennett's modification
of end point requirements, insisting on a formal treaty or renunciation
of claims, may be a step in the right direction but it is not enough to
delineate when participant perceptions of rivalry actually end. That also
is another empirical question in rivalry analysis that we have yet to answer.
Some "nonrivalries" will meet the empirical criteria, therefore, and some
genuine rivalries will be overlooked, and/or ended too early. Given the
emphasis on militarized disputes, the bias toward higher capability actors
should also be manifested in the Bennett and Maoz and Mor rivalry lists.

Thus, we possess at least five different approaches to defining and measuring rivalry that assume militarized conflict and one that does not. Of
course, if we had an earlier established convention that rivalry requires
militarization, the dispute-focused assumption would be more plausible.
But we have no such convention. Nor do we know that a sense of rivalry

demands militarization. It would seem preferable, then, to leave the role of militarization as an open question, not unlike the role of capability symmetry. We could then ask what kind of rivalries become militarized as part of inquiries into conflict-escalation dynamics. The operational approach taken by Bennett, Klein, Diehl, Goertz, Maoz, and Mor precludes this question by delimiting rivalries to situations that have already escalated considerably. If they said that they were interested for whatever reasons in dyadic situations involving serial militarized dispute behavior, that would be one thing. It becomes a different matter when the term "rivalry" is equated with, and restricted to serial militarized dispute behavior. The rich potential of rivalry analysis does not deserve to be handicapped in this fashion. Alternatively, the potential of rivalry analysis is unlikely to be fully realized, we think, if we choose to restrict our analytical attention to some "small" proportion of the rivalry pool from the very outset.[19] The analytical problem will only be complicated further if some of the dyads so identified satisfy serial dispute-density criteria without also delineating accurately the rivalries in the pool. At the very least, we risk losing possibly important observations on the pre-militarization phase of rivalries. The risk is minimal if all rivalries begin with a militarized bang. It is much greater if only some do so. Yet the question remains just how divergent are the lists?

Three factors interfere with a full comparison of the six data sets. One is that it is not possible to discuss each and every case in dispute. There are too many cases and too little space to address the disagreements.[20] Given the conceptual disagreements, there is also no real way to resolve identification disagreements. A third and lesser problem is that each list has a different ending point (in the 1980s, 1990s, or the early 2000s). Yet a dispute-density rivalry in an 1816–1992 dispute-density list must end by 1982 to count as having terminated. A number of rivalries terminated toward the end of the twentieth century but we cannot always be sure how the interstate and enduring rivalry identification systems might have treated them if their databases were longer in duration. There are, nevertheless, a number of observations that can be made about agreement, disagreement, and various biases in the six lists.

One way to capture the extent of disagreement is to note that of some 355 dyads presented as rivalry candidates, there are only 23 cases (6.5 percent) on which all 6 agree in some respect. That is, they may dispute the years in which they were rivals but they do at least agree that

---

[19] Klein, Goertz, and Diehl (2006) suggest that a focus on serial militarized conflict need not generate a small list.

[20] Bennett (1997b: 392) reports some fairly slight differences in outcome using enduring and interstate rivalry data.

Table 2.2 *"Consensus" rivalries*

Afghanistan–Pakistan	Greece–Turkey
Argentina–Chile	India–Pakistan
Britain–Germany	Israel–Jordan
Britain–United States	Israel–Syria
China–India	Italy–Turkey
China–Japan	Japan–Russia
China–Russia	N. Korea–S. Korea
China–United States	Mexico–United States
Ecuador–Peru	Russia–United States
Egypt–Israel	Spain–United States
Ethiopia–Somalia	Turkey–Russia
France–Germany	

the cases listed in Table 2.2 should be considered rivalries. More than half involve great power dyads and, therefore, are fairly well known. The non-great power dyads are also quite prominent in the conflict annals as well. But twenty-three cases is only a small fraction of the identifications made in the six lists. What are we to make of the remainder?

Another way to summarize quickly the level of agreement/disagreement is to calculate the number of agreements in proportional relation to the number of agreements and disagreements. In this calculation, empty cells (both identifications have no entry) are ignored. The specific dating information provided for the duration of the rivalries is also ignored. One might think that a score somewhat in the order of 0.5 makes a good benchmark for some moderate level of convergence. To achieve such a score, the number of agreements must equal the number of disagreements. Yet, as revealed in Table 2.3, only one pairing manages to rise above the 0.5 threshold. The second Bennett listing (interstate rivalries II) resembles closely the first Diehl and Goertz identification (enduring rivalries I) with an agreement index of 0.838. No other score comes close to approximating this level of agreement.

The strategic rivalry identification does not overlap very well with any of the other five. The best score is a 0.349 correspondence with the Klein, Goertz, and Diehl version of enduring rivalry (II). The mean level of agreement with the other five approaches is 0.249. Equally interesting, though, is that the five approaches to enduring rivalries identification do not generate, for the most part, anything resembling similar lists. Diehl and Goertz's (2000) enduring rivalries I, for instance, correlates poorly with Klein, Goertz, and Diehl's (2006) enduring rivalries II. The level of agreement is only 0.212. The two Bennett measures (interstate rivalries

Table 2.3 *The extent of agreement/disagreement in six rivalry identifications*

	Strategic rivalries	Enduring rivalries I	Enduring rivalries II	Interstate rivalries I	Interstate rivalries II	Enduring rivalries III
Strategic rivalries	–	0.203	0.349	0.183	0.200	0.310
Enduring rivalries I		–	0.212	0.342	0.838	0.370
Enduring rivalries II			–	0.113	0.205	0.325
Interstate rivalries I				–	0.377	0.274
Interstate rivalries II					–	0.396
Enduring rivalries III						–

I and II) do better (agreement = 0.377) but still disagree more than they agree. The Maoz and Mor take on enduring rivalry (enduring rivalries III) also disagrees more than it agrees with the other interpretations of enduring rivalry.

Thus, the level of agreement is almost uniformly low across all six data sets. Since the strategic rivalry and the Klein, Goertz, and Diehl lists have so many more rivalries than the other four lists, a low general level of agreement is inevitable. But that only underscores the extent of disagreement about which dyads should be regarded as rivals. Less inevitable is the substantial level of disagreement found to characterize the four lists based on dispute-density measures. Forty-five enduring rivalries I (72.5 percent of 62) are strategic rivalries while all but one of the first set of interstate rivalries I is a strategic rivalry.[21] Only 27 (43.5 percent of 62) enduring rivalries I are interstate rivalries in the first iteration. Put another way, the enduring and interstate rivalries I lists agree on 25 cases and disagree on forty-eight. The first two enduring rivalries lists (I and II) converge on 62 cases yet disagree on as many as 231. The enduring international rivalries list does not correspond all that well to either of the earlier enduring rivalries identifications. The enduring international rivalries list agrees with 47 of the enduring rivalries I list and 96 of the enduring rivalries II list. But their respective disagreements are 80 and 199. The two interstate lists (I and II) agree on 26 cases and disagree on 43. The best agreement, as noted earlier, is manifested by the enduring I and interstate II lists

---

[21] The Cambodia–Thailand dyad is the exception.

(agreeing on 57 and disagreeing on 11), but then the interstate II list was based on an earlier version of the enduring rivalries I list.[22]

None of the lists, moreover, shows much agreement about specific dates. For instance, the enduring rivalries I and interstate I lists agree only on three cases and are a year apart on a fourth case. The interstate rivalries II periodization, of course, is well designed to minimize dating overlaps. It is, of course, difficult to say anything concrete about the Maoz and Mor datings since they are not published but the duration of their rivalries often fails to correspond closely to the duration of the other list entries. Since the way in which the index of agreement was calculated totally ignored dating, it seems safe to say that if periodization was critical, many of the entries in Table 2.3 would have been more likely to approach 0 than 0.5. Much the same can be said about the "consensus" choices listed in Table 2.2.

Perhaps the level of disagreement should not be surprising given the varying conceptual and measurement emphases. However, one of the asserted advantages of the dispute-density approach is its presumed objectivity. Somewhat more agreement than was found, one might think, should characterize four lists with overlapping operational emphases. The problem is compounded by the fact that there is an even earlier version of the enduring rivalries I and II lists arrayed in Table 2.1 which focuses on forty-five cases. In moving from the earlier list to the 2000 one (enduring rivalries I), six rivalries were dropped and twenty-three added. Presumably, these rather extensive modifications were due to revisions of the MIDs data set, a dispute inventory that has expanded its N size several times since it was first introduced in the early 1980s.[23] Continuing revision of the MIDs data set is probable so that it is quite possible that we may see further changes in the rivalry identification lists based, to whatever extent, on dispute-density indicators. How one manages to keep these changes in mind in conjunction with the shifts in measurement strategy (comparing the 2000 and 2006 approaches) is not at all clear.

If one adds the many earlier studies using different dispute thresholds for rivalry variables, three preliminary implications are clear.[24] One, it is difficult to argue that a reliance on either dispute-density or merely disputes avoids the need for interpretation. There is after all some ambiguity about the appropriate cutoff points that can never be removed because the number of disputes and/or years required for a full-fledged rivalry is fairly

---

[22] However, Bennett (1997b) does express some misgivings about whether some of the rivalries his approach identifies should be viewed as rivalries.

[23] Over the years, MIDs analyses have been based on inventories of disputes ranging from 800 to around 2,000 or more cases.

[24] See Rasler and Thompson (2000) for a comparison of other lists.

arbitrary. That is one reason why so many density variations have been put forward. Hence, the interpretive element in dispute-density approaches is focused on thresholds as opposed to more direct evidence for rivalries. While it may be more convenient to both access, and to argue about, the indirect evidence, it is not yet clear that any consensus has emerged concerning precisely what dispute-density or dispute frequency is a necessary criterion for identifying a rivalry.

Even if a consensus had emerged early on, there still would have been multiple dispute-density lists thanks to the revisions in the MIDs data set. Either way, the outcome is that we have to be very careful in interpreting the analyses done on, or involving, rivalry data in the past two decades. It is not always clear what differences the various rivalry identifications might have made in the findings that have been produced. Given the low level of agreement in the most recent ones, which would only be compounded by citing the earlier identifications, we must assume that some of the existing findings might not have emerged if different rivalry identifications had been introduced. That is another empirical question that remains to be resolved. So while a dispute-density approach may constitute a more objective and replicable practice, the employment of such approaches has not had a salutary effect on the rivalry subfield so far. One cannot assume that the findings of any two empirical rivalry analyses are complementary unless they were done by the same author(s) and actually employed the same rivalry identifications. These two conditions have yet to be satisfied jointly all that often.

If we return to a close focus on the identifications listed in Table 2.1, other observations can be advanced. The enduring rivalry I data set identifies no rivalry before 1830 and lists only four as active after 1992. No new rivalry emerges after 1967. But as captured in Table 2.4, the enduring I list does respond to the increase in new states after World War II. The enduring II list begins slowly in 1816 but increases the number of rivalries at a much faster pace than the enduring I list. It also expands its N size after 1945 at approximately twice the level of the enduring I set. Its peak count is registered in the early 1990s followed by a fairly rapid decline that is presumably related to the availability of MIDs data.

The interstate I set starts with two rivalries and remains relatively flat or constant in number after World War II and throughout the Cold War era. No new rivalry emerges after 1968 but, in fact, most of the "latest" rivalries in the set entered in the 1940s. As a consequence, the interstate I set registers the most modest post-1945 increase of the various identifications while demonstrating an aggregated number of rivalries that is quite similar to the enduring I list prior to 1945. The interstate II set converges on the number recorded by the other two dispute-density series around

Table 2.4 *Five rivalry series*

	Strategic rivalries	Enduring rivalries I	Enduring rivalries II	Interstate I rivalries	Interstate II rivalries
1816	18	0	1	2	0
1817	19	0	2	2	0
1818	19	0	2	2	0
1819	18	0	2	2	0
1820	18	0	2	2	0
1821	19	0	2	2	0
1822	19	0	2	2	0
1823	19	0	2	2	0
1824	20	0	2	2	0
1825	21	0	2	2	0
1826	19	0	1	2	0
1827	21	0	2	2	0
1828	20	0	2	2	0
1829	20	0	2	3	0
1830	22	2	3	3	0
1831	24	2	3	3	0
1832	25	2	3	3	0
1833	25	2	3	4	0
1834	25	2	2	4	0
1835	25	2	2	4	0
1836	26	3	4	5	0
1837	26	4	5	5	0
1838	26	5	6	5	0
1839	27	5	6	5	0
1840	33	5	6	5	0
1841	32	5	6	5	0
1842	32	5	8	5	0
1843	33	5	8	6	0
1844	34	5	8	6	0
1845	35	5	8	6	0
1846	35	5	8	6	0
1847	35	5	7	6	0
1848	35	5	8	6	0
1849	35	5	11	6	0
1850	35	5	12	8	0
1851	35	5	11	8	1
1852	35	5	13	8	1
1853	35	5	12	9	1
1854	35	5	13	9	1
1855	35	5	13	9	1
1856	35	5	13	10	1
1857	35	5	12	11	1
1858	35	5	11	11	1
1859	35	5	12	11	1
1860	35	5	13	11	3
1861	35	5	14	11	3

(cont.)

Table 2.4 (*cont.*)

	Strategic rivalries	Enduring rivalries I	Enduring rivalries II	Interstate I rivalries	Interstate II rivalries
1862	37	5	15	11	3
1863	37	5	16	11	3
1864	37	5	16	11	3
1865	37	5	16	11	3
1866	37	5	15	11	3
1867	37	5	11	10	3
1868	38	5	11	10	3
1869	39	5	11	10	3
1870	36	6	12	10	3
1871	35	6	11	11	3
1872	35	6	12	11	3
1873	37	8	16	12	4
1874	37	8	15	13	4
1875	37	8	15	13	5
1876	37	9	20	13	5
1877	37	9	20	13	5
1878	42	9	20	13	6
1879	43	9	20	14	6
1880	43	10	22	14	6
1881	43	10	23	14	6
1882	43	10	22	14	6
1883	43	10	23	14	6
1884	43	10	23	14	6
1885	43	10	24	14	6
1886	42	10	29	15	6
1887	43	11	31	15	6
1888	43	10	31	15	6
1889	44	10	31	15	6
1890	45	10	31	15	6
1891	44	11	32	16	6
1892	44	11	32	16	7
1893	43	11	32	17	7
1894	42	10	31	17	8
1895	43	12	30	17	8
1896	44	12	30	17	8
1897	45	12	31	17	8
1898	45	13	27	17	8
1899	45	13	24	18	9
1900	43	13	25	18	12
1901	43	13	25	18	11
1902	43	13	25	18	11
1903	44	13	24	18	11
1904	42	13	26	17	10
1905	42	12	26	16	11
1906	42	13	25	16	11
1907	41	13	26	16	11
1908	41	14	24	17	11

Table 2.4 (*cont.*)

	Strategic rivalries	Enduring rivalries I	Enduring rivalries II	Interstate I rivalries	Interstate II rivalries
1909	41	14	30	17	11
1910	41	13	25	16	11
1911	41	14	30	16	12
1912	41	14	30	16	12
1913	42	14	31	16	12
1914	42	14	35	16	12
1915	42	17	37	16	12
1916	42	17	37	16	11
1917	42	17	37	16	12
1918	41	17	38	16	14
1919	43	17	36	16	12
1920	41	17	37	15	14
1921	42	17	36	15	14
1922	42	15	27	15	14
1923	42	16	28	15	14
1924	42	15	26	13	14
1925	42	15	26	11	12
1926	42	14	26	11	13
1927	42	14	26	11	13
1928	42	14	25	11	12
1929	41	14	25	11	12
1930	38	13	24	10	11
1931	38	13	25	10	10
1932	40	12	27	10	10
1933	41	13	27	10	11
1934	42	13	28	10	11
1935	41	12	28	9	11
1936	42	12	29	9	11
1937	41	12	30	9	11
1938	40	12	33	9	12
1939	34	11	33	8	12
1940	33	12	33	8	13
1941	33	11	33	8	13
1942	33	11	32	8	13
1943	29	11	30	8	13
1944	28	10	28	8	13
1945	22	10	28	8	13
1946	26	9	22	9	13
1947	27	10	23	10	13
1948	35	13	32	13	13
1949	37	17	40	17	13
1950	36	20	47	18	13
1951	37	20	50	18	13
1952	37	22	51	17	12
1953	36	24	49	19	13
1954	35	24	49	19	13
1955	34	25	62	19	11

(*cont.*)

Table 2.4 (*cont.*)

	Strategic rivalries	Enduring rivalries I	Enduring rivalries II	Interstate I rivalries	Interstate II rivalries
1956	35	24	57	18	9
1957	34	25	62	17	6
1958	35	28	64	17	6
1959	36	27	64	18	6
1960	42	30	66	19	6
1961	42	31	76	19	7
1962	45	35	77	19	7
1963	47	35	76	19	6
1964	50	35	78	19	6
1965	54	38	80	19	6
1966	53	40	82	19	7
1967	54	39	81	19	8
1968	55	39	81	19	11
1969	53	39	82	19	12
1970	50	39	81	19	13
1971	50	39	83	18	15
1972	51	39	80	18	16
1973	52	37	79	17	16
1974	53	36	74	17	17
1975	55	37	72	17	18
1976	57	37	78	17	19
1977	58	37	82	17	20
1978	57	37	81	17	22
1979	56	37	82	17	24
1980	58	37	79	16	26
1981	58	36	81	16	27
1982	57	35	83	16	27
1983	56	34	82	16	27
1984	56	34	84	16	29
1985	54	34	78	15	29
1986	53	26	79	15	29
1987	51	22	77	15	31
1988	48	15	72	15	32
1989	49	13	66		33
1990	48	8	67		34
1991	45	7	69		35
1992	44	4	82		35
1993	41		85		
1994	38		85		
1995	39		79		
1996	39		79		
1997	39		72		
1998	39		74		
1999	39		68		
2000			55		
2001			29		
2002			2		

the turn of the century and then initially declines as the international system expands after 1945 before ramping upward from the 1960s on. It is quite clear that the enduring rivalry series disagree about whether rivalry propensities are increasing, decreasing, or remaining about the same.

In contrast, the strategic list begins in 1816 with eighteen rivalries carried over from the pre-Waterloo era, rises gradually through the first three-quarters of the nineteenth century – not unlike the other two series – before falling off more precipitously than the other two due to the effects of World War II. As many as twenty-one rivalries are listed as terminated between 1939 and 1945. The number of ongoing rivalries then almost trebles in the post-World War II era before declining in the second half of the 1980s and 1990s. The strategic list suggests, however, that almost as many rivalries have persisted into the twenty-first century as the first enduring list ever recorded in operation at one time. The number of strategic rivalries thought to be operating in 1999 is about three times as many in number as the interstate I list has ongoing in 1988 and about ten times the number of enduring rivalries I listed as still functioning in 1992. In contrast, the enduring rivalries II list indicates a higher rivalry count than the one suggested by the strategic rivalry list by some 25–33 percent. The number of interstate II rivalries is actually converging on the number of strategic rivalries toward the end of the twentieth century but, in part, only because the two series are characterized by opposing trends in that time period. Thus, in general, there are some discernible similarities in profile across all five series, but each one has some distinctive characteristics as to when and how much the aggregate number fluctuates.

One of the more striking features of the enduring rivalries I list is that we must presume that the following rivalries have ended: Algeria–Morocco (1984), China–India (1987), Cuba–United States (1990), Ecuador–Peru (1955), Greece–Turkey (1989), India–Pakistan (1991), Iraq–Israel (1991), and Israel–Syria (1986). Other rivalries have terminated in this list but the dating of these eight terminations in particular might come as some surprise to the decision-makers involved in them. The Ecuador–Peru rivalry appears to have terminated in the late 1990s but the others seem to be like Mark Twain alive and well at this writing despite rumors to the contrary.[25] Ironically, one of the rivalries declared ended by the enduring rivalries I list has increased its probability of producing a nuclear war primarily since the rivalry was said to be over. The acute dangers associated with the India–Pakistan rivalry offer a dramatic lesson in the

---

[25] The Iraq–Israel rivalry presumably has been suspended by the second Gulf War outcome but it remains open ended whether this rivalry will resume once foreign troops leave Iraq.

problems linked to overrelying on data on overt, militarized dispute activity – although this particular rivalry has certainly continued to exhibit militarized disputes as well.

Of course, one can attribute some unknown portion of this problem to a censoring problem. At any point in time, the length of the MIDs data is finite. In the absence of complete data, one cannot know when or whether some rivalry identifications based on dispute-density measurement principles that were ongoing fairly recently are genuinely terminated. With more MIDs data, some of these rivalries might be seen in a different light. Note, however, that this liability does not appear to encourage much hesitation in assigning end points to rivalry durations. As Goertz and Diehl (1993: 164) themselves once observed:

Another, often unstated, basis for judging any definition of enduring rivalries is that it match our intuition about what cases qualify as enduring rivalries and exclude those from historical knowledge that we think deserve to be excluded. In respect to capturing termination dates accurately, dispute density identifications, especially those based strictly on an absence of militarized disputes and some post-conflict waiting period, leave something to be desired.

Table 2.5 compares the six lists in terms of the types of actors involved in each identified rivalry dyad. It is not possible to say with any great authority what the distribution across the three dyadic types should be, although it was hypothesized earlier that the distribution should look something like a dumb bell, with major–majors and minor–minors more prevalent than major–minors. In all six lists, minor–minor rivalries are the largest category as predicted, however, the four dispute-density lists have quite a few cases involving major powers, and almost as many as the number of cases involving minor powers only. Since there have been only a handful of major powers and quite a few minor powers, such distributions should be worrisome. Either major power cases are overrepresented or minor power dyads are extraordinarily unlikely to generate rivalries. On the other hand, the problem may simply be that major powers are more likely to engage in militarized disputes than are minor powers.

For instance, if there have been something in the order of 170 minor powers in the past 200 years, that suggests there have been roughly 14,365 minor power dyads in the same time period. The 34 minor power dyads reported in the enduring rivalry I list would then suggest that only 1 of every 500 minor power dyads might be expected to generate a rivalry. The 19 minor power dyads in the interstate list I suggest the ratio of 1.3 to every 1,000 minor power dyads. The interstate II list suggests the ratio is 2.4 per 1,000. In contrast, the strategic rivalry list would predict the probability of a minor power rivalry at about nine in every thousand.

Table 2.5 *Rivalry distributions by types of dyads*

Rivalry types	Major–major	Major–minor	Minor–minor
Strategic rivalries	20 (11.6%)	25 (14.5%)	128 (74.0%)
Enduring rivalries I	10 (15.6%)	20 (31.3%)	34 (53.1%)
Enduring rivalries II	27 (9.3%)	105 (36.1%)	159 (54.6%)
Interstate rivalries I	7 (20.6%)	8 (23.5%)	19 (55.9%)
Interstate rivalries II	8 (13.1%)	19 (31.1%)	34 (55.7%)
Enduring rivalries III	14 (12.7%)	37 (33.6%)	59 (53.6%)

All three estimates are strikingly low. Minor power rivalries are not very probable by any measure, but there is still a rather wide range between 1.3 and 8.8 per 1,000.

There is also disagreement about the frequency of major–minor rivalries. About a third of the three types of enduring rivalries and the interstate rivalries II constitute major–minors. About a fifth of the interstate I combine strong and weak powers, while the same category accounts for only 10 percent of the strategic rivalries. If we have reasons to anticipate that major–minor rivalries are plausible but not all that common, the data set with the fewest such cases, proportionately speaking, should have greater face validity. Then, again, this difference no doubt underscores the differences in definitional intention. If it is correct to say that the primary enduring rivalry focus is on states that have problems with each other, it should not be surprising to find them stressing dyads involving major powers. The real question is whether problems between, say, Belgium and Germany (enduring rivalries I, enduring international rivalries, and interstate rivalries II), Canada and the United States (enduring rivalries II), Haiti and the United States (enduring rivalries II) or Bulgaria and Russia (enduring rivalries III) should be treated as problems of genuine rivals or something else. One might say much the same about the interstate rivalries II listing of NATO states involved in Yugoslavia in the 1990s as rivalries. Pairings such as Iceland–Yugoslavia and Portugal–Yugoslavia (see Table 2.1) strongly suggest a focus on something other than the conventional meaning of interstate rivalry, or even competitors.

Another type of bias to look for concerns the starting dates of rivalries. We are interested in rivalries either as a control variable or as a subject in its own right. Either way, we need to capture the full life cycle of each rivalry as accurately as possible. If one stipulates that rivalries must begin with some sort of coercive bang, linking the start to militarized dispute activity is one way to proceed even though we have seen that there is not a great deal of agreement over which dispute with which to begin. If, on the

Table 2.6 *Starting date biases*

	Strategic rivalries	Enduring rivalries I	Enduring rivalries II	Interstate rivalries I	Interstate rivalries II
Absolute number of years "missed"	365	810	2134	421	2151
Average number of years "missed"	15.9	27.0	28.8	21.1	37.7

Note: The number of years estimate is based on accepting the earliest beginning rivalry as a baseline in cases of conflicting dating and calculating the deviation of the other starting dates from the baseline.

other hand, we have no reason to assume that rivalries must begin with a bang or a bang density, then we need to try capturing when decision-makers begin thinking and acting as if a rivalry existed. Without consensus on this starting point, it is difficult to say whose rivalry starting dates are right or wrong. But we can assess the potential for temporal distortion associated with each approach. Assuming we are better off erring on the liberal side than the conservative side on such an issue, let us separate the rivalry identifications in Table 2.1 that have more than one possible periodization advanced from those that only have one candidate. Then we need to establish the earliest date advanced as a baseline and compute how far off each of the other candidate starting dates is in relation to the earliest one. Such a test is imperfect but it does provide one more indicator of possible bias.

Table 2.6 summarizes the outcome in terms of two numbers. The first number is the number of years that a given rivalry identification missed vis-à-vis another identification of the same rivalry that began earlier. But this absolute number should be qualified by the number of times an identification did not provide the earliest starting date. Otherwise, a list with the fewest overlapping identifications might appear to be the least biased in this respect. The second number is thus the absolute deviation from the earliest start date divided by the number of times another identification commenced at an earlier date.

If earlier starting rivalries, other things being equal, are advantageous, the least bias is associated with the strategic rivalry list which usually advances the earliest date, in part because it is not tied to dispute-densities. Only in a handful of cases do one of the other lists suggest an earlier start date. On average, about sixteen years are "lost" with this approach to identification. Not surprisingly, the most years lost are found in the interstate II list, at an average of almost thirty-eight years per rivalry.

The next most biased on the starting date dimension is the enduring II list at nearly twenty-nine years per rivalry. The enduring I and interstate I lists show very similar averages for the number of years "missed" – indices that are not much different from the enduring rivalries II list.

Of course, putting forward the earliest starting date cannot be equated with possessing the most accuracy. But since we cannot know for sure which starting date is most accurate without privileging one approach over the others, it seems a reasonable test. Based on this test, all six lists possess some propensity for error on starting dates but the one with the least likely amount of error (compared to the other five) on this dimension appears to be the strategic rivalry list. The list with the most likely amount of starting date error is the interstate II list. We might conduct the same test with ending dates, giving the benefit of the doubt in this case to the latest date advanced, but there is simply too much ambiguity about which list actually advances the latest ending dates after 1982 to take us very far. Presumably, we would have to ignore all of the cases that are listed as ongoing. Even without doing any specific analysis of this question, however, the shortest rivalry durations are found in the enduring II list, and it has already been noted that the enduring list I tends to end a number of rivalries prematurely. The likelihood is that ending date biases mirror starting date biases.

Table 2.7 examines geographical distributions. The regional categories used in this table are fairly crude. It is possible to be more discriminating and to distinguish, for instance, among the three subregions in Europe (western, north-central eastern, and southeastern), three subregions of the Middle East (Mashriq, Maghrib, Gulf), the four subregions in sub-Saharan Africa (west, east, central, and southern), or even the continental and maritime distinctions in southeast Asia. But, the relatively small numbers associated with the two of the dispute-density lists would result in a large number of empty cells if a more refined regional breakdown was imposed on the data.

The geographical distribution for the 173 strategic rivalries is quite evenly dispersed among the five areas.[26] Each broadly defined area has generated 31–8 rivalries. The enduring rivalries I list has a slight Asian bias/Middle Eastern bias. Only sub-Saharan Africa appears to be slighted with much less representation than the other regions. Less macroscopically but not demonstrated in Table 2.7, no or very few enduring rivalries are associated with Central America (1), the northern rim of South America (0), north-central eastern Europe (0), western and southern

[26] As much as is possible, the rivalry dyads are located in the areas in which they are primarily concerned. Dyads that cannot be restricted easily in one region are assigned to the "other" category.

Table 2.7 *The geographical distribution of rivalries*

Regions	Strategic rivalries	Enduring rivalries I	Enduring rivalries II	Interstate rivalries I	Interstate rivalries II	Enduring rivalries III
America	33 (19.1%)	11 (17.2%)	52 (17.9%)	9 (26.5%)	11 (18.0%)	23 (20.9%)
Europe	38 (22.0%)	12 (18.8%)	83 (28.6%)	6 (17.6%)	12 (19.7%)	27 (24.5%)
Sub–Saharan Africa	33 (19.1%)	5 (7.8%)	29 (10.0%)	1 (2.9%)	4 (6.6%)	9 (8.2%)
Middle East/ North Africa	34 (19.7%)	16 (25.0%)	52 (17.9%)	6 (17.6%)	15 (24.6%)	22 (20.0%)
Asia	31 (17.9%)	17 (26.6%)	63 (21.7%)	11 (32.4%)	16 (26.2%)	26 (23.6%)
Other	4 (2.3%)	3 (4.7%)	11 (3.8%)	1 (2.9%)	3 (4.9%)	3 (2.7%)
Total	173	64	290	34	61	110

Africa (0), maritime southeast Asia (0), or central Eurasia (0). The same omissions do not apply to the enduring II list but its bias is toward European rivalries, presumably reflecting its emphasis on major powers. The interstate rivalries I list places more than half of its rivalries in the Americas and Asia. Europe is in third place, with comparatively few rivalries assigned to the Middle East and Africa. Yet the interstate I list is especially weak in the same places that are poorly represented in the enduring rivalry I list (Central America, the northern rim of South America, north-central eastern Europe, western and southern Africa, maritime southeast Asia, and central Eurasia). The interstate I list is also quite weakly represented in east Africa (1), southwest Asia (1), and continental southeast Asia (1). The interstate II list shows more geographical balance than interstate I, but it, like the enduring I list, also discriminates against sub-Saharan Africa. The enduring international list most closely resembles the enduring II list with its bias toward Europe and against sub-Saharan Africa. Asian rivalries, however, are proportionately more common in the enduring international rivalries list than they are in the enduring rivalries II list.

Each list, then, has a different geographical slant. Strategic rivalries have been found everywhere. Enduring and interstate rivalries are comparatively thin in sub-Saharan Africa, while the interstate rivalry I list detects little rivalry activity in the Middle East and Africa. All four of the dispute-density lists are noticeably weak in scattered parts of the globe located within the broader macroregions. Presumably, the areas that are discernibly underrepresented in these lists are the other side of the major power bias also found to be linked to dispute-density approaches. More specifically, what that means is that the dispute-density approaches over-look some important rivalry complexes, such as the many intra-Arab feuds, the southern African ones over Apartheid, more obscure ones in East Africa, and new ones in southeastern Europe and central Eurasia.

Conclusion

There are no free lunches in choosing among alternative identifications of rivalries between states. Each list has advantages and disadvantages. The dispute-density lists reduce the need for subjective interpretation, even if they do not dispense with it altogether. Their liabilities include the overrepresentation of rivalries involving major powers and the underrepresentation of hostile interstate activity in various parts of the world. They explicitly exclude cases that do not involve fairly high levels of militarized competition. Their dates of onset and termination, which, after all, have some significance for studies attempting to explain the timing of onsets and terminations, are rendered awkward by reliance on formal indicators that may or may not accurately capture the beginning and ending of the phenomena at hand. Since none of the dispute-density approaches yield rivalry identifications that are very congruent with other dispute-density identifications, there must be considerable room for identification error – both in terms of including the appropriate cases and excluding inappropriate cases. There have also been a number of different dispute-density thresholds, all with different rivalry identifications, applied in the last two decades which suggests that all findings linked to these approaches must be viewed as highly tentative until some consensus should ultimately emerge.

An alternative approach is now available but it relies on an intensive interpretation of historical evidence and a conceptualization of rivalry that emphasizes perceptions, rather than militarized conflict. As such, it avoids artificially censoring and truncating the rivalry data, in terms of specifying onset and termination dates, in terms of excluding less militarized conflicts, and in terms of slighting some parts of the world. But the nature of its construction makes the rivalry identifications clearly less easy to replicate. Acquiring systematic information on apparent decision-maker perceptions is not quite the same thing as recording the number of times two states have clashed. A substantial amount of interpretation seems inevitable if one seeks data on past, present, and future expectations in world politics for a large number of states and for a respectable length of time.

Given a very small country and temporal N, one might be able to reduce substantially the amount of historical interpretation involved. Ultimately, one might even be able to extend these intensive case studies through-out the planet. But we are not there yet. In the interim, we are forced to choose among various types of "quick" and dirty shortcuts to the empir-ical categorizations that we seek.

Choosing among the alternatives, nonetheless, also should reduce, in part, to what we think rivalry relationships are most about. Are they about a process of categorizing some competitors as threatening enemies with variable outcomes in the level of explicit conflict, as the strategic rivalry approach contends? Or, should the concept of rivalry be restricted for all practicable purposes to dyads that engage in a large number of mil-itarized disputes? Most conceptual definitions of rivalry, outside of the dispute-density group, do not insist explicitly on a high level of dispu-tatiousness. The nature of dispute-density measurements, however, pre-cludes a focus on anything but highly conflictual dyads – whether they regard one another as rivals or not. In the final analysis, the significance of rivalry analyses for the study of international conflict may simply be too important to leave them hostage to the existence of data collected earlier and for other purposes. At the same time, there is no reason why there must be only one definition of what interstate rivalry is about. Analysts who prefer the high conflict emphasis are likely to be more comfort-able with dispute-density approaches. Analysts who are uncomfortable with equating rivalry with intense conflict should be uncomfortable with dispute-density approaches. As long as we keep in mind what the differ-ent conceptualizations and measurement approaches entail and imply, we should be able to maximize the digestion and utilization of what we learn from analyses of "rivalry," even as we continue to disagree about how best to approach its identification. For some questions, it may not make all that much difference what approach is adopted. For others, it is likely to make considerable difference. One of the things we need to do now is to determine which questions fall into which category.

Many of the chapters that follow will focus on the basic questions of whether and how rivalries matter. Before pursuing these questions, however, we would do well to pause and consider what strategic rivalries represent as a type of behavior. Are they short in duration? Who par-ticipates in them? How many actually engage in militarized disputes and wars? Are they found equally in all parts of the world? Are they increasing or decreasing in number? Chapter 3 answers these and other questions by describing selectively some of the attributes of strategic rivalries. Empir-ical description certainly cannot resolve all of our questions but it is a good place to start.

3   Describing strategic rivalries

The beginnings of new millennia suggest, accurately or otherwise, openings and opportunities for new forms of behavior. We enter the twenty-first century with several recent and dramatic legacies in interstate conflict. The Soviet-American Cold War ended. Russia and China managed to de-escalate their feud at almost the same time and, of course, not coincidentally. Southern Africa fairly quickly changed from a highly conflictual and potentially explosive region to one characterized by unusually pacific interaction. Several components of the conflicts linking Israel and its immediate neighbors have been defused at least temporarily and work continues intermittently on reducing the remaining conflict issues. In South America, the ABC powers seem more interested currently in economic integration than in maintaining their traditional rivalries. Argentina and Britain seem most unlikely to fight again over the Falklands and even Ecuador and Peru have devised a formula for de-escalating their long-running conflict.

At the same time, though, the Indo-Pakistani feud refuses to go away. The United States, China, and Russia often seem on the verge of resuming one or more of their former rivalries. China and Taiwan continue to exchange missiles and declarations of independence. North and South Korea persist in maintaining their hostile divided status. The boundaries of Iraq remain potentially elastic, with a number of implications for its rivals. Turkey and Greece remain at loggerheads, although their hostility may also be waning. In northeastern Africa, the Somali-Ethiopian conflict petered out with the disintegration of Somalia only to be replaced by new or revived rivalries involving, among others, Ethiopia, Eritrea, and Sudan, and continuing Ethiopian intervention in Somalia. The new states of Central Eurasia have yet to create many new rivalries but the ones involving Armenia–Azerbaijan and Kazakhstan–Uzbekistan came into existence either before or almost from the outset of independence.

The question remains then whether we have any reason to anticipate fewer or greater tendencies toward rivalry in the twenty-first century – in contrast to earlier centuries and, most especially, the past 200 years or so. It is not a trivial question. As we argued in Chapter 2, most intensive forms of interstate conflict emerge from the hostile interaction of rivals. To understand the genesis of the conflicts, we must first decipher how rivalry processes work. Similarly, if all or most of the rivalries disappeared, we might also expect a significant diminishment in propensities toward conflict behavior.

One rationale for the study of these conflicts is that they have histories that influence how the rivals interact in the present and, to variable degrees, how they are likely to interact in the future. Paralleling this logic, we are unlikely to formulate reasonable expectations about the future of interstate rivalry in general unless we know something about its past and present parameters. This chapter offers one perspective on the past, present, and future of rivalry behavior in world politics by outlining selected descriptive characteristics of the behavior of 173 strategic rivalries in existence between 1816 and 1999.

Five sets of characteristics are examined. The first question to be addressed is how has the frequency of strategic rivalries varied over time, if indeed it has? Have rivalries become more or less common? A second question pertains to how we might categorize different types of rivalry and who participates in these interstate feuds. Do rivalries over the control of space outnumber those over position? Are positional rivalries the exclusive province of the major powers or do minor powers participate in them just as much? Do all states have some experience with one or more rivalry? Or, are there a few states that seem to have a special propensity for developing rivalry relations?

A third cluster of questions centers around the timing of escalation and de-escalation. Do states enter into rivalries gradually or are they almost "givens" bestowed on states at birth because of their location and who their neighbors are? How long do they last? Why do they terminate? The fourth cluster focuses on questions about wars and militarized disputes. Are all wars linked to specific rivalries? Or, is it only a few wars that can be so identified? Do all rivalries go to war eventually or only some? What about militarized disputes? Are all rivalries equally likely to escalate to militarized clashes or, again, are only a few likely to do so? Finally, there is the question of geographical distribution. Different regions appear to have different propensities to engage in rivalry behavior. Which regions are most rivalry-prone? Has rivalry-proneness changed over time? Have some regions become rivalry-free?

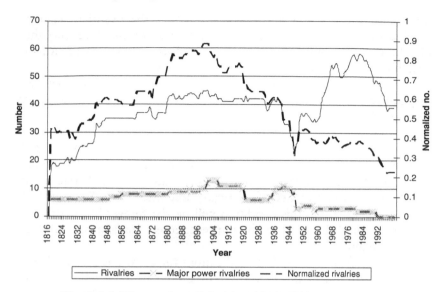

Figure 3.1 The number of rivalries, 1816–1999.

Trends in strategic rivalry

Figure 3.1 aggregates the number of ongoing rivalries between 1816 and 1999. Three series are shown. One is based on the total number of rivalries existing each year. A second series normalizes this frequency count by controlling for the number of states in the system. The third series is restricted to rivalries between major powers. It could be normalized as well but since the major power subsystem, historically, has been more rivalry-prone than the total system (up to about 1978), it would not facilitate the data presentation to add a fourth series to Figure 3.1.

Focusing first on the total number of rivalries, the general movement was upward to the late 1870s when a plateau was obtained through the period leading up to World War II. The Second World War contributed to the termination of a number of extant rivalries but the effect was short-lived, with the number of rivalries again on the upswing in the late 1940s, stabilizing briefly, and then moving upward again to a peak in the late 1970s/early 1980s. Immediately afterwards, the total number of strategic rivalries has been clearly on the downswing. Yet this same period was characterized by a considerable expansion of the number of states in the system. When one controls for this expansion, a different picture emerges. The normalized number of rivalries increased through the nineteenth century and decreased throughout the twentieth century. Obviously, the state system expanded faster in the twentieth century than did the rivalry population, despite some effort on the part of rivals to "catch up" in the second half of the last century.

Interestingly, the major power subsystem approximates the movement displayed by the normalized total series, with the exception of the period around World War II. The number of major power rivalries increased slowly to roughly the beginning of the twentieth century before trending downward, subject to the exception of the 1930s and early 1940s. This downward trend, of course, was aided by the reduction in the number of major powers after 1945. Even so, the major power subsystem outdid the total system by becoming rivalry-free after 1989. We have little reason to believe that this condition will persist forever but it still represents a remarkable, and totally unprecedented, transformation of the elite subsystem.

The transformation also has implications for the whole system. Fewer rivalries in the major power subsystem should be expected to at least restrain rivalry escalation, if not rivalry-proneness, in the larger system. This expectation is based on the assumption that minor powers have their own reasons for developing rivalries with neighbors, but do not always have the means to prosecute these rivalries fully. The de-escalation of the US–Soviet Cold War and the Sino-Soviet rivalry literally pulled the material rug out from underneath a number of minor power rivalries located throughout Afro-Eurasia.[1] Not all of these minor power rivalries disappeared but their participants did adopt lower profiles in the 1990s.

The evidence plotted in Figure 3.1 provides an initial answer to the "whither strategic rivalries" question. We have no reason to anticipate that rivalries will vanish completely in the near future. New rivalries are likely to emerge, both between major powers and between minor powers. Yet, as reinforced by Table 3.1, there does not seem to be any continuous movement toward increasing rivalry-proneness. On the contrary, the world appears to have been characterized by some decrease in rivalry-proneness for the past century. While we have been distracted by questions about whether warfare has been increasing or decreasing, or whether the proliferation of democracies makes some difference, we may have overlooked an important development in international relations. Rivalry-proneness should have some impact on warfare – just

---

[1] More specifically, rivalries in southeast Asia (China–Vietnam), South Asia (India–Pakistan), the Middle East (Syria–Israel), and southern Africa (South Africa versus its front-line foes prior to the end of apartheid) come to mind most readily.

Table 3.1 *The net number of rivalries in the system*

Decade	Number beginning	Number ending	Net number
1816–19	19	1	18
1820–29	5	3	20
1830–39	7	0	27
1840–49	10	2	35
1850–59	1	1	35
1860–69	4	0	39
1870–79	8	4	43
1880–89	5	4	44
1890–99	4	3	45
1900–09	2	6	41
1910–19	9	7	43
1920–29	1	3	41
1930–39	9	16	34
1940–49	19	16	37
1950–59	11	12	36
1960–69	24	7	53
1970–79	17	14	56
1980–89	8	15	49
1990–99	11	21	38

how much will become more clear in a later section (as well as in later chapters). How rivalry-proneness interacts with democratization, economic interdependence, and possibly important processes remains to be seen.

Types of rivalry and participation

Table 3.2 outlines the distribution of rivalry types according to the respective ranks of the rivals. Almost three-quarters of the 1816–1999 rivalry list have been generated by minor–minor pairings. The remainder are split almost evenly between minor–major and major–major matches, with a smaller residual of rivalries in which the participants changed their ranks during the rivalry. In most cases, these rank changes involve an initial major–minor pair in which the rival with the minor rank has been promoted to major power rank. Demotions in rank usually coincide with de-escalations of the rivalry because the demotion is associated with a serious defeat in war. Either the sources of interest conflicts are resolved coercively or one or more parties to the rivalry lose their ability to sustain the competition.

Table 3.2 *Number and type of rivalries by dyadic type*

Strategic rivalries	All		minor–minor		minor–major		major–major		Mixed	
	No.	%	No.	%	No.	%	No.	%	No.	%
Number	173	100.0	127	73.4	17	9.8	20	11.6	9	5.2
Pre–1816	18	10.3	4	22.2	2	11.1	7	38.9	5	27.8
Principals	37	21.3	27	73.0	0	0.0	9	24.3	1	2.7
Main types										
Spatial	122	70.1	91	74.6	15	12.3	8	6.6	8	6.6
Positional	94	54.0	55	58.5	11	11.7	20	21.3	8	8.5
Ideological	71	40.8	51	71.8	4	5.6	14	19.7	2	2.8
Secondary types										
Ethnic	46	26.4	42	91.3	3	6.5	1	3.6	0	0.0
Dissidents	58	33.3	56	96.6	2	3.4	0	0.0	0	0.0
Resources	28	16.1	27	96.4	1	3.6	0	0.0	0	0.0

Note: The first column's percentages are calculated down the column while all other percentages are calculated across the row.

Two other characteristics of rivalries are noted immediately below the row for frequencies. The second row identifies the number and distribution of rivalries that began before 1816 and that were still ongoing after the conclusion of the Napoleonic warfare. Most of these cases involved major powers in one way or another. Either they were European legacies of the "ancien regime" years, as in the case of Britain and France, or they were newer variations as in cases pitting the United States, Russia, or Burma against Britain. The "Principal" category refers to rivalries encompassing situations in which both rivals regard the other rival as their primary adversary (Thompson, 1995). States with multiple rivals tend to rank order their significance. In some cases, one rival stands out from the pack as the most salient one.

To use Britain once again as an example, its top three rivals throughout much of the nineteenth century were France, Russia, and the United States. Of the three, France and Russia oscillated in and out of the number one rival position and both were regarded as principal rivals, whereas the United States never quite attained this distinction. The utility of this principal categorization remains to be demonstrated empirically, but it is conceivable that rivals may treat principals differently than non-principal rivals. The levels of threat, hostility, distrust, and the stakes involved should all be greater for principal rivals than for other types of cases.

As in conflict in general, the three main types of rivalry are spatial, positional, and ideological in nature. As defined in Table 3.3, spatial rivalries

Table 3.3 *Types of strategic rivalry*

Main types

Spatial – Rivals contest the exclusive control of territory

Positional – Rivals contest relative shares of influence over activities and prestige within a system or subsystem.

Ideological – Rivals contest the relative virtues of different belief systems relating to political, economic, societal, or religious activities.

Secondary types

Ethnic – Rivals contest the treatment of minorities within one or more parties to the rivalry. The minority group shares some type of perceived kindred bond with members of the population of a second state, and, as a consequence, the welfare of the minority group is championed by decision-makers of the second state.

Dissidents – Decision-makers in one state protect and encourage a second state's rebels by providing refuge, financial aid, and military training.

Resources – Some valuable commodity is newly discovered or believed to exist within a contested territory, thereby increasing the value of the territory and the contest stakes.

Access – Rivals contest territorial space because of its strategic value and/or because it provides a route to some desired destination.

---

are contests over the exclusive control of territory. Positional rivalries are contests over relative influence and status, either in the world system at large and/or in regional subsystems. Ideological rivalries are contests over the relative superiority of belief systems – whether they refer to economic, political, or religious beliefs. None of these main types is mutually exclusive.[2] A rivalry may well encompass all three simultaneously.[3] However, one reason for categorizing them is that there is an argument in the conflict literature that links conflict type to termination probabilities.[4] Of the three main types, spatial conflict should be the easiest to conclude because they require concessions on territory. Positional conflicts require

[2] The ideological type is not really as "main" as the spatial–positional types.

[3] Three ethnic/dissident rivalries involving Sudan (Chad–Sudan, 1964–9; Sudan–Uganda I, 1963–72; Sudan–Uganda II, 1994–continuing) defied coding in terms of the tripartite, spatial–positional–ideological conceptualization. Of the remaining 170 cases, the largest bloc (32.7 percent) is composed of the purely spatial cases. The next two largest clusters are composed of spatial–positional (21.6 percent) and positional–ideological (15.8 percent) combinations. Rivalries involving all three main elements account for 11.1 percent, while the purely positional and the purely ideological are not that common (6.4 percent each). Equally uncommon is the combination of spatial and ideological issues (5.8 percent).

[4] See Fisher (1990) for an excellent source and interpretative review of the pertinent social psychological material that should be better known than it is.

concessions on relative pecking order, which is thought to be more awkward to surrender than territory that can be more divisible. Ideological conflicts require either the acceptance or tolerance of an alien belief system and, therefore, are thought to be the most difficult to bring to an end. When rivalries do mix two or more types, one can imagine that the prospects for termination are even dimmer, if only because there are more conflicts to disentangle and resolve. Another reason for classifying rivalry motivations is to be able to better assess the contended significance of spatial factors in the escalation of conflicts to war.

Based on the observed distribution of rivalry types in general, spatial rivalries are distributed proportionately as one might expect in rivalries that involve one or more minor states. They are much less likely to be associated with major–major rivalries. Somewhat the converse applies to positional rivalries. They are less likely to be found in minor–minor rivalries but more prevalent in rivalries involving one or more major powers. In fact, all major–major rivalries have possessed a positional element. The ideological component, far more prevalent after 1945 than before at least for minor–minor rivalries, is also most likely to appear in major–major pairings than it is in the other types of dyads.

Table 3.2 also provides some distributional information on four secondary types of rivalry. These types, also defined in Table 3.3, are considered secondary only because they were expected to be more restricted in their application and also to be less definitive in describing what any rivalry might be about. They should be regarded simply as distinctive features that appear in some rivalries, and which may provide some additional clues about the probabilities of escalation or de-escalation.[5] Ethnic rivalries certainly became familiar in the second half of the twentieth century in part because there were almost more than twice as many after 1945 as before (twenty-nine of the forty-six began after 1945). Ethnic rivalries are about situations in which one state champions a kindred group that is a minority in another state. Domestic persecution of the minority may invoke demands for external protection and thus interstate conflict. While ethnic tensions emerged in one out of four rivalries overall, they have appeared in one out of three of the rivalries beginning after 1945. They are also overwhelmingly concentrated in minor–minor dyads.

"Dissident" rivalries involve situations in which one state encourages political unrest in its rival's domestic political system by providing sanctuaries, equipment, and training for rebels from that other political system. This type of activity is also more common after 1945 than before and is also highly concentrated in minor–minor dyads. One reason is that it

[5] These types of conflict issues are used to good advantage in Huth (1996b).

represents a less costly way to engage in militarized hostility with a rival than outright combat between the armies of two states. Therefore, it is a particularly attractive strategy for weaker states. It is also conceivable that newer states, which are more likely to lack territorial cohesion and political legitimacy at the outset, are more likely to experience political rebellion than are older states. Hence, supply and demand factors work together to encourage this factor's appearance in slightly over half (53 percent) of all post-1945 rivalries, while it appeared in only about 13 percent of the rivalries that began before 1945.

"Access" rivalries appear to be becoming less common. These conflicts are at least in part about contests over territory regarded to have strategic importance and/or providing a route toward some desired destination. For instance, in South America, various rivers could provide a way for trade to reach Atlantic ports but access to the river system was denied by an intervening state. As a matter of fact, these types of rivalries were particularly important in generating and fueling many of the older South American feuds and have been less predominant in more contemporary conflicts. "Resource" conflicts have also been quite familiar in South America but, unlike the access conflicts, they are more universal in appearance.

Resource conflicts pertain to contested territories that are abruptly perceived to be more valuable and more worthy of fighting over. The discovery of oil or the expectation of the discovery of oil has been the primary culprit in the past and, again, this is a factor that is primarily found in minor–minor dyads. The distinctiveness of this rivalry type is that while they are apt to be spatial rivalries by definition, it is not the territory *per se* that causes conflict escalation. Rather, it is resources located within the contested space that are increasing tensions. If the resource discovery appears to be incorrect, its extraction becomes too expensive, some sort of equitable allocation scheme is developed, or the resource becomes economically obsolete, presumably, then, the contested space would not be sufficient in and of itself to maintain the rivalry for long.

While this resource factor is not all that common in rivalries (present in about 15 percent), it does suggest another useful qualification of the nature of spatial motivations in interstate rivalry. As in the cases of the ethnic and access features, states may fight over territory but sometimes it is not the territory *per se* that is of main interest. Sometimes it is oil, gold or water, sometimes access to salt water ports, and sometimes it is a matter of protecting the perceived welfare of the territory's inhabitants, or at least some portion of the inhabitants. The question that remains open is whether these different obsessions make some difference in the way the rivalries behave.

Table 3.4 *Participation in rivalries*

		Ten rivalries or more		
Russia (13)	United States (11)	Britain (10)	China (10)	Egypt (10)
Germany (10)	Iran (10)			

		Five to nine rivalries		
Ottoman E./Turkey (9)	Serbia/Yugoslavia/ Serbia (9)	France (8)	Iraq (8)	Sudan (8)
Italy (7)	Austria–Hungary (6)	Nicaragua (6)	Vietnam (6)	Ethiopia (5)
Guatemala (5)	Greece (5)	Israel (5)		

		One to four rivalries		
Argentina (4)	Bulgaria (4)	Chile (4)	Colombia (4)	Honduras (4)
Japan (4)	Jordan (4)	Kenya (4)	Libya (4)	Peru (4)
Poland (4)	South Africa (4)	Syria (4)	Uganda (4)	
Afghanistan (3)	Bolivia (3)	Costa Rica (3)	Czechoslovakia (3)	Ghana (3)
Hungary (3)	Morocco (3)	Paraguay (3)	Tanzania (3)	Thailand (3)
Yemen (3)	Zambia (3)			
Angola (2)	Bosnia (2)	Brazil (2)	Burma (2)	Cambodia (2)
Chad (2)	Croatia (2)	Ecuador (2)	El Salvador (2)	Eritrea (2)
India (2)	Indonesia (2)	Malawi (2)	Mauritania (2)	Mexico (2)
Mozambique (2)	Nigeria (2)	Pakistan (2)	Rhodesia (2)	Romania (2)
S. Vietnam (2)	S. Yemen (2)	Senegal (2)	Somalia (2)	Spain (2)
Venezuela (2)				
Albania (1)	Algeria (1)	Armenia (1)	Azerbaijan (1)	Bahrain (1)
Belize (1)	Burkino Faso (1)	Burundi (1)	Cameroon (1)	Cuba (1)
Dominican Rep. (1)	E. Germany (1)	Eq. Guinea (1)	Gabon (1)	Guinea– Bissau (1)
Guyana (1)	Haiti (1)	Ivory Coast (1)	Kazakhstan (1)	N. Korea (1)
S. Korea (1)	Kuwait (1)	Lithuania (1)	Malaysia (1)	Mali (1)
Netherlands (1)	Oman (1)	Panama (1)	Qatar (1)	Rwanda (1)
Thailand (1)	Togo (1)	Uzbekistan (1)	W. Germany (1)	Zaire (1)
Zimbabwe (1)				

How many states have actually participated in rivalries? For the 1816–1999 period, the answer is that 108 states have engaged in one or more rivalries. Rivalry behavior thus is fairly widespread in the sense that more than half of the international system's state population has participated in them at one time or another. However, as delineated in Table 3.4, rivalry propensity, even among the 108 states, is unevenly distributed. Exactly a third of the 108 (36), have been involved in only one rivalry and almost invariably with an adjacent state. Roughly another third (thirty-eight) have participated in two or three rivalries. Exactly where one should draw the threshold for "most contentious" states is not self-evident but one candidate is the four-or-more-rivalries set of states that encompasses thirty-four states.

The states with the highest rivalry propensity have been a heterogeneous group. All the major powers of the nineteenth and twentieth centuries have been members of this group.[6] The two superpowers of the late twentieth century have been among the most rivalry-prone of all (with thirteen and eleven rivalries respectively). Britain, Germany, and China's rivalry propensity has not been much different. But there are two other types of states in this contentious group. One type of state might be labeled "overachievers," at least in terms of their affinity for conflict. These are relatively weak states that nevertheless mount ambitious foreign policy agendas. Serbia, Iraq, Vietnam, Nicaragua, Syria, and Libya are good examples.

Another group of states is not always easily distinguishable from the overachievers but it seems more accurate to categorize them as located in especially tough neighborhoods. Ethiopia, Sudan, Israel, Kenya, and Peru come to mind most readily. Which group one assigns states such as Greece, Poland, and Bulgaria seems more a matter of taste than anything else. The overachievers tend to be located in tough regional neighborhoods, thanks in part to their own overachieving. If there is some point in reducing the "noise" in interstate conflictual interactions by focusing on those states that are most likely to engage in conflict, states that have participated in rivalries is one good filter. The states with the highest rivalry-proneness may prove to be an even better one.

Origins, duration, and de-escalation

It is sometimes argued that conflict formation, escalation/de-escalation, and termination are entirely different processes that require completely or partially different explanatory models. In general, this differentiation of conflict processes may have considerable validity. Nevertheless, some problems do emerge when the maxim is applied to the analysis of rivalries. Table 3.5 gives one reason for this awkwardness. Most rivalries begin early. Of the 128 rivalries in which the one or both participants became independent after 1816, 72 (about 56 percent) began at the onset of independence for one or more of the rivals. Apparently, the formation process is strongly biased by the nature of the state(s) that are involved, their location(s), or both. One might almost say that sovereignty came

---

[6] A number of pertinent case studies on major power rivalries may be found in Thompson (1999).

Table 3.5 *Number of*
years between rivalry
onset and independence

Years	Number
0	72
1–10	18
11–20	14
21–30	11
31–40	3
41–50	3
51–60	2
61–70	2
71–149	3

with rivalry strings attached. When one considers the circumstances surrounding the independence of the United States, Bulgaria, Serbia, Pakistan, India, Israel, and Somalia, to name just a few, the odds of evading the simultaneous development of strategic rivalries were rather slim. Decision-makers made their choices, to be sure, but it is not as if they had a wide range of choices to make.

This observation about biases in the rivalry-formation process does not imply that formation processes cannot be examined autonomously. It may even provide additional justification for doing so. Why is it that rivalries tend to emerge fairly early or almost not at all? Table 3.5 suggests that almost 90 percent of the appropriate rivalries began within thirty years of independence. This would seem to suggest that as states age, they become less rivalry-prone. Analyses that focus on satisfied versus dissatisfied states might suggest that the sources of dissatisfaction tend to emerge early. Older states may be more likely to be relatively satisfied. Alternatively, perhaps it is spatial conflicts that tend to emerge early or not at all. States are "born" with boundaries that do not always make a great deal of political, economic, or socio-cultural sense. Since these boundaries that seem illogical to some members of the population breed dissatisfaction, the two explanatory approaches may not be all that different. Even so, what remains unclear is why only some boundary problems lead to strategic rivalry while others, perhaps the majority, do not.

One of the hallmarks of current rivalry research is the assumption that these affairs tend to be "enduring," or, alternatively, that the more

Table 3.6 *Mean rivalry duration in years by dyadic rank type*

	All	minor–minor	minor–major	major–major	Mixed
Mean	42.1	38.3	30.3	55.2	71
Years			Number of rivalries		
1–5	9	7	1	0	1
6–10	23	17	3	3	0
11–20	24	20	2	2	0
21–30	21	16	2	2	1
31–60	20	10	3	6	1
61–100	22	14	2	3	3
101–168	16	9	0	4	3

enduring rivalries are likely to be the most important ones to investigate.[7] In this project, these assumptions were tested in part by not establishing any minimal duration in order to qualify as a rivalry. If history is important to conflict processes, one would certainly expect those with more history to behave differently than those with less history. But what is not so clear is just what length of time is necessary for a conflict to begin behaving as a rivalry. The perceived threatening competitor definition employed here says nothing about the effect of time on perceptions. A rivalry begins as soon as the definitional preconditions are met and ends when they are no longer being satisfied. In this context, duration is merely another attribute that may be of interest in explaining rivalry dynamics.

Table 3.6 lists the mean durations for the 135 rivalries that have terminated according to dyadic type. The numbers suggest that the "average" rivalry is fairly long-lasting. Without distinguishing among the dyadic types, the average duration was roughly forty-two years. The average for minor–minor rivalries was slightly less (38.3 years) while major–major rivalries tended to last longer (55.2 years). Still, these averages are based on a considerable range of experiences. The shortest rivalry lasted only two years. The longest rivalry lasted 168 years.[8] The mean duration, therefore, may not be the most useful statistic.

---

[7] See, for instance, the analysis of various approaches to enduring rivalries in Chapter 2.

[8] One might reasonably suggest that very short rivalries should have been excluded by definition. This data collection, however, proceeded with as few initial thresholds as possible. Very short rivalries have existed but they are not numerous. They tend to be linked to two types of circumstances: cases involving rivalry processes that preceded a debatable independence date and/or cases that are resolved quickly by force. In the case of the shortest rivalry in the data base (Saudi Arabia–Yemen I, 1932–4), both circumstances apply. The Saudi expansion had been going on for at least fifteen years, if

More useful are the breakdowns by duration also reported in Table 3.6. Of those that have terminated, less than 7 percent have lasted only one to five years. About 12 percent have persisted for more than 100 years. More than half (57 percent) are finished by thirty years. That suggests that the modal duration is roughly only the equivalent of a generation or so in length. But that is an aggregated statistic. Close to half (47 percent) of all minor–minor power rivalries end within twenty years. Major–major power rivalries have tended to last longer. Their modal duration has been about fifty years, suggesting, in passing, that the Cold War's duration was about what one might have expected – subject, of course, to the usual caveats about other things being equal.

No major effort was made to collect information on the reputed reasons for de-escalation on the principle that this is a question that deserves a specialized research undertaking of its own. However, some rudimentary information was collected for those cases for which authors did advance reasons for termination. The open-ended data collection yielded four-teen categories of response that can be collapsed for our purposes into several encompassing clusters which account for all of the responses. If strategic rivalries are to terminate, it follows that there are several possible ways in which this might come about. The two fundamental paths are: (1) one or both states in the rivalry lose their competitive status and/or (2) one or both states cease being perceived as projecting threat. The actual number of pathways multiplies though when one considers the variety of circumstances that might lead to one of the two main paths.

The loss of competitive status can be achieved if: (1) one side is defeated decisively and acknowledges it; (2) one side acknowledges defeat without going to war; or (3) one or both sides experience(s) political–economic exhaustion and/or intensive civil war. Table 3.7 suggests that the loss of competitive status in one of these fashions is reasonably common. Roughly a fourth (45 of 173) have done so in the past two centuries. Another sixteen cases terminated after one side acknowledged inferiority without suffering a war. If we add all of these cases, close to half of the cases that have terminated ended along what might be viewed as realist outcomes. One side or another lacked the ability to continue the competition.

The main alternative pathway – the downscaling of threat perception – can be realized if one or both sides: (1) changes its strategic priorities; (2) changes its leadership; (3) changes its regime; or (4) negotiates a

not more, prior to the 1932 independence date (in Gleditsch and Ward, 1999) and Yemeni behavior toward Saudi Arabia changed abruptly after Yemen was beaten in war. For the record, the longest rivalries in the data set (at 168 years in duration) are Argentina–Brazil (1817–1985) and Ecuador–Peru (1830–1998).

Table 3.7 *Primary reasons for rivalry termination*

	All	minor–minor	Major–Minor	major–major	Mixed
Still active	38	33	5	0	0
Unspecified terminations	39	36	0	1	2
Pertaining to competitive status	62	30	12	14	6
Coerced loss of competitive status	45	23	6	12	4
Acknowledgment of inferiority	17	7	6	2	2
Pertaining to enemy status	34	27	1	4	2
Change in strategy	17	12	0	3	2
Change in leader/regime	17	15	1	1	0
	173	126	18	19	10

mutual lessening of tension without changing anything in terms of priorities, leadership, or regime. The thirty-four cases that fit the first three situations are equally split between cases involving a change in priorities (seventeen cases) and cases predicated on leader/regime changes (also seventeen cases). Twenty-nine cases involved negotiations that achieve de-escalation without altering the first three categories.

Note that these most prevalent responses mix realist and liberal styles of interpretation. Rivalries can be resolved coercively. They can also be resolved peacefully if appropriate external and domestic changes take place. Given the conceptual proximity of rivalry to conflict, it may be surprising that the realist cases seem to be slightly less prevalent numerically. Still, we have much to learn about rivalry termination processes. Tables 3.7 only scratches the surface of the developments that lead to the end of adversarial relations.[9]

Dispute and war escalation tendencies

One question the strategic rivalry data set cannot address without additional information is whether rivalries are more likely to escalate to higher levels of conflict – militarized disputes and war – than non-rivalry dyads. That is a separate question that can only be tackled with a database that encompasses all states, not just rivalry dyads. But there are related questions that can be answered with the rivalry data set alone. How many wars appear to have roots in rivalries? How often do rivalries escalate

[9] Thompson (2001), Rasler (2001), and Rasler, Thompson, and Ganguly (unpublished) develop a model of rivalry termination that pursues this question in more depth. See, as well, Colaresi (2005) for an alternative approach to explaining termination.

Table 3.8 *Wars with apparent strategic rivalry roots*

Present		Absent
Russo–Turkish (1828–29)	Sino–Soviet (1929)	Franco–Spanish (1823)
Mexican–American (1846–48)	Manchurian (1931–33)	1st Schleswig–Holstein (1848–49)
Austro–Sardinian (1848–49)	Chaco (1932–35)	Anglo–Persian (1856–57)
Roman Republic (1849)	Italo–Ethiopian (1935–36)	Italo–Roman (1860)
La Plata (1851–52)	Sino–Japanese (1937–41)	Italo–Sicilian (1860–61)
Crimean (1853–56)	Changkufeng (1938)	Franco–Mexican (1862–67)
Italian Unification (1859)	Nomohan (1939)	2nd Schleswig–Holstein (1864)
Ecuadorian–Colombian (1863)	World War II (1939–45)	Spanish–Chilean (1865–66)
Lopez (1864–70)	Palestine (1948–49)	Franco–Thai (1893)
Seven Weeks (1866)	Korean (1950–53)	Spanish–American (1898)
Franco–Prussian (1870–71)	Sinai (1956)	Spanish–Moroccan (1909–10)
Russo–Turkish (1877–78)	Sino–Indian (1962)	Franco–Turkish (1919–21)
Pacific (1879–83)	Vietnamese (1965–75)	Russo–Finnish (1939–40)
Sino–French (1884–85)	Second Kashmir (1965)	Franco–Thai (1940–41)
Central American (1885)	Six Day (1967)	Russo–Hungarian (1956)
Sino–Japanese (1894–95)	Israeli–Egyptian (1969–70)	Turco–Cypriot (1974)
Greco–Turkish (1897)	Football (1969)	
Boxer Rebellion (1900)	Bangladesh (1971)	
Russo–Japanese (1904–05)	Yom Kippur (1973)	
Central American (1906)	Vietnamese–Cambodian (1975–79)	
Central American (1907)	Ethiopian–Somalian (1977–78)	
Italo–Turkish (1911–12)	Ugandan–Tanzanian (1978–79)	
First Balkan (1912–13)	Sino–Vietnamese (1979)	
Second Balkan (1914–18)	Iran–Iraq (1980–88)	
World War I (1914–18)	Falklands (1982)	
Lithuanian–Polish (1919–20)	Sino–Vietnamese (1985–87)	
Russo–Polish (1919–20)	Israel–Syria (1982)	
Hungarian–Allies (1919)	Gulf War (1990–91)	
Greco–Turkish (1919–21)	Azeri–Armenian (1992–94)	

to outbreaks of war or militarized disputes? What proportion of rivalries engages in multiple wars?

How many wars appear to have their roots in rivalry processes? The most direct way to answer this question is to examine a list of opponents in warfare and then separate the wars that have rivals opposing each other from the wars in which no rivals are opponents. Table 3.8 reports the outcome of this simple test. The two columns representing wars with rivals on opposite sides list fifty-eight interstate wars. Sixteen wars without rivals as opponents are listed in the third column. That suggests that at least three of every four wars (78.4 percent) have been linked in some way to antecedent rivalry processes. Complicating matters further, though, the employment of Gleditsch–Ward rules for counting independent states would appear to add about twenty-four wars that are regarded currently as "extra-systemic" by more conservative

Correlates of War (Small and Singer, 1982) rules for counting independent states. Of these twenty-four additional wars, most of which take
place in the nineteenth century, sixteen involved rivalries and eight did
not.[10] If these twenty-four wars are added to the seventy-four listed in
Table 3.8, the proportion of wars linked to rivalries drops only slightly
to 75 percent. Interestingly, the three of every four wars rule is capable
of surviving a 33 percent increase in the number of wars despite the fact
that there were more wars without rivalry roots in the nineteenth century when most of the "new" wars were introduced than in the twentieth
century.

The observation that there were more wars in the nineteenth century
century without apparent roots in strategic rivalries than was the case in
the twentieth century raises the question of precisely how much stronger
are the apparent roots in the twentieth century, as opposed to the nineteenth century? If we look only at wars after 1899 (as listed in Table 3.8),
the proportion of rivalry-rooted war is forty-one of forty-seven, or
87.2 percent. If we take this sort of examination one step further and
ask about the record after 1945, the rooted proportion is twenty-one
of twenty-three, or 91.3 percent. Thus, even though wars and rivalries
may be on the numerical decline, these numbers suggest that wars are
becoming increasingly likely to emerge from strategic rivalries. One might
also suggest that an examination of the wars without rivalry roots would
probably reveal at least one common denominator. The "rootless" wars
tend to be reactions to opportunities or problems that decision-makers
have not spent a great deal of time preparing for or premeditating. The
1898 Spanish–American War, the 1940 Thai attempt to take advantage
of a weakened France, or the Soviet invasion of Hungary in 1956 are
exemplars of this type of war. In contrast, wars with roots in rivalries
take time to develop. They may also reflect degrees of opportunism and
short-term reactions to abruptly emerging crises, but the difference is
that they unfold in a historical context that makes overt conflict more

---

[10] The twenty-four extra-systemic wars to which we are referring include the following:
Turco–Persian (1821), First Anglo–Burmese (1823–6), Russo–Persian (1826–8), First
Syrian (1831–2), First British–Afghan (1838–42), First Opium (1839–40), Second
Syrian (1839–40), Franco–Algerian (1839–47), Peruvian–Bolivian (1841), Franco–
Moroccan (1844), Burmese (1852–3), Second Opium (1856–60), French Indochinese
(1858), First Buenos Aires (1859), Tonkin (1873–85), Egypto–Ethiopian (1875–6),
Second British–Afghan (1878–80), Tunisian (1881–2), Franco–Indochinese (1882–4),
Russo–Afghan (1885), Serbo–Bulgarian (1885), First Italo–Ethiopian (1887), Italo–
Ethiopian (1895–6), and Boer (1899–1902). No claim is made that these wars qualify
without doubt – only that they would appear to qualify if one expands the international
system's state population according to Gleditsch and Ward rules. It is also possible that
one or two others might qualify as well.

probable at some point. The same cannot be said for the "rootless" wars.

Even so, these observations do not mean that only rivalries were responsible for that much warfare, but it does suggest that rivalry behavior was probably involved in some causal fashion. Obviously, the summary statistics cannot tell us precisely how the rivalries were involved. That is the role of theory, much of which is yet to be developed. Yet these same summary statistics understate the full extent of involvement in the sense that complex, multiple actor wars are counted in the same way as more simple, dyadic wars. World Wars I and II and the Gulf War – all three of which involved multiple rivalries – are given no more weight than the Anglo-Persian, Italo-Sicilian, or Russo-Finnish Wars, which did not involve interstate rivalries between the main antagonists. Understanding better how rivalries intersect and overlap to create wars involving broad coalitions should be a high theoretical priority. The summary statistics also omit the wars that are indirectly related to other rivalries. For instance, the 1856 Anglo-Persian War took place within the context of the Anglo-Russian contest in Eurasia in general and Persia in particular, the Russo-Finnish War was connected to the Russo-German rivalry in eastern Europe, and the 1974 war between Turkey and Cyprus most evidently was related to the Greco-Turkish rivalry.

Yet the very fact that there have been 76–100 interstate wars since 1816 and 173 rivalries suggests another interesting characteristic of rivalry behavior. Unless a large number of rivalries managed to crowd into the wars with large coalitions, there would appear to be a number of rivalries that are not linked to warfare. It turns out that a slight plurality of strategic rivalries (94 of 173 or 54 percent) have not gone to war. This unexpected pacific characteristic is most pronounced among minor–minor dyads (62.2 percent) and least characteristic of major–major dyads (15 percent). The proportion of rivalries that have engaged in no, one, or more than one war declines in a more or less expected fashion. About twice as many rivalries, counting both major, minor, and mixed power varieties, have engaged in no wars as have engaged in one war. Similarly, about twice as many rivalries have engaged in one war as have engaged in multiple wars. However, this same ratcheting downward effect does not apply exactly to the other three dyadic types. For example, minor–minor rivalries are less likely to engage in any amount of warfare than dyads involving one or more major powers (with one exception). Major–major rivalries are or were clearly the most highly war-prone dyads while rivalries with only one major power have had about a 56:44 chance of breaking out in warfare.

Table 3.9 *Rivalries and militarized dispute years*

Number of militarized dispute years	All	minor–minor	minor–major	major–major	Mixed
0	25	22	3	0	0
1–10	98	74	10	10	4
11–20	25	16	3	5	1
21–30	7	3	2	2	0
31–40	5	3	0	0	2
41–50	7	3	0	2	2
51–90	3	2	0	1	0
Militarized dispute years density					
0	40	35	4	0	1
0.1–0.5	92	64	9	13	6
0.6–1.0	23	13	5	4	1
1.1–1.5	12	8	0	4	0
1.6–2.0	4	3	0	0	1

Note: Militarized dispute year density is militarized dispute years divided by the length of the rivalry. Four rivalries are excluded from the count because they began too late to be included in the militarized dispute data set.

In contrast to the war outcome, most rivalries have engaged in militarized disputes.[11] All but twenty-five (14.4 percent) have had one or more militarized disputes. But most rivalries (72 percent) have only experienced the equivalent of ten years or less of militarized disputes. Table 3.9 provides information on weighted dispute years (number of disputes multiplied by the number of years a dispute is considered ongoing) and weighted dispute year density (weighted dispute years divided by the length of the rivalry). If one controls for the length of the rivalry, fewer than 10 percent of all rivalries have experienced the equivalent of a militarized dispute every year that the rivalry was ongoing. The typical experience, then, is for rivalries to experience only some militarized disputes, and then only intermittently. How this compares to non-rival dyads is a subject taken up in succeeding chapters. Yet one would expect that rivalries would be characterized by more than their fair share of militarized dispute. But the relatively limited dispute activity found to be associated with rivalries, especially in comparison to war behavior, suggests that there may be a looser connection among militarized disputes, war, and rivalry than has hitherto been thought to be the case. The case for a

[11] The source for the dispute data is the Militarized Interstate Disputes 2.1 data set available at www.pss.la.psu.edu/Mid-data.html. The data are described in Jones, Bremer, and Singer (1996).

rivalry–war linkage is quite strong. There may also be a respectable linkage between rivalry and militarized disputes. It is the dispute–war linkage within the context of rivalry that may prove to be the most tenuous.

The regional distribution of strategic rivalries

Highly aggregated findings on rivalry-proneness have their uses but they should not be allowed to conceal the geographical unevenness of rivalry activity. Different parts of the world are more or less susceptible to strategic rivalries. Nor are these regional susceptibilities constant. Several regions have been highly rivalry-prone and have become less so while others have become more prone to interstate feuding. Table 3.10 offers one quick summary view of these nonconstant spatial distributions. The table divides the world into fifteen reasonably conventional geographical categories, although some of the standard categories are further subdivided in terms that make more sense for clustering rivalries. For instance, there is no single Middle East and North Africa although some local actors may be active throughout the larger region. From a rivalry perspective, it seems more appealing to subdivide the region into at least three smaller regions: a Maghribian North Africa, a Mashriq area focused primarily on Israel and the competition for leadership in the Arab world, and a Gulf area focused increasingly around the Iran–Iraq–Saudi Arabia triangle.[12] Similar sorts of subdivisions are made for South America (north vs. southern cone), Eastern Europe (north-central vs. southeast), sub-Saharan Africa (west, eastern, central and southern), Southeast Asia (continental vs. maritime), and Central Eurasia (eastern vs. western/Caspian). To these subdivisions we can add categories for North America, the Caribbean, Central America, South America, Western Europe, South Asia, and East Asia. It should also be noted that we have one category that does not refer to a specific region but rather to rivalries that cut across regional boundaries, as exemplified by the US–Japanese rivalry prior to 1945 or the US–Soviet Cold War. In all, that suggests twenty-two current rivalry regions, along with one residual category.

Table 3.10 divides the information into three main groups: rivalries that began before 1945, those that began after 1945, and rivalries alive in 1999. Two regions have removed themselves from the rivalry distribution list altogether: North America and Western Europe. Several regions are comparatively new to the list reflecting post-World War II independence dates: western, central, and southern Africa; North Africa; South

---

[12] While we need to allocate more resources to the study of rivalry dyads, other combinations such as triangles should not be overlooked. They will probably prove to be more common than anyone knew once we decide to inventory them.

Table 3.10 *The regional distribution of rivalries over time*

Regions	Pre–1946	Post–1946	1999
North America	3	0	0
Caribbean	1	1	1
Central America	9	3	0
South America			
Northern	4	1	2
Southern Cone	9	1	2
Western Europe	6	0	0
Eastern Europe			
North Central	10	1	0
Southern	12	5	4
sub-Saharan Africa			
West	0	8	1
Eastern	2	13	4
Central	0	2	1
Southern	0	6	0
Middle Eastern and North Africa			
Maghrib	0	8	2
Mashriq	4	12	7
Gulf	1	9	7
Southwest Asia	4	1	1
Southern Asia	0	2	0
Southeast Asia			
Continental	4	5	1
Maritime	0	2	0
Central Eurasia			
Eastern	0	1	1
Western	0	1	1
East Asia	5	3	2
Inter-regional	12	3	1

Asia, maritime southeast Asia, and both wings of Central Eurasia. More encouraging perhaps, a number of regions have become discernibly less rivalry-prone: Central America, all of South America, north-central eastern Europe, southwestern Asia, and most of southeast Asia. That leaves the hotbed of rivalry activity at the turn of the century located primarily in southeastern Europe, Africa (especially in the northeast), the Gulf area, south Asia, and east Asia.

Regions becoming less rivalry-prone over time may be a macro-process that is as important as the often-heralded democratic peace in transforming a highly conflictual international system into something less bellicose. Changes in regime type probably do have something to do with this process but it should be clear that "de-rivalization" has preceded or outpaced democratization in several places that have become less rivalry-prone. Presumably, then, other processes are at play about which we need to develop better understanding.[13] Moreover, the emphasis should be on processes in the plural, as opposed to a singular process. The North American regional story suggests a strong role for high levels of capability concentration. The West European regional story suggests a role for processes of long-term, great power exhaustion and demotion, just as the exhaustion of Vietnam has implications for the state of rivalries in its part of the world. The disappearance of rivalries in north-central eastern Europe may be a transitory phenomenon in part linked to inducements attached to NATO membership. The point of this atheoretical speculation is that there are likely to be a variety of processes operating to encourage more and less bellicosity in regional theaters. We have a number of analytical clues but it is not exactly a question that has received much attention as yet.

As we develop more experience with comparative regional analysis of conflict processes, we are also likely to find that the nature of rivalries also varies by region. That is not to say that there is a Latin American rivalry or a Middle Eastern rivalry, both of which differ from African rivalries. But no two regions or subregions have had identical histories and mixes of actors. Nor do they all share the same types of conflict issues. North American rivalries primarily were about US expansion and whether its expansion might be thwarted or contained. South American rivalries primarily were about various spatial questions that became more pressing as the respective populations moved away from the coast and into their interiors, and only then began bumping into neighboring states. Mashriqi rivalries have centered and continue to center on the Israeli question and interrelated question of regional primacy. Southern African rivalries were fixated around apartheid and disintegrated with the collapse or surrender of white supremacy rule in South Africa. Rivalries in northeastern Africa and southeastern Europe have strong elements of ethnicity that have been missing in the rivalries of the Americas and Western Europe. What all of this means is not that rivalry processes are inherently different according to who is fighting them or even where they are being fought. Rather, what is being suggested is that rivalry processes are likely to be characterized by different mixes of elements and subject to different types of influences in different parts of the world. Thus, if we understand the rivalry

---

[13] Suggestively, Rasler and Thompson (2005) find that rivalry information for major powers has stronger explanatory powers than regime type when one is attempting to account for militarized dispute behavior.

de-escalation process in, say, Western Europe, the same explanation may not work in northeastern Africa without considerable translation or conditions pertaining to specific mixes of issues and domestic factors. For that matter, the same explanation may not work at all.

What we need to do is to move away from the regional labels and substitute non-spatial concepts. For instance, it could be argued that regions characterized by high capability concentration can become less rivalry-prone if the strongest actor in the region is either able to establish its hegemony coercively, or at least successfully, or is forced to give up its hegemonic aspirations. Capability concentration alone obviously does not suffice. Compare the histories of rivalries in North America, southern Africa, and South Asia. In North America, the United States gradually defeated its various opponents (Britain, Spain, France, Mexico, and the indigenous native American population) and managed to avoid being splintered into a more multipolar region in the 1860s. South African schemes for regional hegemony go back at least to the days of late nineteenth-century Cecil Rhodes and were ultimately thwarted, unlike the North American story, by a coalition of dissidents from the indigenous population and outside actors. Still, that may not be the end of the regional hegemony story for southern Africa. In South Asia, Indian hegemony has been frustrated to some extent by a relatively weak Pakistan that has also received considerable aid from outside the region.

One might also add Western Europe to this comparison. The Franco-German rivalry became the central rivalry of that region in the second half of the nineteenth century and was only resolved after World War II when German foreign policies made strenuous efforts to avoid traditional realpolitik strategies and when French foreign policy-makers began to believe that a revival of German hegemonic plans was unlikely. There is no doubt that other forces were at work. The Soviet threat and pressures for European integration were intertwined with the Franco-German rivalry de-escalation in ways that we have yet to fully disentangle.[14] But if we sum the four cases, we have three cases of regional hegemonic success and defeat followed or accompanied by rivalry de-escalation and one case of continued hegemonic frustration that continues to be fixated around a dangerous interstate rivalry.[15]

[14] This case received some attention in Chapter 1.
[15] The Egyptian–Israeli rivalry suggests another interesting example of a case in which the emphasis involved Egyptian concerns primarily about its intra-Arab position. The 1967 war highlighted the spatial dimension. After the Camp David accords, the rivalry continued with concerns about a future competition for Middle Eastern or Mashriqi positional primacy.

Regional hegemony is likely to prove to be one important factor in the regional comparison of rivalry de-escalation processes. But it will be only one factor among several in a theoretical effort that has only begun to attract analytical attention. If we are only beginning to explicitly study rivalries as processes, it should not be too surprising to find that we possess only a hazy understanding of regional rivalry (de)escalation processes, let alone how best to proceed in comparing the processes.

Conclusion

It is usually necessary to learn how to crawl before one learns to run. Something similar may be at work with strategic rivalries. We know something about their behavior over the last two centuries. We need to know much more before we can really say much about how they work and impact on other processes. We also will need to learn more about rivalry propensities to be able to say more about the future trajectory of strategic rivalries. In the interim, there appears to be some systematic movement away from rivalry behavior but it has been going on for quite some time, without our catching on to the drift away from the peak attained in the first decade of the twentieth century. What seems most probable is that there will be some fluctuation in the number of rivalries. Yet we have no strong reasons to anticipate abrupt movements either toward increasing rivalry propensity or ending rivalries altogether. Some major power rivalry can be expected to return to the system and it may only take one new major power rivalry to return the world to something resembling the Cold War. Many, but probably not all, of the regions that have become strategically rivalry-free could very well remain so. Such a forecast would suggest a continued, general movement away from rivalry propensities but one which manifested quite unevenly. Some regions are likely to remain quite prone to rivalry formation and persistence. Just why that should be the case must await the development and appropriate testing of theories that speak to these questions. We have hunches, hypotheses, and data but not much more as yet.

On the other hand, we are still debating how best to conceptualize the rivalry terms and where they are to be found. If we are just beginning to come to grips with existential questions, it is hardly surprising that we do not know more. A well-known historian (Gaddis, 1992) criticized international relations theory for not being able to predict the end of the Cold War. He was wrong to think that theory should be able to predict specific events. He was right to imply that we should have known more about rivalry behavior – not just about terminations, but also about rivalry-formation and escalation/de-escalation processes. If we had known more about rivalries in general in the late 1980s, it is just possible that we might have been taken less by surprise than almost all of us were by the turn of events in US–Soviet interactions. That is not the only reason, nor is it the best reason, to study strategic rivalries, but it is certainly one of them. In the next two chapters, we turn to other and more central reasons for studying rivalries – namely, that conflict dynamics within rivalry are more prone to escalation than are conflict dynamics outside of rivalry.

Part II

The dangers of strategic rivalries: Crisis behavior and escalation

4   Protracted conflict and crisis escalation

Underlying the interest in the role of rivalry processes as antecedents to interstate conflict is the simple idea that conflict within the constraints of rivalry works differently than conflict outside of rivalry. Rivalry is by no means necessary for conflict to occur but conflicts associated with rivalry processes erupt with a great deal more historical and psychological baggage than is likely in the absence of rivalry. Rivals have a history of conflict, often over the same issues. Vengeance for past defeats and worries about the probability of future defeats, therefore, intrude into the decision-making processes. Compared to nonrivals, rivals have more reason, whether accurately or not, to mistrust the intentions of their adversaries. They have had time to develop images of their adversaries as threatening opponents with persistent aims to thwart their own objectives. If rivals offer concessions, why should such offers be viewed as anything but attempts at deception? Concessions and movement toward some middle ground, accordingly, are more difficult to attain. The ultimate outcome is that rivals are less likely to settle their disputes than nonrivals. Rivals give themselves fewer opportunities to exit a conflict trajectory, once they are on such a path, than do two opponents coming into conflict for the first time, and, therefore, are also likely to generate more than their fair share of conflict and violence.

But it is also fair to say that analyses of rivalry have outpaced the development of theories and models that explain how pertinent variables might be related. The development of, and the search for, appropriate models should be a high priority. One possibly useful source of theorizing about protracted conflict lies outside the conventional realm of interstate rivalry analyses. It deserves closer scrutiny and, if appropriate, integration into the growing understanding of rivalry processes. More specifically, one of the foci in the International Crisis Behavior (ICB) project (see, for instance, Brecher and Wilkenfeld, 1997) has been on the impact of protracted conflicts on interstate crises. The basic point, very much like the starting point for interstate rivalry analyses, is that crises that erupt within protracted conflicts operate differently than in situations not characterized by a history of conflict between the same opponents over related issues.

The ICB notion of protracted conflicts cannot be equated with inter-state rivalries, despite considerable conceptual and empirical overlap. But the logic underlying the application of protracted conflict to crisis behavior, subject to qualifications, does seem transferable. We first inspect the ICB idea of protracted conflict, discuss some of its problems for our own rivalry analysis purposes, and then apply a protracted conflict model to the analysis of interstate rivalry, with mixed success. In addition, we also appropriate an ICB crisis escalation model, and develop the interaction between rivalry and other variables in the model when predicting crisis escalation to war. Throughout, our basic question concerns what role interstate rivalry plays in crisis behavior. Are the crises of rivals more lethal than those of nonrivals? If so, can we pinpoint why that is the case? To the extent that we are able answer these questions, the outcome should advance both the study of interstate rivalry and crisis behavior.

Strategic rivalry and protracted conflict

The ICB protracted conflict concept stems from earlier conceptualization advanced by Azar, Jureidini, and McLaurin (1978) and possesses the following definitional characteristics:
1. conflict situations in which the stakes are very high;
2. hostile interactions extending over long periods of time;
3. sporadic outbreaks of open warfare fluctuating in frequency and intensity;
4. involving whole societies and acting as agents for defining the scope of national identity and social solidarity;
5. persistence in time with no distinguishable points of termination.

Therefore, protracted conflict embodies intense and violent conflict over important issues persisting for long periods of time.

The concept of rivalry appears quite similar to protracted conflict at first glance. Vasquez (1993), for instance, emphasizes persistent hostility between states of roughly equal power. Diehl and Goertz (2000) stress militarized interstate competition in which some cases are more enduring than others. In Chapter 2, we define strategic rivalry as a competitive relationship between independent states where both states identify the other as an enemy and an explicit threat. All three examples attempt to capture how conflicts can be related over time. Rivalries are not events or brief moments but longitudinal relationships between states that constrain decisions in the past, present, and future.

The similarities between the protracted conflict and rivalry concepts include their emphases on competition between states and the temporal dynamics of those conflicts. Each attempts to extend conflict longitudinally by looking at past interactions between states. The assumption in both is that hostile histories change the present context of an international relationship. Additionally, there is the notion that both rivalries and protracted conflicts involve stakes and issues that the disputants could resolve by force or intense conflict. Thus, for both concepts to apply, there must be some serious goal incompatibility.

Yet, despite these similarities, there are numerous and important differences. First, protracted conflicts by definition must be over "high" stakes issues (see point 1 above), while rivalry conceptualizations usually have no such criteria. For a stake to be of high or low priority there must be an objective criterion by which to judge. Are the disagreements over the Rann of Kutch between India and Pakistan or Turkish airspace incursions over Greece "high" stake issues? While the Rann of Kutch has little strategic/economic value objectively, it served the important purpose of isolating a small force of Indian troops so Pakistan could test its new military equipment without risking war in 1965. Similarly, Turkish airspace intrusions never involved the arming of weapons but were viewed by Greece as a slight to their sovereignty.

In rivalry analysis, issues can take on a life of their own specifically due to the past hostile interactions of the disputants. The Rann of Kutch was an important piece of territory to Pakistan because it allowed them a localized military advantage. The past history of conflict between the states made this issue salient. Likewise, the Turkish slight to Greek airspace was particularly contentious because of the extreme mistrust that had built up between the states since Greek independence. The difference is that protracted conflicts by definition include only objectively high gravity issues while rivalry analysis allows the issues under contention to vary in severity and intensity.

A second difference is that rivalries have not necessarily fought a previous war. The third protracted conflict criterion requires that protracted conflicts have experienced warfare. A rivalry, on the other hand, may or may not have experienced an outbreak of violence. Singling out specific adversaries as explicit threats and therefore worthy of close monitoring can happen with or without war. For example, although Israeli–Egyptian relations were born of war, competition between the United States and the Soviet Union began without a previous war. While some analysts do use conflict to operationalize rivalry, the conflicts that count have a much lower threshold than intense violence (as discussed in Chapter 2). Therefore, rivalries include both states that have escalated their disputes to war, and those that have not. The variation on escalation is of central importance to the current study since we attempt to explain how rivalry affects escalation propensities. If war caused the coding of protracted conflict by definition, it would be impossible to untangle the reciprocal relationship.

Thirdly, rivalries do not necessarily involve "whole societies" or act as "agents for defining the scope of national identity" as protracted conflict suggests. External threats, such as those that may emanate from rivalry, can serve as catalysts for domestic concentration (Desch, 1996) and national identity (Colley, 1992). But they need not do so. In fact, many times divisions within a state arise over which protracted conflict should be considered the most salient. For instance, in late nineteenth-century France, one group of elites picked Germany as the greatest threat to France, while an opposing coalition found Britain to be the real enemy of the French state. Therefore it is unclear as to whether Great Britain–France or France–Germany would have been considered a protracted conflict, though each dyad had gone to war previously. Yet, each dyad was involved in rivalries with the other.

Apart from these conceptual differences, there also are a number of operational complications. Table 4.1 lists the thirty-one cases since the end of World War I identified by the ICB project as qualifying. Since a little more than half (eighteen) are considered to have terminated, it would appear that the fifth characteristic (persistence without termination) should not be taken too literally. More important, however, is the finding that these thirty-one cases encompass 245 crises or 60 percent of the 1918–1995 international crisis data set (Brecher and Wilkenfeld, 1997; and Wilkenfeld and Brecher, 2000).

Given the mix of conflict arenas (e.g., Angola, Rhodesia, Western Sahara, and so forth) and specific interstate dyads (e.g., Chad–Libya, Ethiopia–Somalia, and so on), it is difficult to estimate how many crises would approximate the fair share of these actors if we had no other information. However, the eighteen cases that explicitly involve dyadic inter-state feuds claim 93 of the 245 crises. Thus, eighteen dyads account for about 20 percent of the crisis inventory. The population of the international system has expanded from about 51 at the end of World War I to 186 by 1993. So, the total number of dyads in the system has ranged from a low of 1,275 to a high of 17,205. Let us say that the mean number of states over this time period has been 125. That number of states yields 7,750 dyads. Eighteen dyads out of a field of 7,750 represents 0.2 percent. Therefore, 0.2 percent of the dyads accounts for some 20 percent of the crises. This estimate is in fact quite conservative. If the other thirteen conflict arenas can be translated into multiple feuding dyads or rivalries,

Table 4.1 *Protracted conflicts in the twentieth century*

	Start of PC	End of PC	Number of international crises
Africa			
Angola	1975	1988	11
Chad/Libya	1971	1994	8
Ethiopia/Somalia	1960	present	6
Rhodesia	1965	1980	11
Western Sahara	1975	present	10
Americas			
Costa Rica/ Nicaragua	1918	1955	3
Ecuador/Peru	1935	present	4
Honduras/Nicaragua	1937	present	6
Asia			
Afghanistan/Pakistan	1949	present	3
China/Japan	1927	1945	5
China/Vietnam	1978	present	4
India/Pakistan	1947	present	9
Indochina	1945	1976	7
Indochina	1946	1990	18
Korea	1950	present	6
Europe			
Czech./Germany	1938	1945	3
Finland/Russia	1919	1961	4
France/Germany	1920	1945	5
Italy/Albania/Yugo.	1921	1953	5
Lithuania/Poland	1920	1981	3
Poland/Russia	1920	1981	4
Spain	1936	1939	4
Middle East			
Arab/Israel	1947	present	25
Iran/Iraq	1959	present	7
Iraq/Kuwait	1961	present	6
Yemen	1962	1979	6
Multiregional			
East/West	1918	1989	21
Greece/Turkey	1920	present	9
Iran/USSR	1920	1946	4
Taiwan Strait	1948	present	4
World War II	1939	1945	24

Source: based on Brecher and Wilkenfeld (1997: 821).

the number of dyads involved is approximately thirty-one or 0.4 percent of the mean number of dyads. That observation suggests, then, that less than 1 percent of the possible interstate pairings is responsible for 60 percent of the twentieth century's interstate crises.

That is a remarkable statistic in its own right and certainly reinforces the general notion that much of the world's interstate conflict is generated by a very small number of actors. Most of the world's states simply do not engage in conflict relations with most of the rest of the world's states. A small number of interstate rivalries, on the other hand, do generate much more than their fair share of interstate conflict.

However, there are two problems with Table 4.1's identification of protracted conflicts. Two different types of protracted conflict – situations involving a feuding dyad and more complex arenas involving multiple actors and feuding dyads – are treated similarly. This mixture may be perfectly appropriate for some questions but, in general, it makes it difficult to generalize about crisis behavior in protracted conflict. The processes at work in a dyadic rivalry on the order of Ethiopia and Somalia or Iran and Iraq might be viewed differently if we expanded the unit of analysis to include Northeast Africa (for instance, Sudan–Ethiopia, Kenya–Somalia, Ethiopia–Eritrea, Uganda–Sudan, and Uganda–Tanzania) or the Middle Eastern Gulf area (for instance, Iraq–Saudi Arabia, Iran–Saudi Arabia, Iraq–Kuwait, Iraq–Syria, Saudi Arabia–Yemen, Bahrain–Qatar). The point is that any dyadic rivalry is likely to be embedded in a wider field of protracted conflict. How these dyads interact and intersect may prove to be quite important to understanding the processes of any single dyadic feud. The list in Table 4.1 conflates this issue by treating Indochina, Korea, or East–West as similar in status to Greece–Turkey or China–Vietnam, even though few would deny that Indochina, Korea, Greece–Turkey, or China–Vietnam hardly operated independently of the East–West protracted conflict or that China–Vietnam was tied closely to Indochina (identified as 1946–90 in Table 4.1). One problem, then, is that the cases in Table 4.1 cannot be treated as equivalent units of analysis. Some are dyadic in nature while others are multi-dyadic. Some cases could easily be subsumed by other ones that are identified.

A second problem is that the thirty-one cases represent a selective sample of interstate rivalry in the twentieth century. As far as can be ascertained, the intent of the protracted conflict identification was not to sample. Yet Rhodesia is identified but not South Africa or some larger southern African grouping that would accommodate the conflict in that region that persisted and even grew more intense after 1980 and the transformation of Rhodesia into Zimbabwe. Honduras–El Salvador might qualify in Central America as well as Costa Rica–Nicaragua does. The only South American case in Table 4.1 is Ecuador–Peru.

Bolivia and Paraguay might have been considered. The conflict over the Malvinas/Falkland Islands might have made the list. So, too, might Argentinean-Chilean feuding. In Asia, we have China paired with Japan and Vietnam but not with India. In Europe, we have Poland and Russia but not Germany and Russia. In the Middle East, a number of inter-Arab conflicts do not make the list. In the multiregional category, we have World War II because the ICB project chooses to examine crises that take place within ongoing wars, but we have only some of the conflict processes leading up to the war. That is, China–Japan, Czechoslovakia–Germany, France–Germany, and Poland–Russia are in the list. The United States and Japan or Japan and Russia are not.

The second problem then is that the case universe is less than comprehensive and the nature of the purposive sampling procedure is not clear. It may be that the real problem here is the "protracted conflict" conceptualization. It seems to encourage mixing apples and oranges while overlooking pineapples. We might do better to focus on more readily identifiable units of analysis. Since interstate rivalry seems to be very closely related to the ICB interpretation of protracted conflict, an explicit unit of analysis focused on rivalries should be more persuasive.

Rivalry, context and crisis

Exactly why a small number of states is responsible for so much conflict is not a question that the ICB project has addressed directly. Instead, ICB analysts take the existence of protracted conflict for granted and then attempt to assess the impact of protracted conflict on crisis behavior. Brecher (1993: 822–3) suggests that crises within protracted conflict, as opposed to crises outside of protracted conflict, are characterized by the following:
1. the more visible presence of violence in crisis triggers;
2. higher stakes or a perceived threat to more basic values;
3. greater reliance on violence in crisis management.
4. a resort to more severe types and levels of violence in crisis management;
5. a primary role for violence in crisis management.
The original model includes hypotheses on crisis abatement and termination that we are ignoring to focus exclusively on crisis escalation.

Brecher (Brecher and Wilkenfeld, 1997) also constructs a protracted conflict model, which we think works well as a core statement about the fundamental context of rivalry. At the heart of such a conflict is a dispute over values that are sufficiently basic and important to justify violence. If we add several other characteristics that are apt to emerge in such disputes to the mix (the likelihood of multiple issues coming into conflict, the probability of mutual distrust intensifying, and the likelihood of a series of violent interactions over time), the outcome is prolonged and unresolved hostility. Given this mix, it seems warranted to extract expectations of violence in crisis behavior being more likely to be associated with protracted conflicts than with nonprotracted conflicts. Similarly, there are feedback-effects among the issues and outcomes of crises. As states continue to come into conflict, the number and importance of issues may increase. Therefore crises involving protracted conflict/rivalry should be more prone to multiple and high salience issues, as well as greater violence.

We suggest that crises within rival dyads will evince fundamentally different dynamics than those outside of a rivalry situation. One can conceptualize a crisis situation as a number of tit-for-tat interactions between states, in the form of verbal communication and physical actions. In some cases, the response to one side's signal may increase the level of implied threat. For instance Egypt may verbally threaten Israel, while Israel in response could mobilize its armed forces. Each step is an objective piece of information that needs to be subjectively interpreted and processed. Decision-makers must ask not only "what has happened?" but more importantly "what does it mean?"

The meaning imputed to the opposing side's actions will depend on the context within which the information is processed (Ross, 1998). Was the Egyptian threat meant to signal imminent war or was it just a bluff? Would the same threat be interpreted identically by Israel if it had come from the United States? This decision will be based on an interpretation of the present information in the context of past interactions. Since states' actual intentions are unobservable, decision-makers must make their best guess as to what each action means. Past experience forms the guiding hand of expectation to infer intentionality to action. If one expects cooperative behavior from a state, threats are likely to be interpreted more as warnings or slaps on the wrist as opposed to threats of an oncoming military conflict. Conversely, in a relationship plagued by mistrust and expectations of conflict the same threat may take on a much graver interpretation (Jervis, 1976, 1988; Lebow, 1981; Stoessinger, 1985; and Vertzberger, 1990). As Jervis (1988: 320) suggests, "each new day does not bring a new beginning; severe restrictions are placed on us by the expectations – including our own expectations about ourselves – that constitute the context within which we must behave."

This leads to the general hypothesis that as the context within which information is processed changes, behavior should also change. In the language of rivalry analysis, a rivalry context with its increased mistrust and expectation of conflict will affect the way objective information is processed, all else being equal. The most dramatic implication of this argument is that the action–reaction sequence of crises is likely to be different among rivals. Information passed between rivals must be processed within the conflictual setting of that relationship. Thus, crisis triggers such as verbal threats, sanctions, or military mobilizations are likely to lead to more violent and escalatory responses within rivalry as compared to non-rival interactions (Rioux, 1997; Brecher, James and Wilkenfeld, 2000; Bremer, 2000; Goertz and Diehl, 2000b; Vasquez, 2000). Additionally, attempts to de-escalate the crisis may be less successful due to this same mistrust. For example, the success of a cease-fire agreement hinges on the mutual trust between the two groups that neither will take advantage of the situation to improve its strategic position. If there are strong expectations of guile on both sides, agreement and de-escalation will be difficult regardless of objective signals of friendship or peace. This argument leads to our general hypothesis that the context of rivalry should increase the probability of crisis escalation to war.

The escalation model

Knowing something about the relationship of protracted conflict/rivalry to crisis behavior in general is one of our foci. A second focus centers on explaining and predicting crisis escalation with rivalry as only one of the components of the model. Brecher and Wilkenfeld (1997) put forward a sixteen-variable crisis escalation model that can be used to account for crisis escalation to war. While Brecher and Wilkenfeld suggest that each of these variables significantly affects the probability of escalation, we are interested in the interaction between these variables and strategic rivalry. As argued above, a rivalry frame may change the way objective information is processed within a crisis situation. Thus, we intend to examine this escalation model but not necessarily for the reasons originally advanced by the authors of the model.

We hypothesize four mechanisms by which rivalry can interact with other variables to increase the probability of escalation. First, rivalry can trump or overwhelm constraints on conflict escalation. As noted previously, mistrust and conflict can affect the way crisis interaction unfolds. While there may be objective reasons to avoid conflict, for instance norms of conflict resolution, capability differentials, and major power intervention, these are less likely to be effective within a rivalry setting. While a democratic regime is considered a pacifying element in international relations (see Russett, 1993), the effect may be dampened within rivalry (Rasler and Thompson, 2001). Dixon (1994) argues that democracies use peaceful conflict resolution mechanisms like institutionalized mediation both domestically and internationally to avoid overt violence. Yet, when interacting with an adversary that is mistrusted there may be less incentive to pursue peace as vigorously. Further, others have followed Kant (See Russett, 1993) in arguing that democracies are more pacific because they include the public in decision-making. If those that bear the greatest costs in a war (the masses) can constrain elites from foreign adventures, escalation is less likely. But this denies the fact that in many cases public opinion may have helped push leaders into war, for example in the 1898 clash between the Spanish and Americans in reaction to "yellow journalism." If the public is mistrustful of an adversary, as in the case of many rivalries, public pressure may support escalation rather than de-escalation. Therefore, in the presence of rivalry, the pacifying role of democracy may be reduced.

Likewise, capability considerations can serve as less of a constraint on escalation within rivalry. It is generally hypothesized that states of equal capabilities can deter each other from conflict, while relative capability asymmetry removes a constraint on escalation from one of the players.[1] Yet within rivalry, the military costs of escalation and conflict have to be weighed against the benefits of inflicting damage on the enemy and showing resolve for the future. Even relatively weak states may escalate their disputes to violence to show their rival that continued conflict is too costly and that they will resist in the future. For example, Japan attacked the United States at Pearl Harbor, at least in part, due to the hope that this escalation would show the United States that future conflict was too costly to continue. Additionally, Vasquez (1993) notes that rivalries evolve into relationships in which states care more about hurting adversaries, than benefiting themselves. For these reasons, crises within rivalry are less likely to be influenced by capability asymmetry. Both asymmetric and symmetric rival crises should have relatively high escalation probabilities, as compared to nonrival situations.

An additional constraint on escalation is assumed to be major power involvement in a crisis. If a major power attempts to de-escalate a dispute, their international prestige and leverage may prove to be crucial to avoiding war. Yet, when states mistrust each other's intentions and perceive the situation as zero-sum, any mediated solution is unlikely to be helpful. Thus, within rivalry, crises are more likely to escalate despite the involvement of major powers, while outside of rivalry major power intervention may have an ameliorative effect.

---

[1] See Claude, 1962; Waltz, 1979; for a counterargument, see Geller, 1993, 2000.

A second path through which rivalry can affect escalation is by lowering the threshold for escalation while emphasizing the likelihood of military interaction. If states have come into conflict in the past and perceive the other as hostile, decision-makers are likely to fear an attack by the other state. As the states both prepare for war this exacerbates the security dilemma and makes conflict more likely.[2] In extreme examples, both rivals view war as inevitable and then begin to push, not for peace, but for a war they can win. In this high tension situation crises may not take much kindling to explode into a full-scale conflagration.

Outside of rivalry, therefore, a violent trigger, a military issue, and a threat to basic values may be prerequisites for escalation; in a rivalry context even benign events can ignite violence. Thus, non-violent triggers to crises such as regime transitions or military maneuvers may spark an escalatory response. Similarly, states engaged in rivalry are likely to come to blows over issues that objectively may not seem militarily significant or of high salience. As discussed above, India and Pakistan can still fight over the Rann of Kutch, or India and China can tussle over the Aksai Chin despite rather than because of relatively low salience issues.

In a rivalry context, as opposed to more moderate crisis situations, uncertainty is likely to take on a different meaning. There are many circumstances in crisis where states do not know which other states will join, what resources each will bring to bear, or who will defect. How this uncertainty is interpreted depends on the rivalry context of the decision. Within rivalry, this may increase the fear of a dangerous environment where escalation is inevitable and thus encourage hyper-vigilance. Thus, under increased insecurity, rivals are likely to prepare for the worst. Conversely, uncertainty under more cooperative circumstances, where the states do not have a history of conflict, is less threatening since states will have lower expectations of violence and higher levels of trust. For example, the greater uncertainty of a multipolar system as compared to a bipolar crisis setting, with a larger number of major powers and fluid alliance structures, should increase escalation between rivals, but have less effect on nonrival interactions.

Similarly, as the number of actors in a crisis increases so too does the ambiguity of the situation. States cannot be sure of the reactions of each actor to different possible conflict trajectories.[3] Therefore the rivalry context should also interact with the number of actors in a crisis. This logic should apply as well to "system level" (referring to whether crises

---

[2] See Lebow, 1981; Leng, 1983; Hensel, 1994.
[3] Among others, see the arguments put forward in Cusack and Eberwin, 1982; James, 1988; Brecher, 1993.

occur in dominant or subordinate regional subsystems) considerations. Regional subsystems are more likely to be multipolar in structure. The involvement of neighbors and more powerful actors from outside the region is more probable than is likely to be the case in the dominant subsystem. As a consequence, rivalry escalation is more likely to occur in regional than in dominant subsystems.

A final rivalry process that can lead to greater escalation is through the combination of a vulnerable state and an opportunistic enemy. As Blainey (1973) hypothesizes, domestic problems within one state may open a window of opportunity for another state to attack. This "death watch" hypothesis suggests that the attacking state is opportunistically waiting for its adversary to stumble. We believe this process is much more likely to happen in a rivalry setting, as compared to outside rivalry, because rivals, by definition, have singled each other out for special attention. Further, they are likely to expect future conflict with each other, given their history of confrontation. For example, Iraq expected conflict at some point with Iran, and the Iranian revolution decreased Iran's ability to defend itself while maximizing the chances for an Iraqi victory. This calculus is less convincing when future conflict is not expected or when other threats are more salient. We hypothesize, then, that internal instability in at least one country involved in an international crisis will make escalation to war more likely in a rivalry context, but not outside of rivalry.

In addition to these interaction terms we also control for the heterogeneity, age, and contiguity of the actors involved in the crisis and the crisis stress level. Brecher and Wilkenfeld (1997) find that proximity, less age, and greater heterogeneity in the form of different domestic characteristics make escalation more likely. From our perspective, we are unsure what to anticipate with these variables. Heterogeneity should make rivals more mistrustful but that same heterogeneity may have been partially responsible for the development of rivalry in the first place. Thus, we might find ourselves "double counting." In the case of age, we are unsure if it is the age of the state or the age of the rivalry that should matter most. New states may be more prone to developing rivalries, especially over territorial issues, but that propensity does not speak directly to escalation probabilities.[4] Old states and old rivalries will have at least had more opportunities to escalate their conflicts. They may also have learned ways to regulate their conflicts.

Much the same consideration applies to contiguity. If rivals, other than major powers, tend to be contiguous, the potential variance is biased from the outset. Similarly, the argument that the greater the stress level in a crisis, the greater is the probability of escalation, given the constraints on

---

[4] Brecher (1993), Carment (1993), and Maoz (1996) have examined this question.

rational decision-making that this is imposing, could apply equally well to rivalry and nonrivalry cases. However, all of these variables are included in the model to probe the plausibility of the Brecher–Wilkenfeld (1997) escalation model.[5]

Even so, the Brecher–Wilkenfeld model for crisis escalation is fairly complicated. There are quite a few variables and the anticipated relationships are not the straightforward independent variable to dependent variable type.[6] Some of the independent variables are sure to influence some of the other ostensibly independent variables. That is most clearly the case in terms of threat, time pressure, and the expectation of war which are placed midway in the model between the other influences and the crisis outcomes. But we might anticipate other relationships among the independent variables in the model. Systemic structure surely has some impact on the probability of major power involvement. All sorts of selection effects are conceivable. For instance, if a protracted conflict is present (were we to include this variable), we can assume that there is some probability that the adversaries' capabilities are roughly equal, that they are proximate to one another, and that they are unlikely to be a democratic dyad.

Perhaps given these complications, researchers associated with the ICB project have evaded fully testing the implications of these types of models. There is a strong tendency to settle for bivariate examinations of each independent variable's relationship to various dependent variables. This approach leads to calculations of the number of times a variable is present in a crisis and chi-square cross-tabulation tests on an item-by-item basis. But the ICB project also suggests a rank order of significance for the array of variables in the escalation models. System structure is given a maximum weight of 10. System level and regime pair type are both assigned to the next echelon (rank = 7). Protracted conflict, capability, geographic distance, and the number of actors receive the next rank of 6. Political system age, major power activity, and internal instability receive weighted scores of 5, followed by heterogeneity and the number of issues at 4. Trigger and response receive the lowest rank (3).

Brecher (1993: 153) notes that these ranks are assigned on the basis of their likely effects on the other variables in the model. Presumably, then,

---

[5] The variable of crisis management is not included in the analysis because in many cases escalation to war was the management technique. Therefore, including the variable would introduce a substantial endogeneity problem into the analysis. Instead, it may be useful to have a separate research effort attempt to uncover the relationship between crisis triggers and responses.

[6] The Brecher–Wilkenfeld escalation model links system structure, system level, protracted conflict, relative capability, dyadic regime type, geographic distance, state age, internal instability, triggers, responses, the number of actors, actor heterogeneity, major power involvement, multiple issues, value threat, and time pressure to crisis escalation.

system structure was given the highest weight because its effect is likely to be all-pervasive – perhaps influencing all of the other variables in the model in some way. Trigger and response receive the lowest ranks because they are least likely to affect the values of the other variables. While these speculations are interesting, they fall short of predicting which variables are likely to be most influential in terms of crisis outcomes. One way to probe relative explanatory weights empirically is to examine the influence of all of the variables simultaneously. Given the complicated nature of the model, it is obvious that a single multivariate test cannot resolve whether each and every variable is truly significant. What a single test of this sort can do is assess which of these sixteen variables survive a multivariate evaluation. Our primary expectation, guided by our interest in interstate rivalry-protracted conflict, is that knowing something about the rivalry status of the adversaries should be among the most important predictors of escalation and war. Rivals should be much more likely to escalate their crises than nonrivals. Of the other fifteen variables, we would also expect the trigger-response sequence to be particularly enlightening for an interest in escalation and war. One of our most basic understandings of crisis escalation hinges on the tit-for-tat model. If the initial stimulus is violent, more violence can be expected.

As for the rest of the variables in the model, it is hard to handicap which ones are most likely to survive a multivariate examination. Again, this analytical uncertainty has less to do with our confidence in the logic underlying the choice of variables than it does with the probable interrelationships among the explanatory variables. All we can do at this stage is to attempt some very primitive brush clearing, with the debatable assumption that the strongest effects will emerge in a multivariate test. Whether or not our Darwinian assumption is correct, we can be assured that our empirical outcomes will not be the last word on crisis escalation processes. We see the test more as an initial comparison of the rivalry variable's explanatory value *vis-à-vis* the rest of the ensemble. If the rivalry variable survives this test, and only some of the ICB ensemble emerges as significant, we will have a better sense of the significance of rivalry *vis-à-vis* the other fifteen predictors.

Variables and methods

We have a large number of variables to examine but most have been discussed at length in numerous ICB analyses (Brecher and Wilkenfeld, 1997). The ICB variable definitions and operationalizations are thus summarized in Table 4.2 on an alphabetical basis. The one variable that we are introducing from outside the ICB framework has already

Table 4.2 *Variable definitions*

Variable	Description
Age	Time when crisis actor became an autonomous decision-making entity with continuous existence as a sovereign state (pre-1648, 1648–1814, 1815–1918, 1919–1945, post-WWII–1957, 1958–1966, post-1966).
Capability	The extent to which the adversaries' diplomatic, economic, and military resources are asymmetric (from favorable or unfavorable discrepancy).
Centrality of violence	The relative importance decision-makers attach to the use of violence to achieve goals (central vs. non-central).
Crisis management	The level of violence employed in response to trigger (violent vs. non-violent)
Crisis outcome	Assesses the effect of the crisis on the threat level between the participants (escalation in tensions or de-escalation in tensions).
Effectiveness of major power activity	The extent to which major power third party activity was responsible for crisis abatement (ineffective to important).
Geographic distance	The extent to which the locations of the main crisis participants are contiguous or not.
Heterogeneity	The extent of divergence in military capability, economic development, political regime, and culture (one difference to four differences).
Internal instability	The level of domestic turmoil (not present vs. present in at least one state).
Level	The subsystemic location of the crisis (dominant system or regional subsystem).
Major power activity	The extent of major power involvement as third parties, rather than as participants (none to military activity).
Militarized issues	Crisis involved military or strategic concerns (present, not present).
Number of actors	The number of crisis participants exhibiting substantive involvement in the crisis.
Number of issues	Number of distinct issues that were at stake during crisis (from one issue to more than three issues).
Polarity	The type of polarity or power configuration of the dominant system (unipolarity to polycentric).
Regime pair	The type of domestic institutional government form in power at the time of the crisis for each of the actors (at least one actor was democratic, no states were democratic).
Severity of violence	The intensity of violent actions ranging from minor clashes to war (low or none to severe).
Stress	The available time for decision-makers in relation to the deadline for choice.
Trigger	The specific act, event, or situational change that sets in motion a crisis (violent vs. non-violent).
Values threatened	The gravest threat perceived during the crisis (ranging from high – threat to the existence of the state – to low – limited threat to population and property).
Violence used	Was any violence present during crisis (present or not)?

been introduced in Chapter 2. A strategic rivalry is defined as a highly competitive relationship that is separable from more benign conflict by the criteria of mutual identification. Past research has treated threat as all encompassing. Since the international system is anarchic, all states must feel threatened by all other states. While we agree that disagreements between states can be ubiquitous, we argue that not all threats are weighted equally. There are some states that are singled out as particularly dangerous. Many times this identification is reciprocated. For instance, Israel is more mistrustful of Iraq than it is of Saudi Arabia or, in the last decade, Peru expected more conflict with Ecuador than with Colombia. In both cases the parties involved reciprocated conflictual images. We suggest that these perceptions and expectations will lead to more escalatory behavior during crises.

Our research design has two parts. First, we replicate Brecher's (1993) modified protracted conflict model and, to some extent, Brecher and Wilkenfeld's (1997) analysis using rivalry rather than protracted conflict as the key variable of interest. In this section we follow ICB variable coding rules and statistical methods. Thus, chi-square tests of independence are used to explore bivariate patterns and relationships.

One divergence from the Brecher (1993) and Brecher and Wilkenfeld (1997) designs, in this initial component of the testing, is a change in level of analysis. The ICB data are actually two interrelated data sets: one collected at the individual state level, the foreign policy data, and another at the international level, the international crisis data. The difference is that a focus on state level /actor level actions would have an observation for each individual state involved in the crisis. A focus on interaction at the international level would include only one observation for each crisis. Thus, the Baltic Independence crisis in 1918 has four observations at the individual state level and only one at the crisis level.

Brecher and Wilkenfeld (1997) test several of their hypotheses at the state level. We believe this is inappropriate for our purposes for two reasons. Our theory concerns the interaction between states, not just one decision in isolation. Expectations are adapted and reinforced by action both given and received. Our hypotheses thus concern behavior within crises rather than single decisions. Of course these are related issues, but we think a dyadic theory should be tested at the dyadic level, or at least as close to that level as is possible given data restraints.

A second problem deals with statistical assumptions. In short, chi-square tests of independence are designed to determine if fluctuations in observations are random or not. This test is only appropriate if variables are distributed in a random normal fashion. One violation of this assumption would come from data in which autocorrelation is present.

Specifically, this would be the case in an ICB analysis if one decision affected another decision. While this is possible in all social data, the magnitude of contagion between observations is important. In this analysis there are strong theoretical reasons to suspect that decisions within crises are highly related. Reciprocity, rational expectations, and action–reaction sequences have been found to typify some international interactions.[7] By counting each decision as a separate observation the tests will be skewed, possibly in the direction of statistical significance. Our focus on crises as the unit of analysis allows this contagion to be minimized. It is of course likely that crises are related to each other but this contagion should be of much smaller magnitude than within crisis dependence.[8] For these reasons we use the crisis as the unit of analysis for all of the hypotheses examined.

We also include a smaller subset of crises than either Brecher (1993) or Brecher and Wilkenfeld (1997). Our focus on dyadic interaction led us to include only crises that involved at least two state entities. Crises triggered by internal dissent with no external threat present were dropped from the analysis. Also, intra-war crises were not included in the analysis, since we believe they are quite different animals. Our emphasis on escalation in tensions and war seems a bit out of place if war is already occurring. After excluding these cases we are left with 293 interstate crises.[9]

The second stage of our research takes us beyond bivariate relationships and into the testing of the revised, rivalry-interactive, escalation model. We use logit regression to examine our expectations that crises within rivalry are more likely to escalate to war.[10] Given the binary nature of our dependent variables, OLS regression is inappropriate (Long, 1997). As noted above, we realize that crises are not completely independent of each other. While this problem would be more pronounced in a panel setup, for our purposes it could still bias estimates. Therefore, to control for possible autocorrelation in our data we fit cubic splines to the time

---

[7] Pertinent examples may be found in McClelland (1972), Nomikos and North (1976), McGinnis and Williams (1989), and Pevehouse and Goldstein (1997).

[8] See Hensel (1994), Leng (2000a), and Goertz and Diehl (2000b).

[9] The actual number of crises that fit our criterion is 336. Still, 43 contain missing values for either regime or power discrepancy and are dropped from the analysis.

[10] Specification with probit makes no substantive difference in the results since the only significant difference between the methods is the distribution of the errors (Long, 1997). We also investigated the results of a selection model where the first stage model included all states in the system and measured whether a state initiated a crisis or not, and the second stage model was the current escalation equation. The exclusion restrictions were placed on the time to crisis initiation. We found that the 90 percent confidence interval (CI) for the correlation between the error terms of the two equations included zero, and thus our current conditional results are both consistent and more efficient than those estimates. As a result, we present the conditional estimates.

since the last crisis in the data (Beck, Katz, and Tucker, 1998). This helps to account for the dependence of crisis outcomes on the time since the last crisis. Additionally, we use a robust estimate of the error variance clustered on the crisis sequences to account for heteroskedasticity.[11]

The escalation model provided by Brecher and Wilkenfeld (1997) with the matching operationalizations in the ICB data set allow for a thorough testing of these hypotheses. Other theoretical causes of escalation and war can be controlled for from multiple levels of analysis. One potential problem, hinted at earlier, is the conceptual overlap between the variables in the model. This could lead to problems of multicolinearity. While too much covariation between the independent variables does decrease the efficiency of our tests, it does not bias the coefficients. Neglecting to include a portion of the variables in the escalation model in order to avoid colinearity introduces the possibility of omitted variable bias, and spurious relationships being found statistically significant. Since our goal is to devise a test which could falsify our theory concerning rivals' crisis behavior, we choose multicolinearity as the lesser of two evils. In an attempt to test our expectations concerning the interaction between rivalry and the other explanatory variables, interaction terms are included in the analysis. Since rivalry is a dummy variable this was done by multiplying rivalry times the specific variable of interest.

Data analysis

Our first set of analyses addresses the core "protracted conflict" model that we are co-opting as a core rivalry model. That model suggests that rivalry crises will be more likely to be complicated by the presence of multiple issues and issues that are directly related to military security concerns than are nonrivalry crises. Table 4.3 reports support for both dimensions. In rivalries, single issue crises occur in fewer than one of every ten cases in contrast to the one in five distribution that characterizes nonrivalry cases. Militarized issues are found in rivalry crises roughly seven out of eight times, while the comparative distribution in nonrivalry cases is somewhat less common (three of every four cases). In general, most crises are about multiple, militarized issues but rivalry crises are even more so.

One major hypothesis distinguishing rivalry crises from nonrivalry crises predicts that the former will have a stronger likelihood of becoming violent. Table 4.4 summarizes a mixed outcome on this prediction. It depends very much on how one asks the question. Rivalry and

---

[11] Clustering on other variables, including the year of the crisis or the geographic region, did not alter the results substantially.

Table 4.3 *Issues and rivalry*

	Nonrivalry		Rivalry	
	Number	Percentage	Number	Percentage
Number of issues involved				
One issue involved	28	21.2	18	8.8
More than one issue involved	104	78.8	186	91.2
Total	132		204	
	$\chi^2 = 10.41$, $p = 0.001$			
Militarized issues				
Non-militarized issues	33	25.0	25	12.3
Militarized issues	99	75.0	179	87.7
Total	132		204	
	$\chi^2 = 10.41$, $p = 0.001$			

nonrivalry crises are not distinguishable on the basis of whether violence is employed in crisis triggers (action that causes the crisis), whether crisis management techniques tend to be violent (reaction to the trigger), whether severe violence is more or less likely (how severe is violence), and whether violence is central to the crisis (was violence the only type of action and how important was it in relation to other management techniques).

However, rivalry and nonrivalry crises are distinguishable in terms of the types of values that are threatened. Contrary to the expectation, rivalry crises are more likely to involve medium-level threats while nonrivalry crises are twice as likely to be about low-level threats (as are rivalry threats) and somewhat more likely to be about high-level threats. If one dichotomizes crises into low or severe violence, nothing distinctive emerges. But if the possibilities are specified more exactly, rivalry crises are more likely to result in war than nonrivalry crises while nonrivalry crises are more likely to result in serious clashes than rivalry crises. Finally, rivalry crises are decidedly more likely to employ militarized techniques of crisis management than are nonrivalry crises.

Rivalry crises, then, do not have any monopoly on violence or threats of high gravity. But rivalry crises are more likely to involve medium or greater level threats, to employ militarized techniques, and to result in war than are nonrivalry crises. These findings appear to support our basic contention that rivalry crises are generally more dangerous because of the underlying expectations of mistrust that develop in protracted conflict.

Table 4.4 *Rivalry and violence in crises*

	Nonrivalry		Rivalry	
	Number	Percentage	Number	Percentage
Crisis triggers				
Non-violent trigger	79	59.9	121	59.3
Violent trigger	53	40.1	83	40.7
Total	132		204	
	$\chi^2 = 0.01$, $p = 0.922$			
Threatened values				
Low gravity of threat	17	12.9	13	6.4
Medium gravity of threat	88	66.7	157	77.0
High gravity of threat	27	20.4	34	16.6
Total	132		204	
	$\chi^2 = 5.60$, $p = 0.061$			
Crisis management techniques (violence)				
Non-violent	63	47.7	103	50.5
Violent	69	52.3	101	49.5
Total	132		204	
	$\chi^2 = 0.24$, $p = 0.621$			
Severity of violence				
Low or no violence	81	61.4	125	61.3
Severe violence	51	38.6	79	38.7
Total	132		204	
	$\chi^2 = 0.00$, $p = 0.99$			
Violence used				
No violence	36	27.3	64	31.4
Minor clash	45	34.1	61	29.9
Serious clash	39	29.5	44	21.6
War	12	9.1	35	17.2
Total	132		204	
	$\chi^2 = 6.69$, $p = 0.082$			
Type of crisis management (militarized)				
Non-violent	122	92.4	165	80.9
Militarized	10	7.6	39	19.1
Total	132		204	
	$\chi^2 = 8.57$, $p = 0.003$			
Centrality of violence				
Violence not central	67	50.8	107	52.4
Violence central	65	49.2	97	47.6
Total	132		204	
	$\chi^2 = 0.09$, $p = 0.762$			

Multivariate analysis

In Table 4.5, we turn to a more complex approach to the general question of whether interstate rivalry is critical to an understanding of crisis behavior. Table 4.5 lists the outcomes for models concerning crisis escalation and war. Not all of the fifteen variables are expected to be significant in each model, but, by and large, the Brecher–Wilkenfeld argument is that these are the variables that should be most important to crisis onset, escalation, and war. We have noted that the arguments are especially complicated by the underlying expectation that the fifteen independent variables are not independent of one another. Moreover, they are apt to be characterized by substantial selection biases. Thus, it is not a simple matter to devise appropriate assessments of these assembled variables. What is most clear is that it is not entirely reasonable to simply throw all fifteen variables into one model and see what survives as a test of the model's adequacy. But we can do this to see which relationships are strong enough to survive such a formidable test. Thus, our empirical outcomes in Table 4.5 should be viewed as more suggestive than definitive. They suggest, with some unknown possibility of error, that the statistically significant variables are the ones that will prove to be most important in subsequent, more refined examinations of crisis onset, escalation, and war occurrences.

Model 1 suggests that crises are most likely to escalate to war when they involve rival actors fighting over high salience issues in a multipolar system. Further, violent triggers and greater number of actors increase the probability of escalation while democratic actors and a lack of major power involvement decrease the probability of escalation. Specifically, involving a rivalry in a crisis increases the probability of war by 5 percent (90 percent CI: 2 percent, 10 percent).[12] This validates our general hypothesis concerning war and rivalry. Further, if the system is multipolar, this increases the probability of termination by 12 percent (90 percent CI: 4 percent, 26 percent), while a crisis involving a high value threat increases the probability of escalation to war by 5 percent (90 percent CI: 0.7 percent, 13 percent).[13]

Additionally violent triggers and a large number of actors also increase the probability of escalation. A crisis triggered by violence is 2 percent more likely to escalate to war than a crisis with a non-violent trigger

---

[12] To compute the change in the probability of escalation in this example and others we hold the other variables in the model at their medians and the splines and rivalry at zero unless otherwise noted. Confidence intervals are computed by simulating 5,000 draws from the multivariate normal distribution defined by the coefficient vector and covariance matrix.

[13] All three variables are significant at the 0.05 level for a two-tailed test when analyzing the change in the log-odds of escalation.

Table 4.5 *Logit results for war and escalation (N = 293)*

Level	Variable	Model 1		Model 2 (Interactions)	
		Coefficient	Standard error	Coefficient	Standard error
Perceptual	Rivalry	1.012	0.109***	−1.850	2.275
Systemic	Polarity	1.726	0.310***	2.273	0.302***
	Level	0.780	0.613	−0.569	1.155
Interaction	Capability ratio	−0.053	0.043	−0.498	0.143***
	Democracy	−1.040	0.198***	−0.490	0.284*
	Contiguity	0.167	0.773	−0.152	0.353
Actor	Age	0.002	0.003	0.007	0.002***
	Gov't instability	0.633	0.436	1.950	1.017*
Situational	Trigger	0.415	0.236**	1.042	0.220***
	Number of actors	0.206	0.081**	0.059	0.038*
	Heterogeneity	−0.078	0.134	−0.016	0.045
	M.P. involvement	0.944	0.400***	2.035	0.326***
	Millitarized issues	0.466	0.750	0.235	0.132*
	Values threatened	0.747	0.369**	2.647	0.165***
	Stress	0.082	0.089	0.021	0.028
Interactions	Polar*rivalry			−0.581	0.853
	Level*rivalry			2.283	1.608*
	Cap. rat.*rivalry			0.457	0.118***
	Dem.*rivalry			−1.068	0.369***
	Contig.*rivalry			0.227	0.963
	Age*rivalry			−0.004	0.003
	Gov. inst.*rivalry			−1.439	0.886*
	Trig.*rivalry			−0.892	0.199***
	Num. act.*rivalry			0.273	0.061***
	Hetero.*rivalry			−0.073	0.259
	M.P. invol.*rivalry			−0.692	0.858
	Mil. issue*rivalry			0.671	1.237
	Val. threat*rivalry			−1.848	0.585***
	Stress*rivalry			0.124	0.126
Splines	1	0.024	0.011**	0.022	0.012**
	2	0.497	0.353*	0.602	0.395*
	3	−0.332	0.345	−0.435	0.396
	4	−0.033	0.123	−0.001	0.145
Constant	Constant	−8.535	2.094***	−8.635	2.417***
Log-likelihood =		−73.36		−62.83	

* $p < 0.01$ for a two-tailed test
** $p < 0.05$ for a two-tailed test
*** $p < 0.01$ for a two-tailed test

(90 percent CI: 0.2 percent, 3 percent). The number of actors is also significantly related to crisis escalation propensities. Increasing the number of actors from two to ten is expected to increase the probability of escalation by 6 percent (90 percent CI: 3 percent, 9 percent).[14]

Conversely, both democracy and a lack of major power involvement were found to decrease the propensity for crises to escalate. Having at least one democracy involved in a crisis decreases the probability of war by 2 percent (90 percent CI: −5 percent, −0.6 percent). Also, avoiding major power involvement decreases the probability of escalation by 2 percent (90 percent CI: −6 percent, 0.03 percent).[15]

Interaction effects

Both the statistical and substantive significance of the rivalry variable in model 1 supports our arguments concerning rivalries and war. When we control for a wide range of variables from multiple levels of analysis (systemic, interaction, actor, and situational variables), the presence of rivalry still increases the probability of war. We now turn to the interaction between rivalry and the other crisis variables in Model 2. If our explanation for the bellicosity of rivalry is correct, we expect that the effect of other variables will depend directly on the rivalry setting of a crisis.

Table 4.5 (Model 2) is consistent with the presence of numerous significant interactions between rivalry and other crisis variables, although not all are in the hypothesized directions.[16] Our first set of expectations suggested that rivalry should overwhelm constraints on conflict resolution, such as capability asymmetry, democracy, and major power involvement. Figure 4.1 shows the interaction between power discrepancy and rivalry in predicting crisis escalation to war. While asymmetry in nonrival crises quickly decreases the probability of war outside of rivalry, this is not

---

[14] As can be seen from Table 4.5, both crisis triggers and the number of actors also significantly affect the log-odds of escalation at the 0.10 and 0.05 levels for two-tailed tests, respectively.

[15] The coefficients for democracy and major power involvement are significant at the 0.05-level in Table 4.5.

[16] It is important to note that these interaction coefficients do not directly tell us whether a rivalry context changes the effect of other variables, unlike in a linear regression framework. As Allison (1999) notes, coefficient differences across groups could be related to distinct variances rather than distinct causal effects. Further, these coefficients are in a log-odds metric, which is not intuitive. If we were to make inferences from the coefficients alone, we would have to assume that the variances across groups were equal and that we are only interested in the log-odds of conflict. Instead of stopping at the raw coefficients, we calculate predicted probabilities and confidence intervals using simulation methods. This allows us to compare variables across rivalry contexts without assuming variance equality or forcing the reader to calculate log-odds.

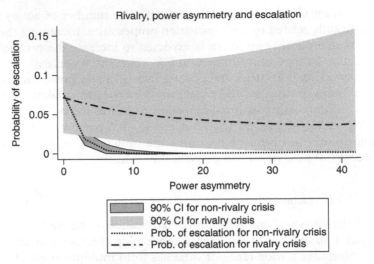

Figure 4.1 The effect of power asymmetry across rivalry contexts.

the case in the presence of rivalry. Instead, as predicted, crises involving rivalries escalate to war despite these asymmetries. Capability symmetry is only a significant predictor of escalation outside of rivalry.[17]

Although there is a significant interaction between rivalry and democracy the direction runs counter to our hypothesis. We suggested that rivalry could overwhelm the democratic peace phenomena since norms of peaceful conflict resolution are not apt to apply under these contentious circumstances. Yet, our findings suggest that democracy has a stronger pacifying effect within rivalry, as compared to outside of rivalry. The first graph in Figure 4.2 illustrates that democracy is expected to decrease the probability of escalation by only 0.18 percent outside of rivalry (90 percent CI: −0.28, −0.002). More dramatically, within a rivalry crisis democracy is expected to decrease the probability of escalation by 3 percent (90 percent CI: −7 percent, −1 percent). The 90 percent confidence interval for the difference between the effect of democracy within and outside of rivalry is −7 percent, −1 percent and does not span zero.[18]

---

[17] We hold the age of the youngest state in the crisis at 70 and the number of actors at four for these simulations.

[18] For these simulations and those that follow, unless noted, we hold power discrepancy at 0, the age of the youngest state at 70 and the number of actors at three. Note that the overlap in confidence intervals for the predictions across rivalry contexts is not analogous to tests that the parameters are different. This is due to the fact that the individual confidence intervals do not take the covariance across contexts into account as well as the fact that the sum of the standard errors around two means does not equal the standard error of the difference in means.

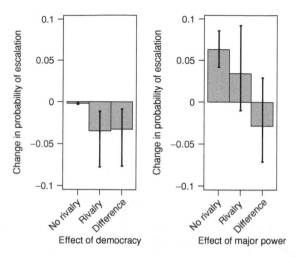

Figure 4.2 The effect of democracy and major powers on probability across rivalry contexts.

The last constraint, major power involvement, turns out not to be a constraint at all. We find that in both contexts (rivalry and nonrivalry), major power involvement increases the risk of escalation, although with varying precision. The probability of escalation to war is estimated to increase by 6 percent (90 percent CI: 4 percent, 8 percent) if a major power is involved in a nonrivalry crisis, as opposed to no major power involvement in a nonrivalry crisis. Similarly, major power intervention in a crisis involving rivals is estimated to increase the probability of escalation by 3 percent (90 percent CI: −0.1 percent, 9 percent).[19] Additionally, as the second graph in Figure 4.2 clarifies, there is no significant difference between the effects of major power intervention across rivalry contexts.[20] In sum, two out of the three constraint variables significantly interacted with the rivalry environment (capability asymmetry and democracy), although the direction of the relationship with democracy was more complicated than hypothesized.

Our second set of hypotheses pointed to the way rivalry can lower the threshold of provocation for escalation while also emphasizing the likelihood of military actions. This led to the expectation that even non-violent triggers, low gravity threats, and non-military issues would produce a significant propensity for a crisis to escalate in a rivalry context, as compared to these same triggers and issues in a nonrivalry setting. Empirically,

[19] The 90 percent confidence interval just overlaps zero.
[20] The 90 percent confidence interval for the difference between the contexts overlaps zero.

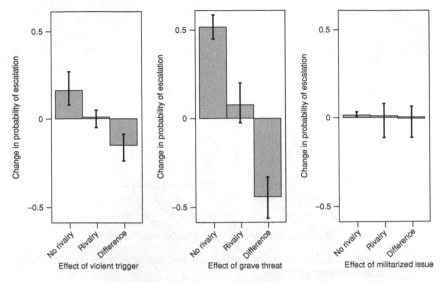

Figure 4.3 The effect of violent triggers, grave threats and militarized issues across rivalry contexts.

lowering the threshold for provocation should depress the relative effect of triggers and issues in rivalry contexts. For example, both violent and non-violent triggers might lead to violence in a rivalry, while it is only violent triggers that precipitate violence outside of rivalry.

In two out of the three cases these hypotheses were confirmed, as violent triggers and high gravity threats produced significantly greater changes in escalation propensities outside of rivalry. Figure 4.3 compares the relative effects of triggers, the gravity of threat, and military issues in rivalry and nonrivalry contexts. While a violent trigger increases the probability of escalation by 16 percent outside of rivalry (90 percent CI: 8 percent, 27 percent), the same change in trigger results in a much smaller, down to .6 percent, and insignificant change in a rivalry crisis context (90 percent CI: −3 percent, 3 percent). Further, the 90 percent confidence interval for the difference between the rivalry and non-rivalry contexts (15 percent) does not span zero (90 percent CI: −0.24, −9 percent). The jump from non-violent to violent triggers is less extreme within rivalry crises as compared to nonrivalry settings.

A similar pattern is reflected in the relationship between rivalry and low gravity threats. Outside of rivalry a move from a low to high gravity threat increases the probability of escalation by 52 percent (90 percent CI: 45 percent, 59 percent). Yet, the expected increase in the probability of escalation is a more modest 7 percent in a rivalry context for the same adjustment in threat (90 percent CI: −2 percent, 20 percent), and the 90 percent confidence interval for the difference between the two contexts again does not span zero (90 percent CI: −56 percent, −33 percent). Conversely, the presence or absence of military issues did not significantly influence the probability of escalation to war in either conflict setting, and there was no statistically significant interaction between military issues and rivalry, as can be seen from the third graph in Figure 4.3. The danger and distinctiveness of rivalry crisis thresholds can be seen in the increased risk of escalation even in non-threatening situations. The model predicts that a rivalry crisis, involving a non-violent trigger, low gravity threats and non-militarized issues[21] has an eleven times greater probability of escalating to war than a non-rivalry crisis with those same seemingly innocuous traits.[22]

There is mixed support for our contention that rivalry reinforces the ambiguity and uncertainty within a crisis. We hypothesized that as the number of actors in a crisis increased and the system moved toward multipolarity that the greater ambiguity of these crisis situations would expand the influence of rivalry. This relationship was supported when analyzing the number of actors in a crisis. While the number of actors in a crisis was positively related to the probability of war in both a rivalry and nonrivalry context, the magnitude of the relationship was markedly different in each setting. Specifically, the interaction between the number of actors and rivalry is significant and positive as predicted. Figure 4.4 illustrates the trivariate relationship between rivalry, the number of actors, and the probability of escalation. Outside of rivalry, the increase in escalation is quite small as the number of actors gets larger, but within rivalry the number of actors has a profound impact on the probability of war. The model predicts that the probability of escalation rises by 28 percent in a rivalry crisis when the number of actors changes from 2 to 10 (90 percent CI: 17 percent, 41 percent). However, the equivalent change in the number of actors leads to only a 0.3 percent increase in the probability of war outside of rivalry (90 percent CI: −0.1 percent, 0.4 percent).[23]

When turning to the effect of multipolarity, we find that a multipolar system increases the probability of escalation in both rivalry and non-rivalry settings, but that there is no significant interaction between the variables. The interaction between rivalry and multipolarity is presented in the first graph in Figure 4.5. The 90 percent confidence intervals

---

[21] Other variables are set as above, excepting power discrepancy and the number of actors that are set at their respective means.

[22] The 90 percent confidence interval for this relative risk does span one (0.78, 134), which is not surprising given the relative dearth of crises involving each of these traits simultaneously.

[23] The difference between the contexts given these settings is approximately 28 percent (90 percent CI: 16 percent, 42 percent).

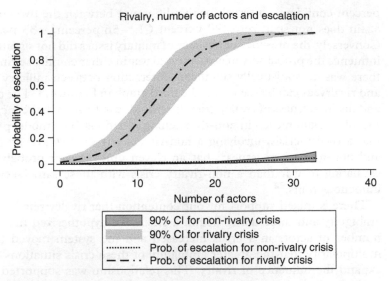

Figure 4.4 The effect of the number of actors across rivalry contexts.

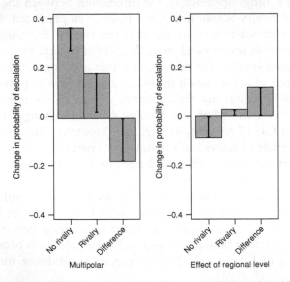

Figure 4.5 The effect of system polarity and regional level across rivalry contexts.

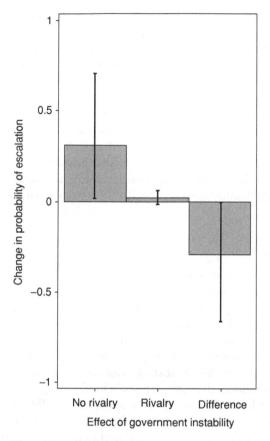

Figure 4.6 The effect of government instability across rivalry contexts.

representing the uncertainties around the effects of multipolarity in both contexts do not overlap zero, representing positive and statistically significant effects. However, the estimated 90 percent confidence interval for the difference between the two changes in the probability of escalation includes zero (90 percent CI: −35 percent, 3 percent).

System level also does not significantly interact with the rivalry context. This is mainly due to the ambiguity of the effect of system level outside of rivalry. The second graph in Figure 4.5 illustrates both the large uncertainty surrounding the effect of crisis level on escalation, and the relative precision in predicting escalation within rivalry. While the effects across rivalry context are in opposite directions, with regional level crises involving rivals increasing the probability of escalation, the 90 percent confidence interval for the difference between rivalry and nonrivalry effects overlaps zero. This suggests that we do not have significant evidence of contextual differences in this case.

Our fourth expectation, that vulnerabilities such as internal instability would be exploited more readily within rivalry was not supported. As shown in Figure 4.6, government instability is estimated to increase the probability of escalation by 28 percent outside of rivalry (90 percent CI: 5 percent, 62 percent), and by 3 percent within rivalry (90 percent CI: −0.2 percent, 6 percent). The fact that the effect of government instability is estimated to be stronger outside of a rivalry context refutes our last hypothesis that rivals are more likely to take advantage of internal instability than nonrivals. Alternatively, neither contiguity, age, heterogeneity nor stress significantly interacted with the rivalry environments.

Conclusion

This analysis is the first confrontation of 1918–1994 crisis and strategic rivalry data. We began with the anticipation that our analyses would enhance our understanding of the dynamics of crisis, rivalry, and their interaction by redirecting ICB concepts of protracted conflict and crisis escalation. While the outcomes associated with utilizing the ICB models in a different setting than the one for which they were designed are mixed, we can claim some success in generating new information. First, the empirical outcomes reinforce the main rationale for focusing on interstate rivalries. Most actors in world politics do not engage conflictually with most other actors. Instead, a small number of pairs of states are responsible for a vastly disproportionate share of total conflict. We now know that this generalization subsumes crises between states as well. Between 1918 and 1994, 204 interstate crises, 67 percent of the total, can be traced to 92 strategic rivalries. Such findings suggest that we are missing a rather good analytical bet if we choose to ignore this rather strong bias and insist on assuming that all state actors are equally likely to engage in conflict (or cooperation) with all other actors. Yet it is precisely this assumption that underlies the lion's share of empirical knowledge on international conflict and cooperation. In this respect, rivalries are much like needles in the haystack except that, in this case, we know where the needles are located. Armed with such information, we may be able to dispense with some of our thrashing about in the hay of world politics.

Moreover, we can also now be more specific about what it is that differentiates crises involving rivalries from those that do not involve rivalries. Crises in rivalry dyads, as opposed to nonrivalry crises, are more likely to entail mid-level threats, militarized techniques, and war. The issues at stake are likely to be multiple and considered worthy of building up one's military force in order to defend them.

On the other hand, while a handful of the crisis escalation model's variables were significant, in many cases these relationships were dependent on the rivalry setting of the crisis. For instance, the escalatory effect of democracy, capability ratios, the crisis trigger, the issues and number of actors involved each either grew stronger or weaker depending on the presence or absence of rivalry. These account for four of the six variables that were significant in the model without interactions. Rivalry not only has an independent effect on escalation, but also indirectly manipulates the uncertainty and constraints in the crisis to make escalation more likely. Such findings, by any stretch of the imagination, do not mean that we now know all that we need to know about crises and crisis escalation in rivalry settings. But they constitute a start. We have increased the justification for focusing on rivalries as especially dangerous incubators of conflict, crisis, and war.[24] We also have some better idea of which explanatory variables interact with the social psychology of protracted conflictual relationships to generate militarization and violence in disputes between states. But these are aggregate findings and crises within rivalries do not erupt in the aggregate. They emerge within rivalry relationships. What we may need then is a better understanding of how serial crises within protracted conflict relationships escalate in severity. Is it repeated crises involving the same actors over time (Leng, 1983) that provides the principal path to war escalation? If so, what is it about serial confrontations that moves rivalry crises out of their more customary, mid-level, threat range? Is the answer related to how many and which actors become involved in the crisis, the location of the crisis, and the nature of the response to the initial trigger? Alternatively, the repetitive nature of rivalry crises may prove to be a red herring. No one has yet examined the full sample of crisis recidivism between rivals. We may discover that it is not repetition *per se* that is most dangerous. Rather, escalation may hinge more basically on whether the right mix of conducive factors comes together, regardless of the number of crises already experienced. The serial nature of rivalry crises could thus be spurious as a direct promoter of escalation even though repeated crises, no doubt, work toward maintaining the psychological underpinnings of ongoing rivalry expectations. If so, repetitive crises may at least be indirectly related to crisis escalation. These are some of the questions pursued next in Chapter 5. What exactly is the relationship between serial crisis behavior and conflict escalation?

---

[24] Gartzke and Simon (1999) take an opposite viewpoint that we examine more closely in the next chapter.

5   Serial crisis behavior and escalating risks

Over the last decade considerable progress has been made in deciphering the causes of international war and conflict. Theoretical advances have been matched by empirical evidence uncovering for instance the democratic peace phenomena. Yet one potentially important research question has gone nearly untouched. How are crises between the same adversaries related to each other, if, indeed, they are? This question is important in its own right: does previous conflict predict future conflict? But it also addresses the prevailing tendency to examine conflict events as if they were entirely independent confrontations. If previous conflict predicts future conflict, the independence assumption will be difficult to sustain. Third, the serial crisis question also addresses the very conceptual foundations of rivalry analysis. If previous conflict does not predict systematically future conflict, an important premise for examining rivalries is eliminated. The problem is that we do not know whether and how past and future conflict is related. We assume that they are related but whether they are remains an interesting empirical question and, as noted, has implications for other analytical assumptions.

Most quantitative research on international conflict has treated confrontations between the same set of states as independent events. For example, it is conventional to treat the 1961 US-Soviet Berlin Crisis as a separate and distinct case from the 1962 Cuban Missile Crisis. It would be equally conventional to treat the sequences of Egyptian-Israeli or Indo-Pakistani crises as if the latest ones had nothing to do with earlier ones. Methodologically, this convention leads to identifying assumptions for statistical models, while theoretically it guides the explanatory variables upon which researchers rely. The independence assumption steers researchers away from variables that measure the interaction between crises and toward variables that can be applied to each crisis cross-sectionally, without discerning past crisis behavior. In many ways this has furthered research into the relationship between international crises and such variables as regime type, contiguity, and capability ratios, but it is important to realize what might be overlooked – namely, that earlier conflicts may very well have some, and perhaps even considerable, influence on the probability of subsequent confrontations.

One of the more curious facets of this prevailing analytical tendency is that a number of analysts have explicitly assumed otherwise – that is, that conflicts are not temporally independent. McClelland (1972) argued that repeated clashes could reduce both uncertainty and the probability of conflict escalation. Bell (1971) coined the term "crisis slide" for serial confrontations that tend to lead to war. While Snyder and Diesing (1977: 19) preferred to leave the situation ambiguous: "Some crises embitter and worsen subsequent relations, others improve them," Lebow (1981: 317) argued that successive crises between adversaries in a short time period "significantly increase international tension and expectation of war." Although his findings are based on a small, selected sample of crises, Leng's (1983) argument that dyads tend to go to war by their third crisis is frequently cited as if it were an established fact about serial crisis behavior. A decade later, Hensel (1994) also found that previous dispute outcomes affected the likelihood of dispute recurrence but his study was restricted to Latin American militarized disputes. Levy (2000b) uses serial crisis behavior as an illustration of a behavioral phenomenon that prospect theory can help explain, while Vasquez (1993, 2000) has incorporated serial crisis behavior as an integral component of his "steps-to-war" realpolitik model. In general, many conflict analysts, if surveyed, would probably agree with the proposition that conflict begets more conflict (or, in some cases, conflict management), which is one of the things that we have learned in contemporary conflict analyses. Yet the "lesson" remains largely restricted to the realm of assumption.

It has also been recognized that the same pair of states can be involved in multiple disputes, and, further, that only a few dyads account for the majority of the total conflict in the international system (Goertz and Diehl 1992a; Vasquez 1993; Diehl and Goertz 2000). These observations are in fact one of the primary reasons for the study of rivalries. Rivalries constitute competitive relationships that persist over time, through successive conflictual encounters, and account for a disproportionate amount of the world's conflict. The major implication is that a respectable portion of conflict is largely undecipherable outside of the rivalry context. Yet most conflict studies have proceeded without explicit reference to the ostensibly critical historical context within which events occur. Thus, if rivalry analysts are right, we should anticipate some major advances in our understanding of interstate conflict thanks to a movement away from the notion that disputes and crises are independent events.

Yet other analysts (most prominently, Gartzke and Simon, 1999) have suggested that these temporal linkages in a small number of interstate dyads have largely been assumed and may have occurred simply due to random chance. Instead of relying on the counter-assumption that these events are interdependent over time, the rival hypothesis is that other variables, such as regime type or capability ratios, are actually responsible for what only seem to be temporal dependencies. Given the quite narrow empirical basis in support of crisis/dispute interdependence, it is difficult to dismiss this rival explanation out of hand.

The question thus remains whether a dyad's conflict at one time impacts on the probability of that same dyad's conflict at some later date. If it does, the idea of focusing more specifically on rivalries makes more sense than if it does not. If conflicts within some dyads are not temporally interdependent in some fashion, the very concept of rivalry would have little meaning. Thus, assessing whether there is serial interdependence in conflict behavior is necessary to provide (or to deny) a firm empirical foundation for the prospects of rivalry analysis generating Goertz and Diehl's (2000a) "dramatic shift in theoretical and methodological perspectives" for international relations research. If conflicts are substantially independent events, history would not seem to matter much. But, if some dyads' conflicts are temporally interdependent, we would need to rethink the way we treat conflicts as inherently autonomous events.

We agree that the proposition that conflicts between adversaries are related over time remains only weakly substantiated. Conflict interdependence over time should neither be assumed nor discounted. Instead, the proposition should be tested empirically. If crises are serially related, conflict propensities should fluctuate systematically with previous behavior. If they are not serially related, previous behavior should exert no systematic influence on subsequent behavior. We also choose to focus upon crises in this analysis, as opposed to some more generic measure of conflict, because it is serial crises and "slides to war" that are thought to be one of the verities of international relations lore. Yet we actually lack a systematic test of whether serial crises have implications for more crises and greater levels of violence.

Therefore, our motivation is dual. We wish to examine crisis behavior over time to test systematically for evidence of conflict interdependence. We do this in part because international relations analysts already assume that serial crisis behavior is one of the established causes of war. We think this idea is not yet established. We are also interested in utilizing this opportunity to respond to Gartzke and Simon's challenge of a central rationale for engaging in studies of rivalry behavior. A basic tenet of rivalry analysis is that a respectable portion of dyadic conflict is conditioned historically by previous encounters. This, too, is a largely untested assumption and richly deserves verification.

To accomplish these twin objectives, we first summarize the limited empirical findings on serial behavior in international politics and their linkage to the study of rivalries. After reviewing the Gartzke and Simon (1999) "hot hands" critique of assumptions about serial influences, several relevant hypotheses are discussed and then tested with 1918–95 data on crises, and other appropriate variables. Our analysis reconfirms the appropriateness of assuming serial influences in crisis sequences but, at the same time, the findings put the issue on a stronger empirical footing than has been the case so far. Our findings also reinforce the inclination to give more emphasis to the analysis of rivalries. The history of dyadic conflict can make some difference. Most dyads have no history of extensive conflict but those few that do find it exceedingly difficult to ignore path dependencies of their own making.

The serial crisis hypothesis

Recent empirical scholarship has begun to treat groups of conflicts as the primary unit of analysis in conflict studies. Most often these conflict streams are termed rivalries. The motivation for the rivalry research program stemmed initially from an intuition that disputes are related over time, and empirical findings on the frequency of confrontations within different dyads (Gochman and Maoz, 1984). Goertz and Diehl (2000b: 222) state that, "Research on (enduring) rivalries begins with [the] observation: a small proportion of dyads accounts for a very large percentage of all militarized disputes and wars . . . these repeated conflicts between the same dyad are related to one another, and . . . explaining war requires understanding the relationship between these disputes." Regardless of how one identifies rivalry, it is a historical sequence of competition, threat, and conflict that alerts us to the existence of such a relationship. By definition, therefore, rivalry analysis is predicated on the notion of a sequence of interdependent perceptual and physical clashes.

Leng's (1983) study on serial crises is highly germane to these observations. Examining a sample of eighteen crises that took place within six dyads, Leng found considerable support for an experiential learning model and the idea that crisis outcomes are related over time. Specifically, the use of a coercive strategy in a previous conflict affects the choice of strategies in a future crisis. As states jockey and bully each other, rather than learning prudence and restraint, Leng argues that leaders learn to use more coercive bargaining strategies. If crisis participants used a coercive strategy successfully, they are more likely to repeat the strategy in the future. If crisis participants were unsuccessful, they are more likely to adopt an even more coercive strategy the next time around. Thus, the greater the number of past crises, assuming some employment of coercive strategies by one or both sides, the more likely are increasingly coercive strategies and war. Only if a crisis initiator lost a war in an earlier round are they likely to move to less coercive strategies. But it is not only previous strategies that are important, their sequencing also makes a difference. In fact, by the time a third crisis has occurred between a pair of states, Leng argued that war is highly probable. Still, Leng's sample was too small to allow for a comparison between crisis dyads that did not repeat and those that did. It may be that he simply picked the most war-prone cases.

Hensel (1994) also found support for a relationship between disputes involving the same states. Focusing on Latin American dyads that had experienced militarized disputes, a relatively complex pattern of inter-actions between disputes emerged. Most importantly, Hensel found that previous dispute outcomes generally influenced the likelihood and timing of dispute recurrence. For example, a stalemate in the previous dispute lowers the time until a subsequent confrontation by about six years, as compared to decisive outcomes. But Hensel did not examine the disputes as specific sequences that would allow one to say anything about the like-lihood of a first or second dispute leading to additional confrontations. All militarized disputes are not crises. Nor are Latin American conflict patterns necessarily representative of the rest of the world.

From the available evidence, however limited, multiple researchers have deduced that conflicts between the same adversaries are related over time. Assuming a concrete relationship, there are three possible connec-tions between past and future conflicts: there can be a positive relation-ship, a non-linear relationship, or a negative relationship. The most often cited rationale for crisis dependence is that past crises make future wars more likely. Vasquez (1993: 75) is representative when he writes that wars "do not break out unless there has been a long history of conflict and hos-tility between disputants." In this view past conflict increases the influence of hard-liners and hawks on each side, while also increasing suspicions between the adversaries. Together, the co-evolution of decision-makers who are more likely to go to war and perceptions that an adversary is becoming increasingly threatening make a future war more likely.

Alternatively, a more contingent, non-linear, position is possible. Adversarial relations prior to war need not reflect an ever-increasing hard-ening of positions. If decision-maker choices are constrained by their understandings of what strategies have or have not worked in the past with a particular rival and different strategies are employed in different circumstances, it is possible that rivalry relationships will oscillate over time. Past conflict, therefore, may increase or decrease the propensities for conflict depending on the nature of choices made in the past, but regardless of the specific correlation of events, crises are related to each other, if non-linearly. This idea is similar to Leng's (1984, 2000a) realist experiential learning model in which the future propensity for war depends on the strategy choice in the past crisis and the success of that choice.[1]

Finally, it is possible that past conflict can make future conflict less likely. McClelland (1972) hypothesized that, through repeated crisis interaction with the same adversary, participants gain experience in ways of coping with each other and reduce uncertainty. While threats may still be made, the probability of overt hostilities declines. It is also conceivable that a confrontation will bring about reduced conflict without involving a sequence of learning experiences. This outcome could occur in two different ways. Crisis participants may go to the brink and realize that continuing the conflict is not in either side's best interests. This sentiment could be due to the realization that one side is simply too powerful to resist successfully. The adversaries may realize that they have more in common (such as a mutual enemy) than they have in dispute. Or, it could also be that the crisis catalyzes a perception that the two parties do not really have much to fight about (Lebow, 1981; Rock, 1989) and that their adversarial relationship has continued to exist due primarily to perceptual inertia. When decision-makers are forced to confront why and what they may be fighting about, as well as the likelihood of limited payoffs in continuing the relationship as in the past, there can be a realization that conflict de-escalation is a more attractive option.

These assertions are similar in spirit to the war-weariness proposition, whereby states are less likely to go to war with each other after a past war. Toynbee (1954; see as well, Wright, 1942/65; Blainey, 1973) maintained that political leaders who have directly experienced the devastation of war will be averse to a future war due to the high costs they have experienced. Whether "war-weariness" should be expected to apply to crisis sequences is debatable. Unlike most crises, wars cause variable destruction and devastation that requires periods of reconstruction. Earlier war participants who wish to resume hostilities tend to be handicapped by the need to rebuild their resource base before they go to war again. Crisis participants can usually avoid incurring heavy costs if they end the crisis before the shooting commences. For that matter, the empirical evidence for the war-weariness hypothesis (Singer and Small, 1974; Singer and Cusack, 1980; Siverson, 1980; Stoll, 1984; Levy and Morgan, 1986; Goldstein, 1988) is decidedly mixed. If the weariness linkages between wars are weak, they may be even weaker between crises.

---

[1] Basically, the idea is that losers in one crisis are likely to try harder the next time around.

Hot spots or hot hands?

Not all researchers accept that there are relationships between crises over time. Gartzke and Simon (1999) offer a methodological and empirical critique of the serial crisis hypothesis. They note that, while states "with histories of disputes are more likely to engage in additional disputes . . . it does not follow, however, that previous disputes are causal" (Gartzke and Simon, 1999: 782). Instead Gartzke and Simon suggest that other variables should be given priority. For instance, in a series of crises between states, something must have caused the first dispute. The "prime mover" in this case cannot be past conflict behavior (since there is no past behavior by definition). Any theory that can account for the first dispute in a series should, *a priori*, be considered as a cause of subsequent disputes. This observation suggests that the appearance of a dispute's linkages to earlier disputes is somewhat spurious. It is not so much repeated disputes that lead to increasing conflict, but the lack of resolution of the underlying grievance, or at least the persistence of other reasons for conflict other than previous outcomes.

The main methodological critique of the enduring rivalry program is that there is omitted variable bias.[2] The observation that a few dyads have a disproportionate share of the total number of crises could be explained by contiguity or some other criterion other than dispute interdependence over time. They argue that it is not surprising that some dyads have fought many times. The presence of one crisis shows that the states have both the opportunity and the willingness to fight, while this is lacking in most dyads. Thus the presence of past crises does not increase the probability of conflict, but instead signals that there is a higher probability of conflict propensity in these states.

Further, Gartzke and Simon attempt to show empirically that these serial disputes could have been generated by chance. Statisticians refer to the phenomenon of human pattern recognition in randomness as the "hot hand." The conventional metaphor comes from basketball, where it seems as if players "get hot" and will hit four or five shots in a row, and then "get cold," missing a few in a row. Yet, statistical research has shown that the probability of making a shot is unaffected by the success of the last attempt (see Dixit and Nalebuff 1991). Gartzke and Simon remind us that probability theory suggests that we will see long strings of low-probability events occurring sometimes, even when events are independent.

---

[2] Gartzke and Simon (1999) refer to the problem as the "instrumental variable problem," which is also correct since endogeneity problems can be reduced to omitted variable bias (King, Keohane, and Verba, 1994).

They hypothesize that enduring rivalries are "hot hands" rather than evidence of serially related disputes. While a few dyads have suffered through a disproportionate share of conflicts, it is possible that this observation could have been generated by a series of independent events. Using a Poisson model to calculate the probability of observing a certain number of confrontations between a dyad, Gartzke and Simon (1999: 784) find that the observed frequency of crises between a few dyads could indeed be generated by a sequence of independent events.

Obviously, if dyadic disputes are independent, considerable doubt is cast on the claim by rivalry researchers that the links between disputes are important causes of war because they are related over time.[3] As Gartzke and Simon (1999: 784) observe, enduring rivalry research "depends on the claim that disputes in series are different from isolated disputes."

We believe that the Gartzke and Simon test should not be the final word on the validity of rivalry research or the serial crisis hypothesis. First, their test is univariate. Only one parameter, the probability of a dispute, was estimated. Research on international relations has produced numerous theories on the variables influencing crisis propensities, including the effects of democracy, contiguity, major power status, and capability ratios. In statistical terms these unmeasured variables introduce unobserved heterogeneity into the estimation of the Poisson model. This heterogeneity biases standard errors downward and exaggerates statistical significance.[4]

Second, while Gartzke and Simon show that a model that assumes independence fits the observations reasonably well, they never compare the Poisson results to a model that assumes event interdependence such as the negative binomial. Thus, we are left wondering whether a model that takes dependence into account could better account for the crisis clustering.

Finally, we see no reason to assume that repeated conflict is due solely, primarily, or even marginally to the persistence of underlying causes or grievances. That is very much an empirical question. Even if there are core, unresolved grievances, the psychological baggage associated with

---

[3] Approaches that do not use disputes as coding rules for rivalry are less affected by this finding, as Gartzke and Simon (1999: 777 and fn 1) themselves point out. Nonetheless, this is a nuance that not all readers are likely to keep in mind.

[4] Gartzke and Simon (1999: 797–8) realize that the Poisson model that they use is dependent on the assumption that the expected number of conflicts per dyad is constant for each draw. Apart from the number of previous conflicts, there are a large number of possible influences (for instance, polarity or alliance ties) on the expected number of conflicts per dyad. Omitting these other influences introduces "unobserved heterogeneity" into the model which can result in biased estimates of the expected counts (Long, 1997). For an attempt to statistically control for event dependence in a logit framework rather than counts, see Beck, Katz, and Tucker (1998). See, as well, Crescenzi and Enterline (2001).

repeated confrontations might be expected to have an additive effect. Consequently, a more specific test of conflict propensities over time is necessary to invalidate the serial crises assumption. Only if we find that sequential confrontations are unrelated will we then be in a position to say that there is no systematic interdependence among strings of conflict events. If we find that these conflict strings are related, we will still not know precisely how much causal credit or blame to allot to conflict recidivism, but we will at least have some better idea of whether it is warranted to assume the probability of conflict interdependence. In the process of assessing this proposition, we can also check on some related possibilities.

Hypotheses

Building on past studies, we develop four hypotheses in this section relating past crisis behavior to present and future conflict propensities. While earlier work has focused alternatively on militarized disputes, crises, and wars, we limit our attention in this analysis solely to interstate crises. Further, we relate sequencing to different dependent variables, the risk of another crisis, and the risk of another violent crisis/war.

Sequencing

As stated above, there are two theoretical perspectives on sequencing in international crises. The first and probably most prevalent is that past crises make subsequent crises more likely within a dyad. Vasquez (2000) describes the repeated "probing" of adversaries through crises as a "step to war," whereby hard-liners and those most likely to be mistrustful of an adversary gain the most influence in decision-making (on this point, see as well Lockhart, 1978: 594; Lebow, 1981: 316). Vasquez (2000: 378) also states that "the repetition of crises is the real engine of war." Adversarial images harden on both sides and stereotypes are formed that make conflict resolution more difficult (see also Jervis 1976). Thus, past conflict makes another crisis more likely. It also increases the probability of that next crisis being violent. This leads to the two elementary serial crisis hypotheses:[5]

[5] Brecher, James, and Wilkenfeld (2000: 43) include the argument that previous crises make subsequent crises more likely in their inventory of ICB propositions that have been tested and supported, but this issue remains relatively underdeveloped in their research program. Brecher and Wilkenfeld (1997) also devote some attention to protracted conflicts that sometimes overlap with dyadic rivalries but also sometimes encompass multiple rivalries.

H1: The greater the number of past crises, the higher is the propensity for future crises.

H2: The greater the number of past crises, the higher is the propensity for future violent crises.

Contrary to the increasing conflict argument is McClelland's (1972) coordination argument, the war-weariness hypotheses, and Lebow's (1981) and Rock's (1989) crisis catalyst thesis. All three arguments suggest that previous experience with crises, in some circumstances, could lead to a lesser likelihood of future crises. In the coordination case, less conflict occurs due to the reduction of uncertainty through repeated interaction, and through the higher salience of the costs of crisis to decision-makers. Thus there will be fewer subsequent crises and/or fewer subsequent violent crises.

The war-weariness argument is that experience with a past traumatic event deters another occurrence in order to avoid additional pain and suffering. The problem here is that crises may or may not be sufficiently traumatic experiences to make decision-makers reluctant to re-engage. Similarly, the Rock argument cannot be applied generically. Some crises (for example, Fashoda) are said to be catalytic for reorienting rivalry relationships, but certainly not all or even most crises are likely to qualify. Still, these arguments do lend some support to the possibility of earlier conflict experiences leading to less, rather than more, conflict. With low expectations of systematic support on our part:

H3: The greater the number of past crises, the lower is the propensity for future crises.

H4: The greater the number of past crises, the lower is the propensity for future violent crises.

Research design considerations

To test the four hypotheses, we need to be able to distinguish among states that have had no crises, one crisis, and more than one crisis. For this purpose, we have created two sets of data. The first includes all dyads in the international system from 1918 to 1995 and information on their crisis behavior. This allows us to compare the likelihood of crisis occurrence between those states that have been involved in a past crisis and those that have not, while controlling for other factors.

To control for the Gartzke and Simon (1999) spuriousness possibility, that previous crises merely demonstrate opportunity and willingness, our second set of analyses includes only states that have been involved in at least one crisis in the years 1918 to 1995. By looking at the variation in conflict propensities within dyads that have been involved in past crises we are able to control for many of the variables Gartzke and Simon (1999) suggest should be given causal priority. Moreover, we are also able to compare the probability of crisis recurrence after a first crisis, second crisis, and so on, in order to keep variation in our independent variable of interest.[6]

Dependent variables

As in the previous chapter, we utilize the International Crisis Behavior project data set (Brecher and Wilkenfeld, 1997) to measure crisis occurrence and recurrence. The data include the presence or absence of crises among dyads in a particular year, as well as the escalation level of that crisis. This allows us to construct three dependent variables of interest. The first is whether or not any crisis occurred in a given year between the parties of a specific dyad. The second and third are related to the type of crisis that occurred. We include separate variables, in addition to the mere presence or absence of a crisis, for those crises that involved violence and those that escalated to war in order to test the specific hypotheses above that relate the independent variable to the violence of the next crisis.[7]

Finally, some may object to our using ICB coded crises rather than other events such as militarized interstate disputes or even scaled events

[6] Another approach to this problem would be to include an explicit selection component for the model (see Greene, 1999). This would be an interesting future extension of the current project. We do not include this approach for two reasons. First, selection models have been developed for linear and logistic regression, neither of which we use in this project. Second, we report results for all dyads in the system in which selection is not as much of a problem. The confluence of results in both the general model and the smaller model should also increase the confidence in our findings, and help answer the Gartzke and Simon critique.

[7] Brecher, James, and Wilkenfeld (2000: 3) define crises as situations in which decision-makers perceive "a threat to one or more basic values, along with an awareness of finite time for response to the value threat, and a heightened probability of involvement in military hostilities." While we generally have few problems with this definition, our specific purposes require making some alterations along the lines discussed in the previous chapter. First, the ICB data set includes crises that take place within and outside of ongoing warfare. We prefer to delete all intra-war crises as distinctively different phenomena from pre war crises, a practice subscribed to by other non-ICB analysts (Diehl, Reifschneider, and Hensel, 1996; Rousseau, Gelpi, Reiter, and Huth, 1996). Additionally, our hypotheses are dyadic in nature; yet the ICB data set includes many multilateral crises. We code as crises only those cases in which the crisis actors view each other as the primary threat in that particular crisis. The non-directional ICB participant coding encompasses actors that are on the same side, as well as actors that are less than fully involved. We need specific identifications of each crisis' main participants and whom they are confronting. If states are not learning about the adversary, or are not "counting" a certain crisis as part of its sequence with a given adversary, past lessons will not apply and we would not expect any relationship between crises. Another part of our approach is that we exclude "one-sided" crises as non-dyadic behavior (see Hewitt and Wilkenfeld, 1999).

data scores. We focus on crises primarily because Leng's (1983) findings on crises have long been cited as a sort of touchstone in this research area. We are fully prepared to accept Leng's generalizations about serial crisis behavior, including the three crisis-war stipulations. But we do not know whether these generalizations will survive the more comprehensive test we undertake in this analysis, even though Leng's earlier findings are precisely the sort of foundation needed to justify conflict interdependence and rivalry analyses.

We do not rule out the possibility that other indices of conflict may also demonstrate interdependence over time. But there is some possibility that other manifestations of conflict may be more amorphous in terms of whether actors learn from them as we think they do learn, or are capable of learning, from crises, either through analogy (Khong, 1992) or a lesson from history (Jervis, 1976; Neustadt and May, 1988). We accept Eckstein's (1975:119) guidance that tests should first be conducted where evidence is likely to be found. If in these crisis cases no support for the hypotheses is uncovered, then we can conclude that the notion of serial crisis behavior is a less concrete phenomenon than we had thought (see also King, Keohane, and Verba 1994: 209). On the other hand, if we included all militarized disputes as past conflict, or even all Conflict and Peace Databank (COPDAB) or World Event Interaction Survey (WEIS) conflict events, and then found no support for the relationship between crises, it would be quite possible that it was our operationalization that accounted for our (lack of) findings rather than the specific empirical phenomena we most wish to test. To this end we use the more restrictive crisis operationalization of past conflict to ensure that our empirical analysis conforms to the specific nature of the arguments being advanced.[8] This leaves us with a total of 145 crises between 1918 and 1995, 67 of which involved dyads that had engaged in one previous crisis in that time period.

Independent variables

Sequence: We code four dummy variables to account for the number of previous crises between a dyad. The first dummy is equal to 1 if there was only one previous crisis. The second is coded as a 1 if there were two previous crises, and so on. Due to the small number of cases that entailed three or more past crises, the fourth dummy variable encompasses all

---

[8] Allison (1995) notes that one way to check if the incomplete sequencing and left censoring are a problem is to delete the problematic cases and see if the results change. In this case, deleting the incomplete cases does not change any of the substantive findings.

such cases. For the first set of analyses which includes all dyads in the international system, the comparison group comprises those states that have no previous crises. For the second set of regressions, which include only those states that have had at least one past crisis, the comparison group comprises those states that have had only one previous crisis. These reference groups allow us to test the serial crisis hypothesis that different sequences have different conflict propensities. We do not include a straight single variable count of the previous sequences, because we wish to (1) test for specific non-linearities, and (2) relate our findings to Leng's previous work, which calls for a jump in war-propensity after the third crisis. A count of previous crises would not pick this up.

It must be acknowledged that our sequencing is incomplete. We only include information on crises between 1918 and 1995, and it is probable that some states had crises prior to this start time. Yet, this problem only raises the bar for finding a statistically significant difference between first, second, and third crises. Consider the hypothetical case that the first hypothesis is true and past crises make subsequent crises more likely. In this case, if we treat some crises as first crises when they are actually third crises, we are biasing the average propensity of first crises upwards (since we are including a volatile third crisis with a not so volatile first crisis).

The practical result of this enterprise is that we are less likely to find significant differences. The same holds true if we suppose that the third hypothesis is true and past conflict makes subsequent conflict less likely. In this instance, if we treat a third crisis as a first crisis we are mixing a non-volatile later crisis with a volatile early crisis, again making it less likely to find differences among crisis sequences. Of course in the last case, if there is actually no relationship between past crises over time, no bias results because the probability of conflict is constant with respect to sequencing. Therefore, if a significant pattern is found between the sequence of a crisis and crisis recidivism, incomplete sequencing should not invalidate the findings.[9]

Control Variables: Gartzke and Simon (1999) point out that there are other factors that can account for crisis propensity which are not related to past outcomes. Given the impossibility of random selection for this research design, we statistically control for democracy, alliance ties, contiguity, and major power status to reduce the chances of spurious correlation.

It is widely cited that the presence of democracy in a dyad reduces the chances for conflict (see among many others, Chan, 1997). Thus the presence of recurring conflict could be attributed to regime type rather

---

[9] We use the EUGene software (Bennett and Stam, 2000) to generate data for all dyads for the years 1918 to 1995 to code the control variables.

Table 5.1 *Descriptive statistics for control variables*

Variable	Mean	Std. dev.	Min	Max	Description
Contiguity	0.04	0.20	0.00	1.00	1 if dyad is contiguous by land, 0 if not (COW contiguity data).
Major powers	0.00	0.05	0.00	1.00	1 if both states are COW major powers, 0 if not.
Democracy	0.59	0.49	0.00	1.00	1 if at least one state is democratic, 0 if not.
Capability ratio	−6.65	5.30	−38.15	0.00	Equal to the log of the lower capability divided by the higher capability in the dyad.
Alliance	0.09	0.29	0.00	1.00	1 if dyad is allied, 0 if not.

$N = 44,8603$
Note: Democracy score is based on subtracting the autocracy scale score from the democracy scale score. If at least one state has a score of 6 or above the dyad is coded as including a democracy. Data generated using the EUGene program V. 1.95 (Bennett and Stam 2000).

than a sequence of past disputes. That is, autocratic actors might be more likely to engage in crisis recidivism than their democratic counterparts. On the opposite end of the spectrum, a contiguous dyad, and a dyad that consists of major powers is more likely to fight than dyads that lack these characteristics (Bremer 1992, 2000). Additionally, realists stress the role of capability ratios within a dyad and the related concerns over security that will guide crisis propensities. While there is disagreement about the sign of the relationship, whether a balance of capabilities leads to peace or war, its importance is widely cited (see, for instance, Kugler and Lemke, 1996; Brecher and Wilkenfeld, 1997; Geller, 2000).

Finally, as in the case of capability ratios, alliance ties within a dyad have elicited conflicting predictions. Conventional wisdom (Brzezinski and Huntington, 1963) and a number of empirical analyses (among others, Maoz, 2000) suggest that an alliance between states makes war less likely. Yet Bueno de Mesquita (1981) derives and finds support for the proposition that allies are more likely to fight each other, all things equal. Here we take no position on these specific debates but only include these variables to statistically control for factors that analysts typically consider to be alternative and causally prior explanatory variables.[10] Table 5.1 includes a description of these control variables.[11]

---

[10] Different operationalizations of democracy, for instance, including only the low score for the dyad, and, for alliances, coding only defense pacts, did not alter the results substantively.
[11] Logistic regression is a special case of the exponential hazard model (see Beck, Katz, and Tucker, 1998; Allison, 1995).

Methods

We estimate a set of Weibull parametric hazard models to statistically analyze the relationships among these variables. The dependent variable in this model is the hazard rate, or risk of a crisis. Intuitively, we are attempting to model the duration of peace between crises. Variables that speed up a crisis increase the hazard rate, while variables that slow down the risk of another crisis decrease the hazard rate. Interpretation of the exponentiated coefficients is similar to odds ratios from a logit specification. Yet, the parametric hazard method has two major advantages over either linear or logistic regression. First, hazard models allow what are called right-censored observations to convey information. A right-censored observation in this study would be a dyad that has not yet had another crisis by 1995 (the end of the study window). Linear regression would treat this systematically imposed censoring as an end point. Hazard analysis allows for the censoring point to contribute the fact that the observation lasted up to this point.

Additionally, unlike logistic regression, the Weibull model does not assume a constant baseline hazard of international crisis or war.[12] The baseline hazard function is the pure time component in the model, similar to a deterministic trend in linear regression. This is important because an incorrect baseline hazard specification can bias estimates (Allison 1995). Our Weibull specification is more flexible than either a logit model that ignores time or an exponential hazard model that assumes the hazard rate is constant across time. While we report Cox regression results elsewhere (Colaresi and Thompson, 2002), where the baseline hazard is factored with the constant and the partial likelihood is evaluated, we choose to present parametric models here for ease of interpretation. The results are robust to specifying either exponential or Gompertz parametric models.[13]

---

[12] Past research on crisis recidivism has used an arbitrary cutoff date to define recurrence. For instance, Diehl, Reifschneider, and Hensel (1996) only include observations ten years after a crisis. Instead of using an arbitrary cutoff point we include observations until the study as a whole is censored in 1995. This procedure allows us to differentiate between a dyad that is involved in a crisis eleven years after the last crisis and one that is involved in a crisis sixty years after their previous crisis. Empirically, Hensel (1994) notes that disputes between Peru and Chile over the Tacna and Arica areas went fifty-five years between confrontations, while Argentina and Uruguay had a dispute gap over sixty-one years long. In both cases, the dyads were involved in another dispute, and over the same issue. A coding rule that censors observations after a certain deadline would miss these new outbreaks.

[13] Further, a non-parametric plot of the baseline hazard was consistent with the monotonicity that the Weibull model assumes.

Analysis

All dyads

Table 5.2 reports the results of our analyses that include all dyads in the international system. The results show that the risk of a future crisis increases by a factor of 5.5 after the first crisis, as compared to the risk of a clash when there had been no previous crisis within the dyad, and holding other variables constant. The risk increases slightly after the second and third crises as well. In the third crisis and after, the risk of a subsequent crisis increases by a factor of 12, in comparison to dyads with no previous crises. Each of these estimates is significant at the 0.01 level (for two-tailed tests), and the signs support the serial crisis hypothesis that the propensity for future conflict increases with the number of past crises. Further, the null hypothesis that all three coefficients are equal to zero (where the hazard rate would not differ based on sequence), can be rejected (chi-square = 108.8 ($df = 3$), $p < 0.01$). The difference between the risk after the first crisis is significantly smaller than the risk of a future conflict after the third crisis ($p < 0.005$). The escalating spiral of crisis recidivism is illustrated in Figure 5.1. Here we model the expected duration of peace within a dyad.[14] If that dyad has experienced no previous crises, we could expect peace to last approximately 55.5 years (90 percent CI: 23.4, 106.9). However, after the first and then third crises the expected duration of peace decreases to 7.8 years (90 percent CI: 3.4, 14.7) and then 3.2 years (90 percent CI: 1.7, 5.2) respectively.[15]

Other significant predictors of crisis occurrence are democracy, major power dyads, and contiguity. Democracy decreased the risk of crisis by a factor of 1.6, holding other variables constant.[16] Major power and contiguous dyads significantly increased the risk of crisis. Most dramatically, being contiguous increased the risk of a crisis by a factor of 36.7, holding all other variables constant.

[14] Specifically, these predictions are made by calculating the mean time to crisis for a dyad that is contiguous, includes two major powers, has near power parity, is not allied, and does not include any democracies. Similar figures can be drawn by changing any of these settings.

[15] These predictions and confidence intervals, as well as those that follow, were calculated by parametrically bootstrapping expected values from a Weibull distribution defined by the estimated coefficient vector, variables setting described above, and the estimated variance–covariance matrix.

[16] This finding appears to support the idea that the democratic peace applies at the monadic level as well as at the dyadic level. For arguments about revising the former consensus that the democratic peace is strictly a dyadic phenomenon, see Russett and Starr (2000) and Ray (2000).

Table 5.2 Weibull regressions results for all dyads ("no previous crisis" is comparison group)

Variables	Any crisis			Violent crisis			War		
	Haz. rat.	S.E.	p-value	Haz. rat.	S.E.	p-value	Haz. rat.	S.E.	p-value
One prev. crisis	5.50	1.49	<0.01	3.70	1.29	<0.01	4.51	2.82	<0.05
Two prev. crises	9.50	3.03	<0.01	9.61	3.51	<0.01	17.37	9.59	<0.01
Three or more prev. crises	11.81	4.22	<0.01	10.73	4.88	<0.01	19.97	21.96	<0.01
Democracy	0.63	0.11	<0.01	0.51	0.12	<0.01	0.44	0.19	<.10
Major power dyad	6.01	2.23	<0.01	6.52	3.87	<0.01	2.15	2.31	N/S
Capability ratio	1.02	0.03	N/S	1.01	0.02	N/S	1.10	0.05	<.10
Alliance	1.18	0.26	N/S	1.14	0.29	N/S	0.69	0.33	N/S
Contiguity	36.75	10.20	<0.01	42.04	13.61	<0.01	36.10	21.26	<0.01
ln(Weibull Shape)	−0.13	0.06	<0.05	−0.16	0.08	<0.05	−0.34	0.13	<0.01
N-size	448,063			448,063			448,063		
Number of failures	146			96			27		
Log likelihood	−610.60			−446.02			−156.32		
Wald chi-square ($df = 8$)	1438.5		$p < 0.01$	832.6		$p < 0.01$	256.43		$p < 0.01$

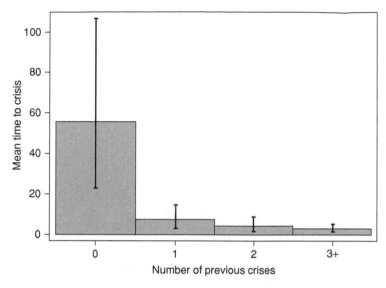

Figure 5.1 The effect of the number of previous crises on the average time till the next crisis, with 90 percent confidence intervals (no previous crises included).

When we turn to the outbreak of violent crises and war, the positive relationship between past crises and conflagrations continues. The three sequencing variables are significant at the 0.01 level (for a two-tailed test) in columns 2 and 3 in Table 5.2. The risk of a violent crisis increases by a factor of 3.7 after the first crisis, and 9.6 after the second crisis, in comparison to a dyad with no previous crises. Figure 5.2 shows the acceleration in violence from crisis to crisis. A dyad with no previous history of crises would be expected to persist for 75.4 years (90 percent CI: 22.6, 173.5) without violence, while the duration of peace without violence descends consistently down to 4.3 years (90 percent CI: 1.8, 8.0) after the third crisis. Similarly, the risk of war increases by a factor of 4.5 after the first crisis, and 3.8 after the second crisis,[17] holding all other variables constant. While there is not a statistically significant jump after the third crisis, the risk of a future violent crisis and war does significantly increase after the second crisis ($p < 0.05$). Likewise, we can reject the null hypothesis that sequences do not affect crisis behavior (that all three coefficients are equal to zero) at the 0.01 level (chi-square = 34.3, $df = 3$).

---

[17] Which is 17.8 times greater than the risk of violence when no previous crises have been observed.

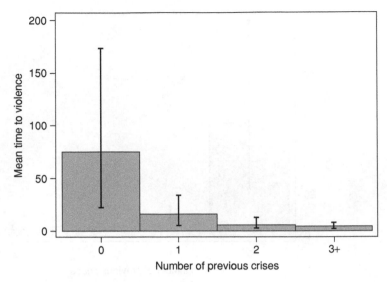

Figure 5.2 The effect of the number of previous crises on the average time till violence, with 90 percent confidence intervals (no previous crises included).

Crisis recurrence

Table 5.3 reports the results of the second set of Weibull regressions that include only those dyads that had been involved in at least one crisis between 1918 and 1995.[18] This test allows for us to isolate those dyads that have previously shown the opportunity and willingness to fight in the past. Due to severe colinearity in this reduced sample, the effects of neither contiguity nor major power status can be estimated. Therefore, we hold these variables constant, modeling only contiguous, non-major power dyads (including mixed power dyads) that have fought at least one previous crisis.

The results strongly support the proposition that the propensity for conflict is dependent on the number of past crises within a dyad. When we analyze the likelihood of any crisis recurring, the risk of recurrence increases by a factor of 1.9 after the second crisis, as compared to after the first crisis, holding other variables constant. Moreover, after the fourth or later crisis, the risk of recurrence is 7.5 times greater than after the

---

[18] As an alternative modeling strategy, we estimated a two-stage selection model where the first-stage dependent variable was whether a dyad had one crisis or not, and the second stage measured future crises or escalation. None of the error term correlations were significant. We therefore report the Weibull estimates here.

Table 5.3 *Weibull regressions results for contiguous non-major power dyads with at least one previous crisis ("one previous crisis" is comparison group)*

Variables	Any crisis			Violent crisis			War		
	Haz. rat.	S.E.	p-value	Haz. rat.	S.E.	p-value	Haz. rat.	S.E.	p-value
Two prev. crisis	16.15	9.76	<0.01	13.21	8.12	<0.01	3.73	2.30	<0.05
Three prev. crises	17.64	12.52	<0.01	15.75	12.72	<0.01	9.43	7.31	<0.01
Four or more prev. crises	79.93	61.57	<0.01	52.42	41.85	<0.01	29.99	20.74	<0.01
Democracy	0.32	0.17	<0.05	0.26	0.16	<0.05	0.18	0.16	<0.05
Capability ratio	0.90	0.04	<0.05	0.92	0.04	<0.10	1.20	0.13	N/S
Alliance	0.62	0.18	N/S	0.61	0.20	N/S	0.32	0.23	N/S
N-size	3005			3005			3005		
Number of failures	67			51			16		
Log likelihood	−245.75			−192.81			−58.12		
Wald chi-square (df)	151.83 (8)			128.24 (8)			58.06 (7)		

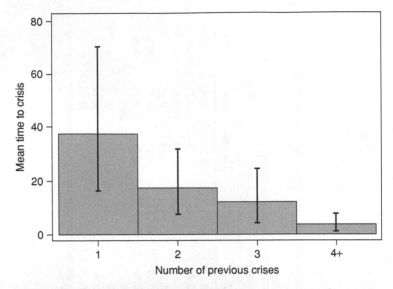

Figure 5.3 The effect of the number of previous crises on the average time till the next crisis, with 90 percent confidence intervals (dyads with one or more previous crises).

first crisis. The 90 percent confidence intervals for each of the three crisis sequence coefficients exclude zero,[19] and we can reject the hypothesis that sequences do not affect the risk of crisis recurrence (chi-square 17.6, df = 3, $p < 0.01$). Substantively, Figure 5.3 shows the now familiar pattern of accelerating crisis recidivism. A dyad with only one previous crisis[20] is expected to avoid a crisis setting for 38 years (90 percent CI: 16.4, 70.1). In contrast, a dyad with four or more previous crises would expect to have crises recur every 3.6 years (90 percent CI: 1.2, 7.7).

While the coefficients support the serial crisis story that the likelihood of crisis recurrence increases as the number of past crises increases, there are non-linear trends that need further research. But to be more specific about the ups and downs of fluctuations in dyads over time, and successive probabilities of greater and lesser conflict, we would need to move to a much more different type of analysis that entails more comprehensive information on dyadic relations than their occasional crises. In other words, we need more case-specific, serial examinations of dyadic events

[19] Thus, the 90 percent CI for the exponential coefficients, the hazard ratios, does not include 1.
[20] The settings for these predictions are the same as for those above excepting the coding of all dyads as major power above, and here they are non-major power dyads.

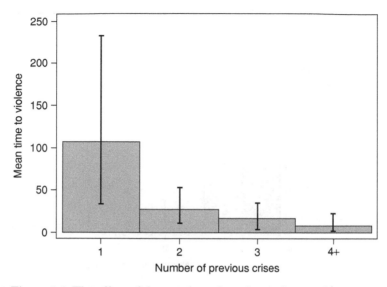

Figure 5.4 The effect of the number of previous crises on the average time till violence, with 90 percent confidence intervals (dyads with one or more previous crises).

data to go beyond the aggregated data with which we are currently working. Such analyses are definitely worth pursuing but their pursuit will have to be postponed for future analyses.

When we look at the probability of crises recurring violently or escalating to war, the hazard ratios again highlight the importance of sequences. Sequences not only make crises more likely, they make violent crises more likely. The risk of a crisis reoccurring violently is 9.5 times greater after the fourth crisis than it is after the first crisis between adversaries, holding all other variables constant, and the risk of war is 14 times greater than the same benchmark. In Figures 5.4 and 5.5, when we look at only contiguous non-major power dyads that have experienced at least one crisis, the expected duration of non-violence is 107 years (90 percent CI: 34.04, 231.9) and war-avoidance is 326.5 years (90 percent CI: 45.0, 957.7), while in comparison the temporal gap between violent incidents after the fourth crisis is only 8.1 years (90 percent CI: 1.4, 22.0). Similarly, war is expected to recur every 8.8 years after the fourth crisis (90 percent CI: 0.4, 30.7).

As for the control variables, conventional wisdom is supported in most cases. Dyads including at least one democracy are 3.4 times less likely to suffer a crisis recurrence, 3.5 times less likely to be involved in a subsequent violent crisis, and 4.9 times less likely to be involved in a future

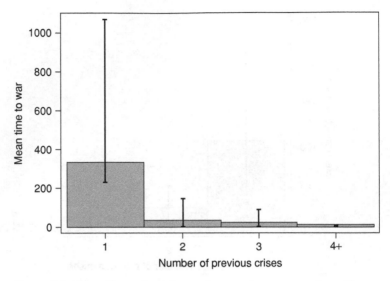

Figure 5.5 The effect of previous crises on the average time till war, with 90 percent confidence intervals (dyads with one or more previous crises).

war, holding other variables constant. Conversely, neither alliance ties nor capability ratios proved to be robust predictors of crisis recurrence in this sample.[21] In many ways the finding that even an asymmetrical dyad may fight repeatedly supports our intuition in Chapter 4 that rivalry and recurrent conflict contexts might be distinct from other types of relationships.

If one looks at the identities of crisis recidivists, the number of asymmetrical pairs is difficult to miss. Table 5.4 lists dyads with two or more crises. Relationships described as strategic rivalries, which involve competitive states that view each other as threatening enemies, are identified with an asterisk.[22] We see at least two processes at work. One involves nonrivalries in which major powers have engaged in some asymmetrical conflicts repeatedly (for instance, China–Vietnam, France–Libya, North Korea–USA). In such cases, the stronger power either has been less than able to project its full strength, has been constrained from a full-scale clash, or

[21] We take up the task of further exploring the interaction between military buildups, alliances, and recurrent crises in later chapters.
[22] The threshold used in the ICB approach to identifying full-scale wars is not always clear. For instance, they have no war outcome between China and Vietnam associated with three crises in the 1980s but they do have a war outcome in the Greek-Turkish 1974 case. In the latter case, they may have the Cypriot-Turkish war in mind when they coded the outcome for the crisis case. Some of this awkwardness may therefore be due to our transformations of the crisis cases into dyadic encounters between the main participants.

Table 5.4 *Dyads involved in multiple crisis sequences*

4–7 crisis sequence	3 crisis sequence	2 crisis sequence
*India–Pakistan (7)	*Afghanistan–Pakistan	*Angola–Zaire
US–USSR	*Algeria–Morocco	*Argentina–Chile
*Egypt–Israel (6)	*China–Vietnam	*Bolivia–Paraguay
*Israel–Syria (5)	*Ethiopia–Somalia	*Cameroon–Nigeria
*Greece–Turkey	France–Libya	*Chad–Libya
*Ecuador–Peru (4)	*Honduras–Nicaragua	*China–India
	*Iraq–Iran	*China–Japan
	*Japan–Russia	*China–US*
	North Korea–US*	*Egypt–Libya
	*Tanzania–Uganda	*France–Germany
		France–Ottoman E.
		*Hungary–Yugoslavia
		Iceland–UK*
		*Indonesia–Netherlands
		Iraq–US*
		*Israel–Jordan
		*Italy–Yugoslavia
		Laos–Thailand
		Libya–US*
		*Lithuania–Poland
		Ott. E.–UK*
		Panama–US*
		*Poland–Russia

Note: *Indicates the dyad is considered a strategic rivalry.

both generalizations apply. While strategic rivalries tend to match states with roughly equal power (i.e., as competitors), that is not always the case as the Indo-Pakistani case most vividly illustrates. Here again, there are various constraints operating on the stronger of the two rival powers to prevent some sort of terminal solution to the tendency to clash repeatedly. Thus, the point is not that a dyadic balance of power makes crisis recurrence less likely but that other factors do not preclude asymmetrical dyads from engaging in multiple crises in greater frequency than one might anticipate.

Table 5.5 exposes more dramatically some of the relationships between rivalry and crisis recurrence. As one moves more deeply into the crisis recurrence chain, the role of rivalry becomes increasingly more evident. The majority of interstate dyads with only one crisis (60 percent) represent nonrivalry situations. But states with more than one crisis tend to involve strategic rivalries. Rivalries claim 65 percent of the two-crisis cases, 80 percent of the three-crisis cases, and 100 percent of the cases

Table 5.5 *Rivalry–nonrivalry crisis sequence comparisons*

	Rivalry		Non rivalry	
Crisis dyads	Number	%	Number	%
1 crisis	24	40.0	36	60.0
2 crises	15	65.2	8	34.8
3 crises	8	80.8	2	19.2
4 or more crises	6	100.0	0	0.0
Serious clashes and war				
1 crisis	15	57.6	13	38.2
2 crises	13	43.3	5	31.3
3 crises	17	70.8	1	16.7
4 or more crises	15	44.1	0	0.0
Escalation in next crisis				
Yes	25	42.4	4	33.3
No	34	57.6	8	66.7
Full-scale ICB wars				
1 crisis	6	85.7	1	14.3
2 crises	3	60.0	2	40.0
3 crises	4	100.0	0	0.0
4 or more crises	9	100.0	0	0.0

Note: crisis dyad and war information is percentagized across the columns.

Percentages are calculated within the rivalry and nonrivalry categories for the clash/war and escalation questions.

with greater than three crises. However, the different behaviors manifested by rivalries and nonrivalries do not translate into a straightforwardly linear progression of a greater risk of serious clashes. Differentiating between cases involving no violence/minor clashes and those leading to serious clashes/full-scale war, nonrivalries become generally less dangerous as they engage in multiple crises.

Crises within rivalries are most likely to be more serious in the first onset or the third. The rivalries with the most crises (more than three) tend to mix serious and not-so-serious confrontations almost equally. At least that is the outcome if we simply aggregate crisis violence outcomes without reference to sequence. If we bring sequence back into the picture, a rivalry crisis is more likely to be followed by another crisis involving greater violence than are non-rivalry crises, but not by a great margin (42 percent versus 33 percent). On the other hand, rivalries involve many more instances of crisis recurrence than nonrivalries

(59 versus 12), so that rivalries are most likely to be associated with the most deadly outcomes. Of the twenty-five full-scale war outcomes associated with the ICB crises on which we are focusing, all but 3 percent or 12 percent were between rivals.

Finally, a word about Leng's (1983) three-crises and war rule is in order. Most of our findings corroborate Leng's early emphasis on crisis sequences and their interdependence. One generalization that is not corroborated is the three-crisis rule. Of the sixteen crisis sequences with three or more confrontations, two (India–Pakistan and Egypt–Israel) went to war before they had experienced their third crisis. Eight sequences did not experience a full-scale war by ICB standards after three crises.[23] Five did and one other case (Israel–Syria) went to war in its fourth crisis. Without doubt, multiple crises increase the probability of conflict, but the number three does not appear to be as critical as Leng's more limited data had suggested.

Conclusion

In sum, the analyses strongly support the serial crises argument. Previous crises make subsequent crises more likely. The subsequent crises are also more likely to be violent. We are now in a position to at least begin to answer Gartzke and Simon's critique of the serial crisis assumption. Serial crises are different from isolated disputes due to their propensity to recur quickly and recur with violence. They are not statistical anomalies. They reflect instead longitudinal processes of persistent mistrust and hostility and, often, rivalry. But if they were only that – reflections of underlying threat and disagreement – we should expect all rivalries to exhibit similar expressions of conflict. They clearly do not. A very small number of rivalries have experienced a string of crises (and wars). A larger number have experienced one or two crises. But a good number have experienced none at all. Then, too, crisis sequences are not monopolized by rivalries, even though crisis recurrence is much more likely in rivalry situations than in non-rivalry situations.

Still, the effects of crisis sequences do not disappear when we control for rivalry relationships, or, for that matter, when we control for contiguity, capability ratios, regime type, or alliances. Crises, therefore, are hardly independent events. Their interdependence over time needs to be highlighted and studied more closely. Hence, the study of rivalry is amply justified. Exactly how rivalry dynamics works remains to be delineated.

---

[23] Between 1918 and 1995, 143 strategic rivalries were in existence. Only 43 experienced ICB reciprocated crises, while 100 dyads experienced no crises.

In that sense, we do not yet have a fully developed theoretical answer to Simon and Gartzke's challenge. But we can be more confident that crisis recurrence linkages are part of the answer – and that we no longer need to assume that crises tend to be independent across time.

Chapters 4 and 5, we think, establish a firm foundation for theorizing further about rivalry and conflict escalation. Rivalry is very important in differentiating states that are likely to engage in conflict from those that are much less likely to do so. One of the reasons for this is that rivalries are more likely to encompass long-running feuds in which conflict is temporally patterned or interdependent across time. What happened before influences what happens next and may hinge as well on what is expected to happen in the future. Assuming rivalry matters, Chapters 6 and 7 develop and examine a theory, first advanced by John Vasquez (1996), that, at least in our version, distinguishes two basic types of rivalry – spatial and positional – and the likelihood that the nature of their escalation to conflict will hinge on the category of rivalry to which they belong.

Part III

Playing to type: Spatial and positional issues in strategic rivalries

6 Contiguity, space, and position in the major power subsystem

Predicated on the finding that most wars stem from a relatively small number of rivalries, some analysts are shifting attention away from general probabilities of state conflict behavior escalating to war and toward modeling why rivalries sometimes (de)escalate in hostility. In this chapter, we reexamine and extend one such effort that is predicated on the assumption that territorial disputes provide the fundamental motor for escalation to war among rivals. Vasquez's (1996) model differentiates two different paths to war for contiguous and noncontiguous rivals. While the model is attractive in many respects, it is doubtful that the major power subsystem, Vasquez's empirical focus in the 1996 study, is the most likely place to find empirical corroboration for an argument stressing territorial issues. Major powers do quarrel over territory but they also have a marked propensity for competing over positional issues. Accordingly, we develop a second theory that allows for variable interests in two types of issues – spatial and positional. Many, but not all, of the same hypotheses that Vasquez derives from his single-issue theoretical focus can also be deduced from the two-issue theory, but now both paths receive equal theoretical attention. Moreover, three more testable hypotheses pertaining to the prevalence of contiguous/noncontiguous rivalries, dyadic versus multilateral wars, and war-joining behavior can also be derived. We can also test the previously assumed linkage between contiguity and territorially focused rivalries. These several new hypotheses and the added explanatory power facilitate choosing between the two war escalation theories.

We are also now in a position to expand our information base on major power rivalries without depending on dispute-density approaches to rivalry identification. The development of a more comprehensive rivalry database for the major power subsystem suggests an additional incentive for reexamining the hypotheses that are shared by the two theories. That is, we cannot focus solely on the hypotheses that differ by theory because it is possible that the outcome depends on which rivalries are included and which ones are ignored. There are also a few other design features that need closer scrutiny – for instance, how one should measure contiguity is less than obvious.

While it is not clear that the more comprehensive rivalry data set or alternative contiguity approaches are critical to the outcome, the empirical evidence clearly supports the two-issue (spatial and positional) theory. Yet this outcome is not as mutually exclusive as it may seem since the two-issue theory can be viewed as really more an expansion and elaboration of the one-issue version than a fully independent rival. Spatial issues remain significant in war escalation processes, but so are positional issues.

In the one-issue theory, positional issues might be said to have lurked as an implicit residual. In the two-issue theory, they receive equal and explicit theoretical attention with spatial issues. Yet the argument is not that their significance is always coequal. Rather, their relative salience is apt to vary from subsystem to subsystem. In some, spatial issues may overwhelm positional issues, while in other subsystems the reverse condition may hold. Nor can we eliminate the possibility that spatial and positional issues are in fact coequal in some places and at some times. Whatever the case, different types of issues lead to differentiated rivalry and war behavior. Thus, not only is the existence of a rivalry a useful predictor of consequent conflict behavior, so, too, is the type of rivalry.

Vasquez's theory of rivalry escalation and earlier analysis

John Vasquez (1996) develops a strikingly parsimonious theory of how rivals escalate to war. The main source of interstate conflict between states of roughly equal power is assumed to be territorial disputes between neighbors. To the extent that systemic conflict resolution institutions are unavailable, disputants are likely to resort to the devices of "power politics" (alliances, military build-ups, and coercive tactics) in efforts to create unilateral solutions to their problems. But the employment of power politics enhances, rather than discourages, the probability of war onset because the techniques increase tension and hostility. The main deduction from these postulates is that rivalries that involve territorial disputes, therefore, are more likely to escalate to war than rivalries that do not.[1]

---

[1] Vasquez assumes that rivals are states of roughly equal power even though that does not apply even to all major power rivalries. We do not share this assumption but it is not an issue that can be explored very far without moving away from a focus on major power dyads. On the other hand, considerable asymmetries can be found within the major power subset that have not precluded the emergence of rivalry.

Vasquez acknowledges the possibility that most rivals are also neighbors and that, as a consequence, most rivalries are likely to be about territorial disputes. What does one then do with noncontiguous and non-territorial disputes that may escalate? To the extent that non-neighboring rivals do exist and do occasionally go to war, Vasquez contends that their war escalations can be explained primarily in terms of being drawn into wars that become more complex by spreading beyond the initial territorial disputants.

Why or how they are drawn into ongoing wars is not discussed. The point of the theory is to differentiate two different paths to war for two types of rivals: neighbors and non-neighbors. They may all end up in war at some point. They may also end up in the same wars. But they did not necessarily become involved in the same way.

Five specific hypotheses (Vasquez, 1996: 539) are extracted from this discussion for testing purposes:

a. Rival dyads that are contiguous are more apt to go to war at some point in their history than rival dyads that are not contiguous.
b. Rivalries involving contiguous states are more apt to end in dyadic war than rivalries involving noncontiguous states.
c. Noncontiguous rivals that go to war are much more apt to be involved in multilateral wars than contiguous rivals that go to war.
d. Noncontiguous rivals that go to war are much more apt to join an ongoing war than contiguous dyads that go to war.
e. In comparison to contiguous rivals, noncontiguous rivals will either have no war or be involved only in multilateral wars with rivals.

To test these hypotheses, data were developed that identify rivals, establish contiguity, code the timing of war joining, and distinguish dyadic from multilateral wars. Vasquez used three different dispute-density rivalry lists: the wars fought between each set of rivals, a standard Correlates of War contiguity dichotomy (present if land borders are adjacent or separated by less than 150 miles of water; absent otherwise), the timing of war participation to differentiate original from subsequent joiners, and the number of war participants to distinguish dyadic from multilateral (more than two participants). In sum, all five hypotheses were supported despite the employment of three different rivalry lists. However, the more restrictive operational definition (Goertz and Diehl, 1995) requiring six disputes (as opposed to five or two in earlier measurement schemes) generated the strongest empirical support. This outcome led Vasquez to conclude that more intense rivalries, as indicated by more dense dispute behavior, were more likely to adhere to his two-path, war escalation model than were less intense rivalries.

Reexamining the Vasquez dual path argument and findings

Vasquez's parsimonious argument and relevant findings are certainly intriguing. If he is right, our understanding of the relationships among rivalry, territorial disputes/contiguity, and war behavior is clearly enhanced significantly. However, there are a variety of interpretive problems that counsel caution on accepting the argument's corroboration without additional analysis. We see possible problems with the basic argument, the rivalry identifications, and other indicator construction decisions that might have influenced the outcome.

We propose an alternative theory that emphasizes two principal types of war motivations. Vasquez's territorial emphasis is encompassed by one, although we will refer to it as the spatial dimension. The second dimension refers to positional considerations. In addition to spatial concerns (i.e., who controls specific territory), decision-makers worry about national status, whether their state's prestige and ranking in the system's (or some subsystem's) hierarchy is being threatened, and whether or to what extent they are able to influence events outside their borders (short of territorial control). As in the case of territory, the circumstances need not be restricted to defensive situations. Decision-makers also seek opportunities to improve their spatial and positional standings. In many respects, this approach preserves Vasquez's two paths interpretation. But the new theory and its operationalization does alter two facets of the original perspective. First, it no longer relies on contiguity as a proxy for territorial disputes. As long as we can distinguish between rivalries that are primarily spatial versus those that are primarily positional in nature, it is possible to investigate the relationship between types of rivalry and contiguity – rather than assume it. Second, we no longer are forced to relegate the non-territorial/noncontiguous disputants to an ambiguous war joiner residual. Positional disputants may or may not be war joiners but they do have specific reasons for fighting that need not be restricted to territorial issues. In the major power subsystem, especially, positional rivalries tend to be the norm – and not the residual.

There are also some other operational questions that deserve reconsideration. Most importantly, Vasquez relies on rivalry identifications that are predicated on their conflict behavior. But if we identify rivalries in this fashion, can we use this conflict behavior-based information to explain conflict behavior? Our answer is that we would prefer to have rivalry identifications that are based on information as independent as is possible from conflict behavior if the ultimate aim is to account for variation in conflict behavior. Thus, we propose substituting strategic rivalries for the dispute-density rivalry identifications. We also take the opportunity to develop somewhat different design approaches to the selection of wars, war participation, and contiguity.

The theory problem

The first problem concerns the correspondence among rivalry, territorial disputes, and contiguity. Vasquez's argument assumes that rivalries (and wars) are mainly about territorial disputes, that territorial disputes are mainly about boundary definitions, and that, therefore, adjacent states are most likely to become involved in these disputes and rivalries. Contiguity thereby becomes a proxy indicator for territorial disputes. But this need not be the case.

The correspondence among rivalry, territorial disputes, and neighbors is greatest for non-major powers, or so we assert, but not evenly manifested throughout the non-major power world. There are strong links between territorial disputes and neighboring rivals, for instance, in the histories of South America, the Horn of Africa, South Asia, eastern/southeastern Europe, and northeastern Asia. That is not quite the whole world but it is a large chunk of the non-major power world. There are also territorial disputes in other parts of the world but it is less clear elsewhere that rivalries are as strongly shaped by territorial disagreements as they are in say South America. Even in the regions listed above, it is not always clear that territorial disputes are primarily about territory, and not other dimensions such as ethnic sentiments, prestige, ideology, and access to other places. But all that means is that territorial disputes can be very complex and more multifaceted than is signified by mere disagreements over landownership or the exact placement of boundaries.

At the very least, it is most safe to assume that the relationship between proximity and rivalry is strongest at the non-major power level. Non-major powers are most unlikely to become involved in a rivalry relationship with nonadjacent states because they lack the opportunity to become embroiled in disputes with more distant competitors. They also usually lack the resources to do anything about it even if they were to find themselves in conflict with non-proximate adversaries. There are exceptions to these generalizations to be sure (for instance, Iraq–Israel) but they are relatively rare unless one also includes rivalries between major and non-major powers. Yet in the case of major–non-major rivalries, it is the resources of the major powers that tend to transcend the geographical barriers to intense conflict.

Major powers, on the other hand, are by definition less constrained by distance barriers. They are also most likely as a categorical group to become involved in disputes over relative position that may or may not involve some territorial manifestation (see Chapter 3). In such cases, it is not always easy to tell whether the positional or the spatial elements are most in contention. Disputes and rivalries are not necessarily one thing or the other, but often some mixture of both. It is just that major power rivalries, we contend, are the ones most likely to have strong positional overtones.

One way to pursue this observation/contention further is to develop an alternative theory to Vasquez's exclusive focus on territorial or spatial disputes. If we begin with the idea that there are two types of dispute (spatial and positional) and two types of rivals (contiguous and noncontiguous), it is fairly easy to suggest that **contiguous rivals are more likely to be embroiled in spatial conflicts than are noncontiguous rivals**. Proximity does not guarantee conflict over territory, but it surely enhances the likelihood of two adjacent states quarreling over space to which both actors have access.

Contrarily, **noncontiguous rivals are more likely to be embroiled in positional conflicts than are contiguous rivals**. This stipulation is not as obvious as the one matching contiguity and spatial rivalry. But as long as we restrict the field of dispute types to only two, it is a logical corollary to the first observation in the sense that nonadjacent rivals are less likely to quarrel over territory that cannot, by definition, be adjacent to both actors. Yet the very existence of a rivalry indicates that the two states are competing over something. If we restrict the types of issues to only two, noncontiguous rivals are more apt to be concerned with positional issues than are contiguous rivals.

Neither of the above statements implies that contiguous rivals never compete over position or that noncontiguous rivals cannot become embroiled in territorial disputes. Nor do they suggest that either type of rivalry cannot compete over both issues simultaneously. The statements only suggest probabilities. Distance cannot determine who becomes unhappy with whom, or what they become unhappy about. Still, proximity does have some influence in world politics. States in two different continents are unlikely to have much interaction, let alone become involved in competition and conflict. When they do become involved in competition and conflict, it is likely to be over matters that go beyond who controls a piece of territory. Proximate states, on the other hand, are likely at some point in their history to dispute boundaries and territorial control.

We also argue that **contests with strong positional overtones are less likely to escalate to war but that once they do escalate, they are more likely to have widespread implications for other states than are contests with predominantly spatial overtones**. There are several reasons why positional contests have relatively less potential for escalation to war than spatial contests. Territorial disputes can arise in all sorts of dyadic power situations – between states of equal power and between states of unequal power. They can also arise in geographical circumstances that may give (or seem to give) one state some sort of logistical advantage over its rival. For instance, Pakistan has long enjoyed an advantage in physical access to contested Kashmir over its more powerful rival, India. Territorial disputes also make excellent domestic weapons to use against incumbents and oppositions, regardless of external asymmetries. Decision-makers may find themselves tempted or forced to do something about ongoing territorial disputes in order to save their domestic political positions. The upshot of these multiple features of incentive structures is that states are episodically attracted to violent resolutions of their territorial disputes.

Positional contests, on the other hand, are more likely to be waged between states with roughly equal capabilities. A state with little prestige is unlikely to fight a state high in the pecking order over issues of whose status is greater. They may fight but it is more likely to be over other issues, unless perhaps the issue is whether the weaker state is choosing to resist subordination to the stronger state. Two states with similar status, though, have strong incentives to make sure that the other state does not pull ahead. Similar status suggests similar capability foundations, and, therefore, greater caution in pursuing the contest more violently. In these circumstances, the uncertainty of the outcome should make decision-makers think twice before resorting to coercion and violence. Relative position is also a more abstract issue than who controls which particular territory. While decision-makers may worry constantly about whether rivals are getting ahead, it may prove more difficult to arouse populations to make sacrifices in the name of prestige, glory, and relative standings alone – unless, of course, they are facilitated by an external attack.

Then, too, positional contests, especially in the major power subsystem, have tended to be fought by different sorts of states. One way to characterize at least the last 500 years of international politics is as an intermittent struggle between ascending regional hegemons and declining global system leaders (Rasler and Thompson, 1994). Regional hegemons tend to base their challenge on land power while system leaders emphasize economic growth, trade, and maritime capability. Whales (sea powers) and elephants (land powers) find it difficult to defeat the other type of rival without substantial help. Whales need elephant allies to defeat elephant challengers. The converse is true as well. This is another reason for exercising caution in escalating positional contests.

Yet once a positional contest has escalated to war, other states are tempted to enter the fray to the extent that their own relative positions may be affected by the outcome. A state aspiring to regional or global hegemony potentially threatens all other states in the same system. Success would mean, among other things, a reduction in relative position for losers and bystanders alike. Bystanders, by definition, are also apt to lose out on opportunities to join the winning side and to enjoy the postwar allocation of war spoils. Whether "balancing" or "bandwagoning," then, there is considerable incentive to take sides in an ongoing positional war. There are also equal incentives for the original participants to induce others to join such contests if they think they stand better chances of winning. More relative position might be gained by going it alone but retaining as much relative position as possible when threatened by a strong adversary encourages the creation of war coalitions – often only after the war has begun.

Some of these same considerations might seem to hold as well for wars with strong spatial overtones. The difference is that territory is more difficult for a coalition to share unless the space available for allocation is situated in a number of different places. A specific piece of territory that is adjacent to the two states quarreling over it is less likely to attract third party involvement unless the third parties are also adjacent, they become involved to ensure that the fighting does not spread beyond the immediate disputants, or they seize the opportunity to gain something from the embattled disputants in a moment of vulnerability.

Yet there is one major caveat to these arguments. Major powers do not fight over territorial issues in a world that is somehow distinct from their positional quarrels. The two types of issues are intertwined and sometimes difficult to tell apart. But some of the constraints that are thought to operate on the escalation of positional disputes may also hold for territorial dispute escalation, at least for major powers and other subsystems in which positional considerations are critical. Two major powers, other things being equal, are more likely to be roughly equal in resources than any other type of dyad. If we think this rough equality may constrain positional conflicts, why should it not also have the same effect on spatial conflicts?

Major powers, unlike minor powers, are more likely to be in a capability position to contest the control of distant territory. But if we think distant territory tends to be less valued than nearby territory, that may also work toward constraining some spatial conflicts between at least major powers. For that matter, spatial gains by major powers imply positional gains and, therefore, there should be some systemic incentive to make sure other major powers do not profit too greatly by winning a spatial dispute.

Major powers then must be especially concerned by the possible multi-lateralization of an initial fight between two major powers. This problem could also serve as an additional constraint on spatial wars in the major power subsystem.

While we suspect that positional rivalries are less war-prone in the larger population, it is not at all clear that this generalization should apply equally well to the major power subsystem where there are sub-stantial constraints on both types of conflict. If we extend the logic of our claim that both types of issues deserve attention, it may well be that the more both types of issues are salient, the more they are equally prone to escalation to war.

This discussion yields three central statements:

1. Contiguous rivals are more likely to be involved in contests with strong spatial overtones while noncontiguous rivals are more likely to be involved in contests with strong positional overtones.
2. In general, contests with strong positional overtones are less likely to escalate to war than are contests with strong spatial overtones. The exceptions to this rule are likely to be subsystems in which both types of issues are equally salient, as in the case of the major power subsystem.
3. Once contests with strong positional overtones do escalate to war, they are more likely to have implications for non-participants than are contests with only strong spatial overtones. Initial non-participants, therefore, are more likely to join such wars than they are to join wars with strong spatial overtones. Put differently, contests with strong positional overtones are less likely to remain strictly dyadic contests; they are more likely to become multilateral contests than are contests with strong spatial overtones.

From these core statements, it is possible to derive some of the same hypotheses that are associated with Vasquez's focus on one type of issue. As we have noted previously, we are retaining Vasquez's two-path approach while at the same time providing equal explanatory rationales for actors following one path versus the other. It is also possible to derive several others that cannot be derived from the singular emphasis on terri-tory. One of these is the exception to the asserted rule about relative posi-tional/spatial propensities for war escalation. But there are three others.

Vasquez's one issue argument would suggest that the following state-ments should hold for all samples (for instance, major power subsystems as well as systems combining both major and non-major powers):

a. Noncontiguous rivalries are more rare than are contiguous rivalries;
b. Dyadic wars are more common than are multilateral wars;
c. Most wars are more likely to be fought by the original participants than they are to be expanded by war joiners.

All three hypotheses stem from the twin assumptions that wars are mainly about territory and that rivalries predominantly involve contiguous adversaries disputing territorial issues. Noncontiguous rivalries should be rare because the rivals are unlikely to be contending over territory – the main cause of escalation. For that matter, what do they have to be rivals about? If noncontiguous rivalries are rare, war joining by noncontiguous rivals should also be rare. Wars would therefore be more likely to remain dyadic in form or at least restricted to the initial disputants in form.

Introducing a second type of issue leads to three different expectations – all very much contingent on the existence and prevalence of contests over position, as opposed primarily to contests over spatial control. If territory is not the only escalator, noncontiguous rivalries are not necessarily any more rare than contiguous rivalries, as long as the adversaries have sufficient resources to engage in noncontiguous conflict. Or, to put it another way, strong positional elements will encourage noncontiguous rivalries.

a. The stronger the presence of positional grievances and concerns, the greater are the number of noncontiguous rivalries.

   If territorial disputes are not the sole or even the primary driver of war escalations, we would have less reason to anticipate that dyadic wars are more common than multilateral wars. Strong positional grievances will encourage multilateral wars.

b. The stronger the presence of positional grievances and concerns, the greater are the tendencies toward multilateral wars.

   The ratio of war joiners to original participants depends on the mix of positional versus spatial issues. Strong positional grievances will encourage war joining because the war outcome is more likely to affect the relative positions of participants and nonparticipants alike than are disputes over adjacent territory.

c. The stronger the presence of positional grievances and concerns, the greater are the tendencies toward war-joining behavior.

   If we add the earlier argument that major power rivals are more likely to contest positions than are non-major power rivals, it follows from the three hypotheses immediately above that we should expect the major power subsystem to be characterized quite strongly by pronounced tendencies toward noncontiguous rivalries, multilateral wars, and war joining. Contiguous rivalries, dyadic wars, and the absence of war joining should be more common among non-major powers. Yet even though our immediate focus is placed entirely on the major power subsystem, there is no reason that these hypotheses could not also be employed in the comparative examination of regional rivalry patterns. The Middle East, for example, is another arena that is characterized by strong positional conflict, especially among Arab rivals. In contrast, South America has its ABC powers but it also has a history of a number of rivalries in which territorial disputes loom large.

More specifically, we propose to test, or at least to begin addressing, the following hypotheses:

H1. In systems characterized by the salience of positional concerns, noncontiguous rivalries are more common than is the case where positional concerns are less salient.

H2. In systems characterized by the salience of positional concerns, war joining and multilateral wars are more common than is the case where positional concerns are less salient.

H3. Contiguous dyads, as opposed to noncontiguous dyads, are more likely to be embroiled in spatial rivalries.

H4. Noncontiguous dyads, as opposed to contiguous dyads, are more likely to be embroiled in positional rivalries.

H5. In general, positional rivalries are less likely to escalate to war than spatial rivalries but in systems characterized by the salience of positional concerns, there may be no significant difference between the war escalation propensities of positional and spatial rivalries.

H6. Once positional rivalries do escalate to war, they are more likely to attract war joiners and to become multilateral affairs than are wars between spatial rivals.

The operational choices

Spatial and positional disputes do not exhaust the possible foci of rivalries. Other issues (see Chapter 3) include such topics as ideological disagreements, the treatment of ethnic minorities, and the assistance of another state's domestic opponents. Sometimes these issues are linked to spatial and positional considerations and sometimes they are not. But that only means that there are other ways to categorize rivalry types. Knowing that there may be other types of issues does not tell us how to distinguish spatial from positional issues and rivalries. The problem is compounded further by the frequent entanglement of spatial and positional issues. Pakistan and India dispute control over Kashmir – a clear spatial issue. Yet they also dispute India's claim to South Asian predominance – a clear positional issue – and it is not always clear whether Kashmir is primarily a spatial contest or another venue for contesting the positional contest.

The approach taken here to distinguish between spatial and positional issues relies on an inventory of the apparent issues at stake in a rivalry. If there is a dispute over territorial control, the rivalry encompasses a spatial issue. If there is a dispute over relative status and influence, ranking, or pecking order in a regional or international hierarchy, the rivalry encompasses a positional issue. If only one of these two types of issues exists, the rivalry can be regarded as either spatial or positional in nature, depending on which type of issue characterizes the dyadic conflict.

When both types of issues are present, the coding situation is more complicated. If both types of issues seemed equally salient, a "mixed" categorization would be inescapable. However, equal salience does not appear to be the rule in the major power cases. Accordingly, we have approached this problem in two ways. The most conservative approach stipulates that if a rivalry encompasses any spatial issues, then the rivalry is a spatial rivalry. Only if no spatial issue is involved and a positional issue is involved can it be viewed as a positional rivalry.

A less conservative approach suggests that a rivalry could encompass one or more spatial issues but still be primarily about position. But how can we determine relative issue weight in a non-arbitrary fashion? Our solution was to make further distinctions about the spatial and positional issues. Spatial issues can be either about local (i.e., adjacent) or distant (e.g., colonial) territory. Positional issues can be either about regional (another type of local) or global hierarchies. Any given rivalry could then be either purely spatial or positional or some combination of spatial and positional issues – which implies some combination of local/distant spatial and regional/global positional issues. We next created the continuum outlined in Table 6.1. Where one draws the line between whether a rivalry is *primarily* spatial or positional is not something that is carved in stone. We chose to draw our line between the combination of local territory–regional/global positional issues and distant territory/regional positional issues. Rivalries on one side of the former scalar point were considered primarily spatial and, if they were on the side of the latter scalar point, they were coded primarily positional. Table 6.2 provides a list of both types of spatial/positional categorizations.

Although we favor the less conservative issue distinction approach as the more appropriate one, we use both approaches in testing hypotheses distinguishing between types of rivalry. Even though we are also focusing exclusively on the major power subsystem, we choose not to censor any information on the conflict behavior of major power dyads that may have occurred before or after they had attained major power status. This approach yields 36 major power dyads listed in Table 6.2. Of the 36,

Table 6.1 *The spatial–positional continuum*

"Pure" spatial
X
X
Local territory – regional position
X
X
Local-distant territory – regional position
X
X
X
Local-distant territory – global position
X
X
X
Local territory – regional/global position
X
X
X
Distant territory – regional position
X
X
X
Distant territory – global position
X
X
X
"Pure" positional

some are major power dyads throughout the 1816–1992 period that we examine.[2] Others are only intermittently major power dyads. Four never attain major power dyadic status because their members were considered major powers in non-overlapping periods. Thirty-six dyads hardly provides a full sample of major and non-major power pairs but it does permit

---

[2] Vasquez includes the Napoleonic Wars for the Anglo-French rivalry on the grounds that one of the rivalry data sources indicated the rivalry preceded 1816. But the same can be said for a number of other major power rivalries that did not have earlier wars included. Moreover, one wonders just how far back in time an analyst would have to move in order to isolate the beginnings of some major power rivalries. In this study, we use the standard Correlates of War identifications of major powers and wars between major powers, with one exception. We balk at accepting COW's elevation of Japan and Germany to major power status in the early 1990s.

Table 6.2 *Major power status, contiguity, rivalry, and rivalry type*

Dyad	Major power	National contiguity	Imperial contiguity	Rivalry	Rivalry type A	Rivalry type B
AUS–BRIT	1816–1918	Absent	Absent	Absent	NA	NA
AUS–CHIN	NA	Absent	Absent	Absent	NA	NA
AUS–FRN	1816–1918	Absent	Absent	1816–1918	P	P
AUS–GER	1816–1918	1816–1992	1816–1992	1816–1870	S	S
AUS–ITL	1860–1918	1816–1992	1816–1992	1848–1918	S	S
AUS–JAP	1895–1918	Absent	Absent	Absent	NA	NA
AUS–RUS	1816–1918	1816–1918	1816–1918	1816–1918	P	P
AUS–USA	1899–1918	Absent	Absent	Absent	NA	NA
BRIT–CHIN	1950–1992	Absent	1840–1992	1831–1941	S	S
BRIT–FRN	1816–1992	1816–1992	1816–1992	1816–1904	S	P
BRIT–GER	1816–1945	Absent	1884–1918	1896–1918	S	P
				1934–1945	P	P
BRIT–ITL	1860–1943	Absent	1889–1943	1934–1943	S	P
BRIT–JAP	1895–1945	Absent	Absent	1932–1945	P	P
BRIT–RUS	1816–1992	Absent	1868–1904	1816–1956	S	P
BRIT–USA	1899–1945	Absent	1816–1992	1816–1904	S	P
CHN–FRN	1950–1992	Absent	1884–1954	1844–1940	S	S
CHN–GER	NA	Absent	1898–1914	Absent	NA	NA
CHN–ITL	NA	Absent	Absent	Absent	NA	NA

Dyad					A	B
CHN–JAP	NA	1816–1992	1816–1992	1873–1945	S	S
CHN–RUS	1950–1992	1816–1992	1816–1992	1816–1949 1958–1989	S S	S S
CHN–USA	1950–1992	Absent	Absent	1949–1978	P	P
FRN–GER	1816–1945	1816–1992	1816–1992	1816–1945	S	P
FRN–ITL	1860–1943	1816–1992	1816–1992	1881–1940	S	S
FRN–JAP	1895–1945	Absent	Absent	Absent	NA	NA
FRN–RUS	1816–1992	Absent	Absent	1816–1894	P	P
FRN–USA	1899–1992	Absent	1862–1866	1863–1871	S	S
GER–ITL	1860–1943	Absent	Absent	Absent	NA	NA
GER–JAP	1895–1945	Absent	Absent	Absent	NA	NA
GER–RUS	1816–1945	1816–1918 1940–1945	1816–1918 1940–1945	1890–1945	S	S
GER–USA	1899–1945	Absent	Absent	1889–1918 1939–1945	S P	P P
ITL–JAP	1895–1943	Absent	Absent	Absent	NA	NA
ITL–RUS	1860–1943	Absent	Absent	1936–1943	P	P
ITL–USA	1899–1943	Absent	Absent	Absent	NA	NA
JAP–RUS	1895–1945	1853–1992	1853–1992	1853–1945	S	S
JAP–USA	1899–1945	Absent	Absent	1900–1945	S	P
RUS–USA	1899–1992	1867–1992	1867–1992	1945–1989	P	P

Note: Rivalry types A and B refer, respectively, to the two approaches to operationalizing the predominant type of issue being contested. Type A codes rivalries as spatial if there is any territorial issue and positional only if there is no spatial issue. Type B codes rivalries as spatial or positional depending on where they fall in the continuum portrayed in this table.

Table 6.3 *A list of dyads and their war involvement*

Dyad	War years	War participation	War type
GB–Germany	1914–18	GB joiner	Multilateral
GB–Germany	1939–45	GB joiner	Multilateral
GB–Russia	1854–56	GB joiner	Multilateral
GB–Italy	1940–43	Italy joiner	Multilateral
GB–Japan	1941–45	Japan joiner	Multilateral
GB–China	1900		Multilateral
GB–China	1950–53	China joiner	Multilateral
France–Germany	1870–71		Multilateral
France–Germany	1914–18	France joiner	Multilateral
France–Germany	1939–40	France joiner	Multilateral
France–Russia	1854–56	France joiner	Multilateral
France–Austria	1859	France joiner	Multilateral
France–Austria	1914–18	France joiner	Multilateral
France–Italy	1940	Italy joiner	Multilateral
France–China	1884–85		Dyadic
France–China	1900		Multilateral
France–China	1951–53	France joiner	Multilateral
Germany–Russia	1914–17	Russia joiner	Multilateral
Germany–Russia	1941–45	Russia joiner	Multilateral
Germany–Austria	1866		Multilateral
Germany–USA	1917–18	USA joiner	Multilateral
Germany–USA	1941–45	Germany joiner	Multilateral
Russia–Austria	1914–17	Russia joiner	Multilateral
Russia–Italy	1855–56	Italy joiner	Multilateral
Russia–Italy	1941–43	Russia joiner	Multilateral
Russia–Japan	1904–05		Dyadic
Russia–Japan	1938		Dyadic
Russia–Japan	1939		Multilateral
Russia–Japan	1945	Russia joiner	Multilateral
Russia–China	1900		Multilateral
Russia–China	1929		Dyadic
Austria–Italy	1848–49		Multilateral
Austria–Italy	1859		Multilateral
Austria–Italy	1866	Italy joiner	Multilateral
Austria–Italy	1915–18	Italy joiner	Multilateral
Japan–USA	1941–45		Multilateral
USA–China	1900		Multilateral
USA–China	1950–53	China joiner	Multilateral
Japan–Germany	1914–18	Japan joiner	Multilateral
Japan–Austria	1914–18	Japan joiner	Multilateral
USA–Austria	1917–18	USA joiner	Multilateral
GB–Austria	1914–18	GB joiner	Multilateral
Italy–Germany	1915–18	Italy joiner	Multilateral
USA–Italy	1941–43	USA joiner	Multilateral
Japan–China	1894–95		Dyadic
Japan–China	1900		Multilateral
Japan–China	1931–33		Dyadic
Japan–China	1937–41		Dyadic
Japan–China	1941–45		Multilateral
China–Germany	1941–45	China joiner	Multilateral
China–Italy	1941–43	China joiner	Multilateral

us to check whether the major powers' status makes some difference to our outcomes (along lines suggested in Lemke and Reed, 1998). In most cases, we will report results with and without the major power filter. As in the Vasquez (1996) study, we examine war onset years in those hypotheses (hypotheses 5 and 6) that explicitly address war behavior. Non-onset war years are removed from the analysis in these instances.

We employ the same contiguity measure that Vasquez relied on but we choose to supplement its analysis with a second measure.[3] Vasquez's contiguity measure is predicated on the distance between the home bases of the major powers and ignores colonial territory. For this reason, we refer to it as the "national" contiguity measure. A second measure, referred to as the "imperial" contiguity measure, incorporates adjacent colonial territory as appropriate.

As far as we can tell, there is no disagreement over the status of dyadic (only two opponents) versus multilateral wars. The last variable to operationalize is war joining. We are unsure how this variable was operationalized in the 1996 study. Our own approach is conservative. Small and Singer (1982) list war participants by the date of war entry. Any participants that choose to enter a war after the earliest date of onset or participation are considered "joiners." We can imagine other approaches – allowing one day, one week, one month, one year, and so on for initial participants to become involved – but we see no compelling reason or rationale for tolerating lapses of time between onset and participation. This information is made available in Table 6.3.

Data analysis

The first two hypotheses concern the ratios of contiguous to noncontiguous rivals, dyadic to multilateral wars, and original participation to war joining. High ratios would support the theory that emphasizes territory as the main issue leading to war escalation. Low ratios would support the possibility that other types of issues, namely positional quarrels, can be as significant in at least some circumstances.

Using Vasquez's contiguity approach, only 9 of 21 (about 43 percent) major power rivalry dyads involve adjacent adversaries. Thus, contiguous rivalries are common but hardly the norm for this particular population. If we look instead at imperial contiguity, the proportion is 13 of 21, or

[3] One exception is the Germany–Russia dyad which Vasquez codes as contiguous. We code it contiguous for all years of rivalry except the 1918–39 period. Another concerns the US–Russian dyad. Vasquez chose to ignore the proximity of Alaska to Russian soil. We make no exceptions. Our contiguity codings are made by the authors based on information found in Haywood with Catchpole, Hall, and Barratt (1997).

about 62 percent. This proportion begins to approximate a norm but one should also keep in mind that the genuinely imperial dimension of such contiguity is often intermittent.

Moreover, seven of the twelve non-adjacent rivalry dyads involve Britain (with Germany, Russia, Japan, and the United States) or the United States (with Germany, Russia, Japan, and China) as one dyadic member.[4] Most of the nonadjacent rivalries are thus overlapping in terms of issue-area and their connections to successive eras of systemic leadership. This observation suggests that the contiguous–noncontiguous division may mask other variables differentiating major power rivalries. Somewhat tangentially, one could also raise the question of whether the respective Anglo-Russian (the nineteenth-century Great Game) and American-Soviet struggles (the twentieth-century Cold War) over control of Eurasia should be viewed strictly speaking as territorial disputes or broader disputes over relative position. We acknowledge that territorial control in places such as Jerusalem, Afghanistan, Persia, Berlin, Korea, and Vietnam was hardly unimportant. But we would also argue that territorial control was in large part important not so much for its own sake, but in terms of what gaining/losing control meant for the relative positions of the major power rivals.

We are also assuming, of course, that contiguity necessarily equates to the likelihood of territorial disputes. Another way to look at this problem is to examine the nine contiguous rivalries. How many obviously involve territorial disputes? How many involve territorial disputes over core or metropolitan territory, as opposed to more peripheral, colonial territories – an argument related to two auxiliary hypotheses also proposed by Vasquez.[5] Four of the nine (France–Germany, Austria–Prussia, Russia–China, and Austria–Hungary–Italy) certainly involved disputes over contested territory and borders, but each involved other issues. France and Germany clashed over western European hegemony. Russia and China, when both had major power status, clashed over leadership of the Communist world. Austria and Prussia clashed over hegemony in the greater German area. Whether one wishes to confine the Austrian–Italian feud to a question of territorial control depends on how one views

---

[4] The other three rivalries are Austria–France, France–Russia, and Italy–Russia. The first two were nineteenth-century carry-overs from the Napoleonic era or earlier and one, Austria–France, had once been contiguous. The Italian-Russian rivalry was short-lived and stemmed initially from their participation in the Spanish Civil War and that conflict's relationship to Italian ambitions *vis-à-vis* Mediterranean position.

[5] More specifically, the auxiliary hypotheses are: (1) rivals in dispute with each other over core territory are more apt to go to war than rivals disputing over peripheral (including colonial) territory; and (2) rivals fighting over core territory are apt to fight more intensely than rivals fighting over peripheral territory.

the Italian state-making process and the need to break free of Austrian control.

Three of the nine (Germany–Russia, Russia–Austria–Hungary, and Russia–Japan) are debatable as to whether one should regard their disputes as ones over core or peripheral territory, just who regarded them as such, and when. The last two cases (France–Italy and Britain–France) had once had core territorial disputes but their overt conflicts were clearly more oriented to relatively peripheral territory in the late nineteenth century and first half of the twentieth.

The general point is that (non)contiguous status in the major power subsystem is not an uncontroversial proxy for either territorial or positional disputes. The connection probably works much better for non-major powers than it does for major powers with their more complex foreign policy agendas.

It is also worth noting that one might make two other motivations as alternative theoretical foundations and arrive at much the same set of hypotheses. If one equated threat intensity with proximity, contiguous (noncontiguous) rivals would be more (less) likely to go to war as original participants. Or, if one equated the opportunity to go to war, or the relative ease of warfare breaking out for whatever reason, with proximity, contiguous (noncontiguous) rivals would also be more (less) likely to go to war as original participants. The bottom line is that if we find a relationship between contiguity and the war behavior of rivals, it is not entirely clear how best to interpret it. It could be traced to issues, the intensity of threat, the convenience of making war, or some combination of all three.[6]

Nevertheless, the possibility of multiple interpretations is not unique to the examination of contiguity. The role of regime type in democratic peace arguments is somewhat similar. If we find a relationship between regime type and war behavior, should we attribute it to institutional restraints, normative constraints, or something else? We are no more likely to fully

---

[6] Huth (1996b) codes specific issues involved in territorial diputes but only after World War I. A number of studies (Holsti, 1991; Kocs, 1995; Hensel, 1996; Senese, 1996; Gibler, 1997; Senese, Vasquez, and Henehan, 1998; Hensel and Sowers, 1998; Lemke and Reed, 1998; and Ben-Yehuda, 1998) introduce issue data from different data sets, but it is clear that they do not help in differentiating spatial from positional issues as discussed in this examination. Ben-Yehuda's (1998) analysis and other studies (Toset and Gleditsch, 1998; and Mitchell and Prins, 1999) are also beginning the task, already well demonstrated in Huth (1996b), that we need more information on what exactly is involved in territorial disputes. It seems most likely that we will need to further specify how different types of disputes involving spatial elements lead to variable types of behavior. In this respect, we would expect spatial issues to be more complex than positional issues. Alternatively put, some types of territorial issues are apt to be more dangerous than other types. Huth (1996b), for instance, finds different types of territorial issues to be important for understanding the genesis, escalation, and/or the termination of disputes.

resolve the ambiguities associated with contiguity than we are to break the interpretation deadlock over the democratic peace in this examination. Our immediate purpose, therefore, is focused on ascertaining whether and to what extent contiguity is important to the conflict behavior in which rivals are engaged.

Table 6.3 summarizes major power war behavior in terms of dyads, war type, and war-joining behavior. It is clear that the major power data are highly skewed. Dyadic warfare is quite rare. Only seven cases are listed (making the ratio 7:44). Of these seven, two (Russia and Japan in 1904–5 and 1938) involved full-fledged major power dyads. The other five involved China at some time prior to its post-civil war, major power status. All seven took place in Eastern Asia before World War II and, therefore, may be telling us as much about the implications of the extra-European diffusion of major power status as they are about war-joining propensities. Major powers have also been much less likely to be original participants than war joiners. The ratio is 6:23 for major power dyads.

Thus, the outcome for our first two hypotheses provides strong support for the two-issue theory. In the major power subsystem, noncontiguous rivals outnumber contiguous rivals, dyadic wars are extremely scarce, and war joining has been the norm. If we accord positional disputes equal theoretical status with spatial issues, this outcome is predictable. It is not if our theory focuses solely on spatial issues.

Table 6.4 displays the first two empirical outcomes (one cross-tabulation for each possible combination of contiguity measure, major power status, and issue measure) for hypotheses 3 and 4 which predict, respectively, that contiguous rivals are more likely to become involved in spatial rivalries while noncontiguous rivals are more likely to become involved in positional disputes. Regardless of the contiguity measure used, the data uniformly support hypothesis 3. Without exception, contiguous rivals are likely to be involved in spatial rivalries and more so than non-contiguous rivals.[7]

Hypothesis 4, linking noncontiguous dyads with positional rivalries, garners its greatest support in the bottom halves of Table 6.4. If we ask only whether there is a spatial component in the rivalry, noncontiguous rivals are more difficult to distinguish than their contiguous counter-parts. For instance, noncontiguous, major power rivals, differentiated by national contiguity (first cross-tabs in Table 6.4), are split virtually 50–50 on this score. If major power status is not controlled, this combination

---

[7] We should note that our analyses in Table 6.4 (as well as in Tables 6.5 and 6.6) depart from the earlier Vasquez study by focusing empirically on the number of rivalry years, as opposed to the number of rivalries. Our results would not change significantly, however, if we adopted the alternative unit of analysis.

Table 6.4 *Contiguity and rivalry type*

RIVALRY TYPE A PROCEDURE
National

	Contiguity	Noncontiguity	Total
Spatial	511 (77.5)	261 (50.3)	772 (66.5)
Positional	148 (22.5)	258 (49.7)	406 (34.5)
Total	659 (100.0)	519 (100.0)	1178 (100.0)

Chi-square 95.5**, $p = 0.00$

RIVALRY TYPE A PROCEDURE
Imperial

	Contiguity	Noncontiguity	Total
Spatial	581 (79.0)	191 (43.1)	772 (65.5)
Positional	154 (21.0)	252 (56.9)	406 (34.5)
Total	735 (100.0)	443 (100.0)	1178 (100.0)

Chi-square 158.0**, $p = 0.00$

RIVALRY TYPE B PROCEDURE
National

	Contiguity	Noncontiguity	Total
Spatial	422 (64.0)	21 (4.0)	443 (37.6)
Positional	237 (36.0)	498 (96.0)	735 (62.4)
Total	659 (100.0)	519 (100.0)	1178 (100.0)

Chi-square 445.3**, $p = 0.00$

RIVALRY TYPE B PROCEDURE
Imperial

	Contiguity	Noncontiguity	Total
Spatial	422 (57.4)	21 (4.7)	443 (37.6)
Positional	313 (42.6)	422 (95.3)	735 (62.4)
Total	735 (100.0)	443 (100.0)	1178 (100.0)

Chi-square = 299.3**, $p = 0.00$

(*cont.*)

Table 6.4 (*cont.*)

RIVALRY TYPE A PROCEDURE
National

	Contiguity	Noncontiguity	Total
Spatial	751 (83.5)	493 (56.2)	1244 (70.1)
Positional	148 (16.5)	384 (43.8)	532 (29.9)
Total	899 (100.0)	877 (100.0)	1776 (100.0)

Chi-square 157.9**, $p = 0.00$

RIVALRY TYPE A PROCEDURE
Imperial

	Contiguity	Noncontiguity	Total
Spatial	980 (80.2)	264 (47.7)	1244 (70.1)
Positional	242 (19.8)	290 (52.3)	532 (29.9)
Total	1222 (100.0)	554 (100.0)	1776 (100.0)

Chi-square 192.4**, $p = 0.00$

RIVALRY TYPE B PROCEDURE
National

	Contiguity	Noncontiguity	Total
Spatial	662 (73.6)	243 (27.7)	905 (51.0)
Positional	237 (26.4)	634 (72.3)	871 (49.0)
Total	899 (100.0)	877 (100.0)	1776 (100.0)

Chi-square 374.7**, $p = 0.00$

RIVALRY TYPE B PROCEDURE
Imperial

	Contiguity	Noncontiguity	Total
Spatial	821 (67.2)	84 (15.2)	905 (51.0)
Positional	401 (32.8)	470 (84.8)	871 (49.0)
Total	1222 (100.0)	554 (100.0)	1776 (100.0)

Chi-square = 412.8**, $p = 0.00$

actually leans toward the spatial end of the spectrum. If one looks instead at imperial contiguity, noncontiguous rivals are somewhat more likely to be positional rivals, which is not what one might expect since an imperial perspective should expand the opportunities for spatial conflicts (second and third cross-tabs in table 6.4).

Nevertheless, six of the eight cross-tabulations suggest that noncontiguous rivals are more positionally inclined than are contiguous rivals – which is what hypotheses 3 and 4 predict. The distinction is particularly noticeable if we look at the more demanding version of rivalry type. When the focus is on whether rivalries are predominantly spatial or positional in emphasis, major power, noncontiguous rivalries are overwhelmingly located in the positional row. Removing the control for major power status makes the distinction less overwhelming, but only marginally so. In general, the evidence provides ample support for hypotheses 3 and 4.

The fifth hypothesis predicts little difference between spatial and positional rivalries in war propensity as long as the two types of grievances are equally salient. Table 6.5 displays four pertinent cross-tabulations: the two upper ones control for major power status and the two lower ones do not. Regardless of which version of issue differentiation is employed, spatial and positional rivalries in the major power subsystem have demonstrated no statistically significant difference in their tendencies to escalate to war. With the more demanding basis for distinguishing issue type (pertaining to the second cross-tabs in Table 6.5), spatial rivalries have escalated to war more often (3.1 versus 2.0 percent), but the difference remains insignificant. If we relax the control for major power status, however, the difference in war propensities is a bit more pronounced (2.8 versus 1.7 percent) and this difference is statistically significant at the 0.11 level (lower fourth cross-tab in Table 6.5).

As in the cases of hypotheses 1 and 2, testing hypothesis 5 ultimately calls for a sample larger than the major powers. We need more variation on issue type salience. Still, the outcome in Table 6.5 is quite supportive. When both types of issues are salient, as we assert they are in the major power subsystem, the war propensities of spatial and positional rivalries are about the same. Spatial rivalries begin to appear more war-like only when we begin to move outside of the major power subsystem. Of course, the data summarized in Table 6.5 do not move very far outside of the major power subsystem. More information on non-major power rivalries will be needed to assess hypothesis 5 more fully.

Hypothesis 6 relates rivalry issue type to war joining and dyadic/ multilateral war participation. Spatial rivals are expected to be more prone to dyadic warfare while positional rivals are expected to specialize in multilateral and war-joining warfare. Tables 6.6 and 6.7 offer eight

Table 6.5 *Rivalry type and war onset*

RIVALRY TYPE A PROCEDURE
Rivalry

	Spatial	Positional	Total
No war	723 (97.6)	369 (97.6)	1092 (97.6)
War	18 (2.4)	9 (2.4)	27 (2.4)
Total	741 (100.0)	378 (100.0)	1119 (100.0)

Chi-square 0.00, $p = 0.96$; excluding war yrs.

RIVALRY TYPE B PROCEDURE
Rivalry

	Spatial	Positional	Total
No war	413 (96.9)	679 (98.0)	1092 (97.6)
War	13 (3.1)	14 (2.0)	27 (2.4)
Total	426 (100.0)	693 (100.0)	1119 (100.0)

Chi-square 1.2, $p = 0.28$; excluding war yrs.

RIVALRY TYPE A PROCEDURE (WITHOUT
MAJOR POWER CONTROL)
Rivalry

	Spatial	Positional	Total
No war	1171 (97.5)	495 (98.2)	1666 (97.7)
War	30 (2.5)	9 (1.8)	39 (2.3)
Total	1201 (100.0)	504 (100.0)	1705 (100.0)

Chi-square 0.81, $p = 0.37$; excluding war yrs.

RIVALRY TYPE B PROCEDURE (WITHOUT
MAJOR POWER CONTROL)
Rivalry

	Spatial	Positional	Total
No war	851 (97.2)	815 (98.3)	1666 (97.7)
War	25 (2.8)	14 (1.7)	39 (2.3)
Total	876 (100.0)	829 (100.0)	1705 (100.0)

Chi-square 2.6*, $p = 0.11$; excluding war yrs.

Table 6.6 *Rivalry type and war types during war onsets*

RIVALRY TYPE A PROCEDURE
Rivalry

	Spatial	Positional	Total
Dyadic	2 (11.1)	0 (0.0)	2 (7.4)
Multilateral	16 (88.9)	9 (100.0)	25 (92.6)
Total	18 (100.0)	9 (100.0)	27 (100.0)

Fisher's exact test: $p = 0.54$

RIVALRY TYPE B PROCEDURE
Rivalry

	Spatial	Positional	Total
Dyadic	2 (15.4)	0 (0.0)	2 (7.4)
Multilateral	11 (84.6)	14 (100.0)	25 (92.6)
Total	13 (100.0)	14 (100.0)	27 (100.0)

Fisher's exact test: $p = 0.22$

RIVALRY TYPE A PROCEDURE (WITHOUT MAJOR POWER CONTROL)
Rivalry

	Spatial	Positional	Total
Dyadic	7 (23.3)	0 (0.0)	7 (17.9)
Multilateral	23 (76.7)	9 (100.0)	32 (82.1)
Total	30 (100.0)	9 (100.0)	39 (100.0)

Fisher's exact test: $p = 0.17$

RIVALRY TYPE B PROCEDURE (WITHOUT MAJOR POWER CONTROL)
Rivalry

	Spatial	Positional	Total
Dyadic	7 (28.0)	0 (0.0)	7 (17.9)
Multilateral	18 (72.0)	14 (100.0)	32 (82.1)
Total	25 (100.0)	14 (100.0)	39 (100.0)

Fisher's exact test: $p = 0.02^{**}$

Table 6.7 *Rivalry type and war joining during war onsets*

RIVALRY TYPE A PROCEDURE
Rivalry

	Spatial	Positional	Total
Nonjoiner	7 (38.9)	1 (11.1)	8 (29.6)
Joiner	11 (61.1)	8 (88.9)	19 (70.4)
Total	18 (100.0)	9 (100.0)	27 (100.0)

Fisher's exact test: $p = 0.15$

RIVALRY TYPE B PROCEDURE
Rivalry

	Spatial	Positional	Total
Nonjoiner	5 (38.5)	3 (21.4)	8 (29.6)
Joiner	8 (61.5)	11 (78.6)	19 (70.4)
Total	13 (100.0)	14 (100.0)	27 (100.0)

Fisher's exact test: $p = 0.29$

RIVALRY TYPE A PROCEDURE (WITHOUT MAJOR POWER CONTROL)
Rivalry

	Spatial	Positional	Total
Nonjoiner	19 (63.3)	1 (11.1)	20 (51.3)
Joiner	11 (36.7)	8 (88.9)	19 (48.7)
Total	30 (100.0)	9 (100.0)	39 (100.0)

Fisher's exact test: $p = 0.01^{**}$

RIVALRY TYPE B PROCEDURE (WITHOUT MAJOR POWER CONTROL)
Rivalry

	Spatial	Positional	Total
Nonjoiner	17 (68.0)	3 (21.4)	20 (51.3)
Joiner	8 (32.0)	11 (78.6)	19 (48.7)
Total	25 (100.0)	14 (100.0)	39 (100.0)

Fisher's exact test: $p = 0.01^{**}$

cross-tabulations pertinent to these expectations. Table 6.6 focuses on dyadic/multilateral warfare while Table 6.7 is restricted to the war-joining phenomenon. As before, both tables first present two cross-tabulations controlling for major power status and then two cross-tabulations in which the major power control is relaxed.

Table 6.6 indicates that hypothesis 6 fails to find empirical support in the major power subsystem. Almost all major power wars have been multilateral in form and the two exceptions, although in the appropriate spatial column, do not suffice to create a significantly differentiated pattern. Only when the major power control is eased and the focus is placed on the more discriminating approach to separating issues is the hypothesis supported in a statistically significant way (fourth cross-tab in Table 6.6).

Much the same type of outcome is realized in Table 6.7. Although there is somewhat more variance on whether major powers choose to join ongoing wars or not than on whether they are dyadic or multilateral, spatial and positional rivalries do not yield significantly different behavioral patterns. Both types of rivalries are biased toward joining versus nonjoining, even though the bias is certainly somewhat more pronounced in positional rivalries. A much different pattern emerges when the major power status control is dropped. In these circumstances, hypothesis 6 receives strong support that does not depend on how one distinguishes the two rivalry issue types. Spatial rivalries are associated with nonjoining while positional rivalries are strongly linked to war joining (fourth cross-tab in Table 6.7).

Conclusions

We have elaborated Vasquez's two-path, single-issue theory into a two-path, two-issue theory. Alternatively, you might say that we have given equal explanatory weight to both paths whereas Vasquez privileged one path, the spatial one, and treated the other one in a residual way. The point remains that the two-path approach is not in dispute. The theoretical question is whether both paths deserve equal attention or whether one can be viewed as more or less derivative of the other. We argue for the former interpretation. Both spatial and positional issues generate rivalries and, in some theaters, positional issues may be just as important, or perhaps even more so, as spatial issues. The major power subsystem, for example, is one such case in which both spatial and positional issues are salient.

The two-path, two-issue theoretical perspective yields a number of expectations about the prevalence of different types of rivalry and differential propensities to war escalation. One expectation is that noncontiguous rivalries should be more common when both spatial and positional issues are salient than would be anticipated if only spatial issues were paramount. Multilateral wars and war-joining tendencies should also be more pronounced in theaters in which both types of issues are found in something approximating equal measure.

In our approach contiguity is not a proxy for spatial issues, but it does influence the types of rivalries that are formed. Proximity encourages spatial rivalries. More distant dyads are more likely to be associated with positional rivalries. While we expect to find that spatial rivalries are more war-prone in general, in subsystems in which spatial and positional issues are both salient, it is less clear that one type of rivalry should be any more or less war-prone than the others. But, once positional rivalries do escalate to war, there is some tendency for them to attract war joiners and to become multilateral. However, this last generalization was not supported in the major power subsystem, strictly speaking. Only when the major power control variable was relaxed within the pool of all states that at one time were major powers did statistical support emerge for this proposition about the expansion of war participation.

Hence, there are analytical limitations in examining comparative propositions within a relatively homogeneous data set. If one wishes to study what is distinctive about major powers, information on non-major power attributes and behavior is also necessary. Alternatively put, we can only proceed so far in testing the hypotheses generated by our two-issue theory with major power data. To the extent that we can test the hypotheses, the empirical support has been encouraging that the theory is on the right track or, better put, the right two spatial and positional tracks. They are not easy to disentangle but it is better to make the attempt than to focus on only one at the expense of the other. Still, determining just how much explanatory power we gain by emphasizing both paths simultaneously must await the analysis of a more ambitious data set on rivalry behavior – and not one restricted to the major powers. That is the task taken up in Chapter 7.

Somewhat similarly, our findings are hardly the last word on rivalry escalation – either for major powers or any other sample. We have shown that certain rivalry characteristics affect the likelihood of war occurrence. However, such a finding is only a beginning and fairly static step in determining the dynamics of why some rivalries go to war while others do not. To go further, we will need to move beyond rivalry attributes and types of contentious issues to rivalry behavior. Chapters 8 through 10 take on this challenge.

7   Initiating and escalating positional and spatial rivalries

According to Bremer (1992), contiguous dyads lacking alliance linkages and composed of less developed autocracies are more prone to war than dyads lacking these features. Less important but still significant are two other characteristics – the absence of preponderance and the presence of one or more major powers – which also contribute to dyadic war-proneness. In the past decade, however, a number of scholars increasingly have turned to a different set of "dangerous dyads" known as rivalries. Instead of assuming that all dyads have an equal probability of friction, why not look more closely at the very small number of dyads that create far more than their share of the world's interstate conflict?

In this chapter, we first view rivalries through the alternative lens of Bremer's "dangerous dyads." Do the attributes found to identify war-proneness in general also inform us about which states are most likely to become rivals? This is a reasonable question to raise given some presumed overlap between rivalry initiation and war-proneness. But we anticipate that there will be a number of reasons to expect that Bremer's profile of most dangerous states, while certainly highlighting important variables, will need considerable modification for use from a rivalry perspective, especially one that does not equate militarized dispute-proneness with rivalry relationships.

Two significant modifications that we will pursue involve putting aside the analysis of potential covariates in a variable-to-variable additive system and, of course, assuming that all actors are equally prone to engage in conflict. We posit instead that some states are particularly prone to conflict escalation based on the development of perceived dyadic relationships between threatening competitors. Moreover, we specify two different types of rivalries that may have distinct causes and effects. Not all dangerous characteristics will be equally associated with both spatial and positional rivalries, as past research has implicitly assumed. We hypothesize that spatial rivalries are more prone to war than positional rivalries, but that both will exhibit similar lower-level conflict dynamics. Even so, both types of rivalries should be more prone to escalation than are nonrivals, even when controlling for Bremer's dangerous characteristics.

We test these arguments using various discrete time event history models. Our findings indicate that Bremer's "dangerous dyads" are of limited help in delineating which dyads initiate rivalry. Yet these findings do support a plural approach to rivalry initiation, as well as underscoring the danger of rivalries. We also find that spatial rivalries are more prone to war, but not lower-level violence, than are positional rivalries, controlling for other factors. Positional rivals are more likely to end up in conflict through joining an ongoing dispute as compared to spatial rivals. Therefore, this analysis adds to an understanding of the various paths that lead to rivalry, as well as the causes of war and conflict. By expanding the sample beyond major powers, it also picks up where Chapter 6 left off.

Dangerous dyads and strategic rivalry

In a highly cited article, Bremer (1992) set out to uncover the "dangerous dyads" in the interstate system. These are the states that have the highest probability of going to war. In the decade since this article's publication, these findings have been both influential and relatively unchallenged. One of the questions that we wish to raise is how this package for predicting dangerous dyads might be utilized for predicting which dyads develop rivalry relationships. A second question is how well information on rivalries fares in comparison to the dangerous dyad set of five variables in predicting escalation to war.

There are some similarities between Bremer's focus on "dangerous dyads" and rivalry analysis. For example, both locate important causes of war at the dyadic level of analysis. It is the traits that characterize the relationships between states or the relationships themselves that are hypothesized to correlate with conflict. Both approaches assume, albeit in very different ways, that some dyads are more prone to conflict than are others. Bremer's approach assumes that we can discern which combination of variables leads to the identification of general dyadic conflict probabilities while rivalry analysis begins with the assumption that the most conflict-prone dyads have already been identified.

Both approaches also rely on patterns of conflict – albeit in different ways – to isolate which pairs of states are most likely to come to blows. Bremer used information on conflict to assess which combinations of dyadic attributes have affected the probability of war in the past. Rivalry analysts identify pairs of states that have developed an adversarial relationship and anticipate, as a consequence, the probability of more conflict to come. Yet, to our knowledge, the two distinctively different approaches have never been compared or used as complements. Nor have they been assessed as "rival" paths to improving our ability to identify trouble-making dyads for they do constitute distinctively different approaches. One important difference that we will pursue in this analysis is that the "dangerous dyad" approach assumes that one set of variables can predict all forms of war-proneness while rivalry approaches are more open to the idea of there being more than one causal path to more dangerous relations.

Bremer's "dangerous dyads"

Bremer arrived at the conclusion that contiguity, alliance status, regime type, development, preponderance, and major power status were the most important attributes predicting escalation to war by first scanning the literature for prominent generalizations, asking whether there was any direct evidence, and then measuring each of the six variables (in addition to one other, militarization, that proved to be insignificant). The bivariate and multivariate relationships with war onset were then examined as a prelude to constructing a ladder of relative impact significance. Beginning with a least war-prone dyad (characterized as consisting of noncontiguous, allied minor powers, with at least one dyad member that can be described as democratic, less militarized, and/or overwhelmingly preponderant), each factor is added step-wise before the consequent impact on the expected number of wars is calculated. The actual order of importance is (1) the presence of contiguity, (2) the absence of an alliance, (3) the absence of a more advanced economy, (4) the absence of a democratic polity, (5) the absence of overwhelming preponderance, and (6) the presence of a major power.

How should we evaluate this information? No one would confuse the six factors with a theory about how wars erupt. Instead, they represent a number of assumptions about fairly static dyadic characteristics and war behavior. Some, but not all, are accompanied by a justification. Some, but not all, are associated with direct empirical evidence that was available by the early 1990s. Again, some, but not all, speak more generically to conflict propensities and not just war onset. Table 7.1 illustrates the variability on these dimensions, in addition to clarifying how each indicator is measured.

The dangerous traits were not initially based on a strong empirical foundation because dyadic analyses were still relatively new in the early 1990s.[1] Bremer's own analysis probably was the first to consider all seven

---

[1] The published references cited as direct evidence by Bremer are limited to five: Gleditsch and Singer (1975), Garnham (1976), Weede (1976), Bueno de Mesquita (1981), and Gochman (1990).

Table 7.1 Bremer's seven "dangerous dyad" attributes

Variable	Explicit rationale advanced?	Direct evidence cited?	Non-war relevance?	Measurement
Geographical proximity	Yes	Yes	Yes	Contiguous dyad members are either proximate (adjacent land borders or separated by 150 miles of water or less) or non-proximate.
Relative power	Yes	Yes	No	The dyadic capability ratio is either small (<3:1), medium (3–10:1), or large (>10:1), in which capability is based on the combined average of military capability (combined average shares of system-wide military expenditures), economic capability (combined average shares of system-wide iron/steel production and energy consumption), and demographic capability (combined average shares of system-wide urban and total population sizes). Dichotomously, small and medium ratios are contrasted with large.
Power status	Yes	No	Yes	Dyads pair two major powers, a major and a minor power, or two minor powers, depending on each dyad member's qualifications on a year-by-year basis.
Alliance	No	Yes	No	Dyad members are either members of the same formal alliance or not.
Democracy	No	No	Yes	Dyad members are either democratic or nondemocratic, based on two alternative indexing approaches: (a) the Chan (1984) index requiring a popularly elected chief executive and legislature plus a legislature able to constrain the executive effectively; (b) the Polity II 1–10 democracy scale based on competitiveness of leader selection processes and constraints on executive authority, employing 5 as the threshold.
Development	Yes	No	Yes	Dyad members are either more advanced (system-wide share of economic capability is greater than its system-wide share of demographic capability [see Relative Power index above] or less advanced
Militarization	Yes	No	Yes	Dyad members are either more militarized (system-wide share of military capabilities is greater than its system-wide share of demographic capabilities [see Relative Power index above] or less militarized.

simultaneously. Since then, the Bremer set of seven variables that yielded six statistically significant, postdictive contributions has been accepted without much protest, not so much as stand-alone explanations but as a standard set of controls. Controlling for these factors, do other variables add something to our explanatory power?

But are all 6–7 variables equally pertinent to non-war dyadic analyses, as in the case of our current interest in rivalry initiation and escalation? The answer is probably not.[2] Rivalries represent relationships of mistrust, suspicion, and antagonism. Each side sees the other side as a threatening enemy. Yet they do not necessarily entail intensive conflict in overtly manifested fashions. They may simmer over long periods of time. Verbal and physical conflict levels may oscillate. A few rivalries will break out into war but, by no means, can one equate rivalry with war.

Thus, geographical proximity seems applicable generically, although all rivalries certainly do not involve contiguous adversaries. Major–minor power status distinctions should speak equally to all sorts of conflict behavior. The presumed constraints of democratic regime types should also be useful in a wide variety of conflict circumstances, including rivalries – although democratic dyads are not particularly prone to initiating rivalries.[3] Much the same might be said about economic development and militarization levels. The least generic arguments seem linked to preponderance and alliance. While it might seem foolish for a very weak actor to attack a very strong opponent, other things being equal, the irrationality of asymmetrical disputes is less overt in non-war situations. Weak states can protest verbally against strong opponents and do. In other words, conflict can develop between the weak and the strong. So, too, can rivalries – even though it is not exactly the most common situation for rivalry initiation. Pakistan and India is one example. Cuba and the United States is another. The question is how far the antagonists are willing to push their confrontations. The logical restraints associated with preponderance thus may address the highest levels of conflict better than the middle-to-lower levels.

The alliance variable is something of a question mark. Whether it is applicable to non-war situations depends on why the variable is a useful predictor. Do states ally because they are threatened by a foe that is too powerful to handle alone? Do states ally because they anticipate going to war soon and wish to augment their offensive capability or safeguard a rear flank? Are states that are not allied more vulnerable to attack and,

---

[2] This is not a criticism of Bremer (1992), since this analysis was focused on dyadic wars.
[3] Major power, mixed regime dyads, on the other hand, have been prone to rivalry formation in the late nineteenth century and throughout the twentieth century.

therefore, more likely to be attacked?[4] Or, does it simply reduce to the probability that allies are less likely to fight each other than are non-allies? Whatever motivations are at work, it seems unlikely that the logic would work equally well for conflict behavior short of war, as it might for war situations. Disputes, conceivably, can arise and be pursued without concern about allies as long as the disputes stop short of physical combat that might elicit external assistance as required by treaty.

Nonetheless, another problem with applying Bremer's logic directly to rivalry analysis is that there may not be just one single set of rivalry-prone characteristics. In Bremer's analysis, it is assumed that there is one dyadic syndrome that leads to war: contiguous, non-developed, and nondemocratic states that are not allied, involve at least one major power, and do not involve a large capability disparity.[5] However applicable that is to conflict analysis, we doubt that it applies equally well to rivalries. By this, we mean to suggest that certain characteristics, taken together, may increase the probability of rivalry in one way, while a separate set of characteristics could also lead to rivalry.

Thompson (1995) hypothesizes that two distinct types of rivalries may have different causes. First, two states may compete over territorial issues. These states are likely to be of near equal capability, contiguous, and nondemocratic minor powers. Ecuador–Peru, Somalia–Ethiopia, and Ghana–Togo serve as examples of this type of path to rivalry. Alternatively, states may compete over prestige and bargaining power. This type of conflict can occur in either a regional theater, such as between Egypt and Syria in the Middle East, or the global theater, such as between the United States and Soviet Union during the Cold War. These states are likely to be either regional or major powers, vying for position in their relative regional or global hierarchies. Either of the spatial/territorial or prestige/positional issues could lead to the initiation of rivalry.

If one takes this view of rivalries, simple hypotheses linking contiguity or other factors to rivalry have little meaning. It is not that contiguity and the other factors Bremer identifies are unimportant, but the pieces are only part of the puzzle. Allowing for contiguity and other variables to have differing effects depending on the type of rivalry expected to initiate is a way of arranging the pieces to make a coherent picture of the

---

[4] See Gartner and Siverson (1996) and Rasler and Thompson (1999) on war initiations against vulnerable targets.

[5] Of course it is possible for war to break out when some or all of these traits are absent. However, it is expected that the probability of war will be greatest when all of these traits are present. The possibility that some traits will increase war propensities in certain instances while other traits may increase conflict likelihood in alternative contexts is not discussed.

rivalry world. Ignoring the differing causes of spatial versus positional rivalries, therefore, can lead to biased inferences and conclusions if the causal process is incorrectly assumed to be equal across all rivalry cases.

The causes and effects of spatial and positional rivalries

But why should we think that there are different causes and effects of spatial versus positional rivalries? The positional–spatial rivalry theory that we are addressing is predicated on the interactions among distance, foreign policy ambitions, and conflict. States enter into conflict relationships with other states over a wide range of topics. Yet it is conceivable that this wide range can be reduced to two general categories: conflicts over space and conflicts over position. Spatial conflicts fundamentally are about control of territory. Two states cannot control the same territory simultaneously. Which state will control a given territory exclusively frequently has become a matter of dispute. Nevertheless, territorial conflicts can be more complicated than they seem. Why a state is motivated to control a specific territory can depend on nationalist mythologies, protection of an ethnic group, general concerns about strategic security, material interests in the exploitation of some profit potential from products that can be extracted from the ground or resident taxpayers, claims of aristocratic/royal inheritance, or simply habit. Labeling a dispute territorial or spatial does not necessarily explain the nature of the dispute. The label simply specifies a categorical focus. These disputes are about territorial control.

Even so, all disputes cannot be reduced to questions of territorial control. States quarrel about positional issues as well. Positional issues focus on questions of influence and status. One need not control a given space if it is possible instead to encourage its inhabitants to do whatever is deemed desirable without confronting the high costs of direct control. For example, imagine state X is under attack from people who use bases located in state Y. If state X wishes to eliminate the bases in Y, there are two principal ways to achieve this goal. State X can take physical control of the areas in state Y from which the terrorists operate. Or, it can persuade state Y to eliminate the bases. Putting aside mixed strategies, the options reduce to one of coercively acquiring territorial control or exerting influence in order to persuade someone else to exercise territorial control. For the indirect route of exercising influence to be successful, state X must have sufficient resources to expend in persuading Y to accede to X's preferences. Presumably, state X will have to offer something Y desires in exchange for the base elimination or to threaten harming Y in some way if it does not carry out the base elimination.

One complication in this example might be that state Y falls within the sphere of influence of state Z. State X cannot operate coercively within Y's territory without offending state Z's sense of prerogatives. State Y may not feel that it can accede to state X's wishes without threatening its own relationship to state Z. These complications suggest a hierarchy in which states X and Z are higher in the pecking order than state Y. State Z may fear that an expansion of state X's sphere of influence will come at its own expense. State Z does not directly control Y's territory but X's activities may threaten Z's position *vis-à-vis* both Y and X.

Whether these concerns about relative status and influence are thought sufficiently serious to fight about will vary. Other things being equal, spatial concerns should have a higher threshold for escalating to combat than do positional concerns. But that in turn depends on geography. If state X is contiguous to state Y, X may be sorely tempted to take the direct route of territorial control as the quicker and more permanent solution to its security problem. If state X is not contiguous to state Y and/or lacks the resources necessary to reach state Y, it may have no recourse but to try the influence path. Coercion may simply not be a possibility in this type of scenario.

Alternatively, state X may have the resources to seize portions of Y's territory but not without forcing state Z to come to the rescue of its client. Fighting state Y may be one thing. Fighting state Z is another matter altogether. The spatial issue between X and Y might then escalate to physical conflict relatively quickly if Y is much weaker than X while the positional issue between X and Z might deter action on X's part, assuming Z is much stronger than Y and roughly equal to X. An escalated conflict between X and Z might also be expected to bring in their allies and possibly other states with high status that view the conflict as an opportunity to improve their own relative position or to reduce the status of X and/or Z.

This extended example is hardly far-fetched. Up to a point it fits, for instance, Israeli activities in Lebanon since the 1970s and US activities in Afghanistan immediately following the 9/11 incident. But as an illustration, it is not intended to mirror the real world as much as it is designed to show how contiguity and foreign policy ambitions might interact with spatial and positional issues.[6] If we narrow our focus even more to the creation, and escalation of, strategic rivalry relationships – dyads involving two states that regard the other member of the pair as

---

[6] The foreign policy ambitions refer specifically to the likelihood that positional concerns will be more compelling for states that compete actively among the elites of regional and global political systems. Most states, whether by choice or the reality of limited resource endowments, possess more limited foreign policy aspirations that preclude giving a high priority to positional issues.

competitive (roughly equal in power status), threatening (posing some potential for physical or military harm), and viewing one another as enemies (a social-psychological categorization implying special and specific dangers to the existence and activities of the adversary) – it is plausible to suggest that strategic rivalries tend to be either predominantly spatially oriented, predominantly positionally oriented, or some combination of both. If that is the case, there is no reason to assume that spatial and positional rivalries "work" the same way. They are likely to follow different courses – especially in terms of initial formation and conflict escalation patterns – because they are subject to different pressures, motivations, and decision-making considerations.

Theoretically, we may combine our interests in contiguity, territory, and influence/status problems in the following three propositions:[7]

> H1: Contiguous adversaries are more likely to become involved in contests with strong spatial overtones while noncontiguous adversaries are more likely to become involved in contests with strong positional overtones.
>
> H2: In general, contests with strong positional overtones are less likely to escalate than are contests with strong spatial overtones.
>
> H3: In general, once contests with strong positional overtones do escalate, they are more likely to become multilateral contests because they will have more implications for bystanders than do spatial contests.

Chapter 6 found considerable encouragement in the major power subsystem. Contiguous rivals did possess an affinity for spatial contests and were more likely to be involved in spatial rivalries than were noncontiguous rivals. Noncontiguous rivals were also more likely to be found in positional contests. Escalation tendencies were difficult to test fully since major power rivalries and warfare have been biased toward noncontiguity, multilateral wars, and war joining. However, some less-than-overwhelming evidence was found supporting the idea that conflicts between spatial rivals were more likely to escalate to war than were the conflicts of positional rivalries. Similarly, some weak support for the idea that spatial wars are likely to remain dyadic in structure while positional wars are more susceptible to war joining was also uncovered.

While the empirical evidence for distinct types of rivalries is supportive but not unchallengeable, the major power subsystem is the most likely place to find positional conflicts. The strong prevalence of positional rivalries among the elite nation-states suggests that arguments based on

---

[7] This evolution of this theory can be tracked by examining the arguments in Vasquez (1993), Thompson (1995), Vasquez (1996), and Rasler and Thompson (2000).

spatial considerations alone would be less than helpful in explaining major power conflict. In contrast, there are other subsystems, such as South America and West Africa, in which spatial conflicts clearly predominate. Just how accurate the spatial–positional generalizations prove to be will depend on testing them in a less biased sample. Nonetheless, the very fact that there are such biases, with different types of conflicts more predominant in some parts of the world than in others, supports the fundamental idea that rivalries can follow different trajectories based on the types of issues involved.

Thus, assuming that there may be different causes of spatial and positional rivalries, what are those causes? We expect that capability symmetry, the absence of democracy, and the presence of a contiguous minor power dyad should increase the risk of spatial rivalry more severely than the risk of positional rivalry. Conflict over territory is more likely to break out between proximate states who have the ability to threaten each other. The absence of democratic institutions and accountability may also promote spatial conflicts, as peaceful mechanisms for resolution are wanting. Alternatively, militarized, major, or regional power dyads are the most likely to compete over prestige stakes and thus find themselves in positional rivalry.[8]

Methods

Using the nominal rival categories of positional, spatial, both, or neither (see Chapter 3), we can estimate a competing risks model to predict not only the occurrence of rivalry, but the rivalry type.[9] In the competing

---

[8] Development may also promote positional rivalry, as economic power and reach can lead to an increase in prestige conflict. For states to even aspire to regional or global prestige and power there must be some prerequisite of military or economic power. However, our development indicator is highly colinear with the major/regional power variable and cannot be included in the same model as estimated. Models with positional power status are superior using various fit statistics (Bayesian Information Criteria [BIC] and Akaike Information Criteria [AIC]) than models using only the development indicator. We do not include alliances in our hypotheses here because they do not seem to fit rivalry initiation particularly well. One might expect two states that share an alliance to be less likely to be rivals because they have some interest in common. Alternatively, an alliance could signal increased interactions between two states, raising the number of potentially conflict-prone issues. We do include the variable as a control.

[9] There are several other potential approaches to the problem. For example, in a previous version of the chapter we estimated a bivariate probit model with partial observability/ Boolean probit model (see Braumoeller 2003). This is an effective modeling strategy when no information on rivalry type is available. In this case, we were forced to categorize variables into "paths" and would have been unable to conduct any tests across rivalry types. The competing risks/multinomial logit formulation below allows for a litany of more useful tests, including estimating and comparing all coefficients across rivalry initiation types. Another possibility for future research is to explore fuzzy-set and Boolean logic within each rivalry type (see Ragin 1994, 2000).

risks formulation, a spell of nonrivalry can end in either spatial, positional, a combination, or neither type of rivalry. We expect that certain covariates should predict spatial rivalries, while others will map to positional rivalries. There are several benefits to the competing risks model, over and above a traditional logit model. Since information on rivalry type is available, a model with a nominal dependent variable allows us to differentiate between types in our statistical analysis. Additionally, we can conduct tests of statistical significance on the coefficients across equations in the competing risks model. If our hypotheses are wrong concerning the different causes of spatial rivalry initiation and positional rivalry initiation then coefficients will be equal across equations. We also explicitly test the independence of irrelevant alternatives assumption (IIA), a known weakness of this class of models, and perform a robustness check that relaxes the IIA assumption.

Bremer's seven variables are coded from the Correlates of War data, and described in Table 7.1.[10] Our measurement strategy follows this same coding scheme. We make two changes, however, by adding information on regional powers and shocks. Thompson (1995) explicitly notes that both major and regional powers may compete in positional rivalry. Therefore, we code regional powers by sorting each state by COW region (Small and Singer 1982) and capabilities (Singer 1987). The strongest four states in each region are coded as regional powers.[11] We then code a major/regional power variable equal to one if that dyad includes either two regional powers or two major powers. To avoid omitting variables that may be relevant to rivalry initiation, we also control for two types of international shocks (Diehl and Goertz 2000). World War shocks are relevant since they may alter both the regional and global playing field for positional rivalries. World wars have both winners and losers in the long and short term, therefore settling some positional scores and possibly incubating others.[12] Similarly, an independence shock, where a new territory is created in close proximity to another state, has the potential to

---

[10] See Bennett and Stam (2000). The variables are generated using the EUGENE program downloaded from <www.eugenesoftware.org>.

[11] The number 4 is almost entirely arbitrary. We suspect that a case might be made for the number 3 as the usual upper limit for positional contests. The ABC powers in South America, the Iran–Iraq–Saudi Arabia complex in the Gulf, and the US–USSR–China triangle in East Asia come quickly to mind as examples. But we are unaware of any systematic research on this question. It would also depend very much on how one codified the boundaries of each region (e.g., whether one decomposed the Middle East into several regional subsystems or only one). We adopt 4 (= 3 + 1) here as an interim guesstimate. Using only the top three states does not affect our conclusions.

[12] See Colaresi (2001) for a more detailed treatment of this relationship in the major power system.

Table 7.2 *Competing risks analysis of rivalry initiation type*

Rivalry type:	Model 1-MNL			Model 2-MNL w/shocks			Model 3-Seemingly unrelated bivariate probit		
	Coef.	S.E.	Sig.	Coef.	S.E.	Sig.	Coef.	S.E.	Sig.
Spatial									
Contiguous	4.59	0.32	<0.01	4.59	0.33	<0.01	1.375	0.093	**
Capability diff.	-2.19	0.44	<0.01	-2.11	0.44	<0.01	-0.664	0.129	**
Alliance	-0.17	0.35	N/S	-0.17	0.35	N/S	-0.096	0.114	
Nondemocracy	-0.20	0.29	N/S	-0.07	0.29	N/S	-0.030	0.092	
Militarized	0.47	0.35	N/S	0.20	0.40	N/S	0.142	0.115	
Positional power	-1.193	1.03	N/S	-0.94	1.03	N/S	-0.385	0.302	
WW shock	–	–	–	-0.31	0.32	N/S	–	–	
Indep. shock	–	–	–	2.36	0.54	<0.01	–	–	
Constant	-7.286	0.33	<0.01	-9.28	0.62	<0.01	-3.078	0.106	**
Positional									
Contiguous	2.07	0.33	<0.01	1.88	0.34	<0.01	0.867	0.080	
Capability diff.	-2.75	0.59	<0.01	-2.78	0.60	<0.01	-0.829	0.170	**
Alliance	0.16	0.32	N/S	0.34	0.33	N/S	0.145	0.087	**
Nondemocracy	0.53	0.23	<0.05	0.69	0.25	<0.01	0.163	0.078	
Militarized	2.17	0.202	<0.01	2.11	0.22	<0.01	0.765	0.077	*
Positional power	3.97	0.32	<0.01	3.57	0.32	<0.01	1.491	0.081	**
WW shock	–	–	N/S	1.59	0.26	<0.01	–	–	
Indep. shock	–	–	N/S	-0.15	0.40	N/S	–	–	
Constant	-7.97	0.36	<0.01	-8.80	0.43	<0.01	-3.528	0.146	**

Both

	Coef.	S.E.	p	Coef.	S.E.	p
Contiguous	1.13	0.28	<0.01	0.99	0.30	<0.01
Capability diff.	-2.40	0.51	<0.01	-2.37	0.51	<0.01
Alliance	-0.61	0.32	<0.10	-0.39	0.34	N/S
Nondemocracy	-0.17	0.23	N/S	0.01	0.24	N/S
Militarized	2.14	0.21	<0.01	2.01	0.210	<0.01
Positional power	4.70	0.24	<0.01	4.26	0.265	<0.01
WW shock	—	—	N/S	1.48	0.26	<0.01
Indep. shock	—	—	N/S	0.03	0.39	N/S
Constant	-7.33	0.34	<0.01	-8.17	0.42	<0.01

Neither

	Coef.	S.E.	p	Coef.	S.E.	p
Contiguous	5.28	1.10	<0.01	5.47	1.12	<0.01
Capability diff.	-2.02	1.10	<0.10	-2.10	1.09	<0.10
Alliance	0.68	0.92	N/S	0.42	0.90	N/S
Nondemocracy	0.04	0.79	N/S	-0.09	0.76	N/S
Militarized	-0.28	1.10	N/S	-0.21	1.10	N/S
Positional power	0.57	1.02	N/S	0.70	1.01	N/S
WW shock	—	—	N/S	-1.54	1.21	N/S
Indep. shock	—	—	N/S	-1.29	1.45	N/S
Constant	-9.65	1.11	<0.01	-8.43	1.49	<0.01
N	320000			320000		319875
Pseudo-R^2	0.355			0.376		
ρ						-0.519

trigger spatial conflicts. The creation of Israel in 1948 is the prototypical example of this type of process. Stinnett and Diehl (2001) find mixed support for the effect of international shocks of this type on militarized conflict situations.[13]

To analyze escalation, we control for spatial and positional rivalries as well as Bremer's variables. We measure lower-level conflict using militarized interstate disputes (Jones, Bremer, and Singer 1996), and wars using the dyadic correlates of war data updated by Maoz (1999).[14] These conflict variables are only equal to 1 in the first year of the dispute, marking conflict onset, rather than duration. Additionally, we create a dichotomous variable equal to 1 if a dyad finds itself in a war that has already been initiated, and is equal to zero otherwise. Therefore, if A and B initiate a dispute, and C joins the dispute against B, and the hostility level between B and C reaches war, B and C are coded as joiners. Additionally, if D joins against A, and the hostility level between D and A reaches war, then D and A, as well as D and C, if they also are at war, are coded as joiners. This information comes from EUGene v2.25 (Bennett and Stam 2000), as coded in the Correlates of War MID data. Finally, we include cubic splines to control for time dependence and specify robust standard errors.

Findings

Competing risks and rivalry initiation types

When we predict the type of rivalry initiated, the evidence for distinct causes of spatial and positional rivalry is strong. In the competing risks model presented in Table 7.2,[15] the coefficients represent the effect of a variable on a specific outcome. For example, we see that contiguity is expected to increase the log-odds of spatial rivalry by 4.6, and the log-odds of positional rivalry by 1.9. What we are primarily interested in is whether there are differential effects of variables across rivalry types. Therefore, the estimated distributions/spreads of the differences

---

[13] We also included civil war, regime, and systemic power shocks in various robustness checks. These three shocks were never significant and did not seem to fit within the theoretical apparatus of the paper. A more nuanced approach to shocks/the timing of strategic rivalry initiation would be a profitable avenue for future work. As in Diehl and Stinnett (2001) we code shocks as lasting for ten years after the event. Decreasing or increasing this number significantly affects the findings for the shocks variables but not for any of the other concepts.

[14] We estimate discrete time event history models with a logit functional form and cubic splines to control for time dependence.

[15] Spline coefficients are not shown.

for four variables across the spatial and positional equations are shown in Figure 7.1. The location of the "mountain" tells us the estimated difference between the effect that variable has on positional rivalry initiation minus the effect it has on spatial rivalry initiation. If there is no difference, the distribution would be centered on or near zero.[16] A variable that has a stronger relative effect on spatial rivalries will be negative, and a variable that has a stronger relative effect on positional rivalries will be positive. Here, we see that contiguity has a significantly greater effect on spatial rivalry initiation than it does on positional rivalry onset. Three other variables have substantively larger effects in the positional context. Nondemocracy, militarization and regional or major power status each increase the likelihood of positional rivalry but not the likelihood of spatial contests. Each difference presented in Figure 7.1 is statistically significant at the 0.05 level.

To understand the substantive magnitude of these differences, Figures 7.2 and 7.3 present information on the change in the predicted probability of observing spatial or positional rivalry as the variable of interest changes.[17] Figure 7.2 illustrates that the probability of spatial rivalry initiation increases by almost 7 percent (90 percent CI: 4 percent, 11 percent), while the probability of positional rivalry increases only marginally (90 percent CI: 0.1 percent, 1 percent).[18] The 90 percent confidence interval for the difference in the effect of contiguity on spatial vs. positional rivalry does not include zero (−11 percent, −3 percent).[19] Conversely, attaining major or regional power status has the opposite effect. The available evidence does not allow us to differentiate regional/major power dyads and non-regional/non-major power dyads based on their probability of

---

[16] The height of the "mountain" tells us the precision of our estimate of the difference. The distributions are computed, like the predicted probabilities to follow from a parametric bootstrap using the coefficient vector and the variance–covariance matrix. Note that all four coefficients compared in Figure 7.1 are associated with dichotomous variables.

[17] These predicted probabilities and their respective confidence intervals were computed using a parametric bootstrap of the estimated model 2 in Table 7.1 and a scenario involving a new non-allied, equal power, non-militarized regional or major power dyad, unless otherwise noted both shock variables are also set to one.

[18] The predictions for contiguity were calculated holding regional/major power at 0. Here is it important to note that the small change in the probability of positional contests is statistically significant (the 90 percent CI does not include zero), but is much less substantively significant than the change in spatial contests.

[19] As in previous chapters, one should not necessarily equate the overlapping of 90 percent confidence intervals for two predictions as a lack of evidence of a significant difference. In the figures presented here, however, the inference drawn from looking at confidence interval overlap and the explicit 90 percent confidence interval for the difference does not vary, unless noted. For this reason, we do not graphically represent the redundant 90 percent CI for the difference.

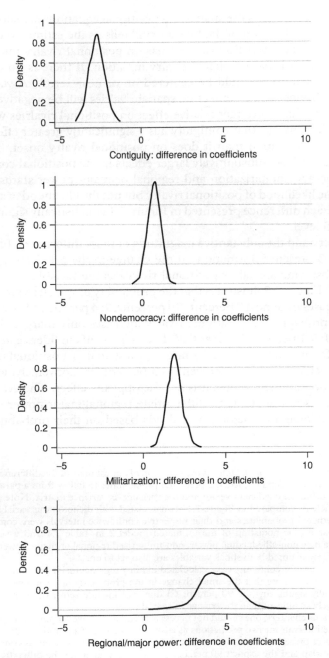

Figure 7.1 The distribution of the difference in the coefficients predicting spatial rivalry versus positional rivalry initiation from a parametric bootstrap. Negative values indicate a greater effect on spatial rivalry initiation.

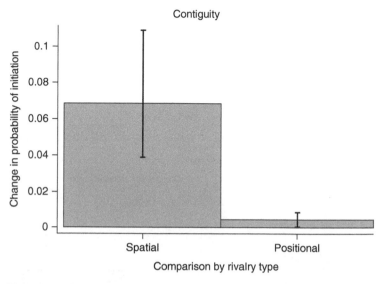

Figure 7.2 The effect of contiguity on the probability of spatial and positional rivalry initiation, with 90 percent confidence intervals.

spatial rivalry, as the 90 percent confidence interval for the effect of regional/major power status includes zero (−0.1 percent, 0.1 percent). However, the probability of a pure spatial rivalry increases by 2 percent, when a dyad gains regional or major power status (90 percent CI: 1 percent, 5 percent). The difference between these effects is significant at the 0.05 level.

Both nondemocracy and militarization also increase the relative probability of positional rivalry. We find in Figure 7.3 that there is evidence that nondemocratic or militarized dyads are more likely to contest with each other over pure positional issues, but we cannot say that either trait leads to the same increased propensity toward spatial rivalry. Specifically, moving from a democratic to a nondemocratic dyad increases the probability of positional rivalry by 2 percent (90 percent CI: 1 percent, 5 percent), while the analogous change leads to a small insignificant decrease in the probability of spatial rivalry initiation (90 percent CI: −0.03 percent, 0.02 percent). A dyad that becomes militarized is expected to have a 9 percent greater probability of pure positional rivalry (90 percent CI: 3 percent, 16 percent), but less than a −0.01 percent lower probability of pure spatial rivalry (90 percent CI: −0.1 percent, 0.02 percent). Additionally, the 90 percent confidence intervals for the estimated differences

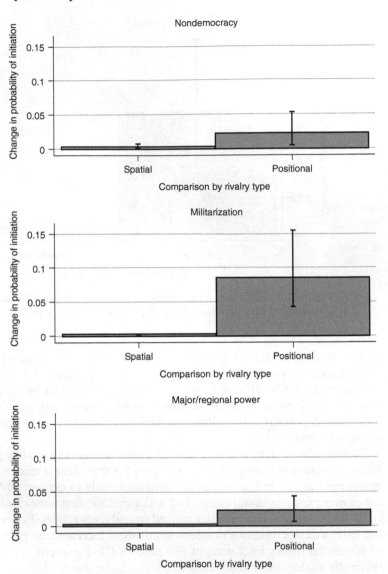

Figure 7.3 The effects of nondemocracy, militarization, and major/regional power on spatial and positional rivalry initiation, with 90 percent confidence intervals.

in the effects of both nondemocracy and militarization on spatial versus positional rivalry initiation do not include zero.

Our analysis did not provide evidence that alliance and capability differences have differential effects on spatial versus positional rivalry initiation. Alternatively, World War and independence shocks were found to have statistically discernible and unique effects on spatial and positional rivalry initiation. A World War shock is expected to increase the odds of positional, but not spatial, rivalry by a factor of approximately 5. This effect is statistically significant at the 0.05 level. Conversely, an independence shock increases the odds of spatial, but not positional, rivalry by a factor of approximately 10.5.[20] These findings again underline the result that rivalries can have plural motivations.

We also analyzed rivalries that involved both spatial and positional issues and those that did not involve either position or spatial issues. The mixed rivalry types seemed to have a profile similar to pure spatial rivalries. They are likely to involve militarized relatively equal regional or major powers. Rivalries that involved neither positional nor spatial issues were rather rare in the data (only ten non-spatial, non-positional rivalries in the data set), it is illustrative that very few of the dyadic characteristics significantly affected this type of rivalry initiation. Only contiguity significantly increases the expected risk of non-spatial non-positional rivalry initiation, as compared to avoiding rivalry (at the 0.05 level). Future research might further illuminate the causes of these mixed and atypical rivalries.

Our analysis highlights the potential biases that result from failing to look at the distinct causes of spatial versus positional rivalries. In fact, for the first time, we can now measure the bias that would result if we predicted rivalry initiation without respect to issue type. Figure 7.4 plots differences between the estimated effects for four variables from a pooled analysis of all rivalry initiations ignoring rivalry type. For example, if we see one member of a dyad gain new territory and become contiguous a pooled analysis would underestimate the probability of spatial rivalry, while overestimating the probability of positional rivalry. The mirror image of this bias appears when we look at the effect of regional/major powers, nondemocracy, and militarization. In each of these cases a naïve pooled analysis would underestimate the probability of positional rivalry, while overestimating the probability of spatial rivalry. In the case of militarization and contiguity the biases are substantively quite large, although even in the less dramatic cases (positional power

---

[20] These odds ratios can be computed from Table 7.2 by exponentiating the coefficient of interest.

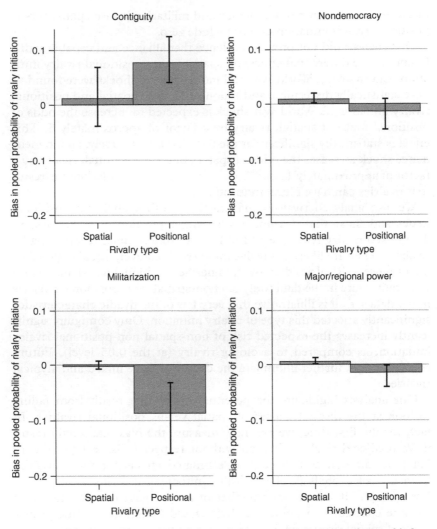

Figure 7.4 The estimate biases that you would find if you ignored information on rivalry initiation types, with 90 percent confidence intervals.

status and nondemocracy), a statistically discernible, and avoidable, bias is measured. Further, Wald and likelihood ratio tests confirmed that none of the rivalry type categories could be combined. The null hypothesis to our rivalry typology logic would be that the coefficients across all four categories would be equal to each other and thus rivalry initiation could be analyzed as a dichotomous variable. Our results lead to a rejection of that simplification of rivalry initiation research. Different variables have distinct effects depending on the rivalry type.[21]

We ran several diagnostic checks on the models and data. Block Wald and likelihood ratio test statistics for each of the coefficients referring to a variable being equal to zero across all equations were insignificant. The only exception was the alliance variable. Therefore, each of the variables included in these models, except possibly alliance linkages, significantly affects the risk of rivalry initiation.

A notorious assumption of competing risks models that use a multinomial logit formulation (referred to as IIA) is that the results are independent of irrelevant alternatives.[22] A Hausman-type test of the IIA assumption cannot reject the null hypothesis that the independence of irrelevant alternatives holds in this case (at the 0.01 level). As a further check on the stability of our results when the IIA assumption is relaxed, we also estimate a seemingly unrelated bivariate probit model, predicting the pure spatial or positional rivalry types. This allows for the error correlation between the two equations to be estimated and tested. If our results differ substantially, it may be that the significant differences found previously were an artifact of the IIA assumption. Instead, we find remarkably consistent results. Although nondemocracy is no longer expected to significantly increase the risk of positional over spatial rivalry, all of the other significant differences between positional and spatial rivalry types remain. The effect of contiguity is significantly greater for spatial rivalry initiation than for positional rivalry initiation. Likewise, major/regional power status and militarization retain their greater effect on positional rivalry development, as compared to spatial rivalry initiation. Finally, the correlation between the error terms of the two equations is negative but insignificant.[23]

Rivalry escalation

Having found some empirical evidence for different causes of spatial and positional rivalry, it remains to be seen whether the two types of rivalries

---

[21] The pooled rivalry results were generated by using a logit model specified in exactly the same way as was the multinomial logit/competing risks Model 2 in Table 7.2. The Wald tests reported above supply evidence that the effects are substantively different across rivalry types.

[22] For a treatment of this problem see Hill, Axinn, and Thorton (1993).

[23] Only three of the five categories are included because of the computational difficulty in estimating and identifying higher-order multinomial probit models (see Hill, Axinn, and Thorton 1993: 247 and Keane 1992). It should be noted that the results in model 3 in Table 7.2 do not include the observations that ended in other rivalry initiation types. If these are added as censored observations the results remain substantively the same.

Table 7.3 Logit results for escalation

Variable	Militarized interstate dispute			War			Joiner		
	Odds ratio	S.E.	Sig.	Odds ratio	S.E.	Sig.	Odds ratio	S.E.	Sig.
Spatial rivalry	2.835	0.784	**	11.837	9.04	**	1.128	0.652	
Positional rivalry	2.38	0.677	**	0.92	0.879		4.559	0.544	**
Contiguous	13.518	2.702	**	3.379	1.588	**	3.397	0.256	**
Capabilities	0.803	0.121		0.23	0.098	**	0.469	0.173	**
Major power	4.727	0.873	**	29.093	14.391	**	17.082	0.206	**
Alliance	1.027	0.134		0.742	0.549		1.112	0.221	
Nondemocracy	1.468	0.188	**	1.487	0.778		2.291	0.197	**
Developed	0.86	0.271	*	0.837	0.738		1.360	0.259	
Militarized	1.756	0.275	**	3.154	1.322	**	2.410	0.205	**
Spline1	0.678	0.047	**	0.001	0.001	*	0.172	0.143	**
Spline2	0.994	0.006		0.472	0.181	*	0.890	0.015	**
Spline3	1.000	0.007		1.869	0.637	*	1.096	0.017	*
Spline4	1.005	0.007		0.753	0.131	*	0.965	0.017	
Spline5	0.993	0.005		1.073	0.066		1.015	0.015	
Spline6	1.006	0.003	*	1.012	0.027		0.995	0.007	
Spline7	0.998	0.001	**	0.953	0.041		1.003	0.002	
Spline8	1.000	0.001	*	1.053	0.048		0.999	0.195	*
R^2	0.319			0.524			0.355		

$N = 305019$; ** $= p < 0.01$; * $= p < 0.05$ for a one-tailed test.

behave differently in terms of escalation propensities. Using the distinction between types of rivalry, we analyze whether the probability and method of escalation is affected by the presence of spatial or positional characteristics. The findings in the first model in Table 7.3 illustrate the influence that rivalry type has on the probability of a militarized interstate dispute (MID). We find that spatial and positional rivals increase the probability of a dispute by 7 percent (90 percent CI: 5 percent, 10 percent) and 5 percent (90 percent CI: 3 percent, 8 percent) respectively, as compared to a nonrival dyad.[24] Further, the difference between spatial and positional rivalries is insignificant on this dimension (90 percent CI for the difference: −6 percent, 3 percent). This finding suggests that rivals in general are characterized by more disputes than nonrivals.

When we turn to the onset of war, the spatial/positional distinction becomes more important. The right-hand columns in Table 7.3 list the results for dyadic (the middle column) and multilateral (the far right column) war and rivalry type. Figure 7.5 translates these coefficients into the predicted probabilities of disputes, wars onset, and war joining. We find that as a dyad moves from no rivalry to contesting over spatial issues the probability of a direct bilateral war increases by 6 percent (90 percent CI: 1 percent, 17 percent). Further, positional rivals do not differ significantly from nonrival war onset dynamics, as the positional rivalry variable is insignificant and the 90 percent positional confidence interval for the predicted probability of war includes zero (90 percent CI: −0.4 percent, 2 percent). However, these is evidence that spatial rivalries are more likely to war with each other directly as the 90 percent confidence interval for the difference between the effects of spatial vs. positional issues does not include zero (90 percent CI: −18 percent, −.2 percent).

Yet positional rivals are more likely to fight each other after joining an ongoing dispute. The positional rivalry variable is positive and significant in the third column, while the spatial rivalry variable is insignificant, controlling for other factors. Specifically, as a dyad moves from no rivalry to positional rivalry the probability of fighting each other as a result of joining an ongoing dispute increases by 9 percent (90 percent CI: 5 percent, 14 percent). The effect of spatial rivalry on joining behavior is insignificant (90 percent CI: −1 percent, 2 percent) and significantly smaller than the positional issue effect (90 percent CI for the difference: 3 percent, 15 percent). Therefore, while both spatial and positional rivals are involved in more militarized disputes than nonrivals, spatial rivalries are involved

---

[24] All of the escalation predicted probabilities are calculated by the same methods as above, except that all other variables are held at zero. The sole exception is contiguity, which is set at one.

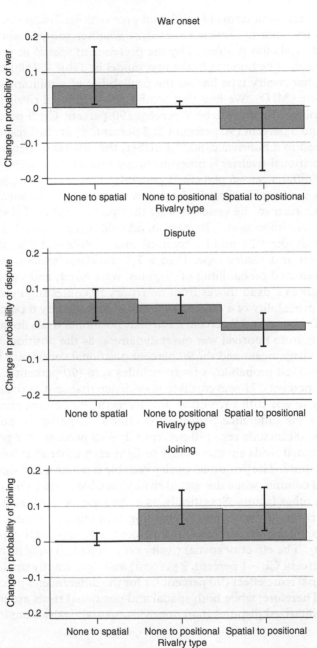

Figure 7.5 Effects of spatial and positional rivalry on the probability of a war onset, any militarized disputes and war joining, with 90 percent confidence intervals. The "Spatial to Positional" entries allow us to test the difference between the effects of spatial versus positional rivalry on war onset, any militarized disputes, and war joining.

in the most dyadic wars. Positional rivals, even so, are far from pacific. Rivals competing over positional issues are more likely to join a war that is ongoing. Thus, we find, literally, two different paths to escalation.

Without a doubt, rivalry information is integral to an understanding of war and conflict dynamics. However, here we have shown that rivalry issue dimensions also tell us something about the way rivalries are likely to fight. If we ignore information on the differences between spatial and positional issues, we are likely to miss one or the other path to war. For example, if we estimate the same escalation models as above for direct war onset and war joining, but control for only pooled rivalries (ignoring issues), we would calculate that rivalry increased the probability of war onset by 5 percent, which would be close to accurate for spatial rivalries, but substantially overstates the risk of this type of conflict for positional rivals. Similarly, we would calculate that the probability of joining an ongoing war for all rivals would be 9 percent, which is accurate only for positional rivals and significantly overstates the threat of joining for spatial rivals.

Our findings regarding the control variables support Bremer's analysis for the most part. We find that contiguity, capability parity, and the presence of at least one major power each increases the probability of war and militarized disputes, as Bremer found. Also, the evidence suggests that alliances are not robust predictors of conflict, again more or less complementing Bremer's analysis.

Yet there are a number of important contrasts also. First, while Bremer ranked major power status as one of the least important predictors of war, we find that when rivalry is controlled, power status becomes a robust predictor of war and conflict. In fact, the presence of at least one major power in the dyad increases the odds of war almost by a factor of 30. Similarly, while Bremer found that militarization was not significant, our results suggest that militarization increases both types of conflict. Also, where Bremer placed emphasis on democracy and development, we find that these variables are only significant when predicting militarized disputes, not war.

Conclusion

We have sought to compare and combine two different approaches to identifying the most dangerous dyads in world politics. Bremer's (1992) approach developed a single set of dyadic attributes on contiguity, capabilities, status, alliances, regime type, development, and militarization that predicted war-proneness. We have contrasted this approach with an approach emphasizing strategic rivalry. One of our questions focused on whether information on rivalry relationships, even controlling for Bremer's dyadic attributes, contributed significantly to our understanding of conflict. There should be no doubt that that is the case. Both sets of information improve our explanatory capability. Combined, they present an even stronger predictive platform.

Another question that was raised is whether the selected dyadic attributes tell us something about rivalry initiation and escalation. Here, we encountered an immediate divergence in assumptions. Whereas Bremer envisioned a single set of war-prone attributes to encompass all cases, it is conceivable that different types of rivalries are associated with different sets of dyadic attributes. It is also plausible that different types of rivalries have different propensities to escalate. Therefore, we needed to modify Bremer's approach to take into account the possibility that spatial and positional rivalries are subject to different influences.

We did find evidence for distinct causes of different rivalry types. Contiguous, minor power dyads that were not asymmetrical in capabilities were most likely to follow the spatial path to conflict over territorial control. Major powers and leading regional powers were most likely to follow the positional path to contention over relative influence and status. Both types of rivalries were prone to militarized dispute behavior but spatial rivalries were more likely to lead to dyadic warfare while positional rivals tended to join wars already in progress. We also found that Bremer's dangerous attributes were differentially useful depending on whether we examined militarized disputes, war, or war expansion. Contiguity, major power status, and militarization were significant in all three contexts. Three of the other variables were significant in one or two of the different conflict contexts. Only the alliance variable proved to have no significant predictive capability.

By introducing the possibility of distinct causes and effects of spatial versus positional rivalries, we have improved our ability to specify how conflicts come about in the first place, and how they escalate to militarized disputes, dyadic war, and multilateral war. There are at least two important and distinctive paths to conflict – one spatial and one positional. Given two paths, a single equation will simply not fit all cases of conflict equally well. We will need to make appropriate theoretical and empirical adjustments that correspond to these findings.

Of course, positional and spatial rivalries do not exist independently of each other. We have good ideas about the dyadic traits and relationships that make conflict more probable. At the same time, it should be clear that our understanding of these conflict processes cannot be dictated by either a single set of traits or even an exclusively dyadic framework. For example, large-scale wars might be most likely when a spatial rivalry breaks into open conflict with positional linkages present. As these positional rivalries are drawn into the spatial fray, the war spreads from localized conflict to regional or even global war. While the spatial component of rivalry may explain bilateral wars, multilateral conflicts may depend on the constellation of positional rivalries and alliances that surround each territorial conflagration. Thus, analysis of rivalry systems may be needed to augment other extra-dyadic explanations of conflict. In the process, a focus on these linkages may help broaden the study of war from a dyadic to a multilateral framework.

Nonetheless, categorizing rivalry types into two basic "species" can only take us so far. We need to draw on other, more classical, dimensions of conflict escalation – such as arms races, alliances, and crises – and to harness our understanding of these processes within a rivalry context. Our last section turns to another theory put forward by John Vasquez – the Steps-to-War theory – in which territorial contests, rivalry, military build-ups, alliances, and crises are brought together, along with other considerations, as a particularly inflammatory, escalatory package leading to war. In Chapter 8, we focus primarily on military build-ups and alliances. The territorial issue is given extensive coverage in Chapter 9 before combining the preliminary outcomes in a more comprehensive way.

Part IV

Filling in some steps to war

8   Arms build-ups and alliances in the steps-to-war theory

A variety of factors have constrained progress on deciphering escalation to war. One is the sheer complexity of the undertaking. International relations are hardly simple and uncomplicated phenomena. Laws of interstate interaction are not readily established and, in any event, will probably prove to be the wrong goal to pursue in unraveling highly complex behavior. A second factor that derives from the complexity is that we tend to focus our explanatory efforts on favored, relatively monovariate, causal elements. One group pursues alliances, another dwells on arms races, and still others specialize in the analysis of rivalry or crises. There is much to be gained from concentrating on specialized topics. But there is also a price to be paid if we remain concentrated too long. Conflict escalation, without doubt, involves multiple causation.

To develop satisfactory explanations of processes subject to multiple stimuli, we need to introduce multiple explanatory factors simultaneously, and possibly interactively, as opposed to separately. However, a third factor that has held us back is that our explanatory apparatuses tend to be linked to the preference for monovariate explorations. We have tended to study individual hypotheses about alliances, or arms races, or crises. Do alliances tend to be followed by war? Are arms races genuinely influential in escalation processes or merely symptomatic of underlying tensions? What types of crises are most likely to lead to war? These are all relevant questions but we need to test more complex arguments that make linkages among alliances, arms races, and crises. For example, are alliances or arms races more dangerous after a series of crises? Of course, it would also help if we had access to many such complex arguments so that we could compare their comparative explanatory values.

We do not assume that we know all that we need to know about each of the factors thought to be related to war escalation. Specialization remains valuable. At the same time, though, we will not know all that we need to know about specialized causes of war until we begin to integrate them. We are also well aware that we lack many integrative theories linking multiple causes of war escalation. Yet as long as we have some (or even one) set of complex statements, presumably, we have enough of a theoretical foundation to begin testing the empirical linkages among a number of escalatory stimuli. Vasquez's (1993) war puzzle theory, replete with some 118 propositions linking a large number of the more prominent variables in the study of war escalation processes, strikes us as an especially good place to begin. While it is simply not feasible to take on all 118 propositions at one time, we can focus on 32 propositions that interrelate territorial disputes, rivalry, alliances, arms races or military build-ups, crises, hostility, cognitive rigidities, domestic politics, and situations leading to war. Examining international behavior over the past two centuries, we find strong empirical support for many of the relationships put forward in Vasquez's integrative theoretical interpretation of multiple steps to war.

One of the ways in which the strong empirical support is registered is that we can examine similar questions from multiple vantage points and arrive at the same answers. In this chapter, for instance, we rely on rivalry information (the spatial versus positional dimension) to capture the presence and absence of territorial disputes. In Chapter 9, we examine questions about the pitfalls of overlapping indicators and strive to develop indicators that are as independent of one another as is possible. One of the changes involves introducing more direct information on territorial disputes and substituting it for the rivalry-related index developed in this chapter. The point is that similar results emerge regardless of how one captures the role of spatial disagreements.

An abridged version of Vasquez's war puzzle argument

There is, of course, a veritable host of variables that have been examined in the context of war outbreaks. Some variables, nonetheless, tend to receive more attention than others. One prominent focus is the idea that states are more likely to fight over territory than any other issue (Hensel, 2000: Huth, 2000). Another is that arms races encourage adversaries to fight either because they lose control of their arms competition (Richardson, 1960) or because they feel more empowered by having acquired the wherewithal to fight (Sample, 2000). There is also a long history of analyses attempting to discern whether the possession of alliances encourages or restrains the outbreak of conflict (Maoz, 2000). Augmenting one's strength by concluding some military arrangement with a stronger power could encourage making a decision to go to war as long as the encouragement was not counterbalanced by a restraining alliance partner or the alliances of the opponent.

One of the more radical departures in recent war analyses has been to highlight the idea that most states are simply unlikely to fight because they are not sufficiently proximate to one another to do so and because they have no history of unresolved grievances and threat perceptions (Goertz and Diehl, 1992a; Thompson, 1995, 2001; Diehl and Goertz, 2000; Wayman, 2000). To the contrary, a small number of dyads dominate the war annals. Rivals are most likely to fight each other and most likely to fight again and again. In a similar vein, the idea that states that clash repeatedly in militarized disputes and crises, and all the more so if they are rivals, are the ones most likely to go war eventually also has received ample support (Leng, 1983; Chapter 5).

The idea that territorial disputes are central to war making is rarely disputed, although it is possible to demur on the extent to which territorial issues actually dominate interstate conflict and whether we should put so many of our theoretical eggs in the spatial basket.[1] The arms race literature largely lacks consensus in part because of the counter argument that military build-ups can be expected to deter opponents, as opposed to empowering the state engaged in a build-up. There are also a number of methodological problems that have plagued analysis, ranging from attempts to capture the mutual stimulation presumably implicit to an arms race to questions about what best captures the process of military build-ups (for instance, military expenditures versus weapon systems) or which cases need to be studied to be able to assess a genuine causal push to war from arms racing.[2]

Alliances possess their own complications due to heterogeneity. Are all types of alliances equally important? Does it matter if an alliance is long-standing or created as part of an anticipation of warfare soon to come? For that matter, are alliance obligations usually honored once invoked? Additionally, we have seemingly contradictory empirical evidence that alliance ties may induce war (Bueno de Mesquita, 1981: 76–8) or deter it (Weede, 1976).

We have good reasons, as a consequence, to suspect that territorial disputes, proximity, arms races, alliances, rivalry, and recurring conflict sequences make important, systematic contributions to the likelihood of war outbreaks. But we have tended to focus our empirical inquiries within largely bivariate frameworks. That is to say we have tended to ask what is the relationship between X and war, usually subject to various control variables, rather than asking what are the relationships between X, Y, and Z and war. As a consequence, we have evidence that X, Y, and Z are individually related to war but we do not know fully the extent to which

[1] See, for example, the argument advanced in Chapter 6.
[2] Compare, among others, Wallace (1979), Smith (1980), Weede (1980), Houweling and Siccama (1981), Altfeld (1983), Diehl (1983, 1985a, 1985b), Siverson and Diehl (1989), Sample (1997, 1998), and Diehl and Crescenzi (1998).

the presence of X and Y influences Z's relationship to war. In particular, if the argument that rivalry as a critical marker of greater-than-average hostility in capturing conflict-prone opponents has validity, it should be all the more critical to assess the causal effects of territorial disputes, arms races and alliances within the context of rivalry – as opposed to analyzing them separately or one at a time (Diehl and Crescenzi, 1998).

Putting aside the inevitable disagreements about how best to measure X, Y, or Z, we have also tended to ask these questions about probability relationships in fairly static ways. We ask, for instance, if a state possesses an alliance or a military build-up or a territorial dispute, is it more or less likely to go to war? Yet these phenomena tend to occur in sequences of conflict. Two states might start with a territorial dispute and then proceed to identify each other as rivals. A border clash might occur which encourages one side to improve its relative capability position by making an alliance leading the other state to seek alliance partners. Failing to find an external relationship, the weaker side might begin a military build-up which, in turn, is reciprocated by the other side. Several more clashes might have transpired before a war finally breaks out.

The paragraph above is not a template for the way in which all wars commence. It is only one possible way in which a war might occur. Some of the steps might be missing altogether in the substitutable etiology of other wars. The alliance or military build-up factors might be absent. Recurring clashes might also be absent. Or, the putative causal factors might come in a different sequence pattern. Alliances might follow a build-up, rather than precede it. Rivalry might precede clashes or follow a number of them. Or, it could be that some of the alleged causes are simply artifacts of underlying tension and will prove to be less significant when examined in a larger complex of factors.

The point is that there is likely to be a dynamic at work that mixes these factors in some mélange that makes war more or less probable. If we look at bivariate relationships, we miss the mélange completely. If we look at the mere presence or absence of possible causal factors any time prior to the outbreak of war, we may also miss the dynamic complex if it makes some difference when alliances or build-ups occur, or whether it makes some difference if a militarized dispute occurs after a rivalry has been terminated – in comparison to occurring within the context of an ongoing rivalry. Unless we examine multiple factors simultaneously, we cannot begin to assess which factors belong in the dynamic complex and which ones are superfluous or spurious.

On the other hand, it is no accident that we have tended to engage in largely static, bivariate examinations. A great deal of preliminary work has been necessary to create the data that make empirical examinations possible. Then, too, bivariate examinations are perfectly appropriate ways

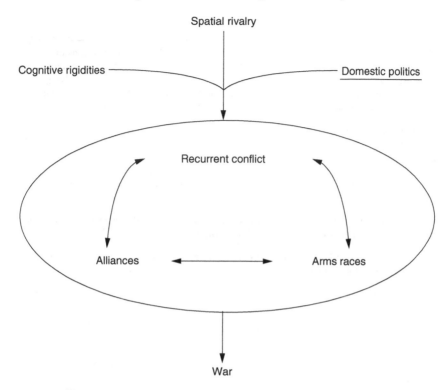

Figure 8.1 An abridged version of Vasquez's steps-to-war theory.

with which to begin empirical study. Finally and not coincidentally, much of our discourse about war causality is couched in highly bivariate terms. We have a large number of bivariate hypotheses but few multivariate theories. Fortunately, Vasquez (1993) is a clear exception to this generalization.

Vasquez (1993) represents a stocktaking of empirical analyses on the outbreak of war. Yet it goes well beyond a simple summary of work done by that date in the sense that an interpretation of how the pieces of the war puzzle fit together is also advanced. The summation and interpretation are specified in part by a list of 118 propositions. Of this assembly, we rely on propositions 11, 12, 12a, 12b, 13–15, 15d, 17, 17a, 19–20, 22–4, 26–9, 29a, 30–3, 36, 36a, 37–8, 38a, 40c, 44a, and 44b for our construction of the abridged Vasquez argument outlined in Figure 8.1 and listed in Table 8.1.

Vasquez is strongly committed to the idea that the single most significant root of modern warfare is disputes over territory. Territorial disputes,

Table 8.1 *Propositions on war escalation*

Enduring rivalries (and protracted conflict between unequals) have their origins in attempts to control space . . . The main difference between rivalries that end in a major war and rivalries that end non-violently is the parties' ability to avoid crises involving territorial contiguity. Rival states that are not contiguous tend not to fight a major war with each other unless they are dragged in by third parties. [propositions 11–12]

Rivals are more concerned with hurting the other than maximizing their own value satisfaction. For this reason they will tend to oppose the position taken by a rival on any issue. Rivals tend to link all issues on the agenda into one grand overarching issue. Linking of issues tends to make disagreements persist. Persistent disagreement produces an over-reliance on negative acts. These in turn increase negative affect (hostility). [propositions 12a–12b]

The more disputes and crises that arise between relative equals, the greater the likelihood of their viewing each other as rivals . . . [proposition 13]

The more disputes and crises that arise between relative equals, the greater the likelihood of their trying to form alliances against each other. [proposition 14]

Ceteris paribus, alliances are more frequently followed by war than by peace. [proposition 15]

Alliances involving major states are more war-prone than alliances without major states. [proposition 15d]

Alliances formed during an ongoing rivalry are much more likely to eventually result in war than alliances formed in other situations. [proposition 17]

The formation of an alliance increases insecurity, uncertainty, and hostility in the target. In a rivalry, the formation of an alliance by one side leads to the formation of a counter-alliance by the other side and/or a military build-up. [proposition 17a]

Alliances followed by military build-ups are much more likely to lead to a war between equals than alliances that are not followed by military build-ups. The formation of an alliance by a rival crystallizes the hostile and threatening image leaders and the public of the other side have of the rival. [propositions 19–20]

Crises, alliance making, and military build-ups form a dynamic in which they interact and reinforce each other to produce increased hostility which in turn institutionalizes and rigidifies images and definitions of the situation. By producing such cognitive rigidities, rising hostility increases the probability of additional crises erupting. [proposition 22]

The presence of hostility produces a step-level effect in subsequent behavior, making actors more sensitive to negative acts and leading them to discount positive ones. Crises repeat if the parties fail to resolve the major issues at hand. This in turn is a function of the kinds of issues they raise and they way they frame those issues. [propositions 23–4]

Arms races presuppose rivalry and intensify that rivalry . . . once they are under way. Arms races also increase insecurity. [proposition 26]

Table 8.1 *(cont.)*

Because leaders are unlikely to get domestic support for a rapid military build-up without some concrete manifestation of the external threat, arms races usually follow a crisis and/or alliance formation rather than precede it. Since crises make threats clear, the greater the number of crises, the greater the probability of an arms race or mutual military build-up of some sort. [propositions 27–8]

In order to gain domestic political support for power politics practices, leaders exaggerate the threat posed by the other side and frame the issue in transcendent terms. This increases fear in the other side and creates constituencies more susceptible to hard-line stances, which make it difficult for leaders to subsequently reduce the salience of the issue or to become more accommodative. This dynamics helps produce an arms race spiral. The presence of this psychological atmosphere and domestic political situation makes it more likely that crises or military disputes that arise during an ongoing arms race will escalate to war than crises or disputes occurring in the absence of an arms race. [propositions 29–29a]

Militarized disputes that occur in the absence of arms races or military build-ups rarely escalate to war. This implies that among equals inadequate defense preparations tend not to be associated with crisis escalation. Adequate defense preparations prior to a militarized dispute between equals make a party less restrained in its crisis bargaining . . . [propositions 30–1]

Arms races and military build-ups increase the number and influence of hard-liners in each side; they in turn push for a military build-up. Arms races (and/or military build-ups of some sort) increase the probability of war between relative equals by increasing hostility, encouraging the outbreak of the kinds of crises most apt to escalate to war, providing adequate military preparation so that bargaining within a crisis need not be restrained, and helping generate a hard-line domestic political context. [propositions 32–3]

Between equals, each side tends to escalate the level of coercion in successive crises. This pattern holds regardless of the success or failure of escalation or decreases in capability. The reason for this is that when actions fail to produce a desired outcome, costlier and riskier actions consistent with the overall policy are tried. Thus, as the underlying issue fails to be resolved by force, bargaining techniques between equals become more coercive and hence more likely to escalate to war. [propositions 36–36a]

In successive crises between equals, leaders rely on the realist emphasis on power and firmness, but have difficulty in heeding realist advice on prudence. Coercion produces hostility which gives leaders a motivated bias to escalate regardless of their immediate prospects of success. In addition, successive crises and escalation increase the willingness to take risks. Even if a particular decision-maker is unaffected by these variables, he or she is biased in favor of escalation by the hard-line domestic political context created by hostility and escalation. [proposition 37]

Escalation from one crisis to the next increases the likelihood of a hostile spiral when the actions of one leader lead the other to reciprocate in a more hostile manner until the end result is war. In the presence of hostility, one expresses hostility. Perceptions of hostility lead to violence. Both sides tend to exaggerate threats and both sides think the other side is being more hostile than it is, while misperceiving their own actions as less hostile than they actually are. [propositions 38–38a]

(cont.)

Table 8.1 (cont.)

Persistent confrontations make leaders and their followers feel that force is the only way to resolve the issue at hand [proposition 40c]

The introduction of each new power politics practice – alliance formation, military build-up, and crisis diplomacy – increases the influence of hard-liners and support for more escalatory actions while simultaneously leading to an increase in hostility and greater insecurity. This process drives out accommodationist influences in each rival, increases the number and influence of hard-liners, and stiffens the leaderships' determination not to give into the opponent. This increases the probability of war. [propositions 44a–44b]

Source: Based on Vasquez (1993: 309–26). We have taken some liberties in combining some propositions as seemed appropriate.

in turn, variably lead to a very complicated complex of five variables critical to escalation: rivalry, militarized disputes/crises, alliances, military build-ups, and hostility. This complex interacts with decision-maker cognitive rigidities and domestic political situations that facilitate decisions to escalate coercion with opponents. War, then, is an outcome made more probable by the combined influences of the seven variables specified in Figure 8.1[3]

Since the escalatory complex is of most interest to this analysis, we need to discuss at length the interactions viewed as most crucial. Rivalries are relationships that emerge in protracted conflict settings between states that are roughly equal in capability. Rivalry relationships are important because the identification of a hostile relationship tends to take over the nature of interactions within the dyad. Different contested issues tend to fuse together, making it more difficult to resolve single issues without settling all of the issues at stake. Subsequent interactions become increasingly negative and hostile. However, violent rivalries are most probable when the main conflict issue concerns a dispute about the possession of territory adjacent to both parties. Noncontiguous rivals, as we saw in Chapter 6, are less likely to come to blows directly unless they are induced to intervene in the conflicts of other states.

An increasing number of disputes and crises between two states not only makes a rivalry relationship more likely to ensue, but it also encourages the relatively equally powerful adversaries to seek alliances that might augment their relative capability. Alliance and counter-alliances further

---

[3] Vasquez's (1993) argument certainly encompasses more than seven variables. We omit polarization, the global institutional/normative context, and many facets of the variables that we do examine.

increase insecurity, uncertainty, and hostility within the rivalry relationship by confirming suspicions about the threatening intentions of an opponent. This dynamic may also encourage military build-ups on one or both sides. An arms race (mutual military build-ups on both sides) probably requires rivalry as a prerequisite but once the prerequisite is satisfied, insecurities are further heightened, as is the sense of rivalry.

Alliance making and arms races also influence crisis behavior. The interaction of alliance making, military build-ups, and repetitive crises facilitates the development of cognitive rigidities in decision-makers who must interpret adversarial intentions and goals and develop appropriate responses. As the negative images of the adversary harden, flexibility is lost. Positive adversarial behavior is likely to be discounted or disbelieved. Negative adversarial behavior is likely to be interpreted in worst-case terms. Responses to adversarial behavior are more likely to be negative than positive. All of these considerations make violent outcomes in crises more probable, especially after a series of crises has been survived without any definitive outcome. Pressures are created to "up the ante" the next time around.

In order to gain and expand domestic political support, decision-makers are encouraged to stress and even to exaggerate the hostility of rivals. To the extent that these efforts are successful, expectations about hard-line stances toward the adversary are cultivated. Leaders may use these expectations to justify military build-ups but, in doing so, they sacrifice flexibility in negotiating with the enemy. If military build-ups create perceptions of adequate defense preparations on one side (while increasing the insecurity of the other side), decision-makers may be more inclined to risk increasingly coercive strategies in crisis bargaining, while at the same time they are less likely to be able to contemplate any accommodation of the adversary's demands.

The combination of these various interactions among the main variables makes escalation to war more probable. Crises encourage hostility and rivalry and rivalry and hostility make crises more likely. Alliance making and military build-ups heighten insecurities and hostility and can encourage decision-makers to escalate in the context of crisis. Cognitive rigidities are apt to encourage exaggerated threats, self-fulfilling prophecies, misperceptions, and fixed preferences for hard-line stances that leave little room for maneuver in crises. Resistance to accommodative strategies within domestic constituencies also makes hard-line stances more probable. In the end, protracted confrontations between rivals should make the use of force more appealing in each successive iteration.

A leitmotif running through all of Vasquez's argument is that decision-makers learn to rely on realpolitik strategies to deal with international problems such as territorial disputes. Arms races, alliances, crisis bargaining, and rivalry are the major conduits of these realpolitik strategies. Therefore, they constitute the primary steps-to-war. To avoid war, the strategies must be recognized as self-defeating and unlearned. Thus, if we are to explain the onset of war (and peace), one basic question is whether the empirical evidence supports this particular multivariate mélange of interactive processes as a significant component of war etiology.

We propose to test several variations on one model that might be extracted from this theoretical argument. It is crucial that we emphasize that our test is only one possible interpretation of how the escalators proceed to increase the probability of heightened conflict. Vasquez's discussion of territorial disputes, rivalry, arms races, alliances, hostility, and recurrent crises suggests that all, or nearly all, six are interrelated reciprocally. This interpretation suggests a reality that is far too complex for our current data and modeling abilities.[4] The sequencing order of half a dozen variables offers a number of alternatives that we will not seek to specify fully at this time. Instead, we focus primarily on the question of whether all of the theoretically sanctioned variables continue to be significant and correctly signed when they are introduced into the same equation. We will also make some initial effort to link their timing in an attempt to avoid the problem of giving too much credit to old alliances, crises, and rivalries. If we find that all of the variables are significant, additional support for Vasquez's steps-to-war theory will have been generated. But since we will not be testing the full theoretical argument but only one, albeit crucial, part of a larger assembly of argumentation about how wars come about, full confirmation of the theory will require much additional testing. In part for the same reason, should we find that only some of the theory's variables are significant, we cannot say that Vasquez's theory must be rejected.[5] We can, however, suggest some possible amendments to the original expression of how the variables are likely to be linked.

[4] We also have reasons to think that not all of these variables are as reciprocally related as Vasquez argues. For instance, Vasquez assumes that a number of disputes and crises precede the development of a sense of rivalry. That is one possible scenario but it is not necessarily the case if one chooses to define rivalry in non-dispute-density terms. Another example is the case of territorial disputes. In Chapter 9, we will find that it is actually quite rare for territorial disputes to precede the beginning of strategic rivalry. More often than not, both begin roughly at the same time.

[5] Any time one operationalizes a theory, the inevitable gap between concepts and indicators always suggests caution in using empirical results to reject (or to confirm) a theory. A different set of operationalizations of the same argument might well yield a different outcome.

Measurement, methodology, and research design

Operational choices must be made in testing complex theories. For instance, we prefer, in conformity with earlier chapters, to use information on strategic rivalries. We choose to examine crises in this chapter as opposed to the more prevalent focus on militarized disputes because crises come closest to the notion of a conflict event that might or might not escalate to war which, in turn, seems to come closer to the processes highlighted in Vasquez's theory. Many militarized disputes probably have only a remote chance of escalating to war. In this particular examination we rely on distinctions already made about our rivalry measure that differentiates rivalries according to their type of contentious issue (spatial versus positional rivalries). While our approach to measuring alliances and war is quite conventional, we have no way to measure the concept of hostility and therefore proceed without any hostility indicator. Nor do we make any effort to measure the cognitive rigidities or domestic politics components sketched in Figure 8.1.[6]

The point remains that we are quite well aware that other analysts might proceed differently. Whether alternative operational choices would have made any empirical difference remains to be seen.[7] Our principal concern at this juncture is that our choices are reasonable – not that they cover every possible contingency.

In order to examine the steps-to-war model empirically, we utilize the data set of recurrent crises and war employed in Chapter 5. The 1918–95 time frame we examine is dictated by the availability of the data. We do not include one-sided or intra-war crises since these have been shown to follow different dynamics than extra-war and dyadic or extra-dyadic crises. Using the crisis data we then create dummy variables for coding the number of previous crises between the dyad.

Having collected information on recurrent crises, we also gathered data on the other main steps-to-war variables. Mutual military build-ups are coded according to Horn's (1987) definition. This procedure defines build-ups as years when two states have above average arms expenditures, and the rate of arms expenditure is increasing over a specified period of time. Specifically, the average arms expenditure over the existence of a state was calculated, and each year's expenditure compared with this baseline. If expenditure was above average in a given year, and was increasing over the last six years, an arms race was present. This measurement rule

---

[6] We hasten to stress that it not unusual to construct only partial tests of theories. Indeed, it is the norm.

[7] The examinations conducted in Chapter 9 make use of different measurements for some variables such as territorial disputes.

was also used by Sample (1997, 1998). Military expenditure data are taken from the Correlates of War project.[8]

For the aggravating effect of external alliances we follow the rules laid out by Senese and Vasquez (2003), whereby a state has an external alliance only if an ally is politically relevant to a dyadic relationship. Political relevance is defined as any major–major or minor–major relationships, as well as minor–minor or major–minor relationships in which the allying parties are in the same region as a potential "target" state. For example, a US–Great Britain alliance is always relevant since they are both major powers, but a US–Canada alliance is only relevant to Canadian and US dyads if the other member of the dyad is in the same region. Regions and alliances are determined by the Correlates of War categorizations (Small and Singer, 1982).

To capture Vasquez's (1993) notion of territorial dispute we include a variable measuring whether or not two states are involved in a spatial rivalry.[9] If two states view each other as threatening competitors and enemies and compete over a spatial issue the variable is coded as one, otherwise it is zero. This variable is not examined in interaction with other variables because we believe that in the steps-to-war explanation, territorial and spatial issues make all situations more dispute prone, rather than being dangerous only in the presence of a military build-up or external alliances. We also code positional rivals using the same data set as a means of comparison.

It is important to note that our measures of both mutual military build-ups and alliances are generalizations of previous work. Sample (1997, 1998), Senese and Vasquez (2003), and Vasquez (2002) only look at observations with an ongoing militarized interstate dispute (MID). We extend these analyses by looking at all dyad years. We view this as a stiffer test of the steps-to-war explanation, not just because of possible selection bias issues, but because of the theoretical confusion between military build-ups (and external alliances) and war. It has been argued (Diehl, 1983; Diehl and Crescenzi, 1999) that mutual military build-ups precede disputes and wars because the potential adversaries already know they are going to war, and thus increase military expenditures. If this were the case,

---

[8] The national material capability data set (v2.1) is available at <www.cow2.la.psu.edu>. The nature of the data is discussed in Singer (1987). We also examined Diehl's (1983) approach to arms race coding, with similar results.

[9] As developed in Chapter 6, the two main types of strategic rivalries are spatial contests over the exclusive control of territory and positional contests over relative influence and status within the world system at large and/or in specific regional subsystems. Rivalries need not be exclusively one type or the other and, in fact, a large number of rivalries combine both foci. In this analysis, any rivalry with a spatial stake is coded as a spatial rivalry, even if there are also positional issues under contention.

then findings derived only from counting backwards from militarized dispute might over-report the danger of increased military expenditures. If military expenditures increased but never led to a militarized dispute this would not show up in a limited dispute-year analysis. Alternatively, by looking at mutual arms build-ups across the board, we can include these types of non-dispute build-ups in our analysis. If we still find a statistically significant build-up or external alliance effect, our confidence in the steps-to-war explanation will be increased. It should be highlighted that we see this type of dyad-year analysis as a complement rather than a competitor to previous dispute-year designs.[10]

Since arms races and external alliances are portrayed as more dangerous within the rubric of recurrent conflict, we include interaction variables between the number of previous crises and the presence or absence of external alliances and mutual military build-ups. These multiplicative interactions represent the product of two dummy variables, whether the dyad has experienced two or more previous crises, and either the external alliance or mutual military build-up variable.[11] Two variables are used to differentiate whether one or both states have an external alliance. This allows us to measure the potentially restraining effect that dual alliance ties may have on states in conflict.

We also control for four other variables that could potentially influence the probability of war. First, contiguity is included in the analysis in part since spatial rivalry could potentially only be measuring a proximity effect.[12] A variable is coded as one if the dyad is contiguous by land, zero otherwise. Second, it is commonly expected that major power dyads may behave differently and more coercively than other types of state pairings. Therefore, we include a dummy variable equal to one if two states are major powers, and zero otherwise. Third, the dyad under analysis could itself be allied, and confound any measure of external alliances. Accordingly, we measure whether two states are allied in any capacity to each other. Again, alliance coding follows the Correlates of War definitions. In acknowledgment of democratic peace arguments, as well as Huth's

[10] A research design similar to Sample (1997, 1998) and Sensese and Vasquez (2003), in which only years with crises are analyzed, leads to similar conclusions. For a middle ground between including all dyad-years and only crisis-years, we analyze a split-population model that relaxes the assumption that either all or none of the non-crisis years are at risk of a war (see below).

[11] Using different dispute cutoffs from two to four yielded substantively identical results. Two seems the best operationalization of "recurrent" crises since this is the earliest point at which one can say conflict has recurred.

[12] See Hensel's (2000) and Vasquez's (2001) discussions and analyses of this issue. Vasquez (1993) argues that territorial disputes between contiguous states are the most likely to escalate to war.

(1996b) argument that autocracies are more likely to fight over territorial disputes, we also include a measure of democracy in the analysis.[13] If at least one state scores a 6 or above on the Polity III democracy scale, the democracy variable is coded one, otherwise it is zero. As many theories, mainly realist in orientation but also encompassing Vasquez's non-realist theory, stress the role that capability ratios play in conflict situations we include a variable measuring the log of the ratio of the weaker powers' capabilities divided by the stronger powers' capabilities (see Brecher and Wilkenfeld, 1997; Geller, 2000).

We analyze the recurrent conflict and steps-to-war variables using event-history techniques. The dependent variable in our analysis is the risk of a war, measured by looking at the spells of peace between crises and wars. Variables that speed up or accelerate the hazard of war will reduce the spells of peace, while variables that slow the hazard of war will increase the spells of peace. Interpretation of the reported hazard ratios is similar to that of odds ratios in logit models. The main benefit of using event-history techniques rather than a logit or probit specification is the probable importance of dynamics in the prediction of wars (see Beck, Katz, and Tucker, 1998). Specifically, we use a Cox hazard model to link the independent and dependent variables because of the flexible baseline hazard (Allison 1995). The baseline hazard is factored with the constant in the Cox model, and the partial likelihood used to estimate the hazard ratios for the independent variables.[14] Robust standard errors are used to account for the non-independence of observations within dyads.

Finally, we also use a split population model to re-analyze the relationship between recurrent conflict and the steps to war. It is possible that not all dyads are continually at risk of war. If that is the case, including all dyads in our risk set could bias the estimated results (Clarke and Regan, 2003). Some scholars attempt to correct for this bias by selecting only dyads that are "politically relevant" for a particular analysis (see Lemke, 1995). The problem with selecting only politically relevant dyads is the possibility of losing some observations that may be informative for the

---

[13] Huth (1996b: 58) argues that autocracies are more likely to apply military pressure while democracies are more likely to accept compromise resolutions in territorial disputes.

[14] Generally, we would prefer to estimate a parametric survival model because the resulting predicted durations, as presented in Chapter 7, are intuitive and easy to understand. However, in this case, the baseline hazard is polytonic, rather than monotonic, and no parametric method we have tried presents an adequate fit for the initial decline, subsequent rise and then final descent of the underlying hazard. Since we take the possibility of duration dependence seriously, as well as to provide a multi-method check on work in other chapters using either bivariate probit or discrete time hazard models, we report the Cox models here. Substantively similar inferences were drawn from logit models fit with time-dependence splines.

analysis. For example, it has been shown that some politically irrelevant dyads have previously fought with each other (see Clarke and Regan, 2003). A split population design avoids many of these pitfalls. All dyads can be included in the analysis, and the probability of a dyad being at risk for war can be estimated based on various covariates. Clarke and Regan (2003) have expressed the split population model in conceptual terms as mirroring the processes of opportunity and willingness. Dyads that have no opportunity to fight are not at risk, while those with opportunity are at risk of war. These split population model results can be compared with the Cox model results to test the robustness of the findings.

Empirical findings

In the first confrontation between recurrent conflict data and the steps-to-war variables, both approaches appear to contribute several important predictors of war. As expected, we find that the greater the number of previous crises, generally, the greater the risk of war. While a dyad with one previous crisis has approximately five times the risk of war as a dyad with no history of crisis, a pair that has two or more crises is found to have approximately twenty-five times the risk of war, as compared to states with no history of crisis (Table 8.2, Model 1). The difference in the hazards of war between one previous crisis and two previous crises is significant at the 0.05 level for a two-tailed test. However, while the difference between one previous crisis and three or more crises is significant by the same measure, there is no statistical and substantive difference between the hazard of war after two, and three or more crises, *ceteris paribus*. The finding that the risk of war escalates over the number of previous crises mirrors the evidence in Chapter 5, but the finding that there is a risk plateau after two crises is a new finding.[15]

As for the other steps-to-war variables, only mutual arms build-ups and spatial rivalry increase the hazard of war. It is estimated that a pair of states involved in a mutual arms build-up increases the risk of war by 380 percent, as compared to a pair of states not involved in this arms competition ($p < 0.05$ for a two-tailed test, Model 1). Neither of the two external alliance variables are estimated to be significantly different from zero. Thus, it does not appear, at first glance, that relevant external alliances increase the risk of war.

In Model 2, we control for spatial rivalry as well as the other steps-to-war and recurrent conflict variables. As predicted by the steps-to-war

---

[15] The difference in findings could be a product of including military build-ups and external alliances, or the increased missing data that is brought on by controlling for these steps-to-war variables.

Table 8.2 Cox regression results for recurrent crises, mutual arms build-ups, alliances, and war

Variables	Model 1			Model 2			Model 3			Model 4		
	Hazard ratio	S.E.	Sig.	Hazard ratio	S.E.	Sig.	Hazard ratio	S.E.	Sig.	Hazard ratio	S.E.	Sig.
Spatial rivalry	—			33.619	39.78	***	15.192	20.397	**	33.178	38.205	***
Positional rivalry							5.481	4.355	**			
One crisis	4.97	3.328	**	2.563	1.682	*	2.973	2.115	*	—	—	
Two crises	24.82	16.092	***	5.906	4.208	***	6.003	4.523	***	—	—	
Three+crises	24.342	19.336	***	6.881	4.614	***	5.167	3.569	***			
Mutual military buildup	3.865	2.225	**	3.814	1.916	***	2.845	1.386	**	1.322	1.169	
Mutual military buildup* two+crises.	—			—						4.924	4.729	**
External ally on one side	1.145	0.633		0.825	0.441		0.730	0.368		0.5	0.372	
External ally* two+crises	—			—						13.991	12.81	***
Both sides have external ally	0.477	0.28		0.63	0.346		0.553	0.352		1.705	1.126	
Both sides have external ally* Two+crises	—			—						0.089	0.093	**
Contiguity	41.583	25.822	***	10.02	12.148	**	8.484	10.223	*	8.984	10.817	**
Alliance	0.979	0.577		1.041	0.565		1.248	0.802		1.24	0.691	
Capability ratio	0.41	0.297		0.383	0.26	*	0.232	0.195	*	0.38	0.233	*
Major powers	4.486	4.751		3.054	2.565	*	1.671	1.431		4.585	3.573	**
Democracy	0.387	0.2	**	0.546	0.304		0.427	0.270	*	0.489	0.273	
Wald chi-square	298.52			409.69			436.07			461.27		
N-size	384744			384744			384744			384744		

Note: The Efron method is used for ties; standard errors are adjusted for clustering within dyads. No main effects are included for dyads with more than two crises in Model 3 due to the fact that almost all of those observations also have mutual arms build-ups.

approach, spatial rivalry increases the risk of war by over 3,300 percent, as compared to a situation outside of spatial rivalry ($p < 0.01$ for a two-tailed test). It is also interesting to note that the inclusion of the spatial rivalry variables decreases the size, although not the significance, of the recurrent conflict variables. This outcome is not surprising since we established in the preceding chapter that spatial rivalries are the most likely to fight recurrently. In Model 3 (Table 8.2), we see that spatial rivalries remain extremely war-prone, but that rivalries with positional components also increase the risk of war by a factor of 5. Thus, Vasquez's focus on territorial issues is justified, but not to the complete exclusion of positional rivalry issues.

As summarized in Model 4, recurrent conflict and the other steps-to-war can be seen as complementary approaches to understanding war. Both external alliances and mutual arms build-ups become significant predictors of war when they are allowed to interact with previous crises. Additionally, in the absence of recurrent conflict (at least two previous crises), mutual military build-ups, previously estimated to increase the risk of war (Models 1 and 2), have no statistically discernible effect (Model 4). It is only after two previous crises that mutual build-ups become dangerous. Likewise, the situation in which one member of a dyad has an external alliance, in comparison to situations in which external alliances are absent, is not estimated to increase the risk of war, outside of a recurrent conflict situation. It is only after two or more crises that the war-proneness of an external alliance significantly increases the hazard of war.

The interconnectedness between recurrent crises and the steps-to-war is illustrated by the fact that no main effect for previous crises can be modeled when these interactions are included. Almost all observations with two or more previous crises have at least one external alliance and/or a mutual arms build-up. A cross-tabulation of the number of previous crises and steps-to-war (arms races, one-sided external alliances, and dual external alliances), shown in Table 8.3, illustrates this phenomenon. While we find that over 20 percent of the time no steps to war are taken in dyads with no previous crises, this percentage decreases significantly with recurring conflict. After a second crisis, over 97 percent of those dyad-years include at least one step to war. This finding reinforces Vasquez's (1993) notion that increased conflict leads to the use of realpolitik foreign policy. Further exploration of this link could be an interesting avenue for future work.[16]

---

[16] A threat to inference remains, however. Since we omitted controlling for recurrent crises in this model, the heightened risk of arms races after two or more crises could

Table 8.3 *Cross-tabulation of steps to war and previous crises (dyad-years)*

	Steps to war				
Previous crises	0	1	2	3	Row total
0	20.43	49.82	28.54	1.21	389,932
1	7.66	31.13	57.39	3.83	1,828
2	2.53	26.75	64.78	5.94	673
3 or more	2.75	32.65	62.54	2.06	291
Column total	79,204	193,628	112,086	4,806	389,724

Note: Numbers represent the row percentage of dyad-years for all states organized by the number of steps to war taken. The steps to war, in this table, are coded as an additive index comprised of whether an arms race (+1), at least one external alliance on one side (+1), or at least one external alliance on both sides (+1) is present. Chi-square = 1700.9 ($df =$ 9), significant at the 0.001 level.

While recurrent conflict helps to illuminate some of the steps-to-war, not all movement is in the direction predicted by that approach. The steps-to-war theory expects that a greater number of external alliance connections to a dyad increases the risk of war; we find that when both states in a dyad have external alliance ties, the risk of war actually decreases. In fact, we find that the risk of war is even lower for two states that have external alliances, after two or more previous crises, than if no external alliances were present. The finding that balanced external alliances decrease the hazard of war, gives some *prima facie* validity to a deterrence understanding of international politics, whereby a state may think twice before starting a war if the target state has a relevant alliance.[17]

Figure 8.2 compares the effect of mutual arms build-ups, and unbalanced and dual external alliances on the risk of war over time. Time is included on the X-axis because we have modeled the hazard of war as a

merely reflect the danger of recurrent crises, shown in previous models and Chapter 5. Therefore, to help to rule out this possibility we ran separate Cox regressions for those states that only had two or more crises and included arms races and dual external alliances. Both variables were in the inferred direction. Specifically, arms racing for states that have a history of crises increases the risk of war by a factor of 7.3 (90 percent CI: 3.2, 16.6) as compared with states with a history of crises but are not locked into an arms race. Dual external alliances reduce the risk of war by a factor of 4.8 (90 percent CI: 1.5, 14.6) for states that have competed in two or more previous crises. Thus in both of these cases we can say that there is evidence of the inferred interactive steps to war. More dramatically, there are no cases of a state without an external alliance, and having at least two prior crises, going to war. Thus, the maximum likelihood estimate for effect of one-sided alliances goes to infinite.

[17] See the analyses of Gartner and Siverson (1996) and Rasler and Thompson (1999) on the tendency of states to initiate wars against states without alliance partners.

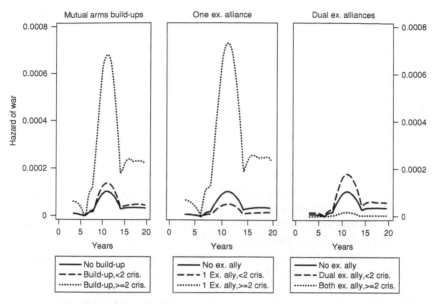

Figure 8.2 The effect of mutual arms build-ups and external alliances on the hazard of war.

time-dependent process. Each line on the figure is calculated by multiplying the estimated hazard ratio from Model 3 times the baseline hazard of a war occurring at each time point.[18] The figure illustrates that the effect of a mutual arms build-up on the hazard of war is equivalent to the war-proneness of unbalanced external alliances, in the presence of recurrent crises. This similarity does not prevail when a dyad has experienced fewer than two previous crises. The third figure illustrates the opposite effect, that dual external alliances decrease the risk of war after two or more crises. In each of the figures the non-linear relationship between time and the risk of war is in evidence.

As a robustness check, we also estimate a split-population model that relaxes the assumption that all dyads are at risk of war. When raw capabilities, mutual military build-ups, political relevance, and democracy are included as predictors of whether an opportunity for war was present, the substantive results remain the same. Mutual military build-ups and one side possessing an external alliance increase the risk of war after two or more previous crises, but not before that. Conversely, dyads with dual external alliances are less likely to go to war after two previous crises. The

[18] The baseline hazard was calculated by numerically differentiating the cumulative baseline hazard, then smoothing the resulting function.

Vuong statistic, a measure comparing non-nested models, suggests that the first-stage model does help to explain why some states may not be at war in a given year. In total, both the Cox and split-population models support a moderately revised steps-to-war model, in which recurrent conflict plays a central role. Similarly, the way in which disputes are handled, if in a realpolitik fashion, helps to explain why recurrent crises are dangerous.

Summary and conclusion

Wars are usually explained in terms of decision-maker attributes, group decision-making dynamics, national attributes, interstate interactions, and systemic structure, or some mixture of these alternative levels of analysis. Within the interstate interactions level, arms racing, alliances, rivalry, and crisis bargaining tend to take center stage as the main foci of analyses. Our question is not so much whether these foci are appropriate but, rather, how these processes come together to increase the probability of war.

We began with a model based on Vasquez's steps-to-war theory that brought together territorial disputes, recurrent crises, rivalry, military build-ups, and external alliances, among other variables and processes. In Vasquez's theory, these variables are closely related and many reciprocally so. In general, we find ample empirical support for many of the relationships predicted by Vasquez. Territorial disputes, to the extent that we capture them by focusing on spatial rivalries, clearly are an important source of interstate issues with high escalatory potential. Rivalry and recurrent crises are two critical processes leading to conflict escalation. Mutual military build-ups increase the probability of escalation. External alliances on only one side also aggravate the escalation potential, but only if a dyad has already experienced two crises.

It may not come as a great surprise to learn that arms races, alliances, recurrent crises, and rivalries enhance the likelihood of escalations to war. After all, we have been proceeding on the assumption for years that this is the case. But that is the problem: we have assumed the validity of their combined contributions to war outbreaks. Multivariate evidence, along with multivariate arguments, has been relatively scarce. Vasquez's steps-to-war theory is a notable exception in the area of multivariate arguments. To the extent that this theory represents a synthesis of a great deal of collective work in progress, the current findings bolster not only the accuracy of the theory but also the probability that we have been on the right empirical track(s) all along.

Much more multivariate work is in order. We have focused primarily on a cluster of interactive, interstate dynamics. There may be other ways to examine their sequencing, or whether it matters which process comes first. There are probably ways to refine our implicit, first-brush assumption that all spatial rivalries, recurrent crises, politically relevant alliances, and military build-ups over a certain threshold should be treated equally. We may well find also that the general model does not hold precisely the same over time or in all parts of the world.

At the same time, we need to move beyond an exclusive focus on one level of analysis. Vasquez's theory is certainly multilevel in combining cognitive rigidities, domestic politics, interstate dynamics, and international norms and structures. If decision-makers learn realpolitik proclivities, international relations analysts also have developed monovariate and mono-level modeling propensities that we, too, need to unlearn. Ideally, an improved appreciation for the substantiated linkages among territorial disputes, rivalries, recurrent crises, arms races, alliances, and war will facilitate this expansion of modeling and theorizing ambitions.

Chapter 9 will attempt to bring all of these factors together. But before we take that challenge on fully, we need to step back a bit and reconsider the role of territorial disputes in these conflict spirals. As it turns out, territorial disputes especially within the context of strategic rivalry prove to be quite crucial and will have a major influence in the construction of a more comprehensive test of Vasquez's steps-to-war theory.

9   Contested territory and conflict escalation

> Enlil, king of the lands, father of the gods, upon his firm command drew
> the border between [Lagash and Umma]. Mesalim, king of Kish, at the
> command of Ishtaran, measured the field and placed a stele. Ush, ruler
> of Umma, acted arrogantly. He ripped out the stele and marched unto
> the plain of Lagash. Ningirsu, the hero of Enlil, at the latter's command
> did battle with Umma. Upon Enlil's command he cast the great battle-
> net upon it. Its great burial mound was set up for him in the plain.
>
> (taken from Van de Mieroop, 2004: 46)

The passage above is an excerpt from a contemporary account of a Sume-
rian border conflict between Lagash and Umma that persisted roughly
between 2500 and 2350 BCE. After the war described in the excerpt, the
boundaries were redrawn by the winners only to be repeatedly contested
by Umma, at least according to the Lagash version of events. Undoubt-
edly, this Lagash–Umma conflict was not the first territorial squabble
between states but it is probably the first one on which we have some doc-
umentation. Since that time, states have multiplied, as have their borders,
and so have their consequent disagreements about where those boundaries should be placed.

Some 4,350 years after the Lagash–Umma conflict, we have learned
a number of things about the role of contested territory in the escalation of interstate conflict.[1] For instance, there is little controversy that
contested territory plays a central role in the escalation of force and the
onset of war.[2] We also know that territorial disagreements tend to recur
(Goertz and Diehl, 1992b; Hensel, 1994; Vasquez, 2001), that contested
territory seems to be associated with dyads that experience more militarized disputes than fewer ones (Tir and Diehl, 2002), and that recurring

---

[1] For those curious about the ultimate outcome of the conflict, Mesopotamia was taken
over by Akkad around 2350 BCE, thereby presumably rendering the dispute moot for
some time.

[2] See Gochman and Leng, 1983; Vasquez, 1993, 1995, 1996, 2001; Hensel, 1994, 1996,
2000; Kocs, 1995; Ben Yehuda, 1997; Vasquez and Henehan, 2001; and Senese and
Vasquez, 2003.

240

disputes have a marked propensity to escalate to war (Leng, 1983; Chapter 5). Furthermore, we know that coercive strategies over territory are most likely to be reciprocated by other states (Hensel and Diehl, 1994; Hensel, 1996; Mitchell and Prins, 1999) and that this behavior results in combat deaths (Senese, 1996; Hensel, 2000). In view of this evidence, it is not surprising that a number of analysts nominate territorially based conflicts as the most significant source of interstate warfare (Hill, 1945; Luard, 1970; Vasquez, 1993; Hensel, 2000).

Contested territory may well prove to be a central clue in the unraveling of war causality. Yet we maintain that territorial disagreements are not the only important factor in escalation processes. Nor are territorial antagonisms the only phenomena that recur, generate reciprocal coercive behavior, or produce combat deaths. Rivalries, for example, possess these same tendencies. We argue that in some cases contested territory leads to the development of rivalries while in others rivalries lead to the development of territorial claims. In still other situations, rivalries and contested territory emerge simultaneously. Presumably, all three types of causality in which rivalry and territorial disputes become fused have a strong potential for escalation.

Our main question at least initially in this chapter, therefore, is how contested territory and interstate rivalries interact to make uses of force and war more probable. We argue that the prevailing idea that contested territorial claims emerge, lead to militarized uses of force when states assert contending claims, and then produce interstate rivalries that occasionally lead to war escalation is not in fact the norm. More commonly, we find that a number of territorial disagreements are embedded within rivalry contexts and that these are the ones that are most likely to escalate into armed clashes. Hence, we hypothesize that contested territory combined with rivalry work together to produce militarized contention. After thoroughly exploring this idea in the first half of the chapter, we move on to consider its robustness when additional factors are introduced.

The conflict potential of contested territory in the context of strategic rivalry

There should be little mystery about why territorial disagreements possess considerable conflict potential.[3] Most territory has some intrinsic value that may be perceived as worth fighting for by at least some groups within a society. For instance, citizens and states desire territory because it

---

[3] See Vasquez (1993), Hensel (2000), and Huth (2000) for good overviews of the conflict potential in territorial disputes.

means control over important resources, populations, or markets even if these commodities are only imagined or have future potential. If these commodities are valued highly enough, states may become involved in extended militarized disputes, as the 1932–5 Chaco War illustrates. Another way that territory can be contentious is when it facilitates access to some other place that is useful for attacking and defending a homeland area or trade route. The Beagle Islands dispute between Argentina and Chile over Chilean access to the Atlantic and Antarctic claims that ended only in 1984 is such an example. Controlling the Golan Heights, on the other hand, is viewed as a critical national security issue by Israel and Syria.

Territory can also overlap with nationalism. When people perceive themselves as belonging to some greater political collectivity that is also associated with territorial boundaries, they are likely to equate defense of the collectivity with the precise location and defense of those boundaries. Since new states tend to inherit boundaries decided by other governments, citizens and leaders are likely to contest these boundaries for a long period of time. These issues, however, can be even more difficult to resolve if the boundaries divide groups of people with common ethnic, linguistic, cultural, or religious identities. Irredentist sentiments and projects for the integration of scattered peoples tend to linger in the political discourse for lengthy periods. The Somali case, involving conflicts with a number of adjacent states over the extent of Greater Somalia and as well as the 1976 Ogaden War, is a prime example of this phenomenon, although the greater Serbian projects of the 1980s and 1990s are more recent examples.

It is often pointed out that territorial issues are also distinctive in terms of their fit with coercive displays of force. The seizure and defense of specified pieces of real estate are what armies are trained to do. Unlike more abstract issues, states know exactly what to do about territorial claims so long as they have the relative means to acquire and maintain control over them. If states do not have adequate coercive power, then they may be able to develop the necessary fire power. Although there might be domestic resistance to the costs or wisdom of such a strategy, leaders find that the defense or expansion of the national homeland is an issue that is less likely to provoke serious criticism than other less nationalistic issues. Such issues become emotional tests of patriotism as opposed to questions of dispassionate logic or rationality.

On the other hand, leaders will find it more difficult to compromise on homeland issues without incurring substantial domestic costs. Consequently, questions about who controls a given territory may never fully be resolved. What may seem a decisive conquest at one time can still be challenged generations later should the issue retain some convenient nationalistic and political appeal. For instance, the Falklands/Malvinas dispute lay dormant for over a century before being resurrected for political purposes a few decades before it escalated to war in 1982. Sino-Soviet fighting in the late 1960s over adjacent territory reflected boundary disputes going back some three centuries. Bolivians still seek access to the Pacific. The question of Gibraltar never quite goes away, even though the intensity of Spanish pressures fluctuates from decade to decade.

In sum, territorial issues can be difficult to paper over or ignore. They can also be quite tempting for politicians who seek messages that are likely to have strong domestic political payoffs. Yet, once adopted as part of a state's foreign policy agenda, territorial issues can prove quite difficult to manage. The territory in question may have little intrinsic value but its symbolic value can easily become inflated. In other cases, though, territorial issues can become imbued with life-or-death urgency if the territory is perceived to be, or is convincingly portrayed as being, critical to national military and/or economic security.

For these reasons, the analytical expectation is that contested territory has some significant probability of leading to militarized disputes and, to the extent that these conflicts are protracted, interstate rivalry and war. There are two questions implicit to this statement. One is the probability question. Is contested territory apt to increase the likelihood of militarized disputes, rivalry, and war? A second question, however, is whether we have the progression of conflict processes correct?

Is the sequence: contested territory → militarized disputes → rivalry → war? There are, of course, several different ways to reorder this chain of variables. But this sequence is based on the widespread view that rivalry should be defined in terms of the density of militarized disputes (see, for instance, Huth, 1996a, 2000; Diehl and Goertz, 2000; Tir and Diehl, 2002). If one accepts that assumption, this particular pattern is redundant because it suggests the following: contested territory → militarized disputes → war. This assumption also sacrifices the explanatory power of interstate rivalry in discriminating among territorial issues that may escalate to militarized clashes and warfare.

To the contrary, we suspect interstate rivalry is an important predictor of the escalations of territorial disagreements. Yet we do not see rivalry as a consequence of clashes over real estate. Rather, we believe that rivalry defines the broader context in which clashes over the control of land (and other things) occur. Rivals, in comparison to nonrivals, are more likely to fight over territory not only because of any intrinsic territorial value but also because they mistrust, fear, and dislike their adversaries. Rivalry injects a psychological flavor to a dispute that can both help magnify the perceived value of the territory and the real domestic costs of making concessions to a rival. As a consequence, we expect the most dangerous territorial contests to be intertwined with rivalry. Territorial issues between nonrivals should be less difficult to manage short of warfare.

Our expectation is predicated on a very specific conceptualization of strategic rivalry that is based on the perceptions that leaders have about their competitors and their enemies. Many state leaders compete with other states without identifying them as threatening or hostile enemies. There are even cases where leaders will perceive other states as threatening but not very competitive. This perception of rivalry will influence how states interact over territorial contests. For instance, Spain and Great Britain were once competitive rivals until Britain definitively established its military primacy *vis-à-vis* Spain in an eighteenth-century war that ensued over a territorial dispute involving Gibraltar. As the rivalry between Great Britain and Spain waned, Spanish attempts to retake Gibraltar by force became less likely in the nineteenth and twentieth centuries. This territorial issue certainly has persisted but in the absence of a strategic rivalry (among other factors), the potential for military escalation has diminished greatly.

Other examples come to mind. Would the Sino-Soviet fighting in the late 1960s over their mutual boundaries have occurred during the brief 1950s interlude in their long-lived rivalry? Or did it become more probable as their strategic rivalry over a variety of issues intensified in the 1960s? Yemeni–Saudi border clashes, similarly, were more evident in the early 1930s and the 1990s and less so in the intervening years. The location of the land in question has not changed over the last eight decades, but Yemeni–Saudi perceptions of their neighbor's hostility have fluctuated. Are repetitive clashes between India and Pakistan over Kashmir to be understood only in terms of the intrinsic value of Kashmiri real estate? Or, is control of Kashmir a stalking horse for a variety of symbolic and material interests? In other words, might the perceptions of threat and hostility be more important than the territorial claims?

Nonetheless, the effect of rivalry on conflict escalation is not a one-way street. The escalatory potential of the Egyptian–Israeli conflict, for instance, became even greater once Israel controlled Egyptian territory after 1967. Before 1967, the Egyptians had more choice in whether they intensified their conflict with Israel. After 1967, the loss of the Sinai left them much less maneuvering room. Likewise, Bolivian–Paraguayan warfare became more probable when the perceived value of the Chaco area was upgraded by beliefs that oil might be extracted from the desert. Moreover, Bolivia's loss of a Pacific access in the late nineteenth century also meant that control of rivers flowing to the east would become more desirable as alternative trade outlets.

Interstate rivalries also become intertwined with territorial disputes that involve the protection of ethnic enclaves in adjacent states. Rivalry perceptions can hinge on the geographical location of key groups who have some claim to cross-national ties and just happen to inhabit adjacent territory that is under the control of another state or rival. The Kashmir example could be said to combine territorial, ethnic, religious, strategic, and ideological issues although not necessarily equally (see Ganguly, 1997). To what extent then or in what sense can we trace the roots of the Indo-Pakistani conflict to a territorial issue? It seems more accurate to say that in this case, and others, territorial issues are intertwined with a number of issues that have led to the emergence and maintenance of the Indo–Pakistani rivalry, in this case from the very outset of independence.

We do not argue, however, that contested territory is unlikely to escalate conflict levels in the absence of a strategic rivalry. Contested territory, presumably, can be sufficiently salient in its own right to lead to shooting matches. We suggest only that they are much more likely to do so within the context of strategic rivalry. Our expectation and main hypothesis, therefore, is that contested territory, especially if a sense of strategic rivalry already exists, leads to militarized disputes, and, in some cases, to war.

> H1: Contested territory, within the context of rivalry, is more prone to militarized disputes and warfare than is contested territory that takes place outside the context of rivalry.

Interpretation of this hypothesis depends in part on how we define rivalry. If we were to take the dispute-density approach to defining rivalry, the proposition essentially says that territorial issues that occur within the context of a number of militarized disputes and over a restricted time frame are more prone to militarized disputes and war. We can avoid this tautology by viewing rivalry as a relationship between adversaries who identify each other as threatening competitors and enemies. Once these perceptions are secured, subsequent interactions between these states are likely to result in suspicion and hostility that can lead to misperceptions, expectations of bad faith behavior, and especially the exaggeration of hostility underlying an adversary's actions. Whether this psychological baggage leads to physical conflict in any specific rivalry relationship remains an open question. In general, we believe that physical conflict is more probable within a rivalry context than outside of it but all strategic rivalries do not by definition engage in militarized disputes.

We maintain that the custom of conceptualizing rivalry as sets of densely timed militarized disputes has led to the expectation that rivalry is an outcome of heightened conflict relations. In other words, one starts with a disagreement of some sort, the disputants clash repeatedly, and then their actions escalate to a series of militarized disputes and rivalry which may or may not escalate further to war. Such a sequence is not implausible, but we believe that it may not be the only or the more probable sequence. For example, a number of territorially oriented conflicts have begun at the very outset of independence of one or more of the disputants. So, too, have a number of rivalries. The combinations of India and Pakistan, Algeria and Morocco, the United States and Mexico in the early nineteenth century, Israel and Jordan, Belize and Guatemala come readily to mind.

Our point here is that the timing of the development of a rivalry context should be an empirical question.[4] Some rivalries begin at the outset of independence and external disputes. Others take time to emerge. Although it may not make much difference to the likelihood of conflict escalation as to when the rivalry developed so long as the rivalry is in place, it should be useful to at least check the apparent sequencing of contested territory, rivalry, and militarized conflict as an auxiliary question.

A third consideration is that territorial disagreements are not always conflicts over contiguous space, especially when rivals are not proximate to one another. Contiguous territorial disputes, however, should be more dangerous than ones separated by some distance. Adjacency makes it much easier to move troops to the contested area. Such "backyard" conflicts are also more difficult to ignore politically. More distant territorial disputes create substantial logistical problems for armed forces to overcome and only some armed forces have the capability to project force afar. "Backyard" conflicts are also more difficult to ignore politically while public and governmental awareness of distant conflicts will wax and wane depending on whether closer-to-home considerations loom larger. Thus, we think that the most potent lethal combination should be contiguous territorial disputes that are embedded in strategic rivalry relationships.[5] On this basis, we hypothesize the following:

> H2: The triadic combination of contiguous contested territory between strategic rivals has significantly more escalatory potential for militarized disputes and warfare than the total absence of these factors or the presence of only one or two of them.

---

[4] This orientation has some linkage to the debate (Goertz and Diehl, 1998, 2000b) over punctuated equilibrium versus evolutionary models of rivalry which is basically about whether the effects of rivalry begin abruptly and stay fairly level thereafter or whether tensions are more gradually developed. However, both sides of this particular debate assume dispute-density which means, in turn, that a sufficient number of militarized disputes must precede the abrupt or gradual onset of rivalry.

[5] This assertion is strongly emphasized in the territorial dispute literature and, in particular, is a core argument in Vasquez's steps-to-war theory. Tir and Diehl (2002) also find support for the combination of territorial dispute and contiguity.

Our final concern relates to the temporal stability of the territorial conflict complex involving disputes, rivalries, contiguity, and regime type. There is reason to think that the influence of territorial disputes as a source of interstate conflict may be on the wane. Huth and Allee (2002: 27), for instance, examine 348 territorial conflicts that occurred during the 1919–95 period in what is the most comprehensive collection of contested territory cases assembled to date. Regionally, the persistence of such disputes appears to vary. The number of ongoing contests in Europe and the Americas is declining: 95 in 1919–45 and 51 in 1946–95. The number in the Middle and Near East (36 to 53), Africa (17 to 31), and Asia (14 to 51) appears to be increasing but not at equal rates in all three regions. Yet there is a problem in interpreting these numbers. There were far fewer states in the 1919–45 period than there have been in the post-1945 era. Let us assume that each conflict involved a different pair of states and that there were 157 territorial disputes in 1919–45 and, say, an average of 60 states in that period and 191 disputes in 1946–95 and an average of roughly 125 states in the more recent period. Then the normalized ratio of 1919–45:1946–95 disputes would be 2.6:1.5 – a reduction of about 43 percent.[6] But even this correction understates the decline in the relative number of disputes. Sixty states create 1,770 dyads while 125 states translate into 7,750 dyads. If we divide the number of conflicts by the number of dyads that could be in contention, the ratio is 0.089:0.025, or about a 72 percent reduction in the relative prevalence of contested territorial cases.

Without becoming too concerned at this point about the exact reduction in the prevalence of contested territory, we infer that a decreased prevalence might alter the way in which contiguity, territorial issues, rivalry, and regime type interact. In addition, there are also regional shifts in the location of territorial contests. In 1919–45, more than half (57 percent) of the cases took place in Europe and the Americas. In 1946–95, less than a third (about 29 percent) occurred in the same regions. So, contested territory is becoming less likely but more Afro-Eurasian in location. These changes might suggest over time behavioral differences but, if so, it is not clear what we should anticipate, other than perhaps a weaker role for regime type differences. Yet, even that may not be the case. In the absence of a clear theoretical clue, we will check the temporal stability of our findings as a potential threat to the validity of our findings.[7]

---

[6] The assumption that each dispute involves a different pair of states is not accurate but it is a reasonable short cut for the sake of the illustration that is being advanced.

[7] We will point out a potential problem along the way that involves the large number of cases associated with World War II. However, this is a problem for which we can develop appropriate controls

Data and variable measurements

Our two hypotheses require data on the timing and location of territorial disputes and rivalry, the proximity of the adversaries, militarized disputes, and war. Several standard control variables (major power status, alliance relationships, and peace years) also need to be examined. In addition, we add a control for dyads pitting democracies versus autocracies. Gleditsch and Hegre (1997) argue and empirically support the notion that this type of dyad is particularly conflict-prone. Rasler and Thompson (2003), moreover, have also found close linkages between conflictual strategic rivalries and dyads of mixed regime type.

Our contested territory data are taken from Huth and Allee's (2002: 305–424) case list.[8] Their cases, encompassing the 1919–95 period, are defined (Huth and Allee, 2002: 300) as:

disagreements between governments over (a) the location of existing international boundaries in particular sectors or along the lengths of their common borders, (b) the refusal of one government to recognize another's claim of sovereign rights over islands, claiming sovereignty for itself instead, or (c) the refusal of one government to recognize another state as a sovereign political-territorial unit, laying claim to the territory of that state.

We convert their case material into dyadic records of the existence of any territorial disputes between two states on a year-by-year basis. Multiple disputes between the same parties ongoing in the same year are treated the same way as single disputes.

As in our other chapters, we rely on the 1816–1999 strategic rivalry data set. Since the span of the territorial dispute data dictates the time span of this analysis, all information on rivalries and territorial disputes that began prior to 1919 is censored.[9] Contiguity (common land border or within 150 miles by sea), major power status (following Correlates of War conventions), and alliances (the members of a dyad are either allied or not) are taken from EUGene (Bennett and Stam, 2000).[10] Polity III (Jaggars and Gurr, 1995) regime type data are employed (democratic dyads are those in which both parties possess a +6 score after subtracting the 1–10 autocracy score from its 1–10 democracy score; mixed dyads

---

[8] We are particularly indebted to Paul Huth and Todd Allee for providing the case material prior to its actual publication.

[9] The absence of some data past 1992 establishes that year as the last year in the data analysis. Information on contested territory and rivalries after 1992 is also eliminated from the analysis.

[10] Keep in mind that contiguity measures the proximity of the dyad members and not whether any territorial disputes involve adjacent territory.

Table 9.1 *Frequency of dyad-years, 1919–1992 (excluding pre-1919 contested territory and rivalries)*

Variable	Militarized interstate disputes are present	Militarized interstate disputes are absent	Total	War is present	War is absent	Total
Contested territory	2,124	256	2,380	78	2,302	2,380
Contested territory with rivalry	145	622	767	58	709	767
Contested territory without rivalry	111	1,502	1,613	20	1,593	1,613
Rivalry	246	1,536	1,782	79	1,703	1,782

Note: Frequency of dyad-years for only militarized interstate disputes and war is 735 and 398 respectively.

are those in which one party qualifies as a democracy and the other does not).[11]

To assess whether our earlier findings are due to relying on crisis information, we look this time at militarized disputes (MIDs), taken from the MID data set (version 2.1 as modified by Zeev Maoz to create dyadic structures) in this chapter. The frequency of dyad-years for contested territory, rivalry, and their combinations in the presence and absence of MIDs and war can be found in Table 9.1. Note that in this table and the other examinations to follow, we restrict our examination to relationships between the presence or absence of territorial grievance, rivalry, and conflict escalation. We do not actually trace, on a case-by-case basis, whether territorial grievances are critical to interstate rivalry or whether conflict escalation is linked closely to territorial grievances *per se.* Such specific tracing is no doubt worth doing but would require a much different and more complicated type of undertaking than the more crude one pursued in this chapter.[12] At this point, we must be content to know whether and to what extent certain dyadic attributes (territorial grievances, rivalry) appear to be linked systematically to subsequent conflict escalation. That

[11] The regime type dummies are coded 1 if they satisfy the joint democracy or mixed dyad criteria and 0 if the dyads are autocracies.

[12] This type of process tracing would require a detailed analysis of the purported causes of each militarized dispute and war. Since the factors thought to be involved would in many cases be either absent or controversial, one would end up writing a history of conflict escalation over the past two centuries that would encompass a great deal of missing "data." An alternative approach would be to focus on a select number of cases for process tracing but this too constitutes another type of analysis than the one undertaken in this chapter.

is something different than knowing precisely when and how often these linkages can be tracked in the historical record.

Methodology

Our methodological strategy combines two approaches. We have two principal interests: one pertains to assessing probabilities of conflict escalation and the other to examining the sequencing of conflict processes. For the latter interest, we examine the timing of disputes and strategic rivalries in order to ascertain the various sequential combinations. We then determine which combinations appear to be most likely to lead to conflict escalation in terms of the occurrence of militarized disputes and wars. The outcome will help us in assessing hypothesis H2. Since this is not a sufficiently sophisticated test to gauge the probabilities of conflict escalation, we also rely on a "unified model" that examines the escalation of MIDs and war.

Reed (2000), Huth and Allee (2002), and Senese and Vasquez (2003) maintain that conflict theorists must be alert to the possibilities of selection bias in studying the causes of militarized interstate disputes and war onsets among dyads.[13] Selection bias is likely to occur when researchers fail to consider that the variables that influence dispute onsets also influence war escalation. Since similar covariates are likely to determine both of these processes, we cannot neglect the indirect effects that certain variables have on war through their direct effects on dispute onsets. By focusing on wars alone, scholars may make the mistake of relying on a biased sample that neglects to include cases in which disputes failed to result in war escalation. One solution to this problem is to estimate a unified model or the joint likelihood of dyads becoming involved in a dispute and the escalation of the dispute to war via a censored probit model (Reed, 2000: 87). Specifically, we estimate two equations (one for dispute initiation and the second for war) simultaneously with a seemingly unrelated probit analysis.[14] We examine the over-time stability of

---

[13] Other scholars have discussed this selection problem. See, among others, Levy (1989), Morrow (1989), Bueno de Mesquita (1996), Gartner and Siverson (1996), and Huth (1996b).

[14] The seemingly unrelated probit analysis produces a nonzero correlation between the residuals of the two equations for each of our dependent variables. If we fail to estimate this residual correlation, the residuals could be confounded with the estimates of the independent variables. Therefore, biased estimates are likely to occur. In an effort to avoid this problem, seemingly unrelated probit analysis assumes that the residuals of our two equations are distributed as a standard bivariate normal distribution, and the coefficients are estimated with a maximum likelihood estimation approach (Greene, 1999). In addition to allowing a nonzero correlation in our probit models, we control for the temporal dependence among dyads across years in the first model of dispute initiation by using the cubic spline technique developed by Beck, Katz, and Tucker (1998).

Table 9.2 *The sequencing of contested territory, militarized disputes, and strategic rivalries*

Dispute-rivalry sequence	Number	Percent
Contested territory → Militarized disputes	56	51.8
Contested territory and rivalry → Militarized disputes	33	30.6
Rivalry → Contested territory → Militarized disputes	4	3.7
Rivalry → Militarized disputes → Contested territory	4	3.7
Contested territory → Rivalry → Militarized disputes	4	3.7
Contested territory → Militarized disputes → Rivalry	3	2.8
Contested territory	3	2.8
Contested territory → Rivalry	1	0.9
Total	108	100.0

the results by redoing our 1919–92 analysis for the more recent 1946–92 period.

Data analysis

We begin with our less complicated examination of the interest in lethality and the distribution of timing sequences. We suspect that the prevailing notion that contested territory leads to militarized disputes which, in turn, lead to rivalries is not likely to find much empirical support. We think rivalry is likely to come much earlier in the sequencing.

Table 9.2 displays the eight sequences discernible when the Huth–Allee territorial conflict 1919–95 database is compared with the timing of strategic rivalry and militarized interstate disputes.[15] The most common sequence is contested territory to militarized dispute (nearly 52 percent). The next most common sequence is the contested territory/rivalry to militarized disputes sequence (not quite 31 percent). This outcome might suggest that our expectation that the more dangerous territorial conflicts are intertwined with strategic rivalry is not supported. There is a very strong difference, however, in the number of militarized disputes that occur in the first two rows. The contested territory → militarized disputes sequence is associated with an average of 1.79 militarized disputes per dyad. The contested territory/rivalry → militarized disputes sequence leads to an average of 5.3 militarized disputes per dyad. Clearly, militarized disputes are possible in the absence of rivalry but they are also much more likely in its presence.

---

[15] The timing of territorial conflicts and strategic rivalries is based strictly on the years in which these issues and relationships are believed to have begun.

If we contrast sequences that involve rivalry and militarized disputes with those that do not involve either one, we find a more balanced distribution. The 56 cases of contested territory and militarized disputes without rivalry still outnumber the 49 cases in which both types of conflict and rivalry are found, but the gap is much less (approximately 6 percent). Yet, two-thirds of the militarized disputes linked to contested territory are associated with the cases in which rivalry is present.[16] This imbalanced proportion translates into a 2.16 average number of militarized disputes for the cases in which interstate rivalry is absent and a 4.98 average for cases in which rivalry is present. Again, we can only conclude that contested territory and rivalry are a more lethal combination than contested territory alone.

Two other features of Table 9.2 also deserve emphasis. One is that what we have described as the predominant image of conflict sequences (contested territory → militarized disputes → rivalry) is rather rare. Only three cases were found that corresponded to this pattern. Equally rare are contested territory cases in the Huth–Allee data set that are not linked in some fashion to subsequent (none of the eight sequences begin with MIDs) militarized disputes. This last fact hints that the Huth–Allee data are biased toward states that have some predisposition to clash with one another. An even more comprehensive collection of territorial dispute cases might then demonstrate a weaker relationship between contested territory and conflict. Nonetheless, this speculation does not mean that the Huth–Allee data are too biased to use. It only means that we need to continue developing more information on the distribution of territorial disagreements before we will be able to assess conclusively the linkages among rivalry and various types of disputes.

In the interim, even stronger evidence for the lethality of combining contested territory with rivalry is forthcoming if we switch the focus to the onset of wars, as opposed to militarized disputes. In Table 9.3, each war participating dyad was coded for the presence/absence of an ongoing territorial conflict and interstate rivalry at the time of the outbreak of war. The numbers that best correspond to the MIDs examination above

---

[16] Tir and Diehl (2002) single out MIDs that have a territorial issue in their analysis of territorial disputes. We do not primarily because we have some uneasiness about the extent to which militarized disputes can be attributed to a single conflict issue. States in conflict are likely to have multiple issues at stake. Choosing to use or threaten force ostensibly over a boundary dispute may conceal other motivations. As a consequence, we prefer to link contested territory to militarized disputes in general, as opposed to specified types of militarized disputes. There is also the related awkwardness of defining conflict, contested territory, and rivalry in terms of the same militarized dispute data. We prefer ostensibly independent measures of these concepts when offered a choice, as we stress later in this chapter.

Table 9.3 *Contested territory, strategic rivalry, and interstate war*

Contested territory present	Strategic rivalry present	All war participant dyads	Percentage	Non-World War II war participant dyads	Percentage
Yes	Yes	49	20.3	40	41.2
Yes	No	10	4.1	5	5.2
No	Yes	16	6.6	6	6.2
No	No	166	68.9	46	47.4
		241	99.9	97	100.0

involve the two combinations in which a territorial disagreement was ongoing at the outset of warfare. One fifth of the cases involved both an ongoing territorial conflict and interstate rivalry. About 4 percent were characterized by an ongoing territorial conflict alone. But these numbers are heavily influenced by the large number of dyads associated with the coalitional warfare of the past sixty-five years.[17] Nearly 60 percent of the total number of dyads is linked to World War II. If we exclude all of the World War II dyads as representing a major source of distortion for present purposes, the ratio of contested territory + rivalry cases to contested territory alone is an even more impressive 41.2 percent:5.2 percent (or 8 to 1).

Thus, there appears to be fairly substantial support for the notion that contested territory is more deadly when it is paired with strategic rivalry. Militarized disputes are more often linked to the former situation by a factor of 2.3 to 1. Wars are linked to contested territory/rivalry settings, in comparison with contested territory alone settings, by a factor of either 5:1 or 8:1, depending on which cases are examined. Moreover, we have ample additional evidence that territorial conflicts have some significant link to militarized disputes and wars. Most of the Huth–Allee cases of territorial conflict have been followed by militarized disputes (92.6 percent) according to Table 9.2. One fourth to nearly one half of the participating war dyads since 1919, depending on which columns are examined, were engaged in a territorial conflict when they escalated their antagonisms to the level of full-scale warfare.

---

[17] Specifically, we are referring to World War II, Korea, Vietnam, and the first Persian Gulf War that involved states as combatants that would most certainly have not been involved in warfare at the time if they had not been encouraged to join relatively large coalitions of states with highly variable contributions to the respective war efforts.

Table 9.4 *Interaction of rivalry and contested territory on militarized interstate disputes and war, 1919–1992 (excluding pre-1919 contested territory and rivalries)*

Variable	Militarized interstate disputes		War onset	
	Coefficient	Z-statistic	Coefficient	Z-statistic
Contested territory with rivalry	**1.14**	17.10	**1.31**	14.56
Contested territory without rivalry	**1.07**	16.56	**0.65**	6.24
Contiguity	**1.04**	22.86	**0.47**	6.87
Allies	0.06	1.34	**−0.37**	−4.76
Major power status	**1.25**	13.75	**1.41**	14.84
Democracies vs. autocracies	**0.09**	3.23	**0.10**	3.02
Peace years[a]	**−0.12**	−12.13	–	–
Constant	**−2.74**	−84.54	**−3.25**	−131.67
Rho $\varepsilon_1\ \varepsilon_2$[b]	**0.14**			
	(0.06)			
Log likelihood no. of observations	**−6805.34**			
	444,460			

Note: Bold coefficients are statistically significant at 0.05 or lower; two-tailed tests. Z-statistics are based on robust standard errors.
[a]Spline coefficients are not reported.
[b]Robust standard error is reported below the rho coefficient.

Even if these numbers eventually require some deflation once more extensive territorial conflict databases become available, they are impressive. Contested territory, rivalries, and militarized conflicts at various levels obviously come together with some frequency. Still, neither Table 9.2 nor Table 9.3 is capable of informing us fully about the probability of contested territory leading to militarized disputes and war, within and outside the context of strategic rivalry. A different and more rigorous research design is needed.

Hypothesis H1 predicts that territorial conflicts that take place within ongoing strategic rivalries will be more prone to escalation than disputes that are not linked to rivalries. Table 9.4 shows the effects of contested territory in a rivalry context (in comparison to contested territory without rivalry) on dispute initiation and war escalation for 1919–92. Considering dispute initiation first, we find that the interaction between contested territory and rivalry has a significant positive effect as does contested territory without rivalry while controlling for contiguity, alliances, major power status, and mixed dyads (democratic vs. autocratic regimes). This relationship holds for war onset as well. Moreover, allied dyads have little association with dispute initiation but a strong negative one with war onset. Mixed dyads (democracies vs. autocracies) are more likely to be associated with both dispute initiation and war onset.

Which variables or combination of variables are more likely to result in dispute initiation and war onset can be determined by calculating the marginal probabilities that are derived from our bivariate probit model in Table 9.4. Table 9.5 lists the probability of a dispute initiation and war onset when changing the value of one or more independent variables from zero to one, while holding the rest of the variables at zero. For militarized interstate disputes, contested territory in combination with rivalry has a slightly higher percent change in probability (17.1 percent) than contested territory that occurs in the absence of rivalry (15 percent; see column "c" of the table). Contiguity, alone, has a significant impact on dispute initiation (13.7 percent), while mixed dyads have little effect (less than 1 percent). Dispute initiation for mixed dyads that occur within the context of contested territory and rivalry (20.7 percent), furthermore, does not increase appreciably more than contested territory that does not occur within the context of either mixed dyads and rivalry (18.3 percent).

The probabilities associated with war onset, however, yield dramatically different results. First, territorial conflicts within the context of rivalry have a stronger association with war, a 44 percent change in probability, than territorial conflicts that occur in the absence of rivalry, a 6.7 percent change in probability (see column "f" in Table 9.5). Moreover, contested territory that occurs in both the context of rivalry and mixed dyads is associated with a 54 percent change in the probability of war onset, relative to a 9 percent change for contested territory that does not occur with rivalry and mixed dyads. Contiguity, on the other hand, has a 4 percent change in probability, while mixed dyads alone have a less than 1 percent change in probability of war onset.

Hypothesis H1 predicts that contested territory that takes place within ongoing strategic rivalries will be more prone to escalation than territorial conflicts that are not linked to rivalries. Tables 9.4 and 9.5 show that this hypothesis is supported for war onsets and less so for dispute initiation. This pattern is also the same for mixed dyads that are involved in territorial conflicts and strategic rivalries. Finally, these results are stable in different time periods: 1919–45 and 1946–92 (see Appendices 9.1–9.4).

The next question is whether the triadic combination of contiguous territorial disputes between strategic rivals has significantly more escalatory potential for militarized disputes and warfare than the presence of only contiguous territorial disputes (H2 hypothesis). Table 9.6 shows that the interaction of territorial disputes, contiguity, and rivalry has a significant positive influence on both dispute initiation and war onset, as

Table 9.5 *Impact of dyadic variables on MIDs and war, 1919–1992*

Change in independent variable from 0 to 1:	Probability of militarized interstate dispute			Probability of war onset		
	(a) Prob. after change (%)	(b) Change in prob. (%)	(c) Percent change in prob.	(d) Prob. after change (%)	(e) Change in prob. (%)	(f) Percent change in prob.
Contested territory with rivalry	5.4	+5.1	+17.1	2.70	+2.64	+44.0
Contested territory w/o rivalry	4.8	+4.5	+15.0	0.46	+0.40	+6.7
Contiguity	4.4	+4.1	+13.7	0.28	+0.24	+4.0
Democracies vs. autocracies	0.4	+0.1	+0.3	0.08	+0.02	+0.3
Contested territory with rivalry and democracies vs. autocracies	6.5	+6.2	+20.7	3.3	+3.24	+54.0
Contested territory w/o rivalry and democracies vs. autocracies	5.8	+5.3	+18.3	0.6	+0.54	+9.0

Note: The probabilities represent the marginal probability of MIDs and war onset from the bivariate probit model in Table 9.3, while holding each of the values of the independent variables constant and changing only the values of the variables above. The initial probability can be calculated by subtracting column (b) from column (a) and column (e) from column (d). Percent change in probability is obtained by dividing columns (b) and (e) by their initial probabilities.

does the interaction of territorial disputes and contiguity in the absence of rivalry.

Table 9.7, which displays the probability estimates, indicates that the triadic combination of contiguity, territorial dispute, and rivalry is associated with a 49 percent probability increase in dispute initiation, while territorial dispute and contiguity are associated with a lower 19 percent probability increase (see column "c" of Table 9.7). The pattern is the same when mixed dyads are combined with territorial disputes, contiguity, and rivalry as opposed to just territorial disputes and contiguity (53 percent vs. 23 percent probability increase; see column "c"). These results are even more dramatic for war onsets. Table 9.7 indicates that the triadic combination (territorial disputes, contiguity, and rivalry) is associated with a 132 percent probability increase in war onset, relative to the 24 percent probability increase for just contiguous territorial disputes (see column "f" of Table 9.7). When mixed dyads are included in the triadic combination, the probability increase in war onsets is 149 percent, relative to the 32 percent probability increase for mixed dyads that are involved in contiguous territorial disputes without rivalry.

Table 9.6 *Interaction effects of contested territory, rivalry, and contiguity on militarized interstate disputes and war, 1919–1992 (excluding pre-1919 contested territory and rivalries)*

Variable	Militarized interstate disputes		War onset	
	Coefficient	Z-statistic	Coefficient	Z-statistic
Contested territory, contiguity and rivalry	**1.89**	31.15	**1.82**	8.02
Contested territory, contiguity without rivalry	**1.30**	14.51	**1.07**	8.18
Allies	**0.36**	9.47	**−0.31**	−5.11
Major power status	**1.39**	17.54	**1.66**	11.59
Democracies vs. autocracies	0.08	3.23	**0.10**	1.87
Peace years[a]	**−0.12**	−13.61	–	–
Constant	**−2.58**	−87.97	**−3.23**	−115.04
Rho $\varepsilon_1 \varepsilon_2$[b]	**0.21**			
	(0.06)			
Log likelihood no. of observations	**−7349.98**			
	444,460			

Note: Bold coefficients are statistically significant at 0.05 or lower; two-tailed tests. Z-statistics are based on robust standard errors.
[a]Spline coefficients are not reported.
[b]Robust standard error is reported below the rho coefficient.

These results support the proposition that contiguous territorial disputes in the context of rivalry have a greater escalatory potential for both dispute initiation and war than the absence of rivalry. In addition, the evidence supports the idea that mixed dyads in addition to contiguity, territorial disputes, and rivalry are a highly combustible situation. The findings are the same for the post-World War II era (see Appendices 9.5–9.6).

The focus of this examination thus far has been on two questions: (1) how critical rivalry is to the escalation of contested territorial issues, and (2) where in the conflict sequence, rivalry fits. Our empirical evidence is relatively unambiguous on the first question. As this chapter establishes once again, rivalry is critical to conflict escalation. Conflict escalation can occur in its absence but the combination of contested territory, contiguity, and strategic rivalry is an impressive recipe for conflict escalation. The empirical answer to the second question is less cut and dried because we found eight different sequential paths in which rivalry could enter the picture at various points. We did find, however, that the notion that contested territory leads to militarized disputes and then to

Table 9.7 *Impact of interactive effects of rivalry, contested territory, and contiguity on MIDs and war, 1919–1992*

Change in independent variable from 0 to 1:	Probability of militarized interstate dispute			Probability of war onset		
	(a) Prob. after change (%)	(b) Change in prob. (%)	(c) Percent change in prob.	(d) Prob. after change (%)	(e) Change in prob. (%)	(f) Percent change in prob.
Contested territory, contiguity and rivalry	25	+24.5	+49	8.0	+7.94	+132.3
Contested territory, contiguity w/o rivalry	10	+9.5	+19	1.5	+1.44	+24.0
Contested territory, rivalry, contiguity and democracies vs. autocracies	27	+26.5	+53	9.0	+8.94	+149.0
Contested territory, contiguity, democracies vs. autocracies w/o rivalry	12	+11.5	+23	2.0	+1.94	+32.3

Note: The probabilities represent the marginal probability of MIDs and war onset from the bivariate probit model in Table 9.6, while holding each of the values of the independent variables constant and changing only the values of the variables above. The initial probability can be calculated by subtracting column (b) from column (a) and column (e) from column (d). Percent change in probability is obtained by dividing columns (b) and (e) by their initial probabilities.

rivalry deserves more consideration. While the prevailing imagery does hinge to a considerable extent on how one defines rivalry, we find that strategic rivalries are more often linked to the onset of territorial conflicts than to subsequent iterations of the conflict sequence. That is probably one of the reasons that rivalry is such an important contributor to the escalation process. Suspicions about intentions and, in general, the level of hostility are heightened from the outset when rivals are involved.

Is this all we need to know about conflict escalation? The answer is obviously no. But it does seem a concrete step forward toward a more comprehensive understanding of the dynamics of conflict escalation. It is not the case that no one has speculated on, written about, or analyzed empirically the combination of contested territory and rivalry. After all, these are two of the principal components of Vasquez's (1993) influential steps-to-war theory. Yet, to our knowledge, this is the first empirical examination combining newly available territorial conflict data with strategic rivalry information.[18] The results are quite robust and they encourage us to continue along this line of inquiry into the causes of conflict escalation.

From territorial disputes to crises to war

One obvious task is the need to combine our analytical efforts in this chapter with the approach taken in Chapter 8. In Chapter 8, we focused on arms build-ups and alliances. This chapter, so far, has stressed territorial disputes but in a fashion that was independent of the types of rivalry focused on in Chapter 8 (that is, spatial rivalries). The theory stipulates that these processes work together. Therefore, we need to unify our various examinations into one combined test.

We also view this integrated testing as an opportunity to examine a potential validity problem in steps-to-war analyses. A number of the tests of the steps-to-war theory have relied quite extensively on multiple measures linked to militarized interstate disputes. The apparent endogeneity of the analyses, as a consequence, tends to leave some doubts about the strength of the relationships uncovered. To what extent is the empirical support due to relying on indicators that are not totally independent of one another? Alternatively, if militarized interstate dispute-based data are used to explain conflict escalation, must we therefore abandon efforts to explain militarized interstate disputes as a type of escalation? There is also some threat of sampling bias if we look only at behavior linked to MIDs. What happens to territorial contests, multiple crises, and rivalries in the absence of militarized disputes?

In this last portion of Chapter 9, we develop a new test of the interactive dynamics portion of the steps-to-war theory that uses simultaneously information on territorial contests, rivalries, alliances, arms build-ups to account for recurring crises and the escalation to war. As it turns out, evading endogeneity/sampling problems of measurement by no means detracts from the explanatory power of the steps-to-war theory. Nor is it necessary to rule out the study of militarized interstate disputes. The main effects of, and interactions among, the main five independent variables constitute a relatively parsimonious but extremely powerful model of war escalation. We do not necessarily find exactly the same findings that others do but the general nature of the outcome certainly corroborates the steps-to-war argument.

---

[18] At the same time, our findings on militarized disputes are fairly compatible with those of Tir and Diehl (2002) who adopt a much different approach to conceptualizing rivalry and a different source of territorial conflict information.

Steps-to-war research and its timing/endogeneity/ sampling problems

The steps-to-war theory of war causation emphasizes that a territorial dispute is the type of grievance that is most likely to be at the heart of interstate conflict. How decision-makers choose to pursue their territorial grievances will strongly influence the probability of escalation to war. Diplomatic negotiations and compromise are always conceivable but the conventional wisdom of international relations prescribes stronger steps as more likely to be effective. The realpolitik path, in particular, involves improving national capability through a build-up of military resources and/or obtaining external assistance through an alliance with another state. If both sides pursue the same strategies, the likelihood of coercive conflict is compounded. Rivalry and recurring crises complicate attempts to resolve the outstanding and highly salient grievance by rendering diplomatic negotiation even less likely and conflict escalation all the more likely. The combination of territorial dispute, external alliances, arms racing or mutual military build-ups, rivalry, and recurring crises interacts to make the escalation to war especially likely.

The evidence compiled to date appears to support this argument. As Vasquez (2004: 24) has put it most recently in summarizing an integrated examination of his theory's claims:

The base probability of dyads . . . going to war at least once is .371, but as one controls for the various conditions specified [in the theory] . . . the predicted probability of war increases to .523 (for dyads dominated by territorial disputes), to .589 (if in addition they both have outside alliances), to .856 (if they are also enduring rivals), to .880 (if they have four or more territorial disputes), and to .951 (if they are enduring rivals, both have outside alliances, and an arms race).

This empirical outcome seems remarkably straightforward and highly supportive of the steps-to-war thesis. Yet even these findings do not come without significant caveats. One of the most obvious criticisms of steps-to-war analyses involves the timing or sequencing of the various processes thought to be steps toward war. Although the argument is that territorial contests, arms races, and alliances increase the probability of war, our research designs often only assess whether territorial contests, arms races, alliances, and war co-occur in general. These findings are not the same thing as specifying which processes came first, or in what sequence. Do states engaged in territorial contests tend as a consequence to also develop arms races and seek alliance partners in order to prepare better for the next war?

Or, is it that these putative antecedents of war are simply and separately linked to the probability of war? Some states have territorial contests and also go to war. Other states have arms races and sometimes go to war. Related to this issue of sequencing is the endogeneity problem of linkages between independent and dependent variables. To what extent do the steps lead to war and/or do wars lead to the steps? In some respects, this problem is simply a variation on the sequencing problem. Which comes first: war or its alleged antecedents, or some mixture of both? This latter problem is made all the more awkward if the same indicators are used in different ways on both sides of a statistical equation. There is always some reason for suspicion that the indicators employed may be themselves partially responsible for the test outcome.

A case in point is the same Vasquez (2004) analysis that produced the confirmatory outcome quoted above. In examining the probability that various hypothesized steps to war influence the probability of an escalation to war, six variables are emphasized: dispute issue, dispute recurrence, enduring rivalry, war, alliance, and military build-up. The problem here is that four of the six are connected closely to militarized interstate disputes. These disputes are coded for several types of grievance, one of which is territorial in nature. Thus a territorial dispute is a militarized interstate dispute that pertains to a territorial issue. Recurrence counts the number of militarized interstate disputes with territorial issues. Enduring rivalry focuses on dyads that engage in some minimal number of militarized disputes within a specified time period. All wars begin as militarized disputes, some of which escalate to higher levels of coercion and lethality.[19]

Should we reject absolutely findings that appear to be characterized by a high degree of conceptual and operational overlap? No, the findings need not be negated by the lack of full independence among the indicators studied. But should we feel uneasy when so many of the measures are interrelated by definition via the conduit of the militarized dispute? The answer must be positive for it is quite possible to see various attributes of militarized disputes being employed to explain the escalation of selected militarized disputes (those that become wars). On the other hand, there is also the strong likelihood of introducing additional sampling bias by linking so many activities to militarized disputes. For instance, if we measure territorial disputes in MIDs terms, the comparison is to dyads without

---

[19] While we are singling out one specific study as illustrative of the problem we are highlighting, the problem is by no means confined to steps-to-war research. Any attempt to explain militarized dispute behavior in terms of "enduring rivalries," invariably measured in MID density terms, for instance, is likely to invoke an endogeneity problem.

territorial disputes *and* MIDs. What is missing is the ability to focus on territorial disputes without MIDs.

Of course, we need not overreact to this conceptual and operational overlap. Data are scarce. Often we must make use of what is available even if it is less than perfectly desirable. Ideally, though, we should work to maximize the apparent independence of the nature of the indicators employed so as to avoid one of several threats to any research design. Still, research does not proceed in an ideal world. Various compromises are made. Tests of theory, as a consequence, are never entirely able to nail down precisely how accurate (or inaccurate) a theory has proven in any given confrontation between theory and data. Theories, therefore, must be tested repeatedly – sometimes changing operational assumptions, sometimes improving the specificity of the test, and sometimes enhancing the perceived validity of the results. Ultimately, then, independent confirmation for theories remains the gold standard of scientific analysis.

In addition, there is a separate conceptual problem in relying heavily on militarized interstate disputes as a proxy for crises or as a mother lode for developing other indicators. Many MIDs fail to qualify as situations that may or may not escalate to war. For instance, a coast guard use of force against fishing vessels from another country is only rarely likely to escalate into something grander, especially if the countries in question have reasonably good relations otherwise. A use-of-force MID (the step immediately prior to the war level) between, say, the United States and Canada is something much different than a similar clash between North and South Korean vessels in the Yellow Sea. We do not claim that MIDs cannot be compared but we do have some qualms about relying on them too heavily – either as proxies for prewar crises or for other conceptual purposes. We also acknowledge that we appear to be in the minority on this question since the analysis of MIDs has become a central focus of quantitative war etiology modeling. Yet the very popularity of MIDs analysis should give pause to analysts who also use MIDs data to construct empirical explanations for militarized interstate disputes.

Our own work, in many respects, has already addressed some of the problems highlighted above. Chapter 8 focused on the relationships among rivalry, alliances, arms build-ups, crises, and war. In this chapter, we have focused primarily on the relationships among territorial contests, rivalry, militarized disputes, and war. We now need to merge these two earlier efforts to create a more comprehensive model encompassing territorial claims, rivalry, alliances, military build-ups, crises, and war with each variable measured as independently of the others as is feasible. We eliminate militarized interstate disputes altogether and focus instead on crises and war. We also can take the opportunity to eliminate some of our own endogeneity. In Chapter 8 we used rivalry data to do double duty as a source of spatial territorial issues and as an index of adversarial relations. Our focus on territorial contests allows us to drop the dependence on spatial rivalries as a proxy for such issues. Even so, such a model still falls short of doing full justice to the complexities of Vasquez's steps-to-war theory. But it does zero in on the interactive dynamics thought to lie at the heart of conflict escalation to war.

Another test of the steps-to-war argument

We propose to continue focusing directly on examining the effects of, and interactions among, territorial contests, rivalry, crises, alliances, and military build-ups on war. These five variables, to some extent, also encompass cognitive rigidities (via rivalries) and hostility (via the interaction of the five variables). Thus, we see this examination as a particularly comprehensive examination of a key portion of Vasquez's steps-to-war synthesis, even if we are unable to address directly all facets of the Vasquez interpretation. We have good reason to anticipate that modeling the five processes on which we are focusing will be successful given our own previous findings reported earlier in this chapter and the preceding one. Merging the modeling thrusts of our earlier work should only strengthen the outcome and give us a better sense of how these processes interact to generate increased probabilities of war from time to time. At the same time, we cannot assume that this will be the case. As it turns out, our integrated results are similar but not identical to our own earlier findings.

In addition to utilizing many of the variables that we have already introduced, our data set on recurrent crises and war is substituted for militarized interstate disputes. Table 9.8 summarizes the frequency of dyad-years for contested territory, rivalry, contiguity, and their combinations in the presence or absence of crises and war.

As we did in the preceding chapter, we estimate a bivariate probit model, this time for crises and wars. In addition, we again control for the temporal dependence among dyads across years by using the cubic spline technique developed by Beck, Katz, and Tucker (1998). We also examine the over-time stability of the results by redoing our 1919–92 analysis for the more recent 1946–92 period.

Analysis

Table 9.9 reports the biprobit outcome for crises and war onsets. We find that contested territory with contiguous actors is a significant predictor

Table 9.8 *Frequency of dyad-years, 1919–1992 (excluding pre-1919 contested territory and rivalries)*

Variable	Crises are present	Crises are absent	Total	War is present	War is absent	Total
Contested territory	54	2,325	2,379	78	2,301	2,379
Contested territory with rivalry	42	724	766	58	708	766
Contested territory without rivalry	12	1,601	1,613	20	1,593	1,613
Contested territory, contiguity with rivalry	31	609	640	48	592	640
Contested territory, contiguity without rivalry	6	576	582	8	574	582

Note: Frequency of dyad-years for only crises and war is 108 and 398 respectively.

Table 9.9 *Interaction of rivalry, contested territory, and contiguity on crises and war, 1919–1992 (excluding pre-1919 contested territory and rivalries)*

Variable	Crises Coefficient	Crises Z-statistic	War onset Coefficient	War onset Z-statistic
Contested territory, contiguity & rivalry	**1.93**	19.45	**1.76**	17.82
Contested territory, contiguity without rivalry	**1.29**	7.50	**1.18**	7.92
Mutual build-up	0.13	0.92	**0.14**	1.70
Mutual build-up * two+ crises	–	–	0.52	1.05
External ally	0.12	1.22	**0.11**	2.05
External ally * two+ crises	–	–	−0.06	−0.34
Both externally allied	**0.16**	2.30	**−0.20**	−4.06
Both externally allied * two+ crises	–	–	−0.06	−0.22
Capability ratio	0.20	1.57	**0.17**	2.01
Major powers	**1.50**	12.33	**1.74**	20.19
Democracies vs. autocracies	**0.25**	3.71	**0.16**	4.11
Crisis years[a]	**−0.07**	−1.75	–	–
Constant	**−3.67**	−29.00	**−3.43**	−64.83
Rho $\varepsilon_1 \varepsilon_2$[b]	**0.45** (0.08)			
Log likelihood no. of observations	**−2638.13** 380,783			

Note: Bold coefficients are statistically significant at 0.10 or lower; two-tailed tests. Z-statistics are based on robust standard errors.
[a]Spline coefficients are not reported.
[b]Robust standard error is reported below the rho coefficient.

of both types of conflict escalation. As we have found before, the addition of a rivalry relationship to contested territory and contiguity creates the strongest foundation for predicting escalation. Even so, contested territory and contiguity without rivalry remain important contributors to the variance explained. Mutual military build-ups and one side with an external ally also increase the probability of war but not crisis. If both sides have external allies, the onset of crisis is not affected significantly but war onsets are less likely. Contrary to our earlier findings, the occurrence of two crises between the members of a dyad does not appear to influence the effects of either mutual military build-ups or external alliances.

The control variables obviously play some explanatory role. The capability ratio indicator's effect is positive in both columns of Table 9.9 signifying that capability symmetry encourages crisis and war onsets. Dyads consisting of two major powers are more likely to escalate their disagreements to the crisis-level or to war than are other types of dyads. Similarly, dyads confronting autocracies and democracies are also prone to crisis and war escalation.[20] Thus there is room for both traditional realist and regime type factors.

Yet what is the relative input of the various escalatory components in the steps-to-war interpretation? Are all equal in explanatory weight? Or, are some slightly or vastly more important than others? Table 9.10 provides some assistance on this question. The importance of the contested territory/contiguity/rivalry triad *vis-à-vis* contested territory/contiguity without any rivalry is a very impressive ratio of about 4 to 1 (4.5 to 1 for crises and 3.9 to 1 for wars) in terms of the percent change in probabilities associated with the two indicators. Equally impressive is the large gap between the contested territory combinations and the other two escalatory variables – mutual build-ups and external alliances. Mutual arms build-ups and the solitary external alliance situation contribute less than 1 percent change in the onset of war. Although we think there is still something to be said for positional conflicts (Chapters 6 and 7), Vazquez's strong emphasis on territorial conflicts clearly has merit.

We view these findings as strongly supportive of the interactive component in the Vasquez steps-to-war theory. Territorial disagreements, contiguity, rivalry, alliances, and arms build-ups definitely come together as a parsimonious and interactive handle on escalatory dynamics. Nevertheless, there are some new findings in this iteration that raise interesting

---

[20] The results reported in Table 9.8 hold for the 1946–92 period suggesting (but hardly demonstrating) that the outcome is not an artifact of the 1919–92 period examined.

Table 9.10 *Impact of dyadic variables on crises and war, 1919–1992*

	Probability of crises			Probability of war onset		
	(a) Prob. after change (%)	(b) Change in prob. (%)	(c) Percent change in prob.	(d) Prob. after change (%)	(e) Change in prob. (%)	(f) Percent change in prob.
Change in independent variable from 0 to 1:						
Contested territory, contiguity & rivalry	6.60	+6.56	+164.0	8.30	+8.21	+91.2
Contested territory, contiguity w/o rivalry	1.50	+1.46	+36.5	2.20	+2.11	+23.4
Mutual build-up	–	–	–	0.13	+0.04	+0.4
Externally allied	–	–	–	0.10	0.01	+0.1

Note: The probabilities represent the average marginal probability of crises and war onset from the bivariate probit model in Table 9.9, while holding each of the values of the independent variables constant and changing only the values of the variables above. The initial probability can be calculated by subtracting column (b) from column (a) and column (e) from column (d). Percent change in probability is obtained by dividing columns (b) and (e) by their initial probabilities.

questions. As reported in Table 9.9, the effects of alliances and arms build-ups do not appear to be contingent on the occurrence of two crises. Table 9.10 suggests, moreover, that the effect of alliances and build-ups is quite weak compared to the other escalatory variables (at least once the other escalatory variables are included in the examination).

There are two interpretation possibilities here, neither of which is mutually exclusive. One is that these outcomes suggest that the roles of alliances and arms races in conflict-escalation dynamics are somewhat variable. What clearly matters most in the types of conflict escalation that we are examining is the combination of territorial contest, contiguous actors, within a rivalry context. Alliance and arms build-ups considerations evidently play sufficient roles to claim statistical significance but they are much less likely to be present in a systematic way – either simultaneously or sequentially – than are the basic dyadic grievance and hostility structures.

Whether this means that we are unlikely to find a single specific sequence – as in contiguity + territorial contest + rivalry + asymmetrical alliance situations + mutual arms build-ups – that fits all or even many cases of escalation remains a topic worthy of further analysis.[21] The present findings hint that such a sequence may prove to be quite unlikely. Sometimes parts of the sequence are there and sometimes they are not, yet conflict escalation can still occur.

A second possibility is that the measure of contiguous territorial contests between rivals absorbs most of the available variance that might otherwise be attributed to alliances, build-ups, and multiple crises because it is precisely these types of dyads that are most likely to seek alliances, engage in military build-ups, and become embroiled in crises. Since these three factors tend to play stronger empirical roles in the absence of the measure combining contiguity with rivalry and territorial contests (see earlier Chapters 5 and 8), we assume that this is likely to be the case. In some respects, then, the dyads that engage in conflict escalation are overdetermined by the steps-to-war framework.

Further advances on understanding these dynamics, no doubt, will require a different approach than the large-N approach that we have relied upon to date. We can use statistical techniques to establish what seems to matter most in escalatory dynamics, but we fall short of establishing a single or even multiple, fully developed paths to crisis and war. Instead, we can distinguish between the "stones" that appear to belong on the paths and those that do not. We think we can also tell which stones are the boulders and which ones are the pebbles. That is certainly better than only suspecting that some stones are part of the escalatory path(s) somewhere. Ultimately, though, we should be able to do better.

Our next and last chapter examines the relevance and significance of strategic rivalry one more time. In earlier chapters, we have looked at other research projects such as the International Crisis Behavior program, the Correlates of War Project's approach to militarized interstate disputes, and the steps-to-war project. In Chapter 10 our focus continues to emphasize the value of rivalries but this time in the context of liberal or Kantian peace arguments. More specifically, we assess the relative explanatory contributions of rivalries versus democratic dyads, economic development, and economic interdependence in accounting for conflict escalation. Without question, the inducements of contiguous rivalries with territorial disagreements are at least as important as the putative constraints of the leading liberal factors. The liberal constraints are significantly discernible but, in the aggregate, do not suffice

---

[21] For that matter, we do not read Vasquez's steps-to-war theory as stipulating that only one sequence should be evident.

to dispense with information on the specific inducements to engage in conflict over space with one's rivals.

Appendices

Appendix 9.A-1 *Interaction of rivalry and contested territory on militarized interstate disputes and war, 1919–1945 (excluding pre-1919 contested territory and rivalries)*

Variable	Militarized interstate disputes		War onset	
	Coefficient	Z-statistic	Coefficient	Z-statistic
Contested territory with rivalry	**1.39**	6.57	**1.23**	5.85
Contested territory without rivalry	**1.26**	9.78	**0.93**	6.98
Contiguity	**0.50**	4.17	0.15	1.15
Allies	−0.03	−0.34	**−0.30**	−2.21
Major power status	**0.94**	6.24	**1.31**	12.26
Democracies vs. autocracies	−0.05	−0.82	**0.20**	3.69
Peace years[a]	**−0.12**	−4.53	–	–
Constant	**−2.56**	−32.69	**−2.87**	−66.59
Rho $\varepsilon_1 \varepsilon_2$[b]	−0.06			
	(.09)			
Log likelihood	**−1957.91**			
No. of observations	49232			

Note: Bold coefficients are statistically significant at 0.05 or lower; two-tailed tests. Z-statistics are based on robust standard errors.
[a] Spline coefficients are not reported.
[b] Robust standard error is reported below the rho coefficient.

Appendix 9.A-2 *Impact of dyadic variables on MIDs and war, 1919–1945*

	Probability of militarized interstate dispute			Probability of war onset		
Change in independent variable from 0 to 1:	(a) Prob. after change (%)	(b) Change in prob. (%)	(c) Percent change in prob.	(d) Prob. after change (%)	(e) Change in prob. (%)	(f) Percent change in prob.
Contested territory with rivalry	12.1	+11.6	+23.2	5.0	+4.8	+24.0
Contested territory w/o rivalry	10.0	+9.5	+19.0	2.6	+2.4	+12.0
Contiguity	2.0	+1.5	+3.0	0.3	+0.1	+0.6
Democracies vs. autocracies	0.4	−1.0	−0.2	0.4	+2.0	+1.0
Contested territory with rivalry and democracies vs. autocracies	11.1	+10.6	+21.2	7.6	+7.4	+37.0
Contested territory w/o rivalry and democracies vs. autocracies	8.9	+8.4	+16.0	4.0	+3.8	+19.0

Note: The probabilities represent the marginal probability of MIDs and war onset from the bivariate probit model in Table 9.A-1, while holding each of the values of the independent variables constant and changing only the values of the variables above. The initial probability can be calculated by subtracting column (b) from column (a) and column (e) from column (d). Percent change in probability is obtained by dividing columns (b) and (e) by their initial probabilities.

Appendix 9.A-3 *Interaction of rivalry and contested territory on militarized interstate disputes and war, 1946–1992 (excluding pre-1919 contested territory and rivalries)*

	Militarized interstate disputes		War onset	
Variable	Coefficient	Z-statistic	Coefficient	Z-statistic
Contested territory with rivalry	**1.06**	14.84	**1.39**	13.48
Contested territory without rivalry	**1.03**	13.53	**0.33**	2.27
Contiguity	**1.18**	22.99	**0.77**	6.92
Allies	0.03	0.62	**−0.40**	−3.96
Major power status	**1.39**	11.12	**0.69**	2.83
Democracies vs. autocracies	**0.15**	4.39	0.06	1.38
Peace years[a]	**−0.09**	−8.22	–	–
Constant	**−2.84**	−74.63	**−3.37**	−106.19
Rho $\varepsilon_1 \varepsilon_2$[b]	**0.18**			
	(0.08)			
Log likelihood no. of observations	**−4556.23**			
	395,228			

Note: Bold coefficients are statistically significant at 0.05 or lower; two-tailed tests. Z-statistics are based on robust standard errors.
[a]Spline coefficients are not reported.
[b]Robust standard error is reported below the rho coefficient.

Appendix 9.A-4 *Impact of dyadic variables on MIDs and war, 1946–1992*

Change in independent variable from 0 to 1:	Probability of militarized interstate dispute			Probability of war onset		
	(a) Prob. after change (%)	(b) Change in prob. (%)	(c) Percent change in prob.	(d) Prob. after change (%)	(e) Change in prob. (%)	(f) Percent change in prob.
Contested territory with rivalry	3.7	+3.5	+17.5	2.40	+2.36	+59.0
Contested territory w/o rivalry	3.5	+3.3	+16.5	0.10	+0.06	+1.5
Contiguity	4.8	+4.6	+23.0	0.30	+0.26	+6.5
Democracies vs. autocracies	0.4	+0.2	+1.0	0.05	+0.01	+0.3
Contested territory with rivalry and democracies vs. autocracies	5.0	+4.8	+24.0	2.70	+2.66	+66.5
Contested territory w/o rivalry and democracies vs. autocracies	4.8	+4.6	+23.0	0.14	+0.10	+2.5

Note: The probabilities represent the marginal probability of MIDs and war onset from the bivariate probit model in Table 9.5, while holding each of the values of the independent variables constant and changing only the values of the variables above. The initial probability can be calculated by subtracting column (b) from column (a) and column (e) from column (d). Percent change in probability is obtained by dividing columns (b) and (e) by their initial probabilities.

Appendix 9.A-5 *Interaction effects of contested territory, rivalry, and contiguity on militarized interstate disputes and war, 1946–1992 (excluding pre-1919 contested territory and rivalries)*

Variable	Militarized interstate disputes		War onset	
	Coefficient	Z-statistic	Coefficient	Z-statistic
Contested territory, contiguity and rivalry	**1.93**	30.81	**1.98**	23.69
Contested territory, contiguity without rivalry	**1.31**	12.75	**0.55**[c]	1.71
Allies	**0.41**	9.46	**−0.30**	−2.72
Major power status	**1.51**	13.99	**1.05**	4.81
Democracies vs. autocracies	0.13	4.26	0.06	1.40
Peace years[a]	**−0.09**	−9.89	–	–
Constant	**−2.64**	−78.93	**−3.36**	−109.22
Rho $\varepsilon_1 \varepsilon_2$[b]	**0.24** (.07)			
Log likelihood no. of observations	−5044.15 395,228			

Note: Bold coefficients are statistically significant at 0.05 or lower; two-tailed tests. Z-statistics are based on robust standard errors.
[a]Spline coefficients are not reported.
[b]Robust standard error is reported below the rho coefficient.
[c]Coefficient is significant at 0.10 level.

Appendix 9.A-6 *Impact of interactive effects of rivalry, contested territory, and contiguity on MIDs and war, 1946–1992*

Change in independent variable from 0 to 1:	Probability of militarized interstate dispute			Probability of war onset		
	(a) Prob. after change (%)	(b) change in prob. (%)	(c) Percent change in prob.	(d) Prob. after change (%)	(e) Change in prob. (%)	(f) Percent change in prob.
Contested territory, contiguity and rivalry	23.7	+23.3	+58.3	8.40	+8.36	+209.0
Contested territory, contiguity w/o rivalry	9.0	+8.6	+21.5	0.25	+0.21	+5.3
Contested territory, rivalry, contiguity, and democracies vs. autocracies	27.8	+27.4	+68.5	9.00	+8.96	+224.0
Contested territory, contiguity, democracies vs. autocracies w/o rivalry	11.2	+10.8	+27.0	0.29	+0.25	+6.5

Note: The probabilities represent the marginal probability of MIDs and war onset from the bivariate probit model in Table 9.9, while holding each of the values of the independent variables constant and changing only the values of the variables above. The initial probability can be calculated by subtracting column (b) from column (a) and column (e) from column (d). Percent change in probability is obtained by dividing columns (b) and (e) by their initial probabilities.

Part V

Strategic rivalries and conflict

10   Inducements, facilitators, and suppressors

In the quantitative analysis of conflict, we have a variety of problems. One is that we tend to adopt a single variable as a principal focus of inquiry for an extended period of time. Over the years, contiguity, arms races, alliances, capability ratios, territorial issues, regime type, rivalries, economic interdependence – to name some of the foci of the past few decades – have sequentially preoccupied much of our attention. There is nothing wrong with an exclusive focus on certain arguments about how conflict comes about. Everything cannot be examined every time we do an empirical analysis. We probably need to develop very specific foci in order to determine what seems to work, as well as what does not seem to work. Still, there is a cost to very specific foci. We tend to either dismiss variables that do not seem to be working or lionize those that do seem to be providing some explanatory and predictive value. The obvious antidote is to at least occasionally avoid relatively narrow foci and try to bring together multiple perspectives simultaneously. But how best to do that?

Another problem is that our arguments tend to be fixed on specific variables. So we have arguments and theories about deterrence, capability, and/or democratic/liberal peace that suggest the utility of examining some variables but not others. By suggesting that we borrow a framework from analysts of disease, Russett (2003) offers an interesting vehicle for getting around this problem. Some factors induce disease while others suppress it. Replace the term "disease" with the concept of conflict: "Conceptually, the implication is that there would be no [conflict] without one or more inducements *and* the weakness or absence of one or more suppressors." Thus, the theoretical task is to assess what combination(s) of inducements and suppressors interact to generate conflict.

While the epidemiology frame is useful, it raises an interesting problem. Many of our analyses have focused on suppressors and facilitators and given much less attention to direct inducements to conflict. Moreover, it is not clear that we fully appreciate the distinctions between inducements – for our purposes, factors that directly bring about conflict – and suppressors/facilitators – or factors that discourage/encourage conflict emerging or escalating. A case in point is Russett's (2003: 166) own treatment when he describes major power status, proximity, contiguity, and a near-equal power ratio as well-known inducements to conflict. In contrast, joint democracy, trade interdependence, trade openness, shared international government organization (IGO) memberships, and alliances are described as potential suppressors. Russett then contends that the inducements are "near-necessary" conditions because without them states are politically irrelevant to one another and therefore unlikely to engage in conflictual interactions, while facilitators encourage conflict when inducers are present. Suppressors, on the other hand, decrease the likelihood that inducers will produce conflict.

But are powerful status, geographical closeness, or capability equality inducements to conflict or simply more potential suppressors and/or facilitators, depending on how we construct these measures?[1] We think more the latter than the former. Relative and absolute power weaknesses, other things being equal, should be expected to inhibit conflict. Distance clearly inhibits conflict because states presumably are unlikely to clash with states with whom they do not come into contact. Capability inequality at least occasionally deters states from taking on other states that are simply too strong to anticipate a favorable outcome. Indeed, all three of these variables can be linked in one way or another to the attribute of relative weakness or strength. Major powers sometimes have the resources to coerce outcomes that smaller powers lack. Strong states can overcome the barriers of distance. It is relatively weak states that are more likely to be on the losing end of a capability inequality ratio.

At the same time, we acknowledge that power, proximity, and/or symmetry might also be thought of as encouraging conflict. But as explanations of the onset of conflict they are usually less than compelling. For

---

[1] If this is simply a disagreement about the term "inducement," we would be guilty of making a conceptual mountain out of a molehill – something that obviously would be undesirable. The verb "induce" actually has several meanings. One is to persuade or influence something to happen. This definition comes close "to facilitate." A second one is to cause or bring something about. It may be that Russett has the first meaning in mind. We definitely are endorsing the second one. Perhaps the difference here is best described as one of expecting "inducements" to do more than simply facilitate or encourage conflict because the suppressing effect is absent. Mixed regime type, for instance, is a facilitator of conflict because there is some likelihood that autocracies and democracies will disagree about preferred outcomes – not merely because they possess different types of political regimes. Another possibility is that joint democratic status in a dyad discourages conflict because for some reason democracies are less likely to disagree about preferred outcomes. Either way, dyadic regime types discourage or encourage conflict but they do not necessarily specify what the cause of conflict might be. States of different ideological stripes might be disagreeing about all sorts of things.

instance, if we say that country X attacked country Y because it could (due either to X's projection capabilities or proximity, or both), are we saying anything other than people climb mountains because they are there to be climbed? If we have to choose between the facilitating feature of proximity versus the barrier of distance, the latter seems somewhat more attractive as a partial explanation of things that do or do not happen.

Similarly, regime type, economic interdependency, and shared IGO membership create structures that conceivably can constrain actors from engaging in or escalating their conflict. But, they all remain potential conflict suppressors of one type or another depending on how one describes them. To the extent that these variables appear frequently in regression equations in our professional journals, we tend to be highlighting (and debating) the relative power of various suppressors to limit conflict without necessarily getting at the root causes of conflict.

One way to evade this problem is to examine root causes or inducers of conflict in conjunction with various suppressors and facilitators. We can then assess just how efficacious suppressors and facilitators might be. Earlier, we have found a factor that seems quite strong in generating conflict – the combination of contiguous rivalries with territorial disagreements.[2] In the context of rivalry, state leaders are more likely to mistrust each other, rely to a greater extent on cognitive rigidities, and be threatened by their adversary. Contiguity makes it possible to clash almost regardless of relative strengths or weaknesses. Disagreements about who should control territory provide rationales for pursuing the argument coercively. In fact a second leading factor in conflict escalation is contiguous territorial contests in the absence of rivalry. Given these two types of territorial inducements to conflict, our question is what suppressors or facilitators seem to make the most, if any, difference?

In contemplating where to look for inducements to conflict there are of course a number of arguments to which to turn. Yet one of the more obvious candidates is contested territory. A number of analyses, as we have demonstrated in Chapter 9, have shown its centrality to conflict escalation. We know that people have found numerous claims to geography worth fighting about and worth dying for. Territory, after all, encompasses scarce resources, populations, strategic positions, markets, and national symbolism. Disputed territory invites military displays of capability and coercion that set up the potential for militarized interstate

---

[2] We recognize that the contiguous rivalry elements in this compound variable would be facilitators if treated separately – as opposed to the direct inducement of territorial disagreements. We use the contiguous rivalry adjectives as types of territorial dispute in distinction from contiguous disputes in the absence of rivalry in order to demonstrate the explanatory power of the former over the latter.

clashes. Territorial issues can be deemed too costly in terms of domestic politics to contemplate negotiation and compromise. Similarly, spatial claims make good political fodder for political entrepreneurs seeking followers or votes. We also know, moreover, that, in some cases, they tend to fight repeatedly over the same land and that recurring disputes are the ones that tend to escalate to war (Chapter 5).

But contested territory does not possess a monopoly on conflict recurrence, escalation, or bloodshed. Strategic rivalries also possess these attributes. While a number of rivalries are at least in part about territorial disagreements, the rivalry phenomenon contributes considerable psychological baggage to interstate disputes. Rivals have little reason to trust their adversaries. By definition, rivals threaten their enemies with the intention of doing harm. In this poisonous context, the ultimate value of contested territory is apt to be inflated – as are the costs of inter-rival compromise. It is not surprising, therefore, that the interaction of rivalry and territorial contest, with the added assistance of contiguity, has been found to be an extraordinarily potent cocktail for conflict escalation for both militarized interstate disputes and war (Chapter 9). Not quite as potent but still considerably significant are contiguous territorial contests in the absence of rivalry. Neither finding means that territorial disagreements are the sole inducement to interstate conflict escalation (see Chapters 6 and 7). But territorial contests do appear to rank among the most significant inducers.

Obviously, though, all territorial disagreements, either between contiguous rivals or not, do not escalate to militarized dispute and war. One possibility is that various suppressors and facilitators intervene to make conflict escalation less or more likely. Some of these factors have already been mentioned and are often included in quantitative examinations usually as control variables. As noted by Russett (2003), these factors include such considerations as capability ratios and major power status. Highly asymmetrical political-military confrontations are thought to be less likely to lead to escalation due to the probability of an outcome, other things being equal, favoring the more powerful actor. If asymmetry is a suppressor, capability symmetry is a facilitator in which disputants can discover empirically which side has better capabilities (Blainey, 1973).

Since major powers have well-defined and widespread foreign policy interests at least in comparison with smaller powers, they can act as a facilitator to conflict escalation. This is so, because major powers are more likely to have the capability to advance or protect their perceived interests, even at some distance from the home base. As a consequence, they are found to be disproportionately involved in militarized interstate disputes and wars. In contrast, the absence of a major power and its ability to project force at greater distances than non-major powers could have a suppressive effect on conflict escalation.

In addition, one of the major emphases of quantitative international politics of the past few years has focused on the claims of the liberal peace. A number of analysts have found strong empirical support for the conflict suppressors of economic development, economic interdependence, and democracy (Mousseau, Hegre, and Oneal, 2003: 277). Since economic and political constraints on decision-making behavior are thought to suppress conflict, liberal factors are not considered to be inducements for conflict. The question remains, however, about whether these liberal factors are significant in the presence of other facilitators or suppressors of conflict escalation.

While the democratic peace effect has survived quite a few empirical trials, several scholars (Mousseau, 2000; Hegre, 2000; Mousseau, Hegre, and Oneal, 2003) have found that the effects of democracy are restricted to more economically developed actors. Or, is the problem that most democracies have also been among the most economically developed states until recently? Either way, there is some question about whether the effects of the democratic peace are conditioned by economic development, and whether we should anticipate the absence of a suppressor effect for dyads that are democratic but less economically developed. As we shall see shortly, there appear to be limits to how far we can pursue this question.

But there are also independent arguments for the suppressor effects of economic development (for example, Rosecrance, 1986) that encourage us to explore this variable's effect on conflict. More developed states may have greater potential capability but they also have more to lose from engaging in the distractions and destructiveness of political-military conflict. Trade, development, and growth become alternative foci to worrying about control over marginal territory. This focus is usually attributed to states with advanced economies as opposed to lesser developed states.

Economic interdependence has a somewhat more checkered record than the analysis of joint democracy effects – as is demonstrated in Table 10.1. One could accurately say that about half of the pertinent findings to date support the suppressor effect of dyadic trading constraints. The other half finds a variety of outcomes, including a positive influence on conflict. Most of the mixed findings appear to be contingent on either categorical groups, or different indicators and different sample sizes.

There is, nonetheless, another more general problem with some of the liberal peace findings. For instance, studies of trade interdependence tend

Table 10.1 *Statistical studies of the trade–conflict relationship*

Positive relationship	Mixed or no relationships	Negative relationships
Russett (1967)	Gasiorowski (1986)	Polachek (1980, 1992, 1997)
Wallensteen (1973)	Domke (1988)	Gasiorowski and Polachek
Barbieri (1996, 1997, 2002)	Reuveny and Kang (1996,	(1982)
Reuveny (1999a, 1999b)	1998)	Polachek and McDonald
	Mansfield, Pevehouse, and	(1992)
	Bearce (1999)	Mansfield (1994)
	Kang and Reuveny (2001)	Polachek, Robst and Chang
	Mansfield and Pevehouse	(1999)
	(2003)	Oneal, Oneal, Maoz, and
	Gelpi and Grieco (2003)	Russett (1996)
	Keshk, Pollins, and Reuveny	Oneal and Ray (1997)
	(2004)	Oneal and Russett (1997,
	Kim and Rousseau (2005)	1999a, 1999b, 2003)
		Mousseau (2000)
		Gartzke, Li, and Boehmer
		(2001)
		Russett and Oneal (2001)
		Oneal (2003)
		Mousseau, Hegre, and Oneal
		(2003)

Source: based primarily on Schneider, Barbieri, and Gleditsch (2003: 17–18) with some updating.

to rely on information about dyadic trade flows and their relative economic significance as denominated by gross domestic product (GDP) indices. Yet, these data, even for more recent years, have been characterized by a very substantial amount of missing data. Kristian Gleditsch (2002), who has labored to ameliorate this problem, estimates that analyses relying on IMF data and Summers's GDP information typically have missing data for as much as 60 percent of the interstate dyad population. Thanks to Gleditsch's improvement of the economic database, it is now possible to analyze information for about 320–400 thousand dyads in the 1950–92 era (depending on data still missing). This number represents a roughly three-fold increase over the number of dyads examined by Mousseau (2000) for the same time period. It is also a 60 percent improvement over the number of dyads examined by analysts who have studied the longer 1885–1992 period. This development suggests that additional analyses need to be conducted in order to discern the extent of the role that liberal variables play in suppressing conflict.

Somewhat as a corollary to the missing data problem, there has also been a tendency to rely on a "politically relevant" selection filter to reduce the sample size to more manageable proportions and to eliminate the "noise" caused by states unlikely to interact, let alone fight. "Politically relevant" states are either contiguous or major powers. The presumption is that these are the states most likely to become involved in violence because other states are simply too far away or too weak to make trouble. There is no question that this filter reduces the sample size.[3] There is some question as to what to make of the non-representative sample that emerges.[4] More to the point, though, the procedure is similar in logic to examining only rival dyads which we construe to be the most likely violent sample. Still, if we wish to assess the impact of rivalry, we would certainly not want to remove all dyads involving nonrivals. Nor does there seem to be much incentive to remove dyads involving noncontiguous actors, especially since contiguity is also an explicit part of our territorial contest inducements to conflict.[5]

Data, variables, and methodology

Our intention is not to replicate any particular study but to address the role of variables that appear in the studies of the liberal peace on militarized disputes and war in the context of our central inducement mix of contiguity, rivalry, and territorial disagreements.[6] Thus, we require data on the timing and location of territorial disputes and rivalry, the proximity of the adversaries, and militarized disputes.[7] At least three standard control variables (major power status, capability ratios, and peace-years) that invariably appear in the liberal peace analyses also need to be examined. Finally, we also need information on economic interdependence,

---

[3] The politically relevant N sizes are about 15 percent the size of what they might have been without employing this filter. But that also means they are about 10–11 percent of what they might have been once much of the missing data for economic indicators have been addressed.

[4] Bennett (2006) documents that political relevance filters do not capture all of the possible conflict, are better at capturing wars than MIDs, and do better encompassing conflict initiators than conflict joiners.

[5] We are also puzzled by previous analyses that first remove non-contiguous actors via the politically relevant filter and then proceed to examine the empirical effects of not only contiguity but also proximity in the same equation.

[6] Actually, we follow most closely some of the analyses carried out in Chapter 9 but do not duplicate all of the emphases of the earlier examination.

[7] We would also have examined war as a dependent variable but found that there was simply too little war variance in the 1950–92 period to warrant the construction of a unified model. A longer time span would be preferable for that type of examination.

economic development, and democracy in order to examine the effects of the main liberal peace suppressors.[8]

Our contested territory data are again taken from Huth and Allee's (2002: 305–424) case list. The availability of the economic development data encourages restricting the time span of this initial analysis to the familiar 1950–92 period. Contiguity (common land border or within 150 miles by sea), major power status (following Correlates of War or COW conventions), capability ratios (the ratio of the weakest to strongest member of the dyad measured in terms of the aggregated, six COW capability measures) are taken from EUGene (Bennett and Stam, 2000).[9] Polity III (Jaggars and Gurr, 1995) regime type data are employed (democratic dyads are those in which both parties possess a +6 score after subtracting the 1–10 autocracy score from its 1–10 democracy score).[10]

Our measures of interdependence and development are based on Gleditsch's (2002) data on trade and gross domestic product (GDP), which are derived primarily from IMF Direction of Trade information and Summers and Heston (1991) GDP indices, but improved for missing data. Interdependence for country A is measured as a function of the sum of A's exports to B and A's imports from B divided by A's GDP. A's economic development is measured as A's GDP per capita. Although there are clear limitations to the interpretation of such measures, we also adopt the weak-link approach that utilizes the lower dyadic scores for interdependence and development.[11] This step assumes that the least interdependent or developed member of a dyad establishes the tenor of the dyad, regardless

---

[8] We do not examine every possible liberal peace indicator. For example, we omit data on international organizations and openness to trade in part because we anticipate substantial colinearity problems in an analysis that is already focused on economic development, economic interdependence, and democracy. One of the more interesting challenges of the liberal peace research movement, we would suggest, is to work out the causal patterns among the arsenal of liberal peace indexes. That is, have economically developed states been more likely to become democratic and/or more open to trade and, therefore, to trade more in general and with democratic states in particular, thereby encouraging joining international organizations designed to provide an institutional infrastructure for international trade? Or, are all of these relationships hopelessly reciprocal?

[9] We do balk at following the COW interpretation that Japan and Germany returned to the major power ranks in 1990. Keep in mind as well that contiguity measures the proximity of the dyad members and not whether any territorial disputes involve adjacent territory. We also dropped an alliance indicator from the analysis after it consistently emerged statistically significant and positive – assuming that this relationship, although hardly central to our present inquiry, may reflect still another colinearity problem of some unknown sort.

[10] The regime type dummies are coded 1 if they satisfy the joint democracy and 0 if the dyads are autocracies.

[11] Dyad democracy also employs the weak-link approach by focusing on the least democratic member of the dyad.

of how interdependent or developed the second member happens to be.[12]

Note that in the investigation to follow, we restrict our examination to relationships between the presence or absence of territorial grievance, rivalry, and conflict escalation. We do not actually trace, on a case-by-case basis, whether territorial grievances are critical to interstate rivalry or whether conflict escalation is linked closely to territorial grievances *per se*. Such specific tracing is no doubt worth doing but would require a much different and more complicated type of undertaking than the more crude one pursued in this chapter.[13] At this point, we must be content to know whether and to what extent certain dyadic attributes (territorial grievances, rivalry) appear to be linked systematically to subsequent conflict escalation. That is something different than knowing precisely when and how often these linkages can be tracked in the historical record. In addition, we control in our logistic regression analysis for the temporal dependence among dyads across years in dispute initiation by using the cubic spline technique developed by Beck, Katz, and Tucker (1998).

Analysis

Table 10.2 summarizes our findings. We examine the relative impact of eight variables (with a ninth added as described below) on the probability of militarized interstate dispute behavior. Two of the variables are considered to be direct inducements to conflict. That is, the two indicators of

---

[12] We also made some attempt to examine the possibility of substantive interactions among the liberal peace indicators (Mousseau, 2000; Mousseau, Hegre, and Oneal, 2003). Specifically, we intended to examine the interaction of democracy and economic development, economic development and economic interdependence, and democracy and economic interdependence. We failed, however, to resolve some major colinearity problems among the interaction between weak-link dyadic measures relying on gross domestic product, trade flows, and regime type. The correlations between economic interdependence and the interactions of democracy and interdependence and development and interdependence, as well as the correlation of democracy with the interaction of democracy and economic development, were all 0.97 or higher. As a consequence, we encountered considerable instability in the signs of liberal peace relationships depending on whether interaction variables were examined bivariately or multivariately. At this time, we do not have a methodological solution for this problem and have chosen to abandon these particular questions for this examination. One puzzle is why we should encounter more colinearity problems with a larger N than earlier studies with smaller Ns found.

[13] This type of process tracing would require a detailed analysis of the purported causes of each militarized dispute and war. Since the factors thought to be involved would in many cases be either absent or controversial, one would end up writing a history of conflict escalation over the past two centuries that would encompass a great deal of missing "data." An alternative approach would be to focus on a select number of cases for process tracing but this too constitutes another type of analysis than the one undertaken in this chapter.

Table 10.2 *Logit regression estimates of militarized interstate disputes, 1950–1992*

Variable	Coefficient	S.E.	p-value
Development $_H$	−0.19	0.07	<0.00
Development $_L$	**0.58**	0.07	<0.00
Dependency $_L$	**−0.15**	0.02	<0.00
Democracy $_L$	**−0.06**	0.01	<0.00
Rivalry, territorial dispute & contiguity	**4.12**	0.14	<0.00
Territorial dispute, & contiguity	**3.28**	0.24	<0.00
Major power dyads	**2.86**	0.37	<0.00
Relative capabilities	**1.09**	0.18	<0.00
Peace years[a]	**−0.33**	0.03	<0.00
Constant	**−8.97**	0.55	<0.00
Log likelihood	−2974.79		
No. of observations	348,613		

Note: Bold coefficients are statistically significant at 0.05 or lower; two-tailed tests. Standard errors are robust Huber/White estimates.
[a]Spline coefficients are not reported.

territorial contests – both involving contiguity and one involving rivalry as well – specify an issue to fight over a psycho-geographical context that is highly facilitative. Four of the variables – two for economic development, one for economic interdependence, and one for regime type – represent some of the anticipated suppressor effects associated with liberal peace contentions. Two others – major power presence and the symmetry of the capability ratio – are more realpolitik in nature and emphasize additional facilitators of conflict escalation.

There are no real surprises in the data outcome. The two territorial disagreement inducers of conflict perform as expected. Both are strongly positive. The presence of a major power in the dyad and greater symmetry in the capability ratios are also positive and therefore serve to facilitate the outbreak of MIDs. Democracy and economic interdependence are both negatively signed and thus constitute suppressors of militarized interstate disputes.

The one finding that may seem odd is associated with the weak-link index of economic development and its significant but positive relationship with conflict escalation. We read this finding as suggesting that the more developed the weaker party in the dyad, the greater the probability of conflict escalation. Mousseau (2000) found the same relationship and attributed it to increasing joint development in turn increasing the likelihood of conflict. Richer states are both more interested in competing outside their borders and more capable of doing so. The finding is certainly not implausible and deserves further examination. As a quick check on the finding, we added a "strong-link" index of economic development – one focusing on the more developed end of the dyad. It performs, as expected – and also as Mousseau (2000) found – as a suppressor of conflict escalation.[14] Economic development in dyadic circumstances, therefore, has a Janus-faced quality depending on how one measures it. Developed states, apparently, are both empowered and constrained in their external behavior with one another.

Thus, the findings reproduce primarily what others have found in analyses that look at some but not all of these variables. The next step would be to assess what the relative weights of these variables are on conflict, but we have opted out of this procedure because the validity of the results would likely be compromised by the varying levels of measurement between the liberal peace variables and the political-military ones. Greater work must be done to take into account the floor and ceiling effects of the liberal factors before we would be in any position to suggest that one set of variables has a greater impact on the probabilities of militarized disputes. Nonetheless, the political-military variables are clearly as strong (and perhaps even stronger depending on future research) as the liberal mix of democracy, development, and interdependence on the probability of conflict escalation.

What do these results suggest for policy-makers who are looking for ways to reduce the odds of conflict escalation? They do suggest that policy-makers should continue their efforts to encourage democratization and interdependence. However, there needs to be some more realistic appraisal as to what the constraints of democratization and interdependence can be expected to deliver.[15] When it comes to reducing the odds of conflict escalation, policy-makers might have more success working on settling territorial disagreements and winding down strategic rivalries than counting on expanded voting rights or trade to do the job alone. At the same time, there is absolutely no theoretical reason why policy-makers cannot work on settling territorial disputes, downscaling strategic rivalries, expanding voting rights, and boosting trade all at the same time. Whether they are likely to do so may be another story.

Finally, Russett's epidemiological frame of inducements and facilitators/suppressors is a useful apparatus for bringing together multiple

---

[14] The positive outcome associated with the weak-link index is also found in a bivariate analysis.

[15] These findings may also be interpreted as lending credence to the argument that we give too much credit to regime type for selective pacification tendencies currently being exhibited. See, for instance, Rasler and Thompson (2005).

arguments for explaining conflict. We should do more rather than fewer multivariate analyses that bring together a range of variables and help in the comparative assessment of multiple research programs. This frame fits well not because conflict is a disease or that we should treat it as if it was a disease. On the contrary, the latter approach would probably represent more of a setback than an advance.[16] What would constitute an advance is to move away from the idea that all conflict is generically similar and subject to a one-equation-fits-all approach. There are surely more forms of disease than there are of conflict but we need to develop greater appreciation for the notion that there are different types of conflict – and quite possibly different explanatory paths for these different types.

Similarly, it seems plausible that suppressors and facilitators can impact some types of conflict but not necessarily all types. Influencing the escalation of territorial disputes may be one thing. Fights over leadership transition in the global system, on the other hand, may be less influenced by the factors that are most pertinent to disagreements of territorial control. That could help explain, for instance, why World War I broke out after a period of intensifying economic interdependence. Or, another way of looking at this phenomenon is that less strong suppressors, such as economic interdependence, can be overwhelmed by strong facilitators such as polarization, non-linear multiple rivalry "ripeness," and system leader relative decline (Thompson, 2003), in addition to intense conflicting grievances.

Yet if conflict over territorial disagreements is one type of conflict, we have some sense for whether various inducements, facilitators, and suppressors influence its escalatory propensities. We should also compare the findings for one conflict path with other possible types of conflict. It may very well be that some suppressors/facilitators work better or worse in the context of different avenues to conflict escalation. What we need to do then is to figure out which inducement paths and contexts matter most and which ones are least important. The goal is not to eradicate conflict as if it were a disease but rather to better understand the etiology of various types of conflict.

Summing up

No doubt there are large-N analyses involving rivalries and escalation yet to do. We certainly cannot claim to have examined every conceivable

[16] Drawing an analogy between disease and conflict suggests that all conflict is bad and must be rooted out and eliminated for political systems to remain healthy and long-lived. Such an analogy has been made before by analysts who presumably preferred stability to the potential of turmoil.

interpretation and possible influence on interstate conflict escalation. We trust that such studies are likely to be executed. Our own best guess, however, is that the next step forward in rivalry studies will come from less aggregated examinations of specific rivalries. We have tried to assess some of the reasons that they escalate into more intense forms of conflict events (as in disputes, crises, and wars). But why do they turn hot and cold, sometimes bitterly hostile and other times marginally peaceful? For that matter, why do they end? Can we be more specific about which dyads are likely to develop rivalry relationships in the first place? These questions can certainly be pursued in the aggregate. However, we suspect that they will be answered better by developing arguments about dynamic interactions over time. That means that we will need to look at rivalries more selectively and with greater nuance, while retaining a systematic approach. Not all rivalries will be susceptible to longitudinal analysis but enough should qualify to take our understanding of rivalry relationships to the next level.

Elsewhere, we have argued that rivalry relationships are based on decision-maker expectations about the intentions of adversaries, their capabilities to do harm, and the availability of capabilities to resist threats.[17] These expectations are first formed and subsequently maintained by external and internal processes, including inertia. They then condition which strategies decision-makers select to cope with domestic demands and external threats. Rivalries thus afford an excellent opportunity to investigate the evolution of foreign policies as a result of interacting psychological processes and interpretations of the internal and external environments in which decision-makers operate. Consequently, there are some central questions to be investigated. Do decision-makers in rivalry relationships select different types of strategies than they select in non-rivalry relationships? Our current findings suggest that is very much the case. But we need to probe more deeply to see exactly where the rivalry context "intervenes" in decision-making.

Once selected, do these strategies evolve over time? What does it take to overcome the inertia, habit, and profound mistrust that presumably build up in old rivalries? We know that a good number of rivalries end coercively (see Chapter 3) but many do not. Therein lies a prime puzzle – explaining why and how rivalries can be terminated in non-coercive ways. To what extent are these terminations, or rivalry dynamics in general, grounded in trial and error experimentation? How often do decision-makers take bold

---

[17] See Thompson (2001, 2005); Rasler (2001, 2005); Colaresi (2005). The first two authors address a theory of rivalry termination while the third author develops and tests a theory of rivalry dynamics.

steps to change the nature of dyadic relationships – as opposed to incremental fumbling around that sometimes leads to unintended outcomes?[18]

Then, too, another area of great interest is the interaction between domestic politics and external rivalries. Politicians play multiple two-level games, often balancing a myriad of issues simultaneously. One audience is domestic while the other is the external foe. In some cases, rivalry dynamics seem more dependent on domestic politics than on interstate calculations. In others, domestic politics appear to play little role. Why is this the case? Can we pin down when, where, and why domestic politics is sometimes salient and other times less so? This is one of the least well explored corners of Vasquez's steps-to-war argument. Can we merge information on domestic politics with the interactive complexes of territorial contests, crises, rivalry, arms build-ups, and alliances? Ultimately, this type of model expansion seems likely to happen. Yet the relatively intractable notion of domestic politics (other than regime type) may also require a more selective examination of rivalry dynamics over time.

Examining rivalry dynamics, rivalry termination, and the domestic politics of rivalries will all pose various types of analytical challenges. Another area that needs more consideration concerns the interactions among rivalries. Rivalry relationships are often nested in regional clusters of multiple and variable power structures. As a consequence, they operate in external environments with something less than full autonomy. How do rivalries intersect? How does conflict and cooperation in one rivalry make belligerence/appeasement more or less likely elsewhere? Are rivalries immune to shifts in power distributions outside of their own narrow dyad? What theoretical bases, for that matter, do we have for answering these questions affirmatively or negatively? In sum, there is much more to do with rivalries and the assessment of their place in the study of world politics.

Where does that leave us at this juncture? We can imagine a number of questions that deserve consideration but what do we know about strategic rivalries?[19] We know where and when they have occurred in the past two centuries. We know something about a number of their attributes, such as duration and proclivities toward violence. More specifically, we know that rivalries are responsible for more than their fair share of contemporary crises and wars. Perhaps not surprisingly, rivalries, in comparison

---

[18] Incremental decision-making fumbling with unintended consequences may prove to be a respectable explanation for the termination of the Soviet-American rivalry. However, this is a complex question which will require its own book.

[19] We are not ignoring the growing literature on what are sometimes called "enduring" rivalries (see Chapter 2) but the conceptual gap between strategic and enduring rivalries cautions against assuming that findings associated with one phenomenon can be applied to what seems to be a different type of phenomenon.

to nonrivalry dyads, are especially prone to conflict escalation – both in the form of crises and wars. Moreover, rivalries have indirect effects, in addition to their direct effects, on other factors that also facilitate conflict escalation. Earlier crises make subsequent crises more probable which, in turn, are more likely to become lethal. This serial nature of crisis recurrence and escalation is especially likely to occur within rivalries. Rivalries, as a consequence, are prime incubators of conflict escalation. Escalation can occur in the absence of rivalry but it is far more probable if adversarial relationships are already in place.

We also have reason to think that rivalries come in two basic types – spatial and positional – although many rivalries may combine both elements. Proximate minor powers, with roughly equal capabilities, tend to generate spatial rivalries. Major powers and strong regional powers tend to create positional rivalries. Spatial rivalries, in comparison to positional rivalries, are more apt to escalate into dyadic wars. Positional rivalries, in contrast, are more likely to join a war already in progress, thereby making it more multilateral than it was initially.

Finally, we have considerable support for the interactive and escalatory nature of territorial contests, capability symmetry, rivalries, crises, arms build-ups, and alliances in generating crises and wars. Most dangerous is the combination of territorial contests between proximate rivals which encourages both types of conflict escalation, as do capability symmetry, major power dyads, and mixed political regime-type dyads. Arms build-ups and alliances on one side encourage war somewhat, but not crises. Alliances on both sides discourage the probability of war.

Yet it is also clear that the relationships among these variables very much depend on what mix of influences is examined. Different findings emerge when subsets of the pool of possible influences are examined. We are most comfortable with the findings associated with the broader pool because they more closely resemble the steps-to-war argument. Theoretical arguments are critical in this regard. One of the main reasons for expending so much energy on the steps-to-war theory is its multivariate nature. A second reason is that a multivariate argument should more closely approximate the real world than a strictly bivariate hypothesis or a restricted set of influences. That does not imply that the more variables we throw at accounting for crises and war, the better off we will necessarily be. Only when we have good reasons to bring together a relatively large number of variables should we follow the directions suggested by a theoretical argument.

The finding(s), overall, that is least sensitive to variations in research design and variable mixes is the strong explanatory value of information on strategic rivalries. We think we have made a strong case for the indispensability of this information. Most pairs of states never become embroiled in conflict relationships with one another. Those that do come to view other states as competitive and threatening enemies are the ones that are most likely to cause trouble for themselves and others in the form of militarized disputes, crises, and, on occasion, wars. Strategic rivalries clearly matter to deciphering international conflict.[20]

---

[20] The most ideal outcome is that the study of rivalry-related processes will become a more prominent activity within the domain of conflict analysis. It is too early to say whether such a forecast is warranted but recent work is promising. See, for instance, Goertz, Jones, and Diehl (2005), Sprecher and DeRouen (2005), and Thies (2005) – all of which pursue rivalry processes *per se* as opposed to using rivalry categorizations as a control variable.

References

Abowd, J. M. and H. S. Farber (1982) "Job Queues and the Union Status of Workers." *Industrial and Labor Relations Review* 35 (3): 354–67.

Alagappa, M. (1993) "International Security in Southeast Asia: Growing Salience of Regional and Domestic Dynamics," in J. Singh and T. Bernauer, eds., *Security of Third World Countries*, pp. 109–49. Aldershot, UK: Dartmouth.

Allison, Paul D. (1995) *Survival Analysis Using the SAS System*. Cary, NC: SAS Institute Inc.

Allison, P. (1999) "Comparing Logit and Probit Coefficients across Groups." *Sociological Methods Research* 28 (2): 186–208.

Altfeld, M. (1983) "Arms Races? And Escalation? A Comment on Wallace." *International Studies Quarterly* 27: 225–31.

Azar, E., P. Jureidini, and R. McLaurin (1978) "Protracted Social Conflict: Theory and Practice in the Middle East." *Journal of Palestine Studies* 29 (1): 41–60.

Barbieri, K. (1996) "Economic Interdependence: A Path to Peace or Source of Interstate Conflict?" *Journal of Peace Research* 33 (1): 29–42.

Barbieri, K. (1997) "Risky Business: The Impact of Trade Linkages on Interstate Conflict, 1870–1985," in Gerald Schneider and Patricia A. Weitsman, eds., *Enforcing Cooperation: "Risky" States and the Intergovernmental Management of Conflict*. London: Macmillan.

Barbieri, K. (2002) *The Liberal Illusion: Does Trade Promote Peace?* Ann Arbor: University of Michigan Press.

Barton, H. A. (1986) *Scandinavia in the Revolutionary Era, 1760–1815*. Minneapolis: University of Minnesota Press.

Beck, N., J. N. Katz, and R. Tucker (1998) "Taking Time Seriously: Time Series-Cross Section Analysis with a Binary Dependent Variable." *American Journal of Political Science* 42 (4): 1260–89.

Bell, C. (1971) *The Conventions of Crisis: A Study in Diplomatic Management*. New York: Oxford University Press.

Bennett, D. Scott (1996) "Security, Bargaining, and the End of Interstate Rivalry." *International Studies Quarterly* 40: 157–83.

Bennett, D. S. (1997a) "Democracy, Regime Change, and Rivalry Termination." *International Interactions* 22: 369–97.

Bennett, D. S. (1997b) "Measuring Rivalry Termination." *Journal of Conflict Resolution* 41: 227–54.

Bennett, D. S. (1998) "Integrating and Testing Models of Rivalry." *American Journal of Political Science* 42: 1200–32.

Bennett, D. S. (2006) "Exploring Operationalizations of Political Relevance." *Conflict Management and Peace Science* 23: 245–61.

Bennett, D. S. and T. Nordstrom (2000) "Foreign Policy Substitutability and Internal Economic Problems in Enduring Rivalries." *Journal of Conflict Resolution* 44 (1): 33–52.

Bennett, D. S. and A. Stam (2000) "EUGene: A Conceptual Manual." *International Interactions* 26: 179–204. website: <http://eugenesoftware.org>.

Ben Yehuda, H. (1997) "Territoriality, Crises, and War: An Examination of Theory and 20th Century Evidence." Paper presented at the annual meeting of the International Studies Association, Toronto, March.

Ben Yehuda, H. (1998) "Territoriality, Crisis and War in the Arab-Israel Conflict, 1947–1994." Paper presented at the Third Pan-European International Relations Conference and Joint Meeting with the International Studies Association, Vienna, Austria, September.

Blainey, G. (1973) *The Causes of War*. New York: Free Press.

Braumoeller, B. F. (2003) "Causal Complexity and the Study of Politics." *Political Analysis* 11: 209–33.

Brecher, M. (1972) *The Foreign Policy System of Israel: Setting, Images, Process*. New Haven, CT: Yale University Press.

Brecher, M. (1984) "International Crises, Protracted Conflicts." *International Interactions* 11: 237–98.

Brecher, M. (1993) *Crises in World Politics: Theory and Reality*. New York: Pergamon Press.

Brecher, M. and J. W. Wilkenfeld (1997) *A Study of Crisis*. Ann Arbor: University of Michigan Press.

Brecher, M., P. James, and J. Wilkenfeld (2000) "Escalation and War in the Twentieth Century: Findings from the International Crisis Behavior Project," in John A. Vasquez, ed., *What Do We Know about War?* Lanham, MD: Rowman and Littlefield.

Bremer, S. (1992) "Dangerous Dyads: Conditions Affecting the Likelihood of Interstate War, 1816–1965." *Journal of Conflict Resolution* 36: 309–41.

Bremer, S. A. (2000) "Who Fights Whom, When, Where, and Why?," in John A. Vasquez, ed., *What Do We Know about War?*, pp. 23–36. Lanham, MD: Rowman and Littlefield.

Brzezinski, Z. and S. P. Huntington (1963) *Political Power: USA/USSR*. New York: Viking Press.

Bueno de Mesquita, B. (1981) *The War Trap*. New Haven, CT: Yale University Press.

Bueno de Mesquita, B. (1996) "The Benefits of a Social-Scientific Approach to Studying International Affairs," in N. Woods, ed., *Explaining International Relations since 1945*. New York: Oxford University Press.

Burke, E. (1976) *Prelude to Protectorate in Morocco: Precolonial Protest and Resistance, 1860–1912*. Chicago: University of Chicago Press.

Burton, H. A. (1986) *Scandinavia in the Revolutionary Era, 1760–1815*. Minneapolis: University of Minnesota Press.

Carment, D. (1993) "The International Dimensions of Ethnic Conflict: Concepts, Indicators, and Theory." *Journal of Peace Research* 30 (2): 137–50.

Chan, S. (1984) "Mirror, Mirror on the Wall: Are the Freer Countries More Pacific?" *Journal of Conflict Resolution* 28: 617–48.

Chan, S. (1997) "In Search of Democratic Peace: Problems and Promise." *Mershon International Studies Review* 41: 59–91.

Choucri, N. and R. S. North (1975) *Nations in Conflict: Prelude to World War I.* San Francisco, CA: Freeman.

Cioffi-Revilla, C. (1998) "The Political Uncertainty of Interstate Rivalries: A Punctuated Equilibrium Model," in P. F. Diehl, ed., *The Dynamics of Enduring Rivalries*, pp. 64–97. Urbana: University of Illinois Press.

Clark, D. H. and P. M. Regan (2003) "Opportunities to Fight: A Statistical Technique for Modeling Unobservable Phenomena." *Journal of Conflict Resolution* 47 (1): 94–115.

Claude, I. (1962) *Power and International Relations.* New York: Random House.

Colaresi, M. (2001) "Shocks to the System: Great Power Rivalries and the Leadership Long Cycle." *Journal of Conflict Resolution* 45 (5): 569–93.

Colaresi, M. (2004) "When Doves Cry: International Rivalry, Unreciprocated Cooperation and Leadership Turnover." *American Journal of Political Science* 48 (3): 555–70.

Colaresi, M. (2005) *Scare Tactics: The Politics of International Rivalry.* Syracuse, NY: Syracuse University Press.

Colaresi, M. P. and W. R. Thompson (2002) "Hot Spots or Hot Hands? Serial Crisis Behavior, Escalating Risks, and Rivalry." *The Journal of Politics* 64 (4) (November): 1175–98.

Colley, L. (1992) *Britons: Forging the Nation, 1707–1837.* New Haven, CT: Yale University Press.

Combs, J. A. (1986) *The History of American Foreign Policy*, vol. I. New York: Alfred A. Knopf.

Cusack, T. and W.-D. Eberwin (1982) "Prelude to War: Incidence, Escalation and Intervention in International Disputes, 1900–1976." *International Interactions* 9 (1): 9–28.

Desch, M. C. (1996) "War and Strong States, Peace and Weak States?" *International Organization* 50 (20): 236–68.

Diehl, P. F. (1983) "Arms Race and Escalation: A Closer Look." *Journal of Peace Research* 22: 249–59.

Diehl, P. F. (1985a) "Arms Races to War: Testing Some Empirical Linkages." *Sociology Quarterly* 26: 331–49.

Diehl, P. F. (1985b) "Armaments without War: An Analysis of Some Underlying Effects." *Journal of Peace Resolution* 22: 249–59.

Diehl, P. F. (1985c) "Contiguity and Military Escalation in Major Power Rivalries, 1816–1980." *Journal of Politics* 47: 1203–11.

Diehl, P. F. (1993) "Enduring Rivalries: Theoretical Constructs and Empirical Patterns." *International Studies Quarterly* 37: 147–71.

Diehl, P. F. (1994) "Substitutes or Complements? The Effects of Alliances on Military Spending in Major Power Rivalries." *International Interactions* 19 (3): 159–76.

Diehl, P. F., ed. (1998) *The Dynamics of Enduring Rivalries*. Urbana: University of Illinois Press.

Diehl, P. F. and M. J. C. Crescenzi (1999) "Reconfiguring the Arms Race-War Debate." *Journal of Peace Research* 35: 111–18.

Diehl, P. F. and G. Goertz (2000) *War and Peace in International Rivalry*. Ann Arbor: University of Michigan Press.

Diehl, P. F. and J. Kingston (1987) "Messenger or Message? Military Buildups and an Initiation of Conflict." *Journal of Politics* 49: 801–13.

Diehl, P. F., J. Reifschneider, and P. R. Hensel (1996) "United Nations Intervention and Recurring Conflict." *International Organization* 50: 683–700.

Dixit, A. K. and B. J. Nalebuff (1991) *Thinking Strategically*. New York: W. W. Norton.

Dixon, W. J. (1994) "Democracy and the Peaceful Settlement of International Conflict." *American Political Science Review* 88 (1): 14–33.

Dokos, T. P. and P. J. Tsakonas (2003) "Greek-Turkish Relations in the Post-Cold War Era," in C. Kollias and G. Gunluk-Senesen, eds., *Greece and Turkey in the 21st Century: Conflict or Cooperation, A Political Economy Perspective*. New York: Nova Science.

Domke, W. K. (1988) *War and the Changing Global System*. New Haven, CT: Yale University Press.

Eckstein, H. (1975) "Case Study and Theory in Political Science," in F. I. Greenstein and N. W. Polsby, eds., *Handbook of Political Science*, vol. I. Reading, MA: Addison-Wesley.

Finlay, D. J., O. R. Holsti, and R. R. Fagan (1967) *Enemies in Politics*. Chicago: Rand McNally.

Fisher, R. J. (1990) *The Social Psychology of Intergroup and International Conflict Resolution*. New York: Springer-Verlag.

Fitzmaurice, J. (1992) *The Baltic: A Regional Future?* New York: St. Martin's Press.

Gaddis, J. L. (1992) "International Relations Theory and the End of the Cold War." *International Security* 17: 5–58.

Ganguly, S. (1997) *The Crisis in Kashmir: Portents of War, Hopes of Peace*. Cambridge: Cambridge University Press.

Ganguly, S. (2001) *Conflict Unending: India-Pakistan Tensions Since 1947*. New York: Columbia University Press.

Garnham, D. (1976) "Dyadic International War, 1816–1965: The Role of Power Parity and Geographical Proximity." *Western Political Quarterly* 29: 231–42.

Gartner, S. S. and R. M. Siverson (1996) "War Expansion and War Outcome." *Journal of Conflict Resolution* 40: 4–15.

Gartzke, E., Q. Li, and C. Boehmer (2001) "Investing in the Peace: Economic Interdependence and International Conflict." *International Organization* 55: 391–438.

Gartzke, E. and M. Simon (1999) "Hot Hand: A Critical Analysis of Enduring Rivalries." *Journal of Politics* 63 (3): 777–98.

Gasiorowski, M. (1986) "Economic Interdependence and International Conflict: Some Cross-National Evidence." *International Studies Quarterly* 30: 23–8.

Gasiorowski, M. and S. Polachek (1982) "Conflict and Interdependence: East-West Trade and Linkages in the Era of Détente." *Journal of Conflict Resolution* 26: 709–29.

Geller, D. S. (1993) "Power Differentials and War in Rival Dyads." *International Studies Quarterly* 37: 173–94.

Geller, D. S. (1998) "The Stability of the Military Balance of War among Great Power Rivals," in P. F. Diehl, ed., *The Dynamics of Enduring Rivalries*, pp. 165–90. Urbana: University of Illinois Press.

Geller, D. S. (2000) "Material Capabilities: Power and International Conflict," in John A. Vasquez, ed., *What Do We Know about War?* pp. 259–77. Lanham, MD: Rowman and Littlefield.

Gelpi, C. and J. M. Grieco (2003) "Economic Interdependence, the Democratic State and the Liberal Peace," in E. D. Mansfield and B. M. Pollins, eds., *Economic Interdependence and International Conflict: New Perspectives on an Enduring Debate*. Ann Arbor: University of Michigan Press.

Gibler, D. (1997) "Control the Issues, Control the Conflict: The Effects of Alliances that Settle Territorial Issues on Interstate Rivalries." *International Interactions* 22: 341–68.

Gleditsch, K. (2002) "Expanded Trade and GDP Data." *Journal of Conflict Resolution* 46: 712–24.

Gleditsch, K. S. and M. D. Ward (1999) "Interstate System Membership: A Revised List of Independent States since 1816." *International Interactions* 25: 393–413.

Gleditsch, N. P. and H. Hegre (1997) "Peace and Democracy: Three Levels of Analysis." *Journal of Conflict Resolution* 41: 283–310.

Gleditsch, N. P. and J. D. Singer (1975) "Distance and International War, 1816–1965," in M. R. Kahn, ed., *Proceedings of the International Peace Research Association, Fifth General Conference*. Oslo, Norway: International Peace Research Association.

Gochman, C. S. (1990) "Capability-Driven Disputes," in C. S. Gochman and A. N. Sabrosky, eds., *Prisoners of War: Nation States in the Modern Era*. Lexington, MA: Lexington Books.

Gochman, C. S. and R. J. Leng (1983) "Realpolitik and the Road to War." *International Studies Quarterly* 27: 97–120.

Gochman, C. and Z. Maoz (1984) "Militarized Interstate Disputes, 1816–1976: Procedures, Patterns, and Insights." *Journal of Conflict Resolution* 28: 585–616.

Goertz, G. and P. F. Diehl (1992a) "The Empirical Importance of Enduring Rivalries." *International Interactions* 18: 151–63.

Goertz, G. and P. F. Diehl (1992b) *Territorial Changes and International Conflict*. London: Routledge.

Goertz, G. and P. F. Diehl (1993) "Enduring Rivalries: Theoretical Constructs and Empirical Patterns." *International Studies Quarterly* 37 (2): 147–72.

Goertz, G. and P. F. Diehl (1995) "The Initiation and Termination of Enduring Rivalries: The Impact of Political Shocks." *American Journal of Political Science* 39: 30–52.

Goertz, G. and P. F. Diehl (1998) "The Volcano Model and Other Patterns in the Evolution of Enduring Rivalries," in P. F. Diehl, ed., *The Dynamics of Enduring Rivalries*. Urbana: University of Illinois Press.

Goertz, Gary and Paul F. Diehl (2000a) "(Enduring) Rivalries," in M. I. Midlarsky, ed., *Handbook of War Studies II*, pp. 222–67. Ann Arbor: University of Michigan Press.

Goertz, G. and P. F. Diehl (2000b) "Rivalries: The Conflict Process," in J. A. Vasquez, ed., *What Do We Know about War?*, pp. 197–217. Lanham, MD: Rowman and Littlefield.

Goertz, G., B. Jones, and P. F. Diehl (2005) "Maintenance Processes in International Rivalries." *Journal of Conflict Resolution* 49: 742–69.

Goldstein, J. S. (1988) *Long Cycles: Prosperity and War in the Modern Age*. New Haven, CT: Yale University Press.

Greene, W. (1999) *Econometric Analysis*, 4th edn. Upper Saddle Valley, NJ: Prentice-Hall.

Haywood, J. with B. Catchpole, S. Hall, and E. Barratt (1997) *Atlas of World History*. New York: Barnes and Noble.

Hegre, H. (2000) "Development and the Liberal Peace: What Does it Take to be a Trading State?" *Journal of Peace Research* 37: 5–30.

Heisbourg, F. (1998) "French and German Approaches to Organizing Europe's Future Security and Defense: A French Perspective," in D. P. Calleo and E. R. Stael, eds., *Europe's Franco-German Engine*, pp. 47–70. Washington, DC: Brookings Institute Press.

Hensel, P. R. (1994) "One Thing Leads to Another: Recurrent Militarized Disputes in Latin America, 1816–1986." *Journal of Peace Research* 31 (3): 281–98.

Hensel, P. R. (1996) "Charting a Course to Conflict: Territorial Issues and Militarized Interstate Disputes, 1816–1992." *Conflict Management and Peace Science* 15: 43–73.

Hensel, P. R. (2000) "Territory: Theory and Evidence on Geography and Conflict," in J. A. Vasquez, ed., *What Do We Know about War?* Lanham, MD: Rowman and Littlefield.

Hensel, P. R. (2001) "Evolution in Domestic Politics and the Development of Rivalry: The Bolivia-Paraguay Case," in W. R. Thompson, ed., *Evolutionary Interpretations of World Politics*. New York: Routledge.

Hensel, P. R. and P. F. Diehl (1994) "It Takes Two to Tango: Non-militarized Responses in Interstate Disputes." *Journal of Conflict Resolution* 38: 479–506.

Hensel, P. R., G. Goertz, and P. F. Diehl (2000) "The Democratic Peace and Rivalries." *Journal of Politics* 62: 1173–88.

Hensel, P. and T. E. Sowers II (1998) "Territorial Claims, Major Power Competition, and the Origins of Enduring Rivalry." Paper presented at the Third Pan-European International Relations Conference and Joint Meeting with the International Studies Association, Vienna, Austria, September.

Herz, M. and J. Pontes Nogueira (2002) *Ecuador vs. Peru: Peacemaking Amid Rivalry*. Boulder, CO: Lynne Rienner.

Hewitt, J. J. and J. Wilkenfeld (1999) "One-Sided Crises in the International System." *Journal of Peace Research* 36: 309–23.

Hill, D. H., W. G. Axinn, and A. Thorton (1993) "Competing Hazards with Shared Unmeasured Risk Factors." *Sociological Methodology* 23 (1): 245–77.

Hill, N. (1945) *Claims to Territory in International Relations.* New York: Oxford University Press.

Hoare, J. E. and S. Pares (1999) *Conflict in Korea: An Encyclopedia.* Santa Barbara, CA: ABC-CLIO.

Holsti, K. J. (1991) *Peace and War: Armed Conflicts and International Order, 1648–1989.* Cambridge: Cambridge University Press.

Horn, M. D. (1987) "Arms Races and the International System." Unpublished PhD dissertation. Department of Political Science: University of Rochester.

Houweling, H. W. and J. G. Siccama (1981) "The Arms Race-War Relationship: Why Serious Disputes Matter." *Arms Control* 2: 157–97.

Huth, P. K. (1996a) "Enduring Rivalries and Territorial Disputes, 1950–1990." *Conflict Management and Peace Science* 15: 7–41.

Huth, P. K. (1996b) *Standing Your Ground: Territorial Disputes and International Conflicts.* Ann Arbor: University of Michigan Press.

Huth, P. K. (2000) "Territory: Why Are Territorial Disputes between States a Central Cause of International Conflict?," in J. A. Vasquez, ed., *What Do We Know about War?* Lanham, MD: Rowman and Littlefield.

Huth, P. K. and T. R. Allee (2002) *The Democratic Peace and Territorial Conflict in the Twentieth Century.* Cambridge: Cambridge University Press.

Huth, P. K., D. S. Bennett, and C. Gelpi (1992) "System Uncertainty, Risk Propensity and International Conflict among the Great Powers." *Journal of Conflict Resolution* 36: 478–517.

Huth, P., C. Gelpi, and D. S. Bennett (1993) "The Escalation of Great Power Militarized Disputes: Testing Rational Deterrence Theory and Structural Realism." *American Political Science Review* 87: 609–23.

Huth, P. K. and B. M. Russett (1993) "General Deterrence Between Enduring Rivals: Testing Three Competing Models." *American Political Science Review* 87: 61–73.

Jaggars, K. and T. R. Gurr (1995) "Tracking Democracy's Third Wave with the Polity III Data." *Journal of Peace Research* 32: 469–82.

James, P. (1988) *Crisis and War.* Montreal: McGill-Queen's University Press.

Jervis, R. (1976) *Perception and Misperception in International Politics.* Princeton, NJ: Princeton University Press.

Jervis, R. (1988) "Perceiving and Coping with Threat," in R. Jervis, R. N. Lebow, and J. Gross Stein, eds., *Psychology and Deterrence,* pp. 1–31. Baltimore, MD: Johns Hopkins University Press.

Jones, D. M., S. A. Bremer, and J. D. Singer (1996) "Militarized Interstate Disputes, 1816–1992: Rationale, Coding Rules and Empirical Patterns." *Conflict Management and Peace Science* 15: 163–213.

Kahler, M. and B. Walter, eds. (2006) *Territoriality and Conflict in an Era of Globalization.* Cambridge: Cambridge University Press.

Kang, H. and R. Reuveny (2001) "Exploring Multi-Country Dynamic Interrelationships between Trade and Conflict." *Defense and Peace Economics* 12: 175–96.

Keane, M. (1992) "A Note on Identification of the Multinomial Probit Model." *Journal of Business and Economic Studies* 10 (2): 193–200.

Kennedy, P. M. (1976) *The Rise and Fall of British Naval Mastery.* New York: Charles Scribner's.

Kennedy, P. M. (1980) *The Rise of the Anglo-German Antagonism, 1860–1914.* London: George Allen & Unwin.

Keshk, O. M. G., B. M. Pollins, and R. Reuveny (2004) "Trade Still Follows the Flag: The Primacy of Politics in a Simultaneous Model of Interdependence and Armed Conflict." *Journal of Politics* 66: 1155–79.

Khong, Y. F. (1992) *Analogies at War: Korea, Munich, Dien Bien Phu, and the Vietnam Decision of 1965.* Princeton, NJ: Princeton University Press.

Kim, H. M. and D. L. Rousseau (2005) "The Classical Liberals Were Half Right (or Half Wrong): New Tests of the Liberal Peace, 1960–88." *Journal of Peace Research* 42 (5): 523–43.

King, G., R. O. Keohane, and S. Verba (1994) *Designing Social Inquiry.* Princeton, NJ: Princeton University Press.

Klein, J. P., G. Goertz, and P. F. Diehl (2006) "The New Rivalry Dataset: Procedures and Patterns." *Journal of Peace Research* 43 (3): 331–48.

Klepak, H. (1998) *Confidence Building Sidestepped: The Peru-Ecuador Conflict of 1995.* Ottawa, Ont.: Centre for International and Security Studies, York University.

Kocs, S. A. (1995) "Territorial Disputes and Interstate War, 1945–1987." *Journal of Politics* 57: 159–75.

Kuenne, R. (1989) "Conflict Management in Mature Rivalry." *Journal of Conflict Resolution* 33: 554–66.

Kugler, J. and D. Lemke, eds. (1996) *Parity and War.* Ann Arbor: University of Michigan Press.

Langley, L. D. (1976) *Struggle for the American Mediterranean: United States-European Rivalry in the Gulf-Caribbean, 1776–1904.* Athens: University of Georgia Press.

Lebow, R. N. (1981) *Between Peace and War: The Nature of International Crisis.* Baltimore, MD: Johns Hopkins University Press.

Lemke, D. (1998) "The Tyranny of Distance: Redefining Relevant Dyads." *International Interactions* 21: 23–38.

Lemke, D. and W. Reed (1998) "Status Quo Evaluations and Interstate Rivalry." Paper presented at the annual meeting of the American Political Science Association, Boston, MA, September.

Leng, R. J. (1983) "When Will They Ever Learn? Coercive Bargaining in Recurrent Crises." *Journal of Conflict Resolution* 21 (5): 379–419.

Leng, R. J. (1984) "Reagan and the Russians: Crisis Bargaining Beliefs and the Historical Record." *American Political Science Review* 78: 338–55.

Leng, R. J. (2000a) *Bargaining and Learning in Recurring Crises: The Soviet-American, Egyptian-Israeli, and Indo-Pakistani Rivalries.* Ann Arbor: University of Michigan Press.

Leng, R. J. (2000b) "Escalation: Crisis Behavior and War," in J. A. Vasquez, ed., *What Do We Know about War?* Lanham, MD: Rowman and Littlefield.

Levy, J. S. (1989) "Quantitative Studies of Deterrence Success and Failure," in P. Stern, R. Axelrod, R. Jervis, and R. Radner, eds., *Perspectives on Deterrence*. Oxford: Oxford University Press.

Levy, J. S. (1999) "Economic Competition, Domestic Politics, and Systematic Change: The Rise and Decline of the Anglo-Dutch Rivalry, 1609–1688," in W. R. Thompson, ed., *Great Power Rivalries*, pp. 172–200. Columbia: University of South Carolina Press.

Levy, J. S. (2000a) "Loss Aversion, Framing Effects, and International Conflict: Perspectives from Prospect Theory," in M. Midlarsky, ed., *Handbook of War Studies II*. Ann Arbor: University of Michigan Press.

Levy, J. S. (2000b) "Reflections on the Scientific Study of War," in J. A. Vasquez, ed., *What Do We Know about War?* Lanham, MD: Rowman and Littlefield.

Levy, J. S. and S. A. Ali (1998) "From Commercial Competition to Strategic Rivalry to War: The Evolution of the Anglo-Dutch Rivalry, 1609–1652," in P. F. Diehl, ed., *The Dynamics of Enduring Rivalries*, pp. 29–63. Urbana: University of Illinois Press.

Levy, J. S. and T. C. Morgan (1986) "The War-Weariness Hypothesis: An Empirical Test." *American Journal of Political Science* 30: 26–50.

Lieberman, E. (1995) "What Makes Deterrence Work? Lessons for the Egyptian-Israeli Enduring Rivalry." *Security Studies* 4: 851–910.

Lisk, J. (1967) *The Struggle for Supremacy in the Baltic, 1600–1725*. New York: Funk and Wagnalls.

Lockhart, C. (1978) "Conflict Actions and Outcomes: Long-Term Impacts." *Journal of Conflict Resolution* 22: 565–98.

Long, J. S. (1997) *Regression Models for Categorical and Limited Dependent Variables*. London: Sage.

Long, J. S. and J. Freese (2006) *Regression Models for Categorical Dependent Variables Using Stata*, 2nd edn. College Station, TX: Stata Press.

Luard, E. (1970) *The International Regulation of Frontier Disuptes*. New York: Praeger.

Luard, E. (1986) *War in International Society*. New Haven, CT: Yale University Press.

Lynch, J. (1985) "The River Plate Republics from Independence to the Paraguayan War," in L. Bethell, ed., *The Cambridge History of Latin America: From Independence to c. 1870*, vol. III. Cambridge: Cambridge University Press.

Mansfield, E. D. (1994) *Power, Trade and War*. Princeton, NJ: Princeton University Press.

Mansfield, E. D. and J. C. Pevehouse (2003) "Institutions, Interdependence and International Conflict," in G. Schneider, K. Barbieri, and N. P. Gleditsch, eds., *Globalization and Armed Conflict*. Lanham, MD: Rowman and Littlefield.

Mansfield, E. D., J. C. Pevehouse, and D. H. Bearce (1999) "Preferential Trading Arrangements and Military Disputes." *Security Studies* 9: 92–118.

Maoz, Z. (1983) "Resolve, Capabilities, and the Outcomes of Interstate Disputes, 1816–1976." *Journal of Conflict Resolution* 27: 195–229.

Maoz, Z. (1984) "Peace by Empire?: Conflict Outcomes and International Stability, 1816–1976." *Journal of Peace Research* 21: 227–41.

Maoz, Z. (1996) *Domestic Sources of Global Change*. Ann Arbor: University of Michigan Press.

Maoz, Z. (1999) "Dyadic Militarized Interstate Disputes (DYMID1.1)" at <http://spirit.tau.ac.il/poli/faculty/maoz/dyadmid.doc>.

Maoz, Z. (2000) "Alliances: The Street Gangs of World Politics – Their Origins, Management and Consequences," in J. A. Vasquez, ed., *What Do We Know about War?* Lanham, MD: Rowman and Littlefield.

Maoz, Z. and B. Mor (1996) "Enduring Rivalries: The Early Years." *International Political Science Review* 17: 141–60.

Maoz, Z. and B. Mor (1998) "Learning, Preference Change and the Evolution of Enduring Rivalries," in P. F. Diehl, ed., *The Dynamics of Enduring Rivalries*, pp. 129–64. Urbana: University of Illinois Press.

Maoz, Z. and Ben Mor (2002) *Bound by Struggle: The Strategic Evolution of Enduring International Rivalries*. Ann Arbor: University of Michigan Press.

Mares, D. R. (1996/7) "Deterrence Bargaining in the Ecuador-Peru Enduring Rivalry: Designing Strategies around Military Weakness." *Security Studies* 6: 91–123.

Mares, D. R. (2001) *Violent Peace: Militarized Interstate Bargaining in Latin America*. New York: Columbia University Press.

Manyin, M. E. (2002) "North-South Korean Relations: A Chronology of Events in 2000 and 2001." Washington, DC: Congressional Research Service, Library of Congress <www.Globalsecurity.org/military/library/report/crs/RL31811.pdf>.

McClelland, C. A. (1972) "The Beginning, Duration, and Abatement of International Crises: Comparisons in Two Conflict Arenas," in C. F. Hermann, ed., *International Crises: Insights from Behavioral Research*, pp. 83–104. New York: Free Press.

McGinnis, M. (1990) "A Rational Model of Regional Rivalry." *International Studies Quarterly* 34: 111–35.

McGinnis, M. and J. Williams (1989) "Change and Stability in Superpower Rivalry." *American Political Science Review* 83: 1101–23.

Milward, A. S. (1984) *The Reconstruction of Western Europe, 1945–51*. Berkeley: University of California Press.

Mitchell, S. M. and B. C. Prins (1999) "Beyond Territorial Contiguity: Issues at Stake in Democratic Militarized Interstate Disputes." *International Studies Quarterly* 44 (1): 503–30.

Modelski, G. and W. R. Thompson (1988) *Sea Power in Global Politics, 1494–1993*. London: Macmillan.

Morrow, J. D. (1989) "Capabilities, Uncertainty, and Resolve: A Limited Information Model of Crisis Bargaining." *American Journal of Political Science* 33: 941–72.

Mousseau, M. (2000) "Market Prosperity, Democratic Consolidation and Democratic Peace." *Journal of Conflict Resolution* 44: 472–507.

Mousseau, M., H. Hegre, and J. R. Oneal (2003) "How the Wealth of Nations Conditions the Liberal Peace." *European Journal of International Relations* 9: 277–314.

Nanto, D. K. (2003) "North Korea: Chronology of Provocations, 1950–2003." Washington, DC: Library of Congress Congressional Research Service <www.fas.org/man/crs/RL3004.pdf>.

Neustadt, R. and E. R. May (1988) *Thinking in Time: The Uses of History for Decision-Makers*. New York: Free Press.

Nomikos, E. V. and R. C. North (1976) *International Crisis: The Outbreak of World War I*. Montreal: McGill-Queen's University Press.

Oberdorfer, D. (2001) *The Two Koreas: A Contemporary History*, rev. edn. New York: Basic Books.

Oneal, J. R. (2003) "Empirical Support for the Liberal Peace," in E. D. Mansfield and B. M. Pollins, eds., *Economic Interdependence and International Conflict: New Perspectives on an Enduring Debate*. Ann Arbor: University of Michigan Press.

Oneal, J. R., F. Oneal, Z. Maoz, and B. M. Russett (1996) "The Liberal Peace: Interdependence, Democracy and International Conflict, 1950–1986." *Journal of Peace Research* 33: 11–28.

Oneal, J. R. and J. Lee Ray (1997) "New Tests of the Democratic Peace: Controlling for Economic Interdependence, 1950–1985." *Political Research Quarterly* 50: 751–75.

Oneal, J. R. and B. M. Russett (1997) "The Classical Liberals Were Right: Democracy, Interdependence and Conflict, 1950–85." *International Studies Quarterly* 41: 267–94.

Oneal, J. R. and B. M. Russett (1999a) "Is the Liberal Peace Just an Artifact of Cold War Interests? Assessing Recent Critiques." *International Interactions* 25: 1–29.

Oneal, J. R. and B. M. Russett (1999b) "The Kantian Peace: The Pacific Benefits of Democracy, Interdependence, and International Organizations, 1885–1992." *World Politics* 52: 1–37.

Oneal, J. R. and B. M. Russett (2003) "Assessing the Liberal Peace with Alternative Specifications: Trade Still Reduces Conflict," in G. Schneider, K. Barbieri and N. P. Gleditsch, eds., *Globalization and Armed Conflict*. Lanham, MD: Rowman and Littlefield.

Paul, T. V., ed. (2005) *The India-Pakistan Conflict: An Enduring Rivalry*. Cambridge: Cambridge University Press.

Parsons, F. V. (1976) *The Origins of the Morocco Question, 1880–1900*. London: Duckworth.

Perry, W. (1986) "Argentina: Regional Power Overstretched," in R. W. Jones and S. A Hildreth, eds., *Emerging Powers: Defense and Security in the Third World*, pp. 343–70. New York: Praeger.

Pevehouse, J. C. and J. S. Goldstein (1997) "Reciprocity, Bullying and International Cooperation: Time Series Analysis of the Bosnian Conflict." *American Political Science Review* 91 (3): 515–32.

Polachek, S. (1980) "Conflict and Trade." *Journal of Conflict Resolution* 24: 55–78.

Polachek, S. (1992) "Conflict and Trade: An Economics Approach to Political International Interactions," in W. Isard and C. H. Anderson, eds., *Economics of Arms Reduction and the Peace Process*. Amsterdam: North-Holland.

Polachek, S. (1997) "Why Do Democracies Cooperate More and Fight Less: The Relationship Between International Trade and Cooperation." *Review of International Economics* 5: 295–309.

Polachek, S. and J. McDonald (1992) "Strategic Trade and the Incentive for Cooperation," in M. Chatterji and L. Rennie Forcey, eds., *Disarmament, Economic Conversion, and Management of Peace*. New York: Praeger.

Polachek, S., J. Robst and Y.-C. Chang (1999) "Liberalism and Interdependence: Extending the Trade-Conflict Model." *Journal of Peace Research* 36 (4): 405–22.

Porter, G. (1990) "Cambodia's Foreign Policy," in D. Wurfel and B. Burton, eds., *The Political Economy of Foreign Policy in Southeast Asia*, pp. 247–72. New York: St. Martin's Press.

Ragin, C. C. (1994) *Constructing Social Research: The Unity and Diversity of Method*. London: Pine Forge Press.

Ragin, C. C. (2000) *Fuzzy-Set Social Science*. Chicago: University of Chicago Press.

Rapkin, D. P. (1999) "The Emergence and Intensification of U.S.-Japan Rivalry in the Early Twentieth Century," in W. R. Thompson, ed., *Great Power Rivalries*, pp. 337–70. Columbia: University of South Carolina Press.

Rasler, K. (2001) "Political Shocks and the De-Escalation of Protracted Conflicts: The Israeli-Palestine Case," in W. R. Thomson, ed., *Evolutionary Interpretations of World Politics*, New York: Routledge.

Rasler, K. (2005) "An Evolutionary Model of Rivalry Termination and the Israeli–Syrian Case, 1948–2000." Paper delivered at the annual meeting of the International Studies Association, Honolulu, Hawai'i, March.

Rasler, K. and W. R. Thompson (1999) "Predatory Initiators and the Changing Landscape for War." *Journal of Conflict Resolution* 43: 411–33.

Rasler, K. and W. R. Thompson (1994) *The Great Powers and Global Struggle, 1490–1990*. Lexington, KY: University of Kentucky Press.

Rasler, K. and W. R. Thompson (2000) "Explaining Escalation to War: Contiguity, Space and Position in the Major Power Subsystem." *International Studies Quarterly* 44 (3): 503–30.

Rasler, K. and W. R. Thompson (2001) "Rivalries and the Democratic Peace in the Major Power Subsystem." *Journal of Peace Research* 38 (6): 659–83.

Rasler, K. and W. R. Thompson (2003) "The Monadic Democratic Peace Puzzle and an 'End of History' Partial Solution?" *International Politics* 40: 657–83.

Rasler, K. and W. R. Thompson (2005) *Puzzles of the Democratic Peace*. New York: Palgrave-Macmillan.

Rasler, K., W. R. Thompson, and S. Ganguly (n.d.) "How Rivalries End." Unpublished Manuscript. Bloomington, IN: Indiana University.

Ray, J. L. (2000) "Democracy: On the Level(s), Does Democracy Correlate with Peace?," in J. A. Vasquez, ed., *What Do We Know about War?* Lanham, MD: Rowman and Littlefield.

Reed, W. (2000) "A Unified Statistical Model of Conflict Onset and Escalation." *American Journal of Political Science* 44: 84–93.

Rennstich, J. (2003) "The Future of Great Power Rivalries," in W. A. Dunaway, ed., *Emerging Issues in the 21st Century World-System*. Westport, Ct.: Praeger.

Reuveny, R. (1999a) "The Political Economy of Israeli-Palestinian Interdependence." *Policy Studies Journal* 27: 643–64.

Reuveny, R. (1999b) "Israeli-Palestinian Economic Interdependence Reconsidered." *Policy Studies Journal* 27: 668–71.

Reuveny, R. and H. Kang (1996) "International Trade. Political Conflict/ Cooperation, and Granger Causality." *International Studies Quarterly* 40: 281–306.

Reuveny, R. and H. Kang (1998) "Bilateral Trade and Political Conflict/ Cooperation: Do Goods Matter?" *Journal of Peace Research* 35 (5): 581–602.

Richardson, L. (1960) *Arms and Insecurity*. Pacific Grove, CA: Boxwood.

Rioux, J. S. (1997) "U.S. Crises and Domestic Politics: Crisis Outcomes, Reputation, and Domestic Consequences." *Southeastern Political Review* 25 (2): 219–29.

Rock, S. R. (1989) *Why Peace Breaks Out: Great Power Rapprochement in Historical Perspective*. Chapel Hill: University of North Carolina Press.

Rosecrance, R. (1986) *The Rise of the Trading State: Commerce and Conquest in the Modern World*. New York: Basic Books.

Ross, M. H. (1998) *The Culture of Conflict: Interpretations and Interests in Comparative Perspective*. New Haven, CT: Yale University Press.

Rousseau, D., C. Gelpi, D. Reiter, and P. Huth (1996) "Assessing the Dyadic Nature of the Democratic Peace, 1918–88." *American Political Science Review* 90: 512–33.

Russett, B. M. (1967) *International Regions and the International System: A Study in Political Ecology*. Chicago: Rand McNally.

Russett, B. M. (1993) *Grasping the Democratic Peace: Principles for a Post-Cold War World*. Princeton, NJ: Princeton University Press.

Russett, B. M. (2003) "Violence and Disease: Trade as Suppressor to Conflict when Suppressors Matter," in E. D. Mansfield and B. M. Pollins, eds., *Economic Interdependence and International Conflict: New Perspectives on an Enduring Debate*. Ann Arbor: University of Michigan Press.

Russett, B. M. and J. R. Oneal (2001) *Triangulating Peace: Democracy, Interdependence, and International Organizations*. New York: Norton.

Russett, B. M. and H. Starr (2000) "From Democratic Peace to Kantian Peace: Democracy and Conflict in the International System," in M. Midlarsky, ed., *Handbook of War II*. Ann Arbor: University of Michigan Press.

Sample, S. (1997) "Arms Races and Dispute Escalation: Resolving the Debate." *Journal of Peace Research* 34: 7–22.

Sample, S. (1998) "Military Buildups, War and Realpolitik: A Multivariate Model." *Journal of Conflict Resolution* 42: 156–75.

Sample, S. (2000) "Military Buildups: Arming and War," in J. A. Vasquez, ed., *What Do We Know about War?* Lanham, MD: Rowman and Littlefield.

Sarkees, M. R. (2000) "The Correlates of War Data on War: An Update to 1997." *Conflict Management and Peace Science* 18: 123–44.

Schneider, G., K. Barbieri, and N. P. Gleditsch (2003) "Does Globalization Contribute to Peace? A Critical Survey of the Literature," in G. Schneider, K. Barbieri, and N. P. Gleditsch, eds., *Globalization and Armed Conflict.* Lanham, MD: Rowman and Littlefield.

Senese, P. D. (1996) "Geographical Proximity and Issue Salience: Their Effects on the Escalation of Miltiarized Interstate Conflict." *Conflict Management and Peace Science* 15: 133–61.

Senese, P. D. (1997) "Dispute to War: The Conditional Importance of Territorial Issue Stakes and Geographic Proximity." Paper delivered to the annual meeting of the International Studies Association, Toronto, Canada, March.

Senese, P. D. and J. A. Vasquez (2003) "Territorial Disputes and the Steps to War, 1816–1945." Paper presented to the annual meeting of the International Studies Association, Portland, OR, February.

Senese, P. D. and J. A. Vasquez (2003) "A Unified Explanation of Territorial Conflict: Testing the Impact of Sampling Bias, 1919–1992." *International Studies Quarterly* 47: 275–98.

Senese, P. D., J. A. Vasquez, and M. T. Henehan (1998) "Testing the Territorial Explanation of War, 1816–1992." Paper presented at the Third Pan-European International Relations Conference and Joint Meeting with the International Studies Association, Vienna, Austria, September.

Singer, J. D. (1987) "Reconstructing the Correlates of War Dataset on Material Capabilities of States, 1816–1985." *International Interactions* 14: 115–32.

Singer, J. D. and T. Cusack (1980) "Periodicity, Inexorability and Steermanship in International War," in R. L. Merritt and B. Russett, eds., *From National Development to Global Community.* London: Allen & Unwin.

Singer, J. D. and M. Small (1974) "Foreign Policy Indicators: Predictions of War in History and in the State of the World Message." *Policy Sciences* 5: 271–96.

Siverson, R. M. (1980) "War and Change in the International System," in O. R. Holsti, R. M. Siverson, and A. L. George, eds., *Change in the International System.* Boulder, CO: Westview.

Siverson, R. M. and P. F. Diehl (1989) "Arms Races, the Conflict Spiral, and the Onset of War," in M. Midlarsky, ed., *Handbook of War Studies.* Boston, MA: Unwin Hyman.

Small, M. and J. D. Singer (1982) *Resort to Arms: International and Civil Wars, 1816–1980.* Beverly Hills, CA: Sage.

Smith, T. C. (1980) "Arms Race Instability and War." *Journal of Conflict Resolution* 24: 253–84.

Snyder, G. H. and P. Diesing (1977) *Conflict among Nations: Bargaining, Decision Making and System Structure in International Crisis.* Princeton, NJ: Princeton University Press.

Sonmezoglu, F. and G. Ayman (2003) "The Roots of Conflict and the Dynamics of Change in Turkish-Greek Relations," in C. Kollias and G. Gunluk-Senesen, eds., *Greece and Turkey in the 21st Century: Conflict or Cooperation, A Political Economy Perspective.* New York: Nova Science.

Sorokin, G. L. (1994) "Arms, Alliances, and Security Trade-offs in Enduring Rivalries." *International Studies Quarterly* 38 (3): 421–47.

Sprecher, C. and K. DeRouen, Jr. (2005) "The Domestic Determinants of Foreign Policy Behavior in Middle Eastern Enduring Rivals, 1948–1998." *Foreign Policy Analysis* 1: 121–41.

Stein, J. G. (1996) "Deterrence and Learning in an Enduring Rivalry: Egypt and Israel, 1948–73." *Security Studies* 6: 104–52.

Stinnett, D. and P. F. Diehl (2001) "The Path(s) to Rivalry: Behavioural and Structural Explanations of Rivalry Development." *Journal of Politics* 63 (3): 717–40.

Stoessinger, J. (1985) *Why Nations Go to War*, 4th edn. New York: St. Martin's Press.

Stoll, R. J. (1984) "From Fire to Frying Pan: The Impact of Major Power War Involvement on Major Power Dispute Involvement, 1816–1975." *Conflict Management and Peace Science* 7: 71–82.

Sturmer, M. (1998) "Deux rêves dan un seul lit: Franco-German Security Cooperation," in D. P. Calleo and E. R. Stael, eds., *Europe's Franco-German Engine*, pp. 71–83. Washington, DC: Brookings Institute Press.

Summers, R. and A. Heston (1991) "The Penn World Table (Mark 5): An Expanded Set of International Comparisons, 1950–1988." *Quarterly Journal of Economics* 106 (2): 263–81.

Thies, Cameron G. (2005) "War, Rivalry and State Making in Latin America." *American Journal of Political Science* 49: 451–65.

Thompson, W. R. (1973) *The Grievances of Military Coup-Makers*. Beverly Hills, CA: Sage.

Thompson, W. R. (1995) "Principal Rivalries." *Journal of Conflict Resolution* 39 (2): 195–223.

Thompson, W. R., ed. (1999) *Great Power Rivalries*. Columbia: University of South Carolina Press.

Thompson, W. R. (2001) "Expectancy Theory, Strategic Rivalries, and the Sino-Soviet Rivalry," in W. R. Thompson, ed., *Evolutionary Interpretations of World Politics*. New York: Routledge.

Thompson, W. R. (2003) "A Streetcar Named Sarajevo: Catalysts, Multiple Rivalries and 'Systemic Accidents.'" *International Studies Quarterly* 47: 453–74.

Thompson, W. R. (2005) "Modeling the De-escalation and Termination of Strategic Rivalries." Paper delivered at the annual meeting of the International Studies Association, Honolulu, Hawai'i, March.

Thompson, W. R. (forthcoming) *Handbook of Interstate Rivalry*. Washington, DC: Congressional Quarterly Press.

Tir, J. and P. F. Diehl (2002) "Geographic Dimensions of Enduring Rivalries." *Political Geography* 21: 263–86.

Toset, H. P. W. and N. P. Gleditsch (1998) "Conflict and Shared Rivers." Paper presented at the Third European International Relations Conference and Joint Meeting with the International Studies Association, Vienna, Austria, September.

Toynbee, A. J. (1954) *A Study of History*, vol. IX. London: Oxford University Press.

Van de Mieroop, M. (2004) *A History of the Ancient Near East, ca. 3000–323 BC.* Malden, MA: Blackwell.

Vasquez, J. A. (1993) *The War Puzzle.* Cambridge: Cambridge University Press.

Vasquez, J. A. (1995) "Why Do Neighbors Fight? Proximity, Interaction, or Territoriality." *Journal of Peace Research* 32: 277–93.

Vasquez, J. A. (1996) Distinguishing Rivals that Go to War from Those that Do Not: A Quantitative Comparative Case Study of the Two Paths to War. *International Studies Quarterly* 40 (4): 531–58.

Vasquez, J. A. (2000) "What Do We Know about War?," in J. A. Vasquez, ed., *What Do We Know about War?*, pp. 335–70. Lanham, MD: Rowman and Littlefield.

Vasquez, J. A. (2001) "Mapping the Probability of War and Analyzing the Possibility of Peace: The Role of Territorial Disputes." *Conflict Management and Peace Science* 18: 145–74.

Vasquez, J. A. (2002) "The Probability of War, 1816–1992." Presidential Address to the International Studies Association, March 25.

Vasquez, J. A. (2004) "The Probability of War, 1816–1992." *International Studies Quarterly* 48: 1–27.

Vasquez, J. A. and M. T. Henehan (2001) "Territorial Disputes and the Probability of War, 1816–1992." *Journal of Peace Research* 38: 123–35.

Vertzberger, Y. (1990) *The World in Their Minds: Information Processing, Cognition, and Perception in Foreign Policy Decision-Making.* Stanford, CA: Stanford University Press.

Wallace, M. (1979) "Arms Races and Escalation: Some New Evidence." *Journal of Conflict Resolution* 23: 3–16.

Wallensteen, P. (1973) *Structure and War: On International Relations, 1920–1968.* Stockholm: Raben and Sjogren.

Waltz, K. N. (1979) *Theory of International Politics.* Reading, MA: McGraw-Hill.

Wayman, F. W. (1996) "Power Shifts and the Onset of War," in J. Kugler and D. Lemke, eds., *Parity and War*, pp. 145–62. Ann Arbor: University of Michigan Press.

Wayman, F. W. (2000) "Rivalries: Recurrent Disputes and Explaining War," in J. A. Vasquez, ed., *What Do We Know about War?*, pp. 219–39. Lanham, MD: Rowman and Littlefield.

Wayman, F. W. and D. M. Jones (1991) "Evolution of Conflict in Enduring Rivalries." Paper presented at the annual meeting of the International Studies Association, Vancouver, British Columbia, March.

Weede, E. (1976) "Overwhelming Preponderance as a Pacifying Condition among Contiguous Asian Dyads, 1950–1969." *Journal of Conflict Resolution* 20: 395–412.

Weede, E. (1980) "Arms Races and Escalation: Some Persisting Doubts." *Journal of Conflict Resolution* 24: 285–7.

Wilkenfeld, J. and M. Brecher (2000) "Interstate Crises and Violence: Twentieth Century Findings," in M. Midlarsky, ed., *Handbook of War Studies II*, pp. 271–300. Ann Arbor: University of Michigan Press.

Wright, Q. (1942/1965) *A Study of War.* Chicago, Il: University of Chicago Press.

Index

ABC powers 73, 167, 171, 199n.11
access rivalry 81
Aegean 7
Afghanistan 178
Akkad 240n.1
Aksai Chin 111
Alagappa, M. 32
Alaska 34
Algeria–Morocco rivalry 34, 35, 65, 246
Ali, S.A. 27n.6
Allee, Todd R. 247, 248, 248n.8, 250, 251, 252, 253, 282
Allison, Paul D. 123n.16, 143n.8, 145n.11, 232
Altfeld, Michael 221n.2
Amazon Basin 5
Anglo–Burmese War, first 89n.10
Anglo–Persian War 90
Angola 104
apartheid 27, 71
  and southern African rivalries 94
Argentina–Britain rivalry 73
Argentina–Brazil rivalry 86n.8
Argentina–Chile rivalry 107, 242, 251
Argentina–Paraguay rivalry 32
Argentina–Uruguay 146n.12
Armenia–Azerbaijan rivalry 73
Asymmetry in capabilities 24, 52
Austria–France rivalry 178n.4
Austria–Italy rivalry 178
Austria–Prussia rivalry 26, 178
Axinn, William G. 209n.22, 209n.23
Ayman, Gulden 7
Azar, Edward 102

Bahrain–Qatar 106
Baltic Independence Crisis 116
Bangladesh 9
Barbieri, Katherine 280
Barratt, E. 177n.3
Barton, H. Arnold 26n.3

Beagle Islands dispute 242
Beck, Nathaniel 118, 139n.4, 145n.11, 232, 250n.14, 263, 283
Belgium–Germany 67
Belize–Guatemala rivalry 246
Bell, Coral 133
Bennett, D. Scott 23, 36, 37n.12, 54, 54n.18, 55, 56, 56n.20, 57, 59n.22, 144n.9, 145, 199n.10, 202, 248, 279, 280, 281n.4
Ben Yehuda, Hemda 179n.6, 240n.2
Berlin 178
Berlin crisis 132
Blainey, Geoffrey 112, 137, 278
Boer War 89n.10
Bolivia 243
Bolivia–Paraguay rivalry 106, 244
Braumoeller, Bear F. 198n.9
Brazil–Paraguay rivalry 32
Brecher, Michael 16, 27n.5, 37n.12, 101, 104, 105, 107, 109, 111n.3, 112, 112n.4, 113, 113n.6, 114, 116, 117, 118, 121, 140n.5, 142, 142n.7, 145, 232
Bremer, Stuart 18, 22, 89n.10, 109, 145, 189, 190, 191, 191n.1, 193, 193n.2, 194, 199, 202, 213, 214
Britain and South American/Caribbean "rivals" 53, rivalry propensity 83
Britain–France rivalry 26, 78, 104, 173n.2, 179
Britain–Germany rivalry 26, 178
Britain–Japan rivalry 178
Britain–Russia rivalry 26, 31, 78, 90, 178
Britain–Spain 244
Britain–United States rivalry 26, 78, 94, 95, 178, 230
British–Afghan Wars
  first 89n.10
  second 89n.10
Brzezinski, Zbigniew 145

307